TOLERANCE, REGULATION AND RESCUE

MANCHESTER
1824

Manchester University Press

TOLERANCE, REGULATION AND RESCUE

Dishonoured women and abandoned children in Italy, 1300–1800

Brian Pullan

Manchester University Press

The right of Brian Pullan to be identified as the author of this work has been asserted by him in accordance with the Copyright, Designs and Patents Act 1988.

Published by Manchester University Press
Altrincham Street, Manchester M1 7JA
www.manchesteruniversitypress.co.uk

British Library Cataloguing-in-Publication Data
A catalogue record for this book is available from the British Library

Library of Congress Cataloging-in-Publication Data applied for

ISBN 978 1 7849 9129 6 hardback

First published 2016

The publisher has no responsibility for the persistence or accuracy of URLs for any external or third-party internet websites referred to in this book, and does not guarantee that any content on such websites is, or will remain, accurate or appropriate.

Typeset by Out of House Publishing
Printed in Great Britain
by TJ International Ltd, Padstow

Contents

Preface

Like many historians, I have long been caught between a desire for cosiness and a kind of wanderlust. On one side there is a wish to shelter within the confines of well-defined subjects and steady archival research among a familiar community of scholars (for me, usually located in Venice and the Venetian State in the sixteenth and seventeenth centuries). On the other is an uneasy feeling that scholars should occasionally chance their arms and grapple with larger, more speculative subjects, venture into the realms of synthesis at the risk of being dubbed charlatans or accused of merely patching together other people's evidence and ideas. After all, academics experience something of this kind whenever they have lectured to first-year students, especially if they have been involved in some enterprise as wide-ranging as Manchester's first-year course, 'Themes in Modern History', launched in the 1970s.

For some years I have been accumulating on my desk an overlarge work, a Penelope's web which was originally designed, far too ambitiously, to be a general history of Catholic charity in western Europe in the late medieval and early modern centuries, but then shrank and became a more modest survey of poverty, charity and social policies in Italian states of the old regime. More sensibly, I hope, I have narrowed the focus still further in this book. Here I have tried to consider the ways in which those societies treated groups of women and children on the margins of mainstream society, and to explore the means by which they came to terms with certain activities which they could not suppress but could only attempt to regulate. The book focuses on prostitution (very broadly interpreted) and on the abandonment of illegitimate children, things regarded as reprehensible in themselves but nevertheless tolerable for the sake of avoiding greater evils.

My warmest thanks are due to a Manchester colleague of many years, Joseph Bergin, for helping me to extract a manageable publishing proposal from a luxuriant typescript, to Manchester University Press for considering and developing it, and to its readers for their constructive, patient and helpful remarks on early proposals and one late draft. Katherine Aron-Beller has read and commented shrewdly and helpfully on several chapters, and my wife Janet, who has had so much of the work inflicted on her over the years, has been enduringly patient and ever ready to issue warnings against humbug, verbosity and over-long sentences. If glaring examples of these have been allowed to survive, the fault is mine and not hers. Our sons William and Thomas have educated me in basic word-processing and put up with my technophobia in an exemplary fashion.

I am hugely grateful to the many colleagues, friends and students who have listened patiently to my half-formed ideas, contributed others of their own, and sometimes responded with a judicious but heartening 'I think you may be on to something.' I think with admiration and affection of the mentors, from John Elliott and the late Peter Laslett in Cambridge in the 1950s and 1960s to the 'modern' historians of Manchester later in the twentieth century, who insisted on the importance of attempting to make comparisons and not retreating too timidly into one's specialist cocoon. Like many users of the university libraries in Cambridge and Manchester, I have reason to be grateful for their fine collections of periodicals, their open shelves, their generous lending policies, and their splendid collections of rare books.

Let me thank the many scholars who have given me valuable references, honoured me with invitations to speak, sent me copies of their work, obtained important material, or otherwise encouraged me. Among them are Giuliana Albini, Joseph Bergin, Michael Biddiss, M.E. Bratchel, Edoardo Bressan, David Chambers and members of the Venetian Seminar, Mark Cohen, Sherrill Cohen, the late Gaetano Cozzi, Stefano D'Amico, Giovanna Farrell-Vinay, Angela Groppi, John Henderson, Peter Higginson, Volker Hunecke, Michael Knapton, Mary Laven, John Law, Lance Gabriel Lazar, Richard Mackenney, Luigi Majno, Reinhold Mueller, Alessandro Pastore, Marina Romanello, the late Nicolai Rubinstein, Guido Ruggiero, Anne Jacobson Schutte, Nelli-Elena Vanzan Marchini, Vera Zamagni and Danilo Zardin.

Abbreviations

B.R.

Bullarium Romanum, i.e. *Bullarum Diplomatum et Privilegiorum Sanctorum Romanorum Pontificum Taurinensis Editio,* 24 vols., Augusta Taurinorum, 1857–1872.

C.J.C.

Corpus Juris Canonici, ed. Emil Ludwig Richter and Emil Friedberg, 2 vols., Leipzig, 1879; photographic reprint, Graz, 1959. Part I: *Decretum Magistri Gratiani.* Part II: *Decretalium Collectiones.*

D.I.P.

Dizionario degli istituti di perfezione, ed. Guerrino Pelliccia and Giancarlo Rocca, 10 vols., Rome 1974–2003.

D.M.S.

I diarii di Marin Sanudo, ed. Rinaldo Fulin *et al.,* 58 vols., Venice, 1879–1903.

E.A.

Enfance abandonné et société en Europe, XIVe–XXe siècle: Collection de l'École Française de Rome 140, Rome, 1991.

Migne P.L. J.P. Migne (ed.)

Patrologiae cursus completus, series latina, 217 vols., Paris, 1847–55.

Pastor. Ludwig, Freiherr von Pastor

The History of the Popes from the Close of the Middle Ages, ed. F.I. Antrobus *et al.,* 40 vols., London, 1891–1953.

T.A.

Fondazione G. Treccani degli Alfieri *Storia di Milano,* 17 vols., Milan, 1953–66.

Biblical references are to the Jerusalem Bible.

References to Shakespeare are to *The Complete Works,* ed. Stanley Wells, Gary Taylor *et al.,* Oxford, 1988.

Introduction

This is a work of synthesis which explores one corner of a sprawling, inexhaustible subject: poverty, charity and social policies in pre-industrial Europe. It concentrates on Italian cities and states and ranges across five centuries from about 1300 to 1800, from the half-century before the Black Death (or Great Mortality) to the Napoleonic invasions. It draws on many monographs composed by painstaking and imaginative scholars, in the hope that by making comparisons, crossing some traditional chronological boundaries and, where practicable, venturing outside the heavily worked fields of Florence, Rome and Venice, it may be possible to produce something more trenchant than a summary of the latest research on a lively subject. The book is equally indebted to the editors and publishers who have made available splendid documentary collections, contemporary descriptions and surveys, correspondence and diaries, travellers' tales, lives of saints or aspiring saints, and a number of satires, short stories and other literary works.

I hope that the authors whose work I have greedily plundered will forgive me for not explicitly engaging in debate with them in the text or expressly conducting a historiographic survey. I have preferred to write about history rather than historians (if the distinction exists), and, for that reason, modern academics seldom make appearances in the text, though I hope to have acknowledged their contributions scrupulously in the references. There is no reigning orthodoxy that I would especially wish to challenge in this book, in which I am more interested in quarrying information than in quarrelling with other scholars, in indulging, like Auden's Housman, in 'savage footnotes on unjust editions' or in some milder form of polemic. The works I have cited are generally excellent as far as they go and very difficult to fault. But they can become even more useful if related, in a synoptic survey, to comparable studies of other communities. Sometimes one can use evidence in ways the original author did not, though I am conscious of being something of a parasite, forever battening on other people's pioneering researches, but not, I trust, distorting or misrepresenting them.

In the past few years I have sometimes been invited to read at learned conferences papers which try to generalise about the theory and practice of charity and social policy in Catholic countries, Italian states especially. Traditionally, this is a subject which has no natural centre or core, nothing to compare with the English poor law; it is often described through studies of particular kinds of institution – confraternities; hospitals and hospices; conservatories for foundlings and orphans and girls at high risk; loan banks offering small-scale credit to 'the poor who are not so poor', and so forth. Can any underlying principles be discerned in these very diverse arrangements, other than a general devotion to the accumulation of merit through works of mercy, and possibly a belief that the poor exist to enable more fortunate people to earn salvation?

In search of another pattern, I shall explore the operation of two related strategies which influenced charity and social policy in Italian states and smaller communities from the late middle ages onwards and gave them a certain coherence. By way of short-hand, the first may be termed the policy of regulation and rescue, the second described as the practice of making a choice of evils and tolerating a so-called lesser evil [*minus malum*] in the hope of averting a much more serious one. Between the early fourteenth and the early sixteenth centuries, many Italian societies decided to acknowledge and try to control, rather than prohibit, certain activities which seemed almost impossible to uproot from a sinful world. These might be both impious and dishonourable in the eyes of strict moralists. But, if skilfully managed, they could, in the view of magistrates, be made to contribute to the common good and to preserve public order. Cities no longer tried to expel all common prostitutes, but began to accommodate them within their own walls, in recognised vice districts or licensed brothels. They allowed prosti-tutes to become, not total outsiders, but marginals, women who attracted official dis-approval, but were nevertheless allowed to live on the edges of mainstream society (see Chapter 2).[1] Prostitutes might, it was hoped, help communities to contain the sexual energies of young, unmarried men in the least harmful way possible. Child abandon-ment began to become a regulated process by which desperate couples, or single par-ents terrified of social disgrace and family revenge, were able to leave base-born infants anonymously and in relative safety at hospitals. These were normally established in cities but served large areas outside them and beyond their immediate environs (see Chapter 7). Moneylending at interest, especially pawnbroking and the small loan business, became a more openly regulated and a more logically defensible trade in the fourteenth and fifteenth centuries. Magistrates increasingly entrusted it to Jewish bank-ers working on contracts of limited duration and living with their families on the edges of Christian communities, sometimes incurring intense hostility, ugly accusations and savage verbal attacks from Christian preachers.

Perhaps these were mere acts of expediency on the part of pragmatic governments and practitioners of poor relief, coming to terms with activities they could not sup-press. Could these policies be reconciled with a Christian conscience? They were applied within Christian communities which courted divine favour and feared divine wrath, sought the protection of the Madonna and saints, subscribed to pious broth-erhoods and sisterhoods, supported clerics and female religious as well as deriding their shortcomings, and sometimes heeded the moral exhortations of the more elo-quent, austere and strictly observant religious orders. Realistic policies had their vic-tims, their lost and endangered souls, in the people they made use of and encouraged in sinful practices. To some extent, Italian societies (not alone in this) compensated for their calculating realism by trying to rescue and redeem some of these victims through pious foundations or other means. They offered them a choice between good and evil, a chance to escape and amend, to recover lost honour. From the fourteenth and fifteenth centuries, city communities supported penitential convents designed to enable women to renounce and atone for their so-called 'evil life [*mala vita*]' (see Chapter 5). From the sixteenth, they made more systematic attempts to rescue unhappily married women and attractive girls, deemed to be in acute danger of being sold or otherwise trapped into prostitution or immoral relationships (see Chapter 6). Some people supposedly benefited from organised child abandonment, including the mothers who escaped social ruin by parting from their illegitimate children. But the process also had victims, in the shape of babies deprived of parental care and the milk of their own mothers. However imperfectly, hospitals made attempts to bring up infants and young children both through foster care and through institutional homes (conservatories), and to equip the survivors for a modest place in mainstream society. As a misbeliever in the eyes of the Christian majority, a Jew was a lost soul, although, as one not bound to obey the gospel's commandments against taking interest, a Jewish banker could be useful to Christian society. Attempts could and should be made to convert Jews to Christianity, by informal persuasion or through houses of instruction for Jewish and other newcomers to the faith. Indeed, a formal justification for licensing some Jewish lenders was the opportunity they received to live on the edge of Christian society and perhaps, inspired by what they had seen, eventually convert to its religion.[2] In all these spheres, it was as if the right hand of society, its charitable, pious side, were seeking to balance the worldliness and moral compromises of the left hand – the expediencies of government, which was often bound to choose, not between good and bad, but between a greater and a lesser evil.

Related to the strategy of regulation and rescue, though not identical with it, was the notion that in some circumstances a so-called lesser evil could be tolerated – that is, left unpunished but not approved or commended – in order to avoid a greater one. From the twelfth century onwards, canon lawyers had uttered such pronouncements as 'Tolerance is a turning away from the greater of two or more evils [*Tolerantia est de maiori duorum vel plurium malorum declinatio*]', or 'Tolerance is concerned with evil and deadly things, where a lesser one is tolerated that a greater may be eliminated [*tolerantia (est) de malis et mortalibus, cum minus toleratur ut maius tollatur*]', or 'For something unlawful to be permitted that something more unlawful may be avoided … is called tolerance [*illicitum permitti, ut magis illicitum vitetur … appellatur tolerantia*]'.[3] Such principles provided some justification, perhaps specious, perhaps sincere, for government action. Other arguments could be found in the writings of eminent theologians, including both Augustine and Aquinas (see Chapter 2). It might seem that the availability of prostitutes had a useful function in diverting lustful men away from more damaging sexual adventures, perhaps in preventing them from assaulting innocent girls and respectable married women. It could be argued that adultery, which undermined marriage, was a far greater evil than simple fornication, so long as this merely involved commercial transactions with far-from-innocent women. So too, it might seem, was sodomy, as the most heinous of carnal sins. Could heterosexual prostitution serve as the lesser evil which averted far greater sins and anti-social practices? To strict moralists of the time, child abandonment was evil and unnatural, a failure on the part of parents who were bound to provide children with milk and bring them up in their proper stations. 'It is a sorry dereliction of duty on the part of parents when they expose or cast away the children they have begotten [*Parentum magna est impietas, dum a se progenitus partus, vel exponunt, vel abiiciunt*]', declared a sixteenth-century professor of law in Milan.[4] To encourage this abuse might be to license immoral conduct, by allowing parents to escape the disgrace and inconvenience of their loose or irresponsible behaviour. But, arguably, abandonment at a hospital was greatly preferable to infanticide and could save souls for baptism and bodies for a useful role in society. As a means of family limitation, it was perhaps less sinful than either abortion or contraception. Jewish pawnbroking might, to many Christian critics at the time, be a violation of gospel precepts. But against this it could be argued that resort to the Jews would reduce the temptation for Christians to sin mortally by lending upon usury to fellow Christians.

The idea that prostitution was a relatively harmless activity, which, though sordid, contributed to the defence of 'honest' women, would be attacked as a dangerous delusion in the sixteenth century by such eminent theologians as Navarre and Mariana. But it would still find defenders in sixteenth-century Rome. In the eighteenth century, even Filangieri, a writer very conscious of the pernicious effects of prostitution, would advise against brothel closure on the grounds that this would seek to 'cure a disorder with one that is even greater' and 'imperil the honour of married folk'. The old argument that prostitution 'must be tolerated in order to avoid greater evils' would still be trotted out in 1876 by a member of a parliamentary commission (see Chapter 3).

This volume will concentrate on two subjects. One is the treatment of women who, in the eyes of late medieval and early modern society, had either lost their honour or were in grave danger of losing it – not just those recognised as so-called 'public sinners' and licensed prostitutes, but also many others whose reputation was tarnished and their good name jeopardised. The other subject is the treatment of abandoned children, especially those thought to be of illegitimate birth. These topics are drawn together by their common concern with the saving of souls and with the defence and restitution of female honour, a quality associated with chastity, though not with that virtue alone. They were both applications of the strategies already outlined, of regulation and rescue and choice of the lesser evil. Both tried to confront the problems which sprang from sexual activity outside wedlock, or outside any kind of stable relationship suited to bringing up children. Both rested on a tacit belief that regulation of certain potentially harmful activities was preferable to their ineffective prohibition. Both had some faith in the therapeutic and protective powers of marriage and of religious communities. For the time being, the third topic mentioned above, Jews and moneylending, must be the subject of another discussion.

The task of this book will be to show how these strategies actually operated over time, to consider their successes and failures, to supply nuances and qualifications: to show how unexpected complications arose, how institutions departed from their original intentions, and how critics questioned the wisdom of these policies. Where possible, every effort will be made, not just to consider the attitudes of the solid citizens and clerics who drafted decrees, founded and ran charities, preached sermons and sat in courts of secular and ecclesiastical law, but also to tell the stories of underlings and survivors – of the ordinary folk who were exploited or protected by the systems described, or employed by them (as were the nurses engaged by the foundling hospitals), and who did their best to use them to their own advantage. Inevitably, we depend on records compiled by a small literate minority and shaped by the preoccupations of, for example, the judges and notaries who compiled trial transcripts and conducted interrogations. But they sometimes afford glimpses of how people perceived and described themselves, and how their neighbours, as distinct from their superiors, chose to see them (see especially Chapters 4, 8, 10 and 11).

How did the subjects of this book, the people and the institutions, relate to general contemporary notions about poverty and charity? It may be helpful to discuss these briefly at the outset. Clergy and laity in late medieval and early modern Italy did not define poverty sharply. Seldom did they measure it exactly. Rather, they came to think in terms of at least five species of poor people, not wholly distinct from each other. These included the 'poor of Christ' (of whom more later); the 'shamefaced poor [*poveri vergognosi*]', i.e. people of standing who had fallen on hard times and shrank from openly revealing their needs, let alone from begging; the fiscal poor (the have-nots or *miserabili* who could not be required to pay direct taxation on their possessions or income); the labouring or industrious poor; and the evil-living, infidel or outcast poor.

Common prostitutes could be said to belong to the last and lowest stratum, existing on the margins of the community and having much in common with vagrants. In the eyes of moralists and social commentators, both prostitutes and vagrants were lost souls, work-shy deceivers, rollers of dice and card-sharpers, confidence tricksters skilled at pitching tales and simulating false emotions, excluded from or given to ignoring the sacraments of the Church and at some risk of dying without Christian burial. At her lowest, a prostitute was a nomad, moving restlessly from country to town and from parish to parish, even crossing Europe in the wake of armies to scrape a living in the brothel quarters of Italian cities, surviving by the sale of sexual services rather than by theft, though the first activity did not exclude the second. Like masculine vagrants, prostitutes were liable to expulsion from the city and its surrounding district. But they were not mere undesirables, since the community could put them to some use, and a few of them could also, by following in the steps of Mary Magdalen and other saints, show the world how the vilest creatures could earn forgiveness by systematic repentance and formal renunciation of their evil way of life.

Certain freelance prostitutes, however, were far from being vagrants, even if they too were regarded as plausible rogues and their tricks were described by satirists. Some charged high fees, prospered for a while, managed to save, acquire property, extract expensive presents from admirers. But they were always vulnerable to the high risks of their profession, including sexually transmitted diseases, vicious acts of revenge from disappointed and jealous lovers, and government expulsion orders. They were poor in the sense of being insecure, pitiable and, in the opinion of moralists and evangelists, probably damned. They too could be in need of redemptive charity which, if it could do nothing more, might persuade a ravaged courtesan to make a good end in a hospital for the incurably ill.

Many occasional prostitutes belonged among the labouring or industrious poor. They were working folk living at least partly by other poorly paid occupations, for example in the textile and garment trades, engaged in a constant struggle for survival, and very much exposed to economic crises or sudden fluctuations in the price of bread. When trade was bad, women were generally the first to be deprived of work, and the offer of sexual services became a means of survival, sometimes a tactic for obtaining such work as there was from the men who had it to give out. Unmarried women and widows might be driven to prostitution occasionally, and so might the wives of absentees, invalids and poor providers. Only reluctantly would they have called themselves prostitutes rather than honest workers who occasionally sold themselves in hard times. Possibly, too, clandestine prostitutes were to be found among the shamefaced poor. In a story in the *Golden Legend*, the great thirteenth-century collection of saints' lives, an impoverished nobleman is about to prostitute his three virgin daughters to salvage the family fortunes. They escape dishonour only because St Nicholas of Myra comes to their rescue by tossing through the window bags of gold which will provide them with dowries and help them to make suitable marriages.[5]

Foundlings, often called *proietti* or *gettatelli*, 'throwaways', were literally outcasts, abandoned by parents. But, being among the most frail and helpless of human creatures, strangers in need of safe havens, they belonged, arguably, among the 'poor of Christ' and were subjects of the traditional works of corporal mercy. Many of the 'poor of Christ' were blameless victims of misfortune, rather resembling the 'impotent poor' of Tudor England (those unable to work or too young to work). In Catholic countries they also included some voluntary poor, such as pilgrims and certain religious (especially those who had no regular income). But the position of foundlings was uncertain. They might be called 'innocents', but their lack of a known father placed them at a very low point in the social hierarchy, and there was often a presumption that they had been doubly conceived in sin and outside wedlock by wayward parents.

The charities most often encountered in this book are hospitals, conservatories and penitential nunneries. In principle, the cities of late medieval and early modern Italy were free to set up and approve their own organisations as they chose (as did some small towns and large villages). These institutions were usually founded by private benefactors, individuals or groups; funded by legacies, gifts and the proceeds of collections; governed, staffed and subsidised by volunteers – though public authorities made token contributions to their finances, granted them a few tax exemptions, and made some effort to ensure that charities were honestly run and testators' wishes honoured. Imitating each other and responding to advice from the same travelling preachers, communities were inclined to set up loosely articulated systems made up of similar parts: especially confraternities, hospitals, conservatories, grain stores and pawn banks (Jewish or Christian or both).

Hospitals were at first mainly concerned with hospitality rather than medical care, with harbouring strangers, travellers and immigrants and homeless and destitute persons. The large centralised hospitals formed in the fourteenth and fifteenth centuries often had three principal concerns, bringing together the various activities already pursued by the older, smaller establishments which they had taken over. They provided for pilgrims and travellers; for sick people, including fever patients, surgical cases, and accident victims who could not be nursed at home; and for orphans and foundlings – abandoned infants of unknown parentage, and other children of less mysterious and more respectable origins. Much of their work was done outside their own premises, by acting as general almonries or farming young children out to wet nurses and foster mothers. Large hospitals were subject to ecclesiastical as well as lay jurisdiction, but they were often supervised by boards which consisted mainly of lay governors and included a few clergymen.

Conservatories were often set up within large general hospitals to provide for older children who had returned from foster homes, though many others functioned independently. Their object was to provide safe houses and residential schools for children and adolescents in need of care and protection, with a view to making them into useful members of society. While boys might be sent out to apprenticeships, girls – generally destined, if possible, for marriage – were usually kept within the walls for longer periods and could become permanent residents. Since many girls were trained in spinning, weaving and needlework, and put to performing basic tasks in the silk industry, some conservatories became capable of functioning as factories or workshops, earning much-needed income for themselves and collaborating with merchant-manufacturers (who found in their girls a useful source of inexpensive and disciplined labour, conveniently concentrated in one place). Certain conservatories were originally designed to receive, not foundlings or orphans, but girls believed to be in danger of losing their virtue and of being drawn into the 'evil life' of common prostitutes, courtesans or concubines.

While conservatories were intended to be places of transit, certain convents, usually known as Convertite, were designed as permanent refuges for 'whores repenting' – in that some of their entrants would take solemn vows and withdraw from the world to perform an unending penance. Less rigorous were the halfway houses (Soccorsi, Depositi, Malmaritate) which offered a breathing-space to women in distress, including married women at loggerheads with their husbands, and allowed women charged with indiscreet behaviour to contemplate ways of recovering their reputation. As Chapters 5 and 6 will show, institutions for women did not, over the centuries, cling to their original brief. For various reasons, they tended to move up the social scale, away from the poorest of the poor and those most exposed to sexual exploitation, and towards admitting residents who, if they were poor at all, belonged to the ranks of the *vergognosi*, enjoyed some favours from influential people, and did not necessarily have a disreputable past.

The most ubiquitous Catholic charity, the confraternity (a band of brothers more often than a sisterhood), will appear occasionally in the book. Usually it consisted mainly of lay persons, often advised but seldom governed by priests, and its members observed a simple religious rule while living at home. Equipped with statutes and ruled by elected officers, they set out to accumulate a store of religious merit by performing good works, usually a mixture of religious observances and ceremonies and of acts of charity. They might range across all the approved works of mercy, both spiritual and corporal, or specialise in one or two. They could assist themselves and their families alone, or look outwards towards a wider clientele. Much favoured was a good deed which was not among the traditional seven works of corporal mercy but became increasingly popular after the mid-fourteenth century, and consisted of contributing to the dowries of poor maidens (usually girls of good reputation). It was a way of helping

impoverished parents to do their duty by their daughters and of keeping the girls themselves on the path of virtue, by equipping them for marriage or, occasionally, convent
life: to both of these they would normally be expected to bring a contribution in cash
or in kind or in both. A confraternity, known by various names, including *compagnia*,
scuola or *consorzio*, could be adapted to almost any charitable purpose and was capable
of administering institutions or providing them with regular financial support.[6]

The first task of the book will be to introduce the women, deemed to be outside or
near the edge of decent, godfearing society, at whom some of these charities directed
their efforts, and whom the law attempted to regulate. There is no satisfactory, concise, inoffensive term which describes all these people. 'Common prostitutes' formed
one, but only one, element among them and that not the most numerous, though it
was the most conspicuous and the most countable. They themselves, their neighbours
and their social superiors could draw on a large descriptive vocabulary. At least since
the nineteenth century analysts of a once-taboo subject have attempted to classify the
people whom they define, sometimes loosely and sometimes narrowly, as prostitutes.
Taxonomies have been presented, for example, in the pioneering study of prostitutes
in Paris (from stylish *panades* to degraded and superannuated *pierreuses*) published
in 1836 by the physician and public hygienist Alexandre Parent-Duchâtelet, or the
essays, *c.*1860, of Henry Mayhew and Bracebridge Hemynge, in which the prostitutes
of London were marshalled into categories which ranged from 'Seclusives' ('kept
women' and 'prima donnas') to 'Park Women' and 'Clandestine Prostitutes' and also
found room for 'Ladies of Intrigue and Assignation'.[7] Following in this tradition,
though without enjoying the benefit of such systematic surveys, the opening chapter
will discuss the different levels of a dedicated prostitute's profession and consider other
women who were liable to attract epithets such as *meretrice* or *puttana*. These words
could well be applied to adulteresses or concubines or to anyone living in a union outside legal marriage or considered by neighbours to be a woman of easy virtue. As several scholars have remarked, they are best translated by elastic if insulting terms such
as 'whore' or 'harlot', rather than the more clinical 'prostitute', which describes a gain-
ful occupation as much as a moral condition. Less objectionable, perhaps, is the term
'women of lost honour', used in the title of the first chapter. Later chapters (especially
4, 5, 6 and 8) will show how and why that honour could be lost; how it might be protected and restored, and how the law and its enforcers attempted to draw sharp lines,
both spatial and social, between respectable and unrespectable, virtuous and corrupt
women, the *oneste* and the *disoneste* (see Chapters 2 and 3). How far did these women,
or some of them, appear to form part of a 'lesser evil', an antidote (if an impure one with
unpleasant side-effects both for them and for society) to profound social disruption
in a sinful world? Alternatively, how far were they perceived as corrupters of innocent
young people, and as a menace to marriage and the family which could not be regulated
and should not be tolerated? Did they undermine or did they protect those sacred institutions which, above all others, bolstered social stability and promised to generate the
abundant population on which strong states were built?

Chapters 7 to 11 consider the efforts made in Italian cities to deal with other consequences of sex outside marriage. How did communities treat illegitimate children,

how did they regulate attempts to abandon them, and how did they rescue single or adulterous mothers from social disgrace and unwanted children from the grave dangers of death by exposure or criminal violence? Chapter 7 introduces the children's wings of general hospitals and outlines the principles on which they functioned. Chapter 8 examines types of illegitimacy and the circumstances in which base-born children were most likely to be kept by their parents, abandoned or otherwise disposed of. It considers the claims of foundling hospitals to have delivered such children from infanticide, an evil which seemed far greater than separation from parents. Chapters 9, 10 and 11 describe the journeys of children to and through the foundling hospitals and into the world beyond them, examining the successes and failures both of systems of wet-nursing and fostering and of conservatories which bore a passing resemblance to the establishments described in Chapters 5 and 6. Did foundling hospitals really save lives by repelling the greater evil of infanticide, or did they, through a mixture of callousness, overcrowding, underfunding and administrative shortcomings, generate other evils of their own and preside over high child mortality? Did they merely substitute mass institutional manslaughter for individual child murder? Did they succeed in rescuing base-born children by giving them a chance to make good in life as farmworkers, artisans or servants, or did they merely release on the world an order of children condemned to poverty and obscurity by the circumstances of their birth?

Notes

1   For the 'semi-inclusive' approach of late medieval Italian cities to deviants, especially prisoners and prostitutes, see (for example) Geltner 2008, pp. 1–3, 104–8; Geltner 2012, pp. 29–37.
2   For an example, see Pope Innocent VIII's concession of 1489 to Leon Norsa at Mantua, in Simonsohn 1977, Appendix, doc. 8, p. 759.
3   See the citations in Bejczy 1997: 369–70. For other remarks on the lesser evil, see Brundage 1976/1993: 844; Brundage 1987, p. 522; Rocke 1996, pp. 30, 263, n. 46; Mormando 1999, pp. 125–6; Pullan 2005: 452–6; Rossiaud 2010, pp. 40–1, 74–7, 84–5, 296–7.
4   Arrivo 1997: 236–8.
5   Jacopo della Voragine ed. Graesse 1890/1965, pp. 22–9; for discussion, see Ricci 1983: 166–8 and Pullan 2000, p. 27.
6   For a comprehensive account of poverty and charity in one early modern Italian city, Turin, see Cavallo 1995. Collections of conference papers on the subject include Politi, Rosa and Della Peruta 1982, Zardin 1995 and Zamagni 2000. For comparative essays, see Pullan 1988 and Pullan 2008.
7   Parent-Duchâtelet ed. Corbin 1981, pp. 119–28; Mayhew 1861–62, republished 1968, IV, pp. 35–272.

1

Women of lost honour: honour and dishonour

'The woman who has lost her honour has lost all her glory and good', wrote Matteo Bandello, the literary friar, diplomat, bishop and mover in courtly circles, who had begun in the 1550s to publish his vast collection of realistic short stories.[1] Less learned people could express the same sentiment in much the same words, perhaps with some help from court notaries. Testifying in 1556 in a breach-of-promise case in the northern diocese of Feltre, a widow declared that she wished both parties well, but hoped the young woman would win because 'when a poor girl has lost her honour she has lost everything she can possibly lose'.[2]

In a general sense, honour was the esteem due to members of a mainstream society who submitted, or at least appeared to submit, to a code of conduct designed to preserve good order and hierarchy. Should persons depart from this code, for example by indulging in improper amorous adventures, they would be well advised to practise discretion and avoid scandal. Honour lay not in a clear conscience so much as in a good reputation, in the image one presented to people who could make life unpleasant for anyone judged to be of questionable conduct.[3] A famous Bandello heroine, Giulia of Gazuolo, a virtuous country girl overpowered and raped in the fields by a love-crazed servant of the bishop of Mantua assisted by a friend, drowns herself for fear of the self-righteous gossips who will blame her for the incident, innocent though she is, and call her a whore. There is no other way to recover her honour, and the bishop respects her, although he cannot bury her in consecrated ground.[4]

Honour was not confined to people of noble or civil condition, or to clergy and religious, though notions of it varied according to one's rank and status. A witness said of Giovanna of Vattaro, another village woman in the diocese of Feltre, 'She lives with her husband, in the sweat of her brow, in the manner of poor people who live honourably' – by obeying the divine commandment to Adam and Eve on their ejection from Eden and accepting the penalty of original sin.[5] A married woman's honour lay partly in her loyal support for a dependable husband, himself no blasphemer, gambler, tavern-haunter, beggar or scrounger, who worked steadily at a respectable occupation. This was generally a trade which provided for essential human needs rather than gross appetites or frivolous entertainments. It was also one which did not incur charges of uncleanness by taking on necessary but despicable tasks of disposing of polluting matter, and one which, at least in theory, had nothing to do with lending money at interest. An honourable woman would contribute a dowry to the household, bear and bring up her husband's and her children, do the housework, supplement family income by doing modestly paid work at home, mind the shop or sell farm produce, work in the fields especially at harvest time, and sometimes carry out the most strenuous tasks on the land in the absence of a husband who had gone to work in the city.

In a narrower sense, a woman's honour, her *onore* or *onestà*, denoted her sexual constancy – her absolute fidelity to a husband or fiancé, her determination to repel the advances of any would-be seducer or tempter. An honourable maiden, the despair of Aretino's procuress (the ex-whore Nanna of Rome), looked forward to marriage or a celibate life as a religious; preserved her virginity to that end; slept with no-one without the approval of her respectable parents and at least the firm promise of a wedding with a seemingly trustworthy man; had access to a dowry which her family had provided, or which she had perhaps earned from an approving employer or been awarded by a charity convinced of her good reputation.[6] Her undoing would be the suspicion of promiscuous conduct, an unwanted pregnancy which she could not conceal, a sexual assault by a predator, especially a stranger who could not be brought to book. There was more to a woman's honour than her reputation for sexual probity.[7] But essential to it was the virginity of a nubile girl, the chastity of a religious, the fidelity of a wife, the decorum of a widow. The honour of a woman's father, brothers and husband was bound up with their control over her sexual behaviour; her looseness, if detected, was their disgrace as well as her own, and their honour might perhaps be retrieved only through her death, which could be more important than her lover's. In a mid-sixteenth-century story by Straparola, a merchant in Venice, Dimitrio, contrives to have his adulterous wife Polissena killed by her brothers and spares her lover, who happens to be a priest.[8]

By definition, a common prostitute (there were other kinds) knew nothing of honour; her portion was infamy. She openly followed one of those occupations which, though many thought them useful if not indispensable to society, incurred contempt by their supposed uncleanness, their dedication to the removal of dirt or human exudations or organic matter. From a social point of view, a common prostitute was a 'specialist in impurity'.[9] From a religious, she was a habitual, public sinner, though she was also one who might justify her existence by diverting others from sins more heinous than fornication, and one who was not beyond redemption. She did not appear to earn her living by manual labour in the sweat of her brow, but by offering the use of her body, by submitting rather than toiling. She might have a lover-protector, but she had no sexually exclusive relationship with him, and overturned the conventions of honourable behaviour by herself becoming the principal earner in their partnership. The antithesis of an honourable woman, she was useful to society partly as the other who was not to be imitated but must be held up to scorn. One of the objects of social policy from the late middle ages onwards was, while harbouring her on the edge of the community, to separate her decisively from decent women, lest they be tempted to join her and lest prowling males upset public order by confusing 'decent' women with common prostitutes. But beyond the common prostitute many other women and girls were poised more uncertainly on the edge of dishonour – the 'good' girl sleeping with her lover and risking a pregnancy outside marriage if he proved to be fickle, the wife living apart from her husband without benefit of an official separation, the housekeeper sharing her employer's bed, the priest's woman, the daughter in a crowded household forced into intimacy with her parents' lodgers, the child sent on errands which exposed her to sexual interference.

Many cities sheltered a cadre of full-time prostitutes, who made no secret of what they did, and a number – probably much larger, but impossible to estimate accurately – of clandestine prostitutes who had other occupations, but made ends meet by occasionally offering sexual services, particularly in hard times. Should they offend neighbours and ignore their reproaches, they would probably be denounced to magistrates, but otherwise they would usually escape official notice. Beyond them were some destitute people, including children, for whom prostitution was not a supplement to low-paid work, still less a craft or profession, but an extension of begging. One of them was Anna Buccelli, whose father, a spirit-seller, left her to seek alms all day in the Campo San Polo in Venice in 1795; not surprisingly, she obliged the stranger who offered her six soldi for sex.[10]

Towns generally included some women working in brothels under the exploitative rule of bawds and pimps. There were also freelance prostitutes. Some of the poorest operated on the streets, while others received and entertained 'friends' in their own rooms, perhaps enjoying the protection of an aggressive male champion or of a soberer *amico fermo*, a regular client willing to foot some of their bills or pay the rent. The standing of independent prostitutes in the larger cities varied with the rank of their clients, the fastidiousness with which they chose them, the dignity of their lodgings, the elegance of the entertainment they offered, the ability of influential patrons to protect them from the attention of the moral police and enable them to flout tedious and humiliating regulations.

In certain cities, it was rumoured, male prostitutes presented females with serious competition. Those of Renaissance Florence were mostly adolescents aged between about twelve and eighteen, beardless, androgynous youths commonly called *bardassi*, perhaps much like those later described by a seventeenth-century Scottish traveller (who was writing about Padua) as 'buggered boys'.[11] In Rome in about 1611, the Piazza Navona and its environs harboured mercenary characters such as Giovannino, alias il Pollarolo, who went there of an evening 'to get picked up by this one and that one, to be sodomised and to earn money from it'.[12] Not always rigorously prosecuted, homosexual prostitution could never be officially condoned, since, with other forms of sodomy, it constituted in the eyes of good citizens one of those greater evils from which heterosexual prostitution was supposed to divert the men of the community.

Prostitutes and harlots

Between the fourteenth and the eighteenth centuries, two of the commonest words for an immoral female were *meretrice* and *puttana*. Both highly insulting and sometimes legally actionable (if misapplied to respectable women), they were elastic rather than exact terms. Each could refer, not just to a commercial prostitute, but to any woman of easy virtue – including an adulteress or a mistress living in an exclusive relationship outside marriage. Several meretricious saints appear in the *Golden Legend*, which became one of the most influential books of the late middle ages. They fall from grace in different ways, before redeeming themselves by heroic penances. St Mary the Egyptian practises as a common prostitute in Alexandria for seventeen years and then works her passage to Jerusalem by offering to pleasure everyone on board ship. Of a different order, but still dubbed a *meretrix*, is Theodora of Alexandria, a married woman who has indulged in one amorous adventure, after falling for a witch's unlikely story that God does not see or know what happens after sunset. The Devil taunts her, 'Being a harlot before all others and an adulteress, you left your husband [*meretrix prae omnibus et adultera reliquisti virum tuum*]', and treats her to a gruesome vision of a huntsman urging on a pack of demons with the cry, 'Feast upon this whore [*comedite meretricem hanc*]!'[13] According to the statutes of a Piedmontese town, Villanova d'Asti, of 1414, an unfaithful wife who defied husbandly reproofs could eventually be expelled from the household as an *immonda meretrix*, 'a filthy whore'.[14] There might be a practical distinction between a *publica meretrix* and a *meretrix*, and the law would treat them differently; but they were on the same moral spectrum, and a woman disgraced for adultery or a discarded mistress might have no option but to become a prostitute. Indeed, at Bergamo in 1399, the adulteress Ricardona was formally escorted to the public brothel with drums beating and flag flying, that she might now be seen in her true colours and work with her own kind as a woman of lost honour.[15]

The word *puttana* could be used in legislation, in court proceedings, in literary or medical treatises, but it was more colloquial than *meretrice*, better adapted, perhaps, to street brawls or domestic altercations. John Florio defined *puttana* in his Italian–English dictionary as 'a whore, a harlot, a strumpet, a quean'.[16] The ill-fated Ferrante Pallavicino, a nobleman of Parma and a licentious Benedictine, writing in about 1642 his *Retorica delle puttane*, admitted that the word was 'not very Tuscan', although it was suitable to light literature and was the unambiguous term that prostitutes and their clients would recognise immediately. In his view, an ambitious and sophisticated prostitute was of a different species from an adulteress driven by affection or passion, since the *puttana*'s sole object was or ought to be profit and the ruthless pursuit of self-interest, and it would be fatal to her career to fall in love with a client and allow sentimentality to cloud her business sense.[17] Others, however, in the sixteenth and seventeenth centuries, would use the word more loosely to mean, for example, a concubine or a former concubine, especially, perhaps, if she was beginning to be unfaithful to the man who had been keeping her.[18]

In some cities, women were officially declared to be prostitutes by magistrates, or registered themselves as such, or entered public brothels, or were conscripted into them. Promiscuity and venality were deemed to be the two strongest characteristics of most prostitutes, though some writers emphasised one more heavily than the other.[19] There was room for argument: at what point should a woman who occasionally fornicated incur the stigma which clung to a professional prostitute and consigned her to the ranks of the *disoneste*, the women without honour? Much could hinge on her local reputation [*fama*]. In fifteenth-century Bologna a woman could be certified a prostitute by the testimony of at least five respectable witnesses from her neighbourhood, and she was entitled to call her own witnesses to clear her name.[20] Several authorities were inclined to count the number of men a woman was known to have bedded rather than the fees, if any, which she exacted. For some, a single lapse would earn the epithet *meretrix*; others were more forgiving. In 1305, the statutes of Savigliano in Piedmont (about thirty miles from Turin) defined as a prostitute a woman who had had four or more lovers.[21] In some cases, though, such precision was not needed. When, in 1401, the Ufficio della Grascia in Florence pronounced Pera di Nicolosa a prostitute, on the testimony of four witnesses, they concluded that she had sold herself 'for monetary gain' 'over and over again, with many, many different persons'.[22]

Common prostitutes: the vocabulary

At the bottom of the hierarchy was the ancestor of W.H. Davies's heroine, 'Here comes Kate Summers who, for gold, Takes any man to bed', though an ordinary prostitute might be lucky to receive cash and would perhaps have to settle for payment in food and drink. In official language she would very likely be called a *meretrice publica*, a *filia* or *mulier comunis*, a *femina comunis et publica*; in the late thirteenth century, a court in Bologna might say of a woman 'that she is a *publica meretrix* and that she openly submits herself to all men who desire her'.[23] In a brief issued in 1199, encouraging pious Christians to marry prostitutes and give them some chance of redemption, Pope Innocent III had written of 'women who live for pleasure and allow anyone to have sexual congress with them [*mulieres voluptuose viventes et admittentes indifferenter quoslibet ad commercium carnis*]'.[24] The archetypal cheap prostitute had no alternative trade and few possessions, and was often on the move, in flight from constables or creditors. At Cuneo in Piedmont in 1441–2 it proved impossible to exact a fine imposed on 'Soya *meretrix*', 'because the culprit is an indigent creature and a vagabond, who neither has nor holds any goods save those which she earns by offering her body, and because, after committing the crime, she left the jurisdiction'.[25]

Other phrases, less formal but more exact, were used to describe prostitutes by alluding to their places of work. *Femina di chiazzo* and *meretrice di postribolo* denoted women working from brothels; some, as in fourteenth-century Bologna, might be both prostitutes and brothel-keepers (*lene* or *ruffiane*), as was the widow Cervaxina, who lived in the district of St Simon and St Jude in 1341. In Bologna in the fifteenth century, a freelance prostitute working from her own lodgings could be called a *caxarega*.[26]

Femina di partito was in use from the early sixteenth century, if no earlier, as witness the diarist Sanudo's implausible estimate that there were over 11,000 such women in Venice in the summer of 1509, when the city was packed with refugees.[27] The phrase suggested women who struck their own bargains and were – as in Florence about 1511 – a cut above the *femmine cantoniere*, who appeared to be street-walkers or possibly brothel prostitutes and were obliged to wear distinguishing signs.[28] Both terms persisted into the seventeenth and eighteenth centuries. In Siena in 1605, Laura Magii described herself as a *donna di partito* who had no other means of support, and explained that in the past few years she had approached her parish priest with a view to confessing and taking communion, but he had refused to absolve her.[29] Ferrante Pallavicino used *femina di partito* as an alternative to *puttana* around 1640, calling such a person 'as scrupulously paid as she is freely enjoyed'.[30] At Bologna in 1689, Caterina Franzaroli admitted that, up to the age of eighteen, about five years earlier, she had been a ' "donna del mondo" or "di partito", as they say, which means that I sold my body, and made it available to anyone who asked me'.[31]

In eighteenth-century Venice, a woman soliciting at a street corner, or standing at her door in some disreputable street, or sitting at a window to attract custom, would probably be called a *cantoniera*. A destitute girl, hanging about in public places and picking up clients in Venetian taverns, might well be described as a *piazzarola*.[32]

The famous concept of the high-class prostitute, the *cortigiana*, came into being (or resurfaced), at least in Rome and Venice, around 1500, but tended with time to descend the social scale towards a much rougher kind of prostitute. Sometimes, in this way, relatively genteel, euphemistic language came to apply to prostitutes of all ranks; sometimes, on the contrary, blunter terms were used for high and low alike, as if to dismiss the pretensions of the more opulent women. In the works of Pietro Fortini, the sixteenth-century playwright and storyteller, the epithet *vil feminella* attaches both to the gorgeous, bejewelled courtesan Dionora of Ferrara and to Caterina, aged sixteen, who lives near the notorious Sistine bridge in Rome, 'a low hussy who gave of her goods for a paltry price to anyone who asked for them'.[33]

Peccatrice, meaning a persistent female sexual sinner, was often (though not solely) used in connection with missions to redeem the souls of 'fallen' women and persuade them to marry, enter convents, or take refuge with charities. Men visiting brothels were seldom if ever referred to as *peccatori*.

Metaphorically, prostitutes were liable to be described not just as women who waited to oblige customers but as anglers and fowlers equipped with cunning techniques for entrapping innocents (sometimes described as *merlotti*, literally fledgling blackbirds) who became entangled in their nets or rose to the bait cast into the waters. 'Your trade is a kind of fishing', a mother advises her daughter in one of the spoof letters of Pallavicino's *Corriere svaligiato*, of about 1640.[34] In 1760 the journalist Gasparo Gozzi called the prostitutes of the via del Carbone 'ensnarers of male birds [*uccellatrici degli uomini*]', allegedly the most sordid practitioners of their trade to be found anywhere in Venice.[35]

Free women

In some cities a woman might call herself a *donna libera* if she had broken free or been released by widowhood from masculine control and chosen to do things in her own way, as an independent prostitute or by combining acts of prostitution with application to some respectable trade. One who asserted her independence might have to resort to her sexual powers in order to live, and would probably be suspected of doing so even if she did not. 'I, sir, am a free woman', testified Chiara Jacobi in Rome in 1628; 'sometimes I work and sometimes I play the courtesan, as opportunity arises, and I live as best I can.'[36] Maria Poggi in Bologna in 1692 was even clearer: 'I am twenty-four years of age, I make stockings when I can get the work, and sometimes, to make a living, I submit to men, because I am neither a child, nor a widow, nor a wife, but a free woman.'[37]

Local usage of the term varied. In the diocese of Monreale in western Sicily in the sixteenth and seventeenth centuries, a *donna libera* was an unmarried prostitute, as distinct from a *donna cortigiana*, a married woman forced to earn extra income by immoral means because her husband was away from home or a bad provider. A *donna libera* might have to deny accusations of becoming what the law then regarded as a greater evil: a concubine or kept woman. Had she allowed herself to enter an exclusive relationship and be supported entirely by one man, in a mockery of marriage, far more subversive of the Christian order promoted by the Catholic hierarchy after the Council of Trent than were the transactions of a prostitute? In the same diocese in 1626, charged with being the mistress of Honofrio Carlino, Ninfa 'La Dulci' pleaded her promiscuity in her defence by declaring that she had 'a thousand friends' and was not especially fond of any of them.[38]

At Siena in 1589, Cecilia di Giovanni, caught with the tailor Giovanni di Giulio, robustly affirmed her position as a free woman, a discerning prostitute who chose her clients, and was nobody's mistress: 'he has seldom been to my house, because no man maintains me [*non sto a posta di nessuno*] and I am free and give pleasure and service to those whom I choose'. Her client confirmed her story – allegedly, he had visited her 'once in a hundred years, so to speak, and I do not support or keep her, and she is free and mistress of herself'. Both were released; there was no evidence of a continuous relationship between them, or any proof that Cecilia had lost her independence.[39]

In Venice, however, *donna libera* was sometimes applied to a less free-roving person, a nobleman's concubine, otherwise his *amica*, a 'female friend' who lived discreetly and faithfully with him as though she were his wife, and as if she were free only in not being legally married to him. A serial adulteress of good family, blessed with a complaisant husband, might well be known by the more derogatory term *donna del mondo*, which was also frequently applied to a commercial prostitute.[40]

Lovers and concubines

In the late middle ages the word *amasia* had been used, sometimes officially as well as colloquially – in the statutes of Verona of 1276, in certain legal contracts, in certain administrative records – to mean a concubine, sometimes a 'servant and concubine', a housekeeper who shared her master's bed, perhaps became his companion and bore him children. Medieval canon lawyers, at least from the twelfth century onwards, were prepared to regard some forms of concubinage as a species of second-rate marriage – so long as there was 'marital affection' between the couple and an intention to form a lasting union. The essence of a valid marriage then lay in the couple's consent rather than in legal formalities, and it could be hard to distinguish between concubinage and clandestine marriage.[41]

In its simplest form, concubinage was a relationship between two people who could legally have married but chose not to do so, perhaps because the woman was of lower status than the man and had no dowry. In a more complex situation, one or both parties might be married to somebody else, or the man, being in holy orders, be forbidden to marry, even if his flock were happy to regard his 'woman' as his wife. In principle, a concubine, living in a continuous if insecure relationship which could be ended far more easily than a legal marriage, was not a prostitute. But some women could be concubine and prostitute simultaneously, if, for example, they went with a pimp or protector who lived off their earnings. In Florence in 1346, an illegal brothel harboured Francisca, 'the woman of Salvestro, nicknamed "Bestial"', and Tessa, 'the concubine of Stefano di ser Giovenchio'.[42]

To be regarded as living in concubinage, as *conviventi*, couples did not have to live under the same roof. They frequently did not, though a man of high rank would be quite capable of installing a mistress in the same house as his wife, as though to display his wealth and status, a move less offensive to the lady if he abstained from treating his mistress as her equal.[43] In Bologna towards 1300, a woman who lived in an unmarried man's house and submitted to his authority would probably be accepted as a second-class wife. But if she did not live with her man, but called and performed personal services (such as washing his hair) in return for financial support, thereby retaining more independence, the magistrates would very likely stigmatise her as a common prostitute. Not all the witnesses who appeared before them would share this harsh opinion.[44]

The severity of the moral climate fluctuated; indeed, the 'ducal decrees of Savoy' of 1430 objected generally to couples being joined together outside marriage.[45] But the most sustained assault on concubinage, a series of attempts, diocese by diocese, to equate it with continuous fornication and treat it as a greater evil than prostitution, began in the sixteenth century. This campaign met defiance on the part of some powerful and devious men. Others, however, became conscience-stricken and yielded to clerical persuasion or other pressure. Sometimes, if they could, they married their paramours themselves; sometimes they sent them away; sometimes they arranged marriages with husbands of inferior rank, who were supposedly more suited to their station; sometimes they left them in the lurch.[46]

Shortly before the Council of Trent, some authorities began to urge that any woman living in an extramarital relationship be regarded as a *meretrice*. In 1543 the Venetian Senate wished this status upon 'those women who, being unmarried, have dealings and intercourse [*comertio et praticha*] with one man or more. It shall also apply to those who have husbands and do not live with them, but are separated from them and have dealings [*comercio*] with one man or more'.[47] This legislation was close in time to a vigorous campaign against concubinage launched about 1541 by Bishop Gian Matteo Giberti in the diocese of Verona, in the heart of Venice's mainland empire: he and his successors were clearly trying to equate concubines with prostitutes and whores.[48] A clause of the Tridentine decree on the reform of matrimony (1563) condemned the practice of maintaining concubines as a grave lapse on the part of unmarried men, which became graver still 'when married men live in this state of damnation and have the boldness at times to maintain and keep them in their own homes even with their own wives'.[49] From the Veneto to Tuscany and in parts of the kingdom of Naples concubines were reviled as *puttane* or *pudorate*. By 1578, Chiara, who had been for seventeen years the mistress of a powerful figure in Pistoia, was attracting the insult, if only because a philandering knight thought her fair game ('the captain's woman, not his wife') and she, oppressed by an increasingly jealous and ailing master, showed signs of yielding to her new admirer's overtures.[50]

In the sixteenth and seventeenth centuries, certainly in Naples and probably generally, there was much movement between concubinage and prostitution. Girls were taken on as mistresses and kept for a few months or years by some man who fancied and then grew tired of them, or prostitutes took refuge with a man who helped them go straight for a while but did not offer marriage. In Naples in 1601–2, Santa, a young Flemish woman, formerly a prostitute, had been living for six years with Giacomo d'Ambrosio, a constable; a witness testified that 'she sins with nobody, apart from the said Giacomo'. When, as an unmarried couple living in sin, they were forced to separate, Santa returned to 'the evil life', though eventually Giacomo did agree to marry her.[51] Investigations of improper unions in the archdioceses of Monreale and Naples revealed *ménages à trois*, one woman with two men and one man with two women, and raised such questions as: could one be a concubine twice over or a prostitute with only two 'friends', and which of one's 'friends', if either, should one be ordered to marry?[52] The line between prostitution and concubinage was often crossed, one condition often exchanged for the other. The law was inclined if it could to put a stop to concubinage, but not to prostitution, which was still regarded as a lesser evil and as such tolerable.

Rural prostitution

Urban prostitution has left most traces for historians to follow. But surviving judicial records have afforded glimpses of prostitution, or something very like it, in small towns and villages. They have preserved, for example, the stories which neighbours repeated to a vicar's court in the Florentine State about the antics of Argentina, a sharecropper's wife at Montagnana, near Pescia, *c.*1427. A lurid incident, in which a lover crept into the house by night and had intercourse with her a few feet away from her sleeping husband and mother-in-law, brought to the surface allegations that resulted in her banishment from the village and enforced separation from her husband. Her reputation damned her, for neighbours said (without supplying detailed proof) that she had had sexual relations 'with many, many men, for many, many years in the past' and had received 'a fee and reward [*premium et mercedem*]' from some of them, including Andrea, her most recent visitor.[53] More organised was the disorderly house kept in the village of Bellante, in the diocese of Teramo (Abruzzi) in 1605, by Palumbina, described as 'a woman of low standing and bad reputation, a *meretrice* who brought scandal to the place', and her colleague Lella. Their convivial establishment, at which, among other things, the 'game of twenty cards' could be enjoyed, attracted punters from nearby villages, and two young clergymen who had frequented this saloon were prosecuted for conduct unbefitting the cloth.[54] About 1607, Castel Lubriano, a small, remote village near Orvieto, became the base for the operations of a mother, a stepfather and a husband, unpopular outsiders who, between them, prostituted young Giulia, aged about sixteen, and took her both to cities and to one neighbouring village to delight the local castellan and some other inhabitants.[55] At Montefollonico, a Tuscan fief near Montepulciano, for much of the seventeenth century, there were at any given time two or three women, regarded by local gossips as prostitutes, who plied their trade in a village of 100–120 households. They charged fees which only the richer inhabitants could afford and were sometimes visited by groups of three or four gregarious pleasure-seekers.[56]

Montefollonico's prostitutes tended to be widows left with children and struggling to maintain them. In the eighteenth century, villages of the Veneto had 'licentious' girls of a different stamp, often fatherless or motherless or both, with no marital prospects and easy prey to sexual assaults and false promises. No doubt some received rewards for their sexual favours. Some, inevitably, became pregnant, and accusations of infanticide could bring them into the records. Domenica Cazzin, accused of killing her child in the region of Padua in 1752, had lapsed into a form of prostitution when her brother and sister-in-law threw her out of their house and forced her to fend for herself. Lucia Cavaliere had lost both parents and was living by vagrancy and prostitution; she was arrested in 1753 for killing a child she had borne on the road. Admitted to a hospice, she died before sentence could be passed. Maria Chiapperina, described as a spinner, had such a bad reputation in her village of Balduina in the jurisdiction of Este that her parish priest hatched plans to send her away; she ascribed her pregnancy to a man who had forced himself on her – perhaps a married man, perhaps a young bachelor tailor, she did not know which. After bearing a child on Holy Thursday 1756 and trying to conceal the birth, she claimed that the infant had been stillborn. But circumstances were suspicious and neighbours hostile. The chief magistrate and governor of Este eventually gaoled Chiapperina for five years for infanticide and her mother for eighteen months for complicity in the crime.[57]

Appointed to the southern bishopric of Sant'Agata dei Goti in 1762, the Neapolitan missionary Alfonso de' Liguori soon encountered one immoral entrepreneur working in a village nearby. This was Carmina Graziano, a kind of Magdalen in reverse, who had descended from piety into devilry and become a madame in Colonna. 'They say that in large cities these women must be tolerated', wrote the bishop to the duke of Maddaloni, urging him to have Carmina banished, 'but in country areas and small towns, such people cannot be tolerated, since they are the ruin of young men and even, at times, of whole families'. Lust, promiscuity and readiness to cater for them were not naturally confined to the wicked metropolis, and were sometimes in season in the Fusaro, marshlands to the south of the diocese and mostly outside its borders, where men and women gathered in the summer to cure flax and hemp, and some prostitutes arrived to service the workers' needs.[58]

Courtesans

Charitable folk, including Alfonso de' Liguori, might be prepared to see ordinary prostitutes, especially the youngest ones, as victims of circumstance, the prey of grinding poverty and the schemes of pimps, procuresses, bawds and bad parents. Some moralists, though, tended to blame the 'unbridled lust [*sfrenata concupiscenza*]' of whores themselves, not the base urges of their clients, or else to ascribe prostitution to the sin of sloth that appeared to underlie all forms of vagrancy.[59] Like *furfanti*, the plausible rogues of literature and legislation, sophisticated city prostitutes were often perceived as skilled deceivers and consummate actors. It seemed that they could wreak far greater havoc than did ordinary vagabonds, for their worst crimes consisted, not of conning almsgivers and diverting their charity from the true poor of Christ, but of ruining youths of good family by ruthless gold-digging. Elegant and intelligent prostitutes with a flair for trickery appear in the *Decameron*, 'honoured', 'renowned' and 'stylish' whores in the Venetian diaries of Marin Sanudo in the early sixteenth century.[60] A clever woman could have her feet in both camps, the honourable and the dishonourable, confuse the categories, become a *meretrice onesta* – know nothing of chastity, but much about courtesy and civilised behaviour, wit and conversation, music and verse, run a salon for the intelligentsia, read Petrarch, Boccaccio and Ariosto or at least display and carry copies of their works. And she might become a published poet herself, sometimes with the help of an amenable gentleman friend.[61]

About 1500, the German master of ceremonies at the papal court, Johann Burchard, used *cortegiana* as an alternative to *meretrix honesta* and first applied it to one Corsetta. Fifty 'courtesans' figured in an orgy in the apartment of Cesare Borgia in October 1501, although that event, which involved nude dancing and called for physical rather than intellectual grace, did not demand all the skills for which courtesans later became famous. In another contemporary report, some of the women were described more mundanely as 'street-walkers [*cantoniere*]'.[62] Within twenty years, however, the expression *curialis* or *curialis meretrix* had entered the papacy's official vocabulary; it appeared more than once in Leo X's bull 'Salvator noster', which established a convent for the reform of *curiales meretrices* 'who live by the pursuit of immoral earnings, outside the modest confines of marriage [*ex illicito quaestu et extra matrimonii claustra et pudorem viventium*]'.[63] Courtesans in the classical sense, a little like the Greek *hetairai*, had perhaps begun a renaissance when, in the second half of the fifteenth century, bachelor humanists serving in the papal administration began to seek female company to enliven their soirées and to find it among the more presentable and witty of the free women whom they already knew and who came to be known as *curiales*, as they themselves were.[64]

Ideally, courtesans were universal women, artistes and hostesses who pleasured all the senses, flattered the intellect, eschewed coarseness, and did not just satisfy physical desire – however imaginative or suggestible they were between their sheets. 'I want you to be as great a whore in bed as you are respectable elsewhere', says Aretino's Nanna to her daughter. 'Nothing unseemly have I ever said, Prudent in speech and crazy in my bed', says Joachim du Bellay's courtesan.[65] A few won personal fame or notoriety, especially in Rome and Venice, with the aid of a literary genre which developed in the 1520s and '30s. By turns admiring, satirical and misogynistic, presented by such authors as Aretino, Francisco Delicado and Lorenzo Venier, and later by Du Bellay and Francesco Pona, it celebrated their qualities, explored their tactics and ruses, provided semi-serious guides to their services and fees, exposed their social pretensions, gloated over their real or imagined humiliations, revealed their underlying coarseness and toughness, and sometimes predicted nastily their descent into abject poverty as victims of middle age and the French evil. A late contribution to the theme was Pallavicino's *Rettorica delle puttane*, of 1642, in which he parodied a reputable treatise on rhetoric by the Jesuit Cipriano Suarez in such a way as to provide fifteen lessons for budding courtesans on how to talk money and presents out of clients. The three ordinary vows of the sophisticated prostitute were to lust, greed, and eternal deception; to these, in the manner of the Jesuits, the apt pupil added a fourth vow, 'never to trust in any man in such a way as to esteem his love or attach any value to his promises'.[66]

Courtesans lived neither in brothels nor in back alleys; in their heyday many rented premises which overlooked spacious thoroughfares or opened on to the Grand Canal. A fortunate few owned property, acquired by inheritance (not all were self-made) or by gifts from generous admirers. For financial support they often relied on fees and presents from a small circle of clients, whom they would be wise to manage tactfully, avoiding outbursts of jealousy which would inevitably recoil on the courtesan herself. 'Behave in such a way that no man can leave angry at you or feeling he's the favourite' – so Aretino's Nanna tells her daughter Pippa.[67] Du Bellay's courtesan has two or three *fermes amis* who pay her a regular retainer of thirty scudi a month and whom she manipulates with great skill.[68] Rows, hard words, woundings and threats of murder were liable to ensue when tetchy, possessive men called on a favoured professional lady and found her entertaining somebody else.[69]

Venetians were no strangers to such incidents, but for some it seemed possible to make more civilised arrangements, which might induce clients to bond rather than quarrel with each other and the courtesan. Here, wrote Bandello, a courtesan might have six or seven patrician lovers and assign each of her regulars his own night of the week, on the understanding that the day would be hers to fill as she would. 'And these lovers, thus constituted, pay so much a month, and it is stipulated in the agreements that the woman may receive and accommodate foreigners overnight.'[70] In the mid-seventeenth century, Francesco Pannocchieschi, nephew to the papal nuncio to Venice, dwelt on the amicable relationship between fellow-clients – on the surprising fact that 'four, five or six people, acting in unison, can keep a woman in whose house they eat, drink and gamble, and there they meet together almost every day, forming friendships out of a thing that normally gives rise to jealousy and enmity'.[71] Elsewhere it was possible for a group of high-ranking citizens to establish and maintain a small group of courtesans who lived together in the same house, as did Filippo Strozzi and certain companions at Pio, near Florence, in about 1514.[72] Did each have his own mistress or were the women held in common? Where a group combined to share courtesans in Rome arrangements had some chance of working smoothly so long as no social inferior pushed his way in – as did the groom Pietro Fiorentino in 1605, when he presumed to frequent two courtesans, Menica and Maddalena, and was probably murdered by their affronted gentlemen friends.[73]

With time, the word 'courtesan' descended to lower levels of the profession; of eighty-four prostitutes invited to describe themselves in court in Rome in the late sixteenth and early seventeenth centuries, half called themselves *cortigiane*, and only twelve used the more derogatory terms *puttana*, *meretrice*, *donna di malavita* or *donna di partito*.[74] Visits even to the less refined prostitutes of Rome, who were hostesses and entertainers if not exactly *salonnières*, could be convivial occasions, not just mechanical couplings on narrow beds in sordid chambers; the woman and her clients would eat together, and perhaps have meals sent in from a neighbouring tavern; even ordinary prostitutes provided plenty of chairs as if expecting company, and might well own guitars and trumpets, if not lutes and clavichords.[75] The expensive prostitute and the public whore were sisters under their skin, divided by income and status and luck, not by any caste-like distinctions, and the fortunes of both were fragile.

Anna Bianchini and Fillide Melandroni both arrived in Rome from Siena in about 1593. The following year they were both arrested on being caught at night outside the brothel quarter, but then their paths diverged. Melandroni became an old-style, cultivated courtesan who kept a salon; from about 1600 she figured prominently in a circle of professional ladies managed and introduced to people of consequence by one Ranuccio Tomassoni. At the age of nineteen, she was acting as mentor to the younger girls. Anna Bianchini was a coarse young woman who, regularly denounced for brawling, went with several painters, and may have been the model for Caravaggio's repentant Magdalen. She passed much of her time in eating houses and taverns, finding lover-protectors among their owners. When Bianchini died in 1604 of complications during a pregnancy, she was buried in the church of Sant'Andrea delle Fratte and described in the parish's death register as a *cortigiana*. But Melandroni too got the wrong side of the law, suffering arrest and imprisonment as a whore when armed men met illegally in her house on Carnival Thursday 1599. Her parish priest denounced her in the jubilee year 1600 as a *corteggiana scandalosa* for being one of a small number of Roman residents who neglected to take communion at Easter. When she died in 1618, without benefit of either communion or confession, it was she who was buried in unconsecrated ground.[76]

The culture of the fashionable, elegant courtesan in Rome survived the expulsion orders of the Counter Reformation popes in the late sixteenth century; by no means everlasting, it probably declined only around 1650 or a little later, when the more affluent clients may have been transferring their allegiance to other accomplished women, better described as singers (*cantarine* or *virtuose*).[77] Domenica Calvi, one of the old school, who had arrived in Rome from Orvieto in 1600, lived on in her mansion in the via dei Greci until her death at the age of about fifty in 1633 and left a fortune to her sister; a Venetian counterpart, Paola Provesin, protégée of the nobleman Tommaso Contarini, died in a luxurious apartment on the Piazza San Marco in 1638.[78] To judge by the vivid testimony of famous foreigners, the splendour of Venetian courtesans was still undimmed about 1740. They included Giulietta, the dazzling call-girl who kept pistols on her dressing table lest clients get out of hand, and famously advised the nervous Jean-Jacques Rousseau: 'Give up the ladies and study mathematics'.[79] More mature and imposing in her palatial surroundings was Madame Bagatina, aged about thirty-five, who was visited by an eager French sightseer, the President De Brosses; he saw her go through a preliminary pretence of being a *marchesa*, but suddenly drop this pantomime in order to get down to business. Her air of the *grande dame* and her furniture and jewellery none the less secured her a handsome tip, for 'I did not wish to put anything measly into a hand sparkling with diamonds'. Venetian courtesans, it seemed to him, were generally prettier if less opulent than she was, exquisitely obliging, and an improvement on their Parisian counterparts. There was nothing to compare with them in Rome, which, thanks to 'clerical decorum', was equally disinclined to tolerate actresses.[80]

Numbers

Not surprisingly, it is impossible to know how many prostitutes there were at any one time in any late medieval or early modern Italian city. Available figures can be divided into partial estimates (usually in hundreds), ingenious speculations, and wild guesses, often in thousands. Most are bedevilled by uncertainty as to the exact meaning of *meretrix*, *cortigiana* or other terms – were they confined to full-time 'public women', or intended to include a much wider range of unchaste females, among them concubines and sexually exploited children?

Official surveys generally concentrated on 'visible' female prostitutes working in brothels, or registered with magistrates, or living in designated vice districts. Willingness to register tended to decrease with time, especially in Bologna and Florence from the seventeenth century onwards, and the figures became even more incomplete. Investigations in Bologna in 1341 brought to light nine houses which appeared to be entirely devoted to brothels and another two which prostitutes occupied intermittently; most were in areas heavily populated by university students, and over 120 prostitutes, not all working from brothels, were identified.[81] In Florence in 1436, four recognised brothels sheltered a total of seventy prostitutes; by 1486–90 prostitutes' numbers had risen to 150. The most comprehensive survey of the next century, conducted in the 1560s, revealed a total of 240, ranging from 'rich' to 'truly poor'. The authorities were usually aware of prostitutes of higher standing who were escaping their control and were not included.[82] Some 'official' figures may represent only one-half to one-third or even less of the total number of *meretrici* in the city.

A Roman census of prostitutes, compiled for tax purposes in 1549, listed a total of 425.[83] Estimates for Rome over the years 1599 to 1605 probably refer to prostitutes living within the area permitted to them by Pope Clement VIII. They suggest that there were then 600–900 among Rome's 37,000–47,000 female inhabitants, approximately 17 per thousand. Prostitution may well have increased during the terrible famines of the early 1590s and numbers may have fallen when, in the jubilee year 1600, the authorities made special efforts to clean up the city.[84] Roman parish priests were now required to consider their flocks annually and identify persons, ranging from the suspect to the scandalous, unfit to receive holy communion. The resulting *Stati delle Anime* suggested that the number of reputed prostitutes in Rome in the first half of the seventeenth century was between 600 and 1,200, equivalent to approximately 3.5 per cent of adult women. But beyond them, very likely, were many others who acted more discreetly, shocked their priests less, and succeeded in taking their Easter communion.[85]

At other times and in other cities, census-takers produced much smaller estimates. They were neither consistent nor candid in describing women's occupations. Most poor female household heads had to do several jobs to eke out a living; to seize on the least respectable activity of some of them would have seemed unjust and misleading. Very likely some census-takers, particularly priests, were reluctant to call them prostitutes, lest the stigma rub off on the parish and bring reproof upon themselves.[86] Indeed, in Milan in 1610, parish priests admitted to only eight public prostitutes in a city of 113,000 inhabitants.[87] But at least one Neapolitan cleric went to the other extreme, when he and his brethren were called on to compile *Stati delle Anime* for large inner-city parishes. The priest of Santi Francesco e Matteo, in 1624, thought he had about four thousand parishioners, of whom three thousand were old enough to take communion, though one thousand of these were prostitutes 'who do not take communion, as he believes'. Admittedly, this was in the Quartieri Spagnoli, where vice was notoriously rampant, but his guesswork probably inclined to exaggeration.[88]

A comprehensive census of Rome, compiled in 1526, listed 9,328 households and institutions, which included 53,689 'mouths'. A number of local censuses [*status animarum*] were drawn up in Venice between 1589 and 1607, mostly in the 1590s, and surviving records cover between them 94,862 persons and 19,444 households.[89] The Roman census identified twenty-nine female heads of households as *cortigiane* or *curiales*; the coarser term *puttana* was added in a later hand to two other names; one woman was more gently described as *Anna amorosa* and another as *Lucretia mamola* (literally a violet). On the roll, too, were seven *stufari*, keepers of stews [*stuphae*] or bath-houses, which were often thinly disguised brothels; they appeared to have forty-eight persons resident on their premises. An earlier census, taken between 1511 and 1518, had identified 193 prostitutes, mostly described as courtesans and almost all foreigners; the 1526 census seemed inclined to caution or euphemism or both.[90] Since about a quarter of Roman households were headed by single women, some historians have guessed that the actual number of prostitutes (including occasional ones) may have run into thousands, perhaps even to nearly five thousand or approximately a quarter of the female population of Rome. This estimate depends partly on counting the number of women who used the same kinds of name and style as the small number listed as *cortigiane*, and partly on supposing that single women in low-paid occupations, for example, washerwomen, must have prostituted themselves occasionally to make ends meet.[91] Arguably, though, the process, while ingenious, assumes too much and is too much at odds with the more sober figures from the turn of the century to be convincing. Safer, no doubt, is the cautious opinion that the 213 women listed as prostitutes in the Venetian censuses mentioned above represented only a tiny fraction of the actual number of prostitutes of all kinds in the city.[92] Centuries later, in the kingdom of Italy around 1900, statisticians would encounter the same problem: only brothel prostitutes and others officially registered could be counted accurately, and clandestine prostitutes, including many children and adolescents, were then believed to be anything from three to ten times as numerous.[93]

Such discrepant figures reflect the complexities of the 'profession' and the 'amateur' activities which lay beyond it; the loose terminology used to describe the industry; the limitations of law enforcement; the subjectivity of census-taking. Myths depicted the unbounded licentiousness of certain cities, especially Venice and Rome, and prompted the English visitor Coryat to report, soon after 1600, that Venice and its lagoon islands sheltered 'at the least twenty thousand' 'Cortezans', 'whereof many are esteemed so loose, that they are said to open their quivers to every arrow'.[94] The 'profession' was layered but not rigidly hierarchical – up aloft, the skilled trade of the courtesan, apparently shaping her own destiny and breaking the chains which shackled respectable women, creating that hybrid, the *meretrice onesta*; at another level, the brothel prostitute exploited but also guarded by pimps and bawds and taxed by the city; in the basement, the street girl desperate to earn her next meal. As moralists liked to point out, the courtesan, down on her luck and disfigured by disease, could swiftly decline into misery and end her days on the Sistine bridge, on the steps of a church, or in a hospital for incurably sick patients.

Conclusion

Since most humans were constant sinners, but some sins were more pardonable than others, a common prostitute ought to have been an uncomplicated and useful creature in the eyes of many pragmatists. To them she should be an easily identified woman of no account who had lost her honour and existed to satisfy pressing physical needs. She should create no lasting emotional attachments or financial responsibilities, should survive but not prosper, should practise one of the simpler sins (not adultery, but fornication), and should receive a fee for each transaction. Prostitution, though, was infinitely more complex in reality. It could be, not a pursuit confined to outcasts or marginal people, but a strategy adopted occasionally by low-paid workers, often widows struggling to survive and perhaps feed children without steady masculine support. It could be practised, sometimes under heavy pressure from husbands, by married women who became, at least technically, adulteresses. Free women and courtesans, not content to be fee-earners, might become mistresses, intruding on households, jeopardising marriages, even upsetting the social order by marrying patrician husbands. The successes of a clever, graceful, uppity courtesan might suggest all too starkly that vice could pay at least as handsomely as virtue.

In Italy, too, prostitution did not remain an impersonal sex industry, free of emotion and passion. Some courtesans, despite warnings, made the fatal mistake of falling in love. As for their clients, Montaigne observed that 'In Italy they play the swooning suitor even with women who sell their favours.' Men in these lands could never be content with possessing the body alone; they must needs conquer the woman's will, which formed no part of the commercial bargain. 'It is her will that the Italians are after, they say. And they are right. What must be courted and ensnared is the will. I am horrified by the thought of a body given to me but lacking love.'[95] Differently disposed, Tommaso Garzoni, discoursing on expensive prostitutes, whom he could hardly bear to call courtesans, inveighed against the sirens who throughout the centuries had misapplied their talents to entrapping not merely men but gods as well.

> Why do you think they take the names of Guinevra, Virginia, Isabella, Olimpia, Helena, Diana, Lidia, Vittoria, Laura, Domitia, Lavinia, Lucretia, Stella, Delia, Flora, if not to captivate the hearts of young men, who are crazy enough to inscribe them in letters of gold and compose madrigals and sonnets in their praise and set the mountains, the hills, the

beaches, the woods, and the wild and verdant places echoing with the names so extravagantly celebrated in their lovesick verses?

The love of prostitutes could do nothing but inflict untold misery. 'So all courtesans should go to the brothel [*chiasso*] and wise men attend to other pursuits which will bring them profit, honour and glory.'[96] But prostitutes, being of many species and going by many names, were not so easily confined.

Notes

1 Bandello ed. Flora 1934, II xxii, vol. I, p. 868.
2 Lazzaretti 1996: 71–2.
3 Di Blasi 1982, pp. 145–55.
4 Bandello ed. Flora 1934, I viii, vol. I, pp. 108–14.
5 Lazzaretti 1996: 52. See Genesis 3:19: 'With sweat on your brow shall you eat your bread until you return to the soil, as you were taken from it.'
6 For Nanna's views on young women determined to get married, see Aretino trans. Rosenthal 1972, pp. 376–7.
7 For some other aspects of female honour, see especially T.V. and E.S. Cohen 1993, pp. 23–4.
8 Straparola ed. Rua and Stocchi 1975, I.v, vol. I, pp. 50–9.
9 For broad treatment of this theme by a social anthropologist, see Blok 2001, pp. 44–86, 261–73.
10 Gambier 1980, p. 552.
11 For Florence, Rocke 1996, pp. 74–5, 106–9, 145–6, 157, 164–5, 209–10, 228; for Padua, Lithgow ed. Kerr 1974, p. 43 – also quoted in Davidson 2002, p. 65.
12 Rocke 2008, p.127.
13 Jacopo da Voragine ed. Graesse 1965, pp. 247–9, 397–400.
14 Comba 1986: 551.
15 Brolis 2001: 646.
16 Florio 1611/1968.
17 Pallavicino ed. Coci 1992, pp. 7, 64.
18 See (for example) Weinstein 2000, especially pp. 58–69.
19 Brundage 1976: 826–8.
20 From a communication by Lucia Ferrante (1983), reported in Buttafuoco 1985, p. 76. For definitions of a prostitute see (for example) V. and B. Bullough 1987, pp. x–xiii, 48, 68–9; Karras 1996, pp. 243–4; Scarabello 2004: 99; Lazar 2005, p. 98.
21 Boulting 1910, p. 243; Comba 1986: 571; Brundage 1987, pp. 464–5; cf. Dean 1998, p. 95.
22 Mazzi 1991, pp. 323–7.
23 For example, Comba 1986: 563–4, 569–70; Dubuis 1986: 582–3, 596, n. 116; Lansing 2003, p. 257, n. 12.
24 Innocent III, 'Inter opera charitatis', Migne P.L. 214, coll. 102–3.
25 Comba 1986: 563.
26 Rinaldi 1991, pp. 108–9, 114–15, 124, n. 36.
27 D.M.S. VIII, col. 414, 15 June 1509.
28 Mazzi 1991, pp. 230–1.
29 Nardi 1989: 23–4.
30 Pallavicino ed. Coci 1992, pp. 25, 26, 55.
31 Ferrante 1996, pp. 222–3.

32 Gozzi ed. Zardo 1915, p. 332, 5 November 1760; Canosa 1993, pp. 227-9.
33 Fortini ed. Mauriello 1995, First Day, Novella ix, vol. II, p. 820; Second Day, Novella xiii, vol. II, pp. 993-4.
34 Pallavicino ed. Marchi 1984, letter xxv, p. 62; letter xxx, pp. 73-4.
35 Gozzi ed. Zardo 1915, p. 414, 24 December 1760.
36 Storey 2001: 275; Storey 2008/2012, pp. 121-2, 226-7.
37 Ferrante 1996, p. 219.
38 Pizzolato 2007: 242-3.
39 Nardi 1989: 60; see also 48, 97.
40 Cowan 2007, pp. 125-6, 147.
41 Brundage 1975: 1-17; Brundage 1976: 828-9.
42 Jansen et al. 2009, pp. 198-9.
43 Comba 1986: 540, n. 46, 548-50, 563; Dubuis 1986: 600-01; Martini 1986-7: 302; Ferrante 1996, pp. 213-17; Eisenach 2004, pp. 136-9.
44 Lansing 2003, pp. 85-6, 91-2, 96-9.
45 Comba 1986: 550, 573-4.
46 For some examples, see Martini 1986-7; Basilico 2008.
47 Leggi e memorie 1870-2, pp. 108-9, as translated in Chambers and Pullan 1992, p. 127.
48 Eisenach 2004, pp. 170-6.
49 Canons of Trent ed. Schroeder 1941, pp. 188, 459.
50 Weinstein 2000, pp. 25-8, 58-69, 89, 92-4, 111-12; Eisenach 2004, pp. 134-5, 149; Basilico 2008, 133-4, 141-3.
51 Romeo 2008, pp. 78-9, 121-2, 127.
52 Pizzolato 2007: 253; Romeo 2008, pp. 116-17, 136, 226-7.
53 Mazzi 1986a: 615-17.
54 Basilico 2008: 126-7.
55 Storey 2008/2012, pp. 150-7.
56 Hanlon 2009: 22-4.
57 Povolo 1978-9: 129-30; Povolo 1979-80: 416-25, 430-1.
58 Jones 1992, pp. 373-4, 392, 516.
59 On this theme, see, for example, the discussion in Muratori ed. Nonis 1961, pp. 726-8.
60 Boccaccio ed. McWilliam 1995, II.5, pp. 97-111; VIII.10, pp. 632-44; IX.5, pp. 668-77; D.M.S., XIX, col. 25, 7 September 1514; XXXIII, coll. 233, 234, 9 May 1522.
61 On courtesans, their tastes, possessions and accomplishments, see, for example, Larivaille 1975; Masson 1975; Lawner 1987; Santore 1988; Rosenthal 1992; Ruggiero 1993, pp. 44-5; Ferrante 1994, p. 920; Camerano 1998: 658-62; Brown 2004, pp. 173-80, 183; Storey 2008/2012, pp. 188-202.
62 Burchard ed. Thuasne 1883-85, II, pp. 442-4, 2 April 1498; III, p. 167, 30 October 1501. The second passage is translated in Burchard ed. Parker 1963, p. 194.
63 Leo X, 'Salvator noster', 19 May 1520, in B.R., V, pp. 745, 747.
64 Cf. Larivaille 1975, pp. 33-5; on the hetairai, see V. and B. Bullough 1987, pp. 35-44.
65 Aretino trans. Rosenthal 1972, p. 117; cf. pp. 283-4; Du Bellay ed. Saulnier 1947, p. 158, lines 241-2; cf. p. 157, lines 227-30. 'Que rien qu'honneur ne sortait de ma bouche: Sage au parler, et follastre à la couche'.
66 Pallavicino ed. Coci 1992, especially pp. xxix-xlii, 102, 108-9.
67 Aretino trans. Rosenthal 1972, p. 221.
68 Du Bellay ed. Saulnier 1947, lines 121-80, pp. 153-5.

69   For some examples, see D.M.S., III, col. 133, 26 February 1500; Brown 2004, p. 163; Ruggiero 1993, pp. 3–8; T.V. and E.S. Cohen 1993, pp. 85–9.

70   Bandello ed. Flora 1934, Part III, novella xxxi, vol. II, pp. 417–19.

71   Pannocchieschi ed. Molmenti 1919, p. 331.

72   Masson 1975, pp. 60–4; Lawner 1987, p. 48.

73   Storey 2008/2012, pp. 215–20.

74   *Ibid.*, p. 122.

75   Camerano 1998: 658–62; Storey 2008/2012, pp. 114, 188–97, 203.

76   Bassani and Bellini 1994, pp. 49–55, 66–77, 182–4, 243–4. See pp. 93–4, 107 for the possibility that Caravaggio employed these women as models. For some scepticism about the practice of identifying paintings as portraits of courtesans, see Schuler 1991.

77   Storey 2008/2012, pp. 249–50.

78   Bassani and Bellini 1994, pp. 127–33, 244; Brown 2004, p. 186.

79   Rousseau trans. Cohen 1953, pp. 298–302.

80   De Brosses ed. Bezard 1931, Letters xv, xvii, I, pp. 176–9, 242; xlv, II, pp. 195–6.

81   Rinaldi 1991, pp. 109, 114–16.

82   Trexler 1981: 987–8, 990; Brackett 1993: 291–2, 296–7; see also Canosa and Colonnello 1989, pp. 109–11.

83   Camerano 1998: 667, n. 46.

84   Delumeau 1957–9, I, pp. 421–4.

85   Storey 2008/2012, pp. 65, 68, 89, 115–16, 241.

86   Burke 1987, pp. 37–8.

87   D'Amico 1994, pp. 142, 163–4.

88   Romeo 2008, p.144.

89   *Descriptio Urbis* ed. Lee 1985, p. 20; Chojnacka 2001, p. 141.

90   Canosa and Colonnello 1989, pp. 47–9.

91   *Descriptio Urbis* ed. Lee, *passim*; see pp. 44 and 101 for the 'mamola' and the 'amorosa', p. 352 for the 'stufari'; Lawner 1987, pp. 5–6, 204; Hufton 1997, p. 329.

92   Chojnacka 2001, pp. 22–3.

93   Buttafuoco 1985, p. 81; Gibson 1986, p. 105.

94   Coryat 1611/1905, I, p. 402.

95   De Montaigne ed. Screech 2003, III.5, p. 997.

96   Garzoni 1616, fo. 258v.–260v.

2

Prostitution, sin and the law

Seldom if ever did princes and magistrates in Italy attempt to forbid women to sell sexual services to men in all parts of their cities and territories. But prostitutes who plied their trade in forbidden places, or at forbidden times, or consented to 'unnatural' acts, were liable to punishment, albeit randomly applied. Their behaviour, to say nothing of their clients' rowdy and sometimes violent antics, could be distressing to neighbours. Much like, for example, butchery or tanning, public prostitution was best confined to its own quarter, prevented from contaminating the most dignified parts of town and from profaning the surroundings of religious houses. Regarded as an unclean and sinful occupation, it was practised by women who suffered restrictions on free movement and risked being denied holy communion. In itself, though, heterosexual prostitution was not a sin against nature, and, unlike sodomy, did not seem to late medieval moralists especially likely to arouse the wrath of God. Hence it proved possible, in the fourteenth and fifteenth centuries, to license prostitution as if it were a civic amenity comparable with pawnbroking: ungodly but necessary, better exposed and controlled than driven into shadows and allowed to permeate a whole society.

In a sense, prostitutes were below the law, privileged in reverse: accept the stigma attached to common women and they would escape the ferocious penalties which lay in store for women of higher status convicted of sexual crimes. Prostitution was not in itself a crime, though procuring and trafficking were regarded as grave offences in principle, and prostitutes were often charged with incidental misdemeanours. Several were confined in Florence's new prison, the Stinche, during the fourteenth century.[1] About 1140, the legal code of King Roger II of Sicily had declared that 'Known prostitutes shall not be thought worthy to observe these laws and shall stand absolutely immune from the judicial punishments for adultery and fornication.' The law should protect a prostitute against violence, but she must not 'dwell among women of good reputation'.[2] Most authorities would uphold this principle, even centuries later. Chaste women and girls might otherwise be scandalised, exposed to bad example, molested by undiscriminating punters, tempted into lewd adventures of their own and even, having lost their honour, be forced to become prostitutes themselves.

'The lesser evil'

Magistrates rarely went to great lengths to explain or justify their actions by legislative preambles or other methods (they were dealing with an indelicate matter), and the reasoning behind their policies has often to be inferred. It would be difficult to prove that hard-headed civic authorities read closely the remarks of doctors of the Church on the subject of tolerating prostitutes or to show that their actions were inspired by theologians rather than by their own pragmatism. But magistrates' policies were compatible with statements of principle made during the thirteenth century by Thomas Aquinas and one of his disciples, and (centuries earlier) by Augustine of Hippo. Aquinas seemed ready to approve the compromises made by human authorities, even dignify them as proper imitations of God.

> Human government derives from divine government and should be modelled on it. Though he is omnipotent and supremely good, God permits some evils in the universe which he could prevent, lest without them greater goods might be lost or greater evils ensue. So, too, in human government the authorities rightly tolerate certain evils lest certain good be impeded or greater evils be incurred.[3]

By way of illustration, he quoted a passage from St Augustine's *De Ordine*, which read in full: 'What can be called more filthy, more worthless, more wicked and dishonourable than whores, pimps, and other such baneful creatures? But take away harlots from human affairs and you will trouble everything with unbridled lust and passion.'[4] This left much to the imagination: did it mean, as it was sometimes taken to mean in later centuries, that chaste maidens and respectable married women would be molested by lustful males if there were no loose women to distract these predators and absorb their sexual energies? Aquinas's treatise on princely government expanded on the theme and supplied some detail. The remarks were really those of his pupil and commentator, Ptolemy of Lucca, as, at least by the eighteenth century, some pundits had come to realise. But they acquired more weight by being attributed to Aquinas himself. Discussing the laws and customs of Sparta, the author commended Aristotle's opinion that soldiers should be allowed wives or women because they were naturally licentious and would otherwise lie with other men: it was 'less evil to have sexual congress with women than to succumb to scandalous vices [*minus malum est mulieribus carnaliter commisceri, quam in vilia declinare flagitia*]'. He added that the function of a prostitute was like that of

> bilge-water at sea or the sewer in a palace: 'Remove the sewer and you will fill the whole palace with the stench', and, likewise, concerning bilge-water, 'Remove prostitutes from the world, and you will fill it with sodomy.' Hence Augustine says, in the thirteenth book of *The City of God*, that 'the earthly city has made resort to prostitutes a legitimate form of wickedness'.[5]

Heterosexual prostitution, it seemed, could provide a defence against greater evils and serve as a form of hygiene – though the women who provided the service would receive few thanks and much dishonour.

Bernardino of Siena, the Franciscan fundamentalist preaching of sin and divine retribution to huge audiences in fifteenth-century city squares, regaled his hearers with a text from Genesis: the story of Lot, the righteous man trapped in Sodom. Besieged at home by degenerate local males determined to 'sin with' the handsome young men under his roof, he had offered them his virgin daughters, to be abused as the lecherous citizens saw fit. The moral of this tale appeared to be that almost any sexual sin involving unmarried women was preferable to coupling between males, and that some women could be sacrificed to provide a diversion.[6] Bernardino was no friend to prostitutes, especially when they corrupted the respectable women of Siena by arousing interest in the latest French fashions. But prostitution and casual fornication were not among the evils which he most passionately denounced.[7] Could they perhaps provide an antidote to unnatural vice?

In a treatise on marriage, Augustine had warned against the fallacy of regarding some sinful acts as harmless because it was possible to imagine something worse: fornication was not good because adultery was worse (nor could adultery be called good because incest was even worse and sodomy heinous).[8] But some people were inclined to excuse visits to prostitutes so long as they entailed only 'simple fornication': 'the coupling of a free man with a free woman by mutual agreement', neither party being tied by marriage, betrothal or religious vows, and there being no danger of incest, no suggestion of rape, no question of indulging in 'unnatural' intercourse. True, distinctions between simple and more elaborate varieties of fornication had not been drawn when St Paul listed sins which barred sinners from God's kingdom, those which Augustine called 'mortal [*mortifera*]' – 'do you think I can take parts of Christ's body and join them to a prostitute? Never! ... Keep away from fornication.'[9] But for centuries a questionable opinion persisted, for all that strict moralists could do to dispel it, to the effect that casual consensual sex between unmarried persons was at worst a trivial offence. The proposition that simple fornication was not a mortal sin would be repeatedly condemned by tribunals of the Spanish Inquisition in the sixteenth and seventeenth centuries, and occasionally surfaced in Sardinia and Sicily in the late sixteenth. A popular preacher, the Franciscan Cornelio Musso of Piacenza, denounced the opinion evidently current in Rome at this time that simple fornication was blameless. In 1665, Pope Alexander VII saw fit to condemn the proposition that a man who had had sexual relations with an unmarried woman could meet his obligations in the confessional by merely saying 'I have committed a serious sin against chastity with an unmarried woman' without giving details.[10] In the late middle ages, lechery, gluttony and sloth, as sins of the flesh, tended to be treated as less grave than sins of aversion, such as pride, envy or anger.[11] Sodomy was the subject of savage vituperation and occasionally of exemplary punishment, but was it the worst of all sins or merely the worst sexual sin, less grievous than blasphemy?[12]

Prostitution was inclined to flourish in societies where men married late after learning a trade or profession, so that they were unmarried at the stage in life when their sexual drive was at its height; or where marriages were limited by propertied families (e.g. to avoid procreating too many heirs to a divisible estate or providing generous marriage portions for too many daughters); or where clerics were called upon to be celibate and did not always respond. Large cities played host to a floating population which included unchaste priests and friars, travelling merchants, migrant artisans, labourers and agricultural workers, pilgrims, soldiers and sailors – men without women who would perhaps threaten the locals less if they had affordable brothels or vice districts to resort to. Studies of the Florentine tax survey of 1427 have shown that the proportion of 'permanent bachelors', defined by the analysts as single men aged between forty-eight and fifty-two, reached 12.1 per cent of the masculine population in the city, while in the countryside it did not exceed 5.3 per cent.[13] Some enforced bachelors, no doubt, visited prostitutes. Arguably, the supply of potential prostitutes (for example, from poor girls drifting from country to town or travelling across Europe in flight from war zones) was ample enough to destroy any realistic prospect of suppressing the trade, even if the authorities had seriously wished to do so.

The clergy's official teachings inclined to the view that all human beings were assailed by lust, corrupted by a hereditary disease of the flesh springing from the rebellion of the first man and woman. At best, this was palliated, not cured, by baptism washing away original sin, for the sacrament did not eliminate concupiscence, 'sensual appetite resistent to reason', like the ungovernable passion which drives the young man to rape Giulia of Gazuolo in Bandello's pathetic story.[14] Lust was part of the human condition, but a good Christian ought to be capable of subduing sensual stirrings and practising restraint, if not total abstention. For ordinary people, marriage was the cure for lust (it was more than that), in accordance with the Pauline advice: 'if they cannot control the sexual urges, they should get married, since it is better to be married than to be tortured'.[15] Celibacy was superior to the married state, and the proper function of sexual intercourse within marriage was to attempt to procreate children; according to Augustine, however, intercourse within marriage designed to satisfy lust was not a grave sin unless it was indulged in to excess and unless it degenerated into 'unnatural' practices, perhaps into anal or oral sex for contraceptive purposes.[16] Indeed, intercourse for pleasure could be defended on the grounds that 'it preserves fidelity to the marriage bed'. Worldly government, though, had to preside over a population in which a fair number of men were not married or cloistered or were away from their wives for long periods. Magistrates were perhaps entitled to make some concessions to human or at least to masculine imperfections, for the sake of preserving good order and preventing worse evils.

Medical opinion sometimes parted company with theological, followers of Galen holding the view that total abstention from sexual activity was harmful to masculine health and that coitus, practised in moderation, was important to a man's wellbeing.[17] This view would be bluntly expressed by the notorious Ferrante Pallavicino in the mid-seventeenth century, when, probably drawing on a pseudo-Galenian text, he reminded his readers that ' "semen retained is poison", says the oracle of the physicians'. By his reckoning, sexual activity was as natural and indeed necessary as eating and drinking. Like excreting, it required a receptacle; perhaps distantly echoing the metaphor of the sewer, he declared that the function of prostitutes was 'to serve as chamberpots and urinals provided for the common benefit of anyone who wishes to relieve himself of a surplus of semen'.[18]

License or tolerate prostitutes and men unfaithful to the marriage bed would visit them, if only on their travels; their clientele would not be confined to bachelors and widowers. Discontented wives in marital disputes of the sixteenth and seventeenth centuries would complain of husbands who resorted to prostitutes close to home.[19] It is possible – as certain modern scholars have suggested – that prostitutes reduced some husbands' demands on their wives, afforded married women some relief from repeated pregnancies, and helped to limit the size of families.[20] Recourse to prostitutes was reprehensible for many reasons, not least because it involved sexual intercourse without the intention of begetting a child or of taking responsibility for nurturing any that might be born. But it was arguably no worse, and perhaps more tolerable, than other practices, such as contraception, abortion or child abandonment, which might be used to dispose of children whom their parents could not or did not wish to support, and were dangerous to the children's bodies and souls.

'Fortresses of lust'

In the thirteenth and early fourteenth centuries, some cities – among them Bergamo, Bologna, Ferrara, Florence, Lucca, Orvieto, Venice, Vercelli – had attempted to expel prostitutes, along with vagrants and gamblers and other undesirables. Often they had forbidden them to ply their trade in the suburbs and the *contado*. Sometimes magistrates proclaimed a general ban; otherwise they compiled ever-lengthening lists of inner-city districts from which prostitutes would henceforth be excluded. Laws sometimes demanded that in any part of the territory they should keep a certain distance from monasteries or convents. Responsible neighbours (in Florence, ideally two from each side of the offending premises) were urged to report disorderly houses to magistrates. Landlords were forbidden to let lodgings for immoral purposes, warned that any house known to have sheltered a prostitute would be demolished and the building materials and furniture confiscated. Venetian legislation forbade tavern-keepers to supply prostitutes with food or drink or allow them beds on their premises. Authorities in Bologna viewed with alarm the tendency of the vice trade to organise itself, with prostitutes working in groups and taking houses, each with a capacity of up to five or six lodgers.[21]

By the 1330s, however, city magistrates and councils in northern and central Italy were beginning to allow, even to encourage, prostitutes and their pimps and managers to set up shop within town walls, so long as they concentrated their activities in a particular area. Sometimes this was in a remote corner, but occasionally (as in Venice, Ferrara, Florence or Macerata in the Marches) near a commercial district where pleasure could be alternated with business. The process went on fitfully for a century and more, the authorities looking, sluggishly or energetically, for suitable sites in which to confine the *ars libidinis*, 'the craft of lust', as it was called in Macerata in 1424.[22] Many towns and cities in southern and eastern France, in Germany, and in Spain were adopting similar tactics, setting up communal brothels or establishing zones of toleration which were sometimes walled, gated and transformed into townships within cities.[23] Official brothels would be less common, indeed unknown, in some parts of northern Europe. But even in England they did exist in Southwark, Sandwich and Southampton, possibly for the convenience of visiting traders and seamen from southern Europe, who expected to find in these ports the amenities they were used to at home.[24]

In Italy the brothel was sometimes a municipal building, supervised or even directly administered by a government agency. Or, more commonly, it would be leased for a term of a year or more to a contractor, male or female, quite likely an experienced pimp or prostitute, or to a couple, who would pay rent to the commune. Alternatively, the civic authorities might designate a brothel-street (in the smaller towns, probably just a blind alley), or several intertwining streets also provided with taverns, inns and bath-houses – an area in which much of the property might well be owned by patricians or well-to-do citizens, as in Florence in the 1430s. In this quarter, the ban on letting to prostitutes would be waived. Landlords would receive rent, but rooming-houses would be managed by their tenants ('hosts and pimps', *hospites et lenones*), and the area super-vised by magistrates responsible for maintaining order and paying some attention to the welfare of the women who worked there.[25] Though still regarded as dishonourable, registered prostitutes were under the city's protection, entitled to fees; unlike usurers, they could not be compelled to restore their gains.[26] Landlords and brothel-keepers were allowed to make profits from the sale of sexual services, and communes were beginning to receive rent or taxes from this, as though they were entitled to receive their own dues for overseeing an activity of some benefit to the public.

In 1334, the statutes of Imola allowed brothels to be set up in the city so long as prostitutes kept their distance from the abbey of Santa Maria in Regola. A year later, the papal marshal of the Romagna authorised the mayor to rent out a public brothel, called a *baratteria* or *biscazzeria* (which suggested a gambling-den as much as a bawdy house), for fifty florins and permitted him to tax gamblers and prostitutes.[27] Other public brothels followed: at Bologna and Lucca in the 1340s, Perugia (the Malacucina) in 1359, Venice in 1360, Genoa by 1363 and Bergamo by 1399, Milan and Pavia in 1390, Florence in 1403. At Pinerolo in Savoy-Piedmont, the possibility of establishing a suitable 'receptacle' for prostitutes, to protect the more decorous parts of town, was discussed in 1379; the sexual needs of students were debated in Turin in 1412.[28] The earliest surviving contract between the commune of Macerata and a brothel-keeper was concluded in 1391.[29] A public brothel was functioning at Pisa by 1427.[30] In a famous course of sermons delivered in Siena that year, Bernardino of Siena rebuked the citizens for the uncharitable act of diverting water supplies from the prison – whose inmates were now sorely neglected – to the brothel quarter, which he referred to elsewhere as 'the evil place', *il mal luogo*.[31] By 1476 there appeared to be two, possibly three brothel compounds in Ferrara, i.e. San Biagio, El Gambaro (owned by the rulers) and Santa Croce.[32]

It is not clear why cities should have changed direction, turning from the expulsion to the internal segregation of common prostitutes, at the time when they did. Perhaps these moves echoed events in thirteenth-century France, where Louis IX, bent on the creation of an orderly Christian society, had tried to outlaw prostitution in 1254, but had found his decrees unenforceable and retreated into regulation rather than prohibi-tion.[33] Measures after the 1340s might have reflected a declining population in the wake of the Great Mortality, pestilence making vacant lots available within city walls and heightening the fear of 'unnatural' vice, or of the sterile practices to which young men might resort if prostitutes were not readily available: these were at once a menace to the birth rate and a provocative sin which threatened the community with more divine displeasure.[34] Nor is it obvious how the word spread between cities – did magistrates study each other's regulations, were they influenced by travellers' or envoys' reports of arrangements in other cities, or moved by the exhortations of travelling preachers concerned for public decency? But in 1430, Amedeo VIII of Savoy did issue a general instruction that all towns in his duchy should establish 'a sordid hidden place, far removed from any respectable women, in which all prostitutes must live'; the following year, Turin was rebuked for past negligence and urged to provide a suitable 'house' for the purpose of eliminating scandal and preserving the honour of good wives, chaste maidens and respectable widows.[35] By the end of the fifteenth century, Florence's subject towns were evidently expected to create reservations for prostitutes, although at Figline, San Cassiano, Montevarchi and elsewhere in 1492 the women were breaking their bounds on market days and roaming freely in search of custom.[36]

Contractors who ran official brothels might be citizens or outsiders. In 1349 the councils of Lucca attempted to concentrate all prostitutes in the Cuoieria (near the tanneries, perhaps?); two years later, the task of managing them fell to a citizen, Nicolò Tepa, who agreed to pay a total of 120 florins in twelve monthly instalments to the city treasurer.[37] But, between 1391 and 1446, the brothel at Macerata was always in the hands of outsiders – some from another Italian city, some from Istria or the Balkans, while after 1416, the contractors were generally described as natives of 'Germany'. Here sixteen annual contracts were made with a female contractor alone, eight with couples and nine with male bawds [ruffiani] alone.[38] Was it considered more seemly that prostitution should be managed by foreigners? In Pisa, c.1427, the brothel was sometimes leased for three years to a Florentine contractor, sometimes administered temporarily by a government agency.[39] A census of the official vice district in Florence, compiled in 1436, listed four inns of ill-fame; at least three of the four hosts were outsiders, one German, one Venetian and one Ferrarese.[40]

An official brothel or vice district was something of a ghetto *avant la lettre*, designed for public sinners rather than religious minorities – places of compulsory residence for professing Jews would spread widely only in the sixteenth and seventeenth centuries – and something of a fortress. Its garrison might have to be defended against rowdy, hot-tempered customers or gangs intent on rape or theft or sloping off without paying. Among the more unruly individuals was the Venetian client of 1392, who, when the matrons denied him access to his favourite, ran amok and set fire to all the beds he could lay hands on.[41] Some establishments, as in Bologna, Pisa or Venice, were called 'castles', as though echoing the French 'castel joyos'; regulations in Bologna (1382) required prostitutes to live 'in the appointed place, which is called a *castelucio* or *bordellum*'.[42] Others were known as *postriboli* or *loci publici*. Brothels might be surrounded by walls seemingly designed to spare the public indecent sights, to frustrate voyeurs, and to create an aura of secrecy. At Lucca (1351) one could enter and leave the premises only through a back door facing the city walls; the side of the building facing the city had to be blank and impenetrable.[43] In Milan in 1390, an area already densely settled by prostitutes was enclosed by a wall and a porter employed to lock the gate at night and reopen it in the morning.[44] At Pinerolo in the mid-fifteenth century, a committee recommended building the house of resort in an angle of the city walls and protecting the establishment by 'stout walls' of its own.[45] Ferrarese rules appeared to prescribe that brothels, though near to markets, should be lodged in back streets, e.g. in nondescript one-storey houses, merging with their surroundings and as inconspicuous as could be.[46]

Venice's first public brothel, set up near Rialto in 1360, occupied houses owned by the patrician families of Venier and Morosini and lasted for a century. After its demolition, another nobleman, Priamo Malipiero, made houses in the same area available to a board composed mainly of a group of police magistrates, the chiefs of the six administrative districts of the city. These gentlemen drew up regulations, determined the rents to be paid by 'sinful women' who took rooms in the building, appointed the *castellans* charged with protecting them, fixed the opening hours, and forbade anyone to enter the brothel bearing a weapon. All women wishing to work there must present themselves to the board for approval. The landlord received the rent, subject to certain deductions, and undertook to keep the premises in good shape and convert the interior so as to provide enough cubicles for sexual congress (in 1496 there were thirty-four).[47] In Macerata, however, the brothel's managers appeared to be free to make their own arrangements with prostitutes, who were not vetted by city authorities.[48] In any town, much of the brothel-keepers' power over their underlings derived, not from their official position, but from the sums which prostitutes owed them for clothes, jewellery, food and rent. Indebtedness could compel women to work for nothing and prevent them from departing without being pursued by the law – as were Lucrezia of Mantua and Lucrezia of Brescia, when they fled the establishment of Iacopo of Germany in Florence in 1498, allegedly bearing 'goods that belonged to him', including, in effect, themselves.[49]

Much medieval legislation restricted the movement of public prostitutes about town (sometimes they could lawfully leave the brothel only on Saturdays) and required them, when they did so, to wear distinctive signs so that they should nowhere pass for respectable women and lecherous men should have no excuse for accosting women who were normally dressed. In the fourteenth and fifteenth centuries, some city regulations favoured the grotesque, employing warning bells, garish colours (red, green and especially yellow), images of beasts and absurd items of dress, presumably outlandish enough not to be taken for the latest fashions. The sixteenth and seventeenth centuries usually favoured simpler arrangements, often resorting to the colour yellow, e.g. for shawls or sleeves, and making some use of caps and veils (including Venice's *velo deshonesto*), but occasionally denying veils to prostitutes and compelling them to go barefaced. Another approach, used at Ancona, was to exempt prostitutes from the city's laws restraining expenditure on clothing and jewellery and lavish entertainment, cunningly suggesting that any extravagantly dressed woman must be one of easy virtue.[50]

There were analogies with the signs imposed on Jews and Saracens by general legislation of the Church since the thirteenth century (though these were less varied and imaginative). The English eulogist of papal Rome, Gregory Martin, did not fail to draw parallels when, about 1580, he was describing the legal oppression of prostitutes:

> as the Jews by their yellow cappe, so they are discerned by their distinct form of attire, whereby they are notoriously knowen and as Marie Magdalen in her citie, shunned but

where there is hope of reclayming them, and subject to all shrewdnes of the boies in the
streetes, who use commonly to mocke and revile them.[51]

These emblems, though, had different purposes: those of prostitutes were at least partly
designed to indicate that they were sexually available, while those worn by Jews and
Saracens were intended, initially at least, to warn Christians against so-called 'ruin-
ous commingling', Christian intimacy with infidel women, or infidel intimacy with
Christian women.[52]

Many official brothels enjoyed, in principle, a monopoly of the vice trade; they
would lose much of their *raison d'être* if prostitutes were allowed to solicit and practise
outside them, to escape the control of their contractors, to reduce profits and taxes. The
rule that sexual services could only be sold 'in the houses in which the brothel is established' was spelled out laboriously in contracts at Macerata.[53] At Ivrea in Piedmont,
from 1433, should a prostitute be caught working elsewhere in the town, the brothel
women were to escort her to their own premises, accompanied by trumpet and bells,
and transform her from competitor into colleague.[54]

During the fifteenth century, however, it was clearly becoming difficult to stop the
trade from creeping away from its official territory and invading other places.[55] No
doubt many prostitutes welcomed the brothel's protection on arrival in town but soon
began chafing against its constraints. Some developed, often in collusion with male protectors who were drumming up their own business, ambitions to set up on their own, to
the annoyance of neighbours – if Betta, in Florence in the 1430s, wished to surrender
to lust, 'she should go to live in the public places allotted for the purpose'.[56] About 1490,
two officials in Ferrara complained that prostitutes were no longer living in brothels
and that revenue from lewdness and drink was being lost; they urged that more rooms
and an inn be provided to accommodate them – in vain for the time being, as it happened, since the ruler, Ercole d'Este, was falling under Savonarola's puritanical spell.[57]

Public brothels offered cheap services affordable by artisans and shopkeepers, or
even by journeymen and labourers and farmworkers in town on market days, or by
soldiers, or travellers, or other foreign visitors. To float financially on small fees, keepers
depended on a swift turnover of clients, who had to be briskly and perhaps brusquely
served. Fastidious citizens at Macerata, reluctant to jostle with plebeian customers
and preferring more leisurely encounters, were entitled to have prostitutes brought
to their homes by appointment.[58] Small private establishments could well prove more
attractive to genteel clients than the sleazy inns or ground-floor hovels of an official
brothel quarter.

If respectable people were seen near a public brothel their intentions would be all
too plain. But should they visit a tavern or a bath-house outside a brothel compound,
they could pretend to be interested only in food, drink, cleanliness and good company,
though these establishments, too, harboured prostitutes.[59] On the premises of stews
[*stuphae*] there would probably be not only wet and dry rooms but also retiring rooms,
where prostitutes, a shade more refined than the 'common girls', could be visited,
and illicit liaisons pursued.[60] Authorities in Turin in the mid-fifteenth century fined
Stephano, a bath-house keeper, for allowing public prostitutes to 'stay' on his premises,

and Perineto, a barber, for having one available in his shop.[61] In Florence, both the Stufa dei Tedeschi, on the way to the Faenza gate, and the stews of San Michele Berteldi, in the vice district, were involved in the trade.[62] But at Moncalieri in Piedmont, the bath-house was a more decorous place that could properly be visited by clergymen and married couples; it seems to have been complementary to the brothel, rather than a rival establishment.[63] In subsequent centuries, however, some baths still had a louche air; when the hirsute Montaigne visited one in Rome in 1581, his interest was chiefly in depilation, but it was usual, he said, to take along female friends, who were 'massaged with you by the boys'.[64]

Encounters with magistrates

In the thirteenth and fourteenth centuries, some cities employed overseers of uncertain status to mediate between mainstream society and the people on its margins, including gamblers and other undesirables as well as prostitutes. Bearing titles such as *potestas marochorum*, *potestas ribaldorum* or *potestas meretricum*, they had affinities to the French *roi des ribauds* or *roi de l'amoureuse vie*. They may not have been public executioners, as was apparently common in France, but they were not patricians or respectable citizens. At Ivrea one of the town criers [*preconi*] became the *potestas meretricum*, endowed with 'authority to guard and preserve prostitutes … and to discipline and punish them'.[65] In Lucca the office of 'king of the riff-raff' was held intermittently in the 1340s by Cecco Dini, a Florentine who wielded authority over all 'public and mercenary women' in Lucca and its suburbs and could compel them to live in suitable places, lest their activities contaminate the whole city. His position disappeared during the great plague of 1348, after which a brothel contractor replaced him.[66]

With time, some cities began to subject prostitutes to more respectable figures, to elected magistrates as well as to brothel-keepers and whoremistresses, and to grant the women some legal rights. An unusually specialised magistracy was set up in Florence in 1403 and generally known as the Onestà, the Office of Public Decency. This panel did not merely award the status of prostitute, as other boards had done before them, they were also to issue residence permits to prostitutes and pimps arriving from abroad, to enforce discipline, to reprimand mavericks who presumed to work outside the area of tolerance, and to punish 'unnatural acts' and other excesses. They made some effort to protect prostitutes from assaults, listened to their grievances as well as to complaints against them, and occasionally considered the formal agreements which were sometimes made between prostitutes and pimps.[67] The Office of Public Decency was to function in Florence from 1403 to 1680.[68] It was sometimes overruled by a superior tribunal, the Otto di Guardia, who were known to release culprits sentenced by the Onestà for assaulting prostitutes.[69]

In sixteenth-century Lucca, similar tasks fell to the Protectors of Prostitutes [*Protettori delle Meretrici*], constituted in 1534. Between 1564 and 1571 about forty women complained to these magistrates, some more than once; several of their grievances concerned groups of rowdies who roamed the city, hammered on prostitutes' doors, stoned the windows, forced an entry, interrupted business, and refused to go away. Very likely they were bullies picking on soft targets, rejected or penniless would-be clients spoiling others' fun, rather than moral crusaders.[70] In Naples, for a time, jurisdiction over recognised prostitutes belonged in the first instance to a court administered by the entrepreneurs who had purchased the right to exact the tax on prostitutes first introduced in 1401. Regulations issued in 1517 allowed the women to apply to another tribunal only if they had been denied justice in the court of the tax-farmers.[71]

Elsewhere, few magistracies concentrated on regulating prostitution alone. In Bologna, the Ufficio delle Bollette or Permit Office was originally charged with keeping an eye on foreigners, but its jurisdiction was later extended to innkeepers, Jews, and (from the late fourteenth century) prostitutes. By the late seventeenth century, it was also concerned with concubines, by which time prostitutes could also be summoned to the archbishop's court.[72] The Ufficio delle Bollette in fifteenth-century Ferrara carried out similar duties and also required prostitutes, once registered, to buy a pass if they wished to leave the city either temporarily or permanently.[73] In early modern Venice, at least three magistracies dealt with aspects of prostitution – the Ufficio della Sanità (matters related to vagrancy and disease), the Esecutori contro la Bestemmia (lewd acts in public places), and the Provveditori alle Pompe (forbidden extravagance, for example, the excesses of courtesans aping gentlewomen).[74] In Rome, police magistrates, especially the governor, dealt with disturbances in or around brothels and courtesans' houses, and listened to prostitutes' complaints of insults, assaults, and attacks on their property launched by disgruntled lovers.[75] On the fief of Montefollonico near Montepulciano, two village prostitutes, Giomma la Lombardina (c.1632) and Francesca Borzelli (c.1656) both urged the local magistrate to punish their tormentors, and Borzelli at least succeeded in having the miscreants fined.[76]

In the early fourteenth century, prostitutes had enjoyed very few legal rights, in that they could not sue to recover fees or accuse anyone else of crimes, and they generally enjoyed little protection against violence. At Susa (north-west Piedmont) in the late middle ages, sexual assaults on prostitutes would be punished, but the fine would be paltry, no more than a quarter to a half of the average. If 'by public repute she is said to be a common prostitute', a woman complaining of rape would start at a disadvantage.[77] But by about 1500, prostitutes had in theory acquired much the same legal capacity as 'reputable' women and some entitlement to protection.[78] They also began to enjoy, in theory if not always in practice, some safeguards against the accumulation of debts for food, drink and clothing which prevented them from escaping from brothel-keepers' clutches.[79] Benefactors in Ferrara occasionally made bequests or grants to prostitutes in the hope of freeing them from debt.[80] And, in Lucca at least, new regulations allowed them during the fifteenth century to move more freely about the city and even to accompany men to the public baths.[81]

Sodomy: a greater evil?

'Remove prostitutes from the world and you will fill it with sodomy', according to the maxim attributed to Aquinas.[82] Was this the greater evil, denounced by preachers and at times severely punished by law courts, that helped to justify the tolerance and regulation of heterosexual prostitution? And were female prostitutes themselves entirely innocent of this crime?

Theologians and moralists used 'sodomy' as an all-embracing term for 'unnatural' sexual acts and sometimes employed it to describe any kind of 'sin against nature'. This generally denoted intercourse between males, but occasionally involved women or girls. Sometimes it consisted of self-abuse, and sometimes it was used to prevent conception.[83] By squandering semen and making conception impossible, one disobeyed the divine commandment to Adam and Eve, 'Be fruitful and multiply, fill the earth and conquer it'.[84] For sodomites deposited the seed in the wrong orifice, *in vase indebito*, or spilled it outside the body, so that no souls could spring from it. It could be said that most sexual encounters in a municipal brothel were intended to assuage lust, not procreate children. But in vaginal intercourse the possibility of conception still existed, and so the offence could be regarded as far less serious. As defined by law courts, legislation and legal treatises, 'sodomy' included buggery, oral sex, simulated sex between the thighs, masturbation (usually regarded as less iniquitous), sexual congress with animals or dead bodies, occasionally cross-dressing, and occasionally intercourse with Jews and infidels.[85]

The gravest legal penalties were generally imposed in cases where sodomy had been aggravated by violence, where it had been part of a series of brutal acts or had combined with other forms of scandalous or irreligious behaviour, involving blasphemy, sacrilege or image desecration, and come close to some mindless form of heresy.[86] Many offences took the form of pederasty: of intercourse between a man in his twenties or thirties and an adolescent or younger boy. Some involved sudden assaults, others a gentler, consensual relationship which unfolded gradually and might last for several years. Seldom were there reports of reciprocal relations, of partners exchanging roles. Usually there was an active, older participant, the dominant *agens*, and a passive, younger one, the *patiens*; older men who submitted to younger partners attracted particular revulsion. The *patiens* might be a homosexual prostitute out for presents or cash or free meals. But he might equally well be an innocent, suffering painful abuse from a person in authority or a strong sexual predator: a master craftsman raping his apprentice, a schoolmaster interfering with his pupils, a cattleman in the Sicilian countryside misusing the teenagers who minded the calves, or a travelling labourer preying on the small boys who did odd jobs on the farms and could easily be lured into lonely places.[87] Courts also heard reports of anal intercourse involving women and girls; prosecution of heterosexual sodomy was particularly vigorous in Florence between about 1492 and 1502, the decade in which Savonarola rose to and fell from power.[88]

Sodomy was commonly described as the abominable vice, the *vizio nefando* or *vizio pessimo*, the greatest imaginable sexual evil; its practitioners were occasionally called *nefandari*, its victims said to have been *nefandati*, horribly misused.[89] Bernardino of Siena called it the sin which revolted the Devil himself, glad though he was of its power to win souls for hell – much like one who empties privies for a living and finds the stench disgusting, but endures it for the sake of the money it brings in.[90] In the fifteenth and sixteenth centuries especially, sodomy was deemed a public danger partly because it could be expected to attract the wrath of God to any community that sheltered sodomites. This would not perhaps be consumed by brimstone and fire, as were the 'cities of the plain' [Genesis 18–19], but the offending society could well suffer a punitive plague, an earthquake, a military defeat, a famine.[91] Girolamo Priuli, a Venetian diarist, attributed Venice's catastrophic defeat in 1509 by the League of Cambrai partly to the rulers' failure to enforce their own rigorous laws against sodomy and to the fondness of mature senators for perverse pleasures.[92] Natural calamities, including an earthquake in the Mugello valley and storm damage to the cathedral dome and a government palace, helped to inspire the harsh law against sodomy issued under Duke Cosimo de' Medici in Florence in 1542.[93] More prosaically, sodomy, as the enemy of procreation, threatened to undermine the State's power, in so far as it depended on a large population. This imagined blow to the birth rate could be a matter of grave concern in the late fourteenth and the fifteenth century, when population was stagnating, far short of the levels attained before the 1340s. Bernardino of Siena, not the most sophisticated demographer, admonished his Tuscan audience in the 1420s that sodomy was 'the reason you have lost half your population over the last twenty-five years'.[94] Heterosexual prostitution would itself be accused, at least by economists in the eighteenth century, of reducing population by spreading hereditary venereal disease and discouraging marriage.[95] But in the late middle ages, the blame seemed to rest on sodomy, which allegedly hindered demographic recovery from repeated epidemics of plague.

Potentially, sodomy was a capital crime as grave as treason or heresy. But patterns of prosecution varied from state to state, courts exercised discretion, paid some attention to noble and clerical privilege, and sometimes imposed lesser punishments, including exile and galley service. Sometimes jurisdiction over the offence was reserved to a high criminal court (in Venice to a committee of the Council of Ten, the standing committee of public safety which dealt with grave threats to public order and the State). Sometimes it was, usually at least, the concern of a relatively minor and specialised magistracy. In Florence after 1432, cases were generally reserved to the Ufficiali di Notte, who treated most of them as misdemeanours deserving of fines or flogging rather than more drastic penalties. In Florence, there were over 2,400 convictions for such offences between 1432 and 1502, compared with 268 in Venice between 1406 and 1500. At Bologna, the supreme criminal court of the Torrone pronounced, between 1540 and 1620, a total of about 20 death sentences for sodomitical acts, most of which had been aggravated by other serious offences. In Palermo, between 1572 and 1664, 77 of 958 judicial executions were for sodomy, while in Lucca, between 1551 and 1580, on average about 30 persons a year were investigated on suspicion of having perpetrated acts of sodomy and 12 punished, though not very harshly. At least in Venice it was probably not until the seventeenth century that sodomy ceased to be regarded as a serious threat to the State, when prosecutions became rarer and the Ten no longer exercised exclusive jurisdiction over the crime.[96]

Repression alone would never suffice; no magistracy would ever command or be capable of imposing penalties savage enough to deter all citizens from indulging in forbidden pleasures. Could female prostitutes provide an antidote to sodomy, or could the need to discourage sodomy serve as a pretext for tolerating female prostitution?

Sometimes, in the early fourteenth century, both vices were equally condemned. In Orvieto, about 1300, the Seven tried to suppress immoral behaviour, not only by fining and humiliating convicted sodomites, but also by banning pimps and prostitutes or excluding them from certain parts of town.[97] But in Florence, soon after 1400, the supreme magistracy, though authorised to set up machinery for suppressing sodomy, changed course and established both a tribunal, the Onestà, which was designed to regulate heterosexual prostitution, and an official brothel. It was as if the government had chosen to try an oblique approach first; the Ufficiali di Notte arrived on the scene only in 1432.[98] Their revelations do not suggest that female prostitutes had cured or would cure Tuscan men of resorting to catamites or molesting boys. Conceivably, though, had female prostitution been driven from the cities, Tuscans might have done even more to provoke the wrath of God.

In Venice there was no apparent link between the establishment of the public brothel in 1360 and the Ten's campaign against sodomy, which began in 1406 and entered a new phase in 1418. But it was sometimes supposed that resort to female prostitutes and indulgence in sodomitical practices were polar opposites: if sexual energy flowed towards one, it would depart from the other. In 1511, the patriarch of Venice told the Venetian cabinet that 'The female whores have sent to him to say that they cannot make a living because no-one now goes to them, so rampant is sodomy; even the old men are getting down to it.'[99] In 1534, a leading magistrate of Lucca told the general council that the ill-treatment of female prostitutes in the city was a major cause of the present increase in the *vizio sodomitico*, and that the women must be properly protected.[100] It was as if heterosexual prostitution was perceived as a counterweight to sodomy, which could be thrown into the scales against it, but that it was far from certain that it would succeed in attracting the male population towards a more moderate and acceptable form of vice.

Arguably, female prostitutes had never been expected to perform the task of shaping or reshaping a person's sexual orientation. It was doubtful whether contemporaries conceived of men whose whole sexual nature diverged from what was considered normal: more likely, they thought of offenders who, out of depraved self-indulgence, committed 'unnatural' acts. Active sodomites usually appeared to be misguided individuals who, generally between adolescence and marriage, used boys as if they were women, and would also lie with women if the opportunity arose. Their appetites did not lead them in one direction alone. Their virility was not in question and there was some prospect that their delight in buggery would be forgotten with advancing age and matrimonial responsibilities.[101] If the city provided a legitimate outlet for sexual energy, inexpensive, safe and free from the risk of retribution, the attractions of lawless sex might dwindle at an earlier stage in life.

One hazard, though, was that female prostitutes could not be trusted to offer 'straight' sex alone and they were suspected of colluding in depraved practices – for example, by dressing as men to titillate their clients. If boys could be used as women, could not women be used as boys? The Onestà in Florence in 1463 set up a pillory to punish prostitutes who, among other things, 'lent their bodies to unnatural acts in the most wicked manner possible'.[102] In the second half of the fifteenth century, the

same magistrates tried several cases in which prostitutes were accused of participating in deviant sex, and the Onestà were accused of allowing a rich notary to buy his
way out of trouble in 1495.[103] Between 1478 and 1492, the Ufficiali di Notte received
information of only 13 cases of heterosexual sodomy, but between 1492 and 1502 they
reviewed as many as 109 such cases and handed out 37 convictions; many of these trials involved prostitutes.[104] The Council of Ten in Venice in 1480 complained of women
wearing their hair in masculine styles and threatened dire penalties for whores caught
sporting a 'mushroom' – 'by means of this coiffure women conceal their sex and strive
to please men by pretending to be men, which is a form of sodomy'.[105] In 1500, the Ten
sentenced a bawd, Rada de Jadra, for employing young prostitutes to be sodomised
by male clients; they noted, too, that other women were keeping girls of seven for the
use of men who delighted in anal intercourse with females.[106] In Rome men's attire
was occasionally listed in inventories of courtesans' possessions – though some of this
clothing was perhaps intended as a disguise to help a woman escape the attention of the
moral police.[107] In Venice in 1608, the priest Alessandro Rubilio had allegedly invited
female prostitutes to his house for the purpose of attracting men, to whom he could
then submit 'as the passive partner'.[108]

It could not be said that the female prostitute and the sodomite inhabited different
worlds, as authority might have liked to imagine, that the lesser and the greater evil
would always be separable, or that the man who enjoyed women would never interfere
with other men. Since prostitutes had an interest in avoiding conception, they may also
have engaged in unorthodox or incomplete sexual intercourse. Rejecting the notion
that they submitted willingly to buggery, Aretino's Nanna doubts the ability of professional women to exhaust the energies of men – 'even after they have them all, they're
not satisfied, but with great industriousness go and satisfy their lust even with the scullions in the filthiest taverns of Rome'. Courtesans might provide a distraction for disorderly desires, but in Nanna's eyes, they could not offer a cure.[109] A century later, the
Aretinesque works of Ferrante Pallavicino contained sly hints that loose young men
were offering strenuous competition to female prostitutes in Rome, Florence, Bologna,
Venice and elsewhere, and that if prostitutes wished to make their pile they should consider unnatural practices themselves, 'for the whore must bear herself like those ships
which sail before every wind'.[110]

Conclusion

By the end of the fifteenth century, the rulers of many cities in northern and central Italy
had openly recognised and were attempting to regulate, rather than suppress, the forms
of vice which they considered least objectionable. Their arrangements were compatible
with the theological argument that a lesser evil could be tolerated if it averted something more dreadful. To some extent, marginal people, visibly stigmatised, could be
used to perform essential services which would demean respectable citizens. To set up
communal brothels and define vice districts was, it might seem, a realistic way of facing
an awkward fact – that the sexual drive of young men was at its most powerful at a stage
in life when marriage was usually impracticable. This was one way of dealing with the

fear, once vaguely evoked by St Augustine, that unless lust was directed into some kind of safe receptacle, committed to its own fortress, it would inflict untold social and moral damage. No doubt it seemed more realistic and practical to accommodate a relatively small group of dishonoured women than to demand that ordinary men, not particularly inclined to piety, should exercise self-control. It was often all too obvious that tolerated prostitution did not have the effect of freeing society entirely from adultery or sodomy, and clear, too, that prostitutes, who were expected to please their clients and were often regarded as mercenaries who would do anything for money or presents, were unlikely to stick to 'straight' sex. But it was always possible to urge, and hard to disprove, the argument that without the services of prostitutes, society would have been more generally corrupted. One of many problems, however, was that public brothels lacked refinement and catered only for a section of the market. Moreover, economic conditions forced many women to resort to occasional prostitution without becoming full-time, registered prostitutes, and much of the industry, if such it was, would always escape public notice and regimentation. Cities could not control vice through public brothels alone, which were unable to maintain their monopoly of the trade against competition from a growing private sector.

Notes

1 Geltner 2013–14: 36–8.
2 From chapters xxviii–xxx, as translated by G.A. Loud in K.L. Jansen *et al.* 2009, pp. 182–3.
3 Aquinas ed. Gilby 1964–81, II.2, qu. 10, art. 11, vol. 32, pp. 72–3.
4 Augustine ed. Green 1955, II.4, p. 125.
5 Aquinas ed. Mathis 1971, IV.14, pp. 82–3; see also Rossiaud 1988, pp. 80–1; Bejczy 1997: 373–4. For the passage in *The City of God*, see Augustine ed. Evans 2003, XIV.18, pp. 579–80. For eighteenth-century comments and criticisms, see Canosa and Colonnello 1989, pp. 182–3, 185.
6 Bernardino of Siena ed. Bargellini 1936, Sermon xxxix, p. 900; Mormando 1999, pp. 124–6. The reference is to Genesis 19:8.
7 Bernardino ed. Bargellini 1936, Sermon xxxvi, p. 829; Sermon xxxvii, pp. 837–8, 840, 852.
8 Augustine ed. Walsh 2001, pp. 18–19.
9 I Corinthians 6: 9–20; Galatians 5: 19–21; Augustine ed. Lombardo 1988, n. 59, p. 80, n. 185, pp. 94–5.
10 Rossiaud 1988, pp. 77–82; Canosa 1993, pp. 28–35, 62, 118–20; also Rossiaud 2010, pp. 74–7, 159–60.
11 See, for example, Bossy 1985, pp. 35–42; Rossiaud 1988, pp. 73–5; Rossiaud 2010, pp. 84–6.
12 Mormando 1999, pp. 122–3.
13 Herlihy and Klapisch-Zuber 1985, pp. 210–11, 216–23.
14 For this definition, see Lansing 1997: 40. For Giulia, see Chapter 1, n. 4.
15 I Corinthians 7:9.
16 Augustine ed. Walsh 2001, Chapter 6, pp. 14–15, Chapters 11–12, pp. 24–7.
17 See Storey 2008/12, pp. 61–2; Rossiaud 2010, p. 60.
18 Pallavicino ed. Coci 1992, pp. 117–18, 129.
19 For examples, see Ferraro 2001, pp. 125–6; Hacke 2004, pp. 131–3.
20 Cf. V. and B. Bullough 1987, p. xv; Rossiaud 2010, pp. 37–8.
21 For Bergamo, Brolis 2001: 645; for Bologna, Rinaldi 1991, pp. 110–15, 122, n. 29, and Lansing 2003, p. 89; for Ferrara, Ghirardo 2001: 406; for Florence, K.L. Jansen *et al.* 2009, pp. 196–7;

for Lucca, Bongi 1863, pp. 373–5; for Orvieto, Lansing 1997: 39; for Venice, Scarabello 2004: 15–22; for Vercelli, Comba 1986: 565.

22 P. Jansen 2001, p. 606.

23 For general accounts of prostitution in late medieval and renaissance Europe, see, for example, V. and B. Bullough 1987, pp. 122–9; Karras 1996, pp. 243–60; Karras 1999: 159–77; Wiesner 1999, pp. 179–80; Rossiaud 2010. Important monographs on European cities in this period include Otis 1985; Roper 1985; Rossiaud 1988.

24 Goldberg 1999, pp. 183–5.

25 Mazzi 1991, pp. 249–53, 256–60.

26 Rossiaud 2010, p. 39.

27 Galassi 1966–70, II, pp. 192–3.

28 Comba 1986: 567–8.

29 P. Jansen 2001, pp. 604–5.

30 Mazzi 1986a: 620–1; Mazzi 1991, pp. 254–5.

31 Bernardino of Siena ed. Bargellini 1936, Sermon xxxv, pp. 810–11; Sermon xxxvi, p. 829; Sermon xxxviii, pp. 870–1.

32 Ghirardo 2001: 414–16.

33 V. and B. Bullough 1987, pp. 122–3; Otis 1985, pp. 19–24; Rossiaud 1988, pp. 55–8.

34 Cf. Rossiaud 2010, p. 134.

35 Comba 1986: 567–8.

36 Mazzi 1991, pp. 180–1.

37 Bongi 1863, pp. 204–5, 384–5. Cf. Bratchel 1995, p. 146.

38 P. Jansen 2001, pp. 608–11.

39 Mazzi 1991, pp. 254–5.

40 Trexler 1981: 990; Mazzi 1991, p. 265.

41 Scarabello 2004: 25.

42 Muzzarelli 1994, pp. 767–8. For the statutes of the Castel Joyos of Pamiers (late fifteenth or early sixteenth century), see Otis 1985, Appendix A, doc. 10, pp. 127–9.

43 Bongi 1863, pp. 384–5.

44 Canosa and Colonnello 1989, pp. 15–16.

45 Comba 1986: 570–1.

46 Ghirardo 2001: 413, 418, 421, 424.

47 Pavan 1980: 242–9; Scarabello 2004: 22–5, 27–9, 36–7. For the regulations of 1460, see *Leggi e memorie* 1870–72, pp. 56–9, and the translation in Chambers and Pullan 1992, pp. 120–3.

48 P. Jansen 2001, pp. 604–5.

49 For examples, see Mazzi 1991, pp. 305–7, 341–5, 385–6.

50 Brucker 1971, doc. 90, p. 191; Larivaille 1975, p. 78; Ferrante in Ciammitti *et al.* 1980, p. 455; Comba 1986: 587; Brundage 1987, pp. 468–9; Brundage 1987a: 346–7, 351–2; Lawner 1987, p. 178; Davidson 1994, p. 92; Muzzarelli 1994, pp. 767–8; E.S. Cohen 1998: 398; Sperling 1999, pp. 148–9; Brolis 2001: 645; Ghirardo 2001: 402, 410; Scarabello 2004: 35; Storey 2008/2012, pp. 75–6.

51 G. Martin ed. Parks 1969, p. 146.

52 Fourth Lateran Council (1215), Canon 68, in Schroeder 1937, pp. 290–1, 584.

53 P. Jansen 2001, pp. 604–6.

54 Comba 1986: 566–7.

55 On this theme, see especially Pavan 1980: 250–5; Mazzi 1991, pp. 271–92; Rossiaud 2010, pp. 47, 88–9.

56 Mazzi 1991, pp. 215–18.

57 Ghirardo 2001: 415.

58   P. Jansen 2001, pp. 606, 612.

59   Rossiaud 2010, p. 39.

60   Lawner 1987, pp. 8–9; Vanzan Marchini 1995, pp. 49, 51.

61   Comba 1986: 540.

62   Mazzi 1991, pp. 276–80.

63   Comba 1986: 574.

64   De Montaigne ed. Dédéyan 1946, p. 230; p. 481, n. 511.

65   For France see Terroine 1978; Rossiaud 1988, pp. 58, 65. For Bologna, see Rinaldi 1991, pp. 112, 121, n. 23, 122, n. 25; for Turin and Ivrea, Comba 1986: 566–7.

66   Bongi 1863, pp. 375–6, 383.

67   Trexler 1981: 996–1001; Mazzi 1991, pp. 202–5, 218, 240–2, 331–4.

68   Brackett 1993: 273–300.

69   Mazzi 1991, pp. 168, 220–30, 276–7, 287–8; Rocke 1996, p. 46.

70   Canosa and Colonnello 1989, pp. 60–4.

71   Ibid., pp. 225–6.

72   Ferrante 1985, pp. 2–3; Rinaldi 1991, p. 105, 125, n. 46; Ferrante 1996, pp. 206–28.

73   Ghirardo 2001: 406–7, 408, 410.

74   For the Provveditori alla Sanità, see Leggi e memorie, passim, and Chambers and Pullan 1992, pp. 126–7; for the Esecutori alla Bestemmia, Derosas 1980 and Canosa 1993, pp. 226–32; for the Provveditori alle Pompe, Newett 1902, Bistort 1912, and Chambers and Pullan 1992, pp. 178–80. In general, see Scarabello 2004: 70–3.

75   For many examples, see E.S. Cohen 1992, T.V. and E.S. Cohen 1993, and Storey 2008/2012.

76   Hanlon 2009: 23.

77   Dubuis 1986: 584, 596, n. 116, 602.

78   Brundage 1987, pp. 465–7, 529.

79   De Spirito 1978: 57–8; Pavan 1980: 260–1; Scarabello 2004: 24, 38.

80   Ghirardo 2001: 410.

81   Bratchel 1995, p. 148.

82   See above, n. 5.

83   Mormando 1999, pp. 113–15.

84   Bernardino of Siena ed. Bargellini 1936, Sermon xxxix, pp. 906–7, 918. The biblical reference is to Genesis 1:28.

85   Labalme 1984: 220; Ruggiero 1985, pp. 114–16; Martini 1986: 164; Martini 1986–87a: 343; Marcello 1992: 118; Rocke 1996, pp. 91–3; Pizzolato 2006: 472–4. See also below, n. 107.

86   For some examples, see Martini 1986: 162–6; Zuccarello 2000: 37–51; Grassi 2007: 140–3.

87   Martini 1986: 162–3; Martini 1986–87a: 345; Marcello 1992: 119–34; Rocke 1996, pp. 10–15, 87–93, 96–7, 162, 171; Zuccarello 2000: 37–47; Pizzolato 2006: 451, 455, 459–64, 466–8; Grassi 2007: 144–6, 148–9.

88   Rocke 1996, pp. 215–16.

89   Martini 1986: 190–1, 195, 197; Pizzolato 2006: 456–8, 462–3.

90   Bernardino of Siena ed. Bargellini 1936, Sermon xxxix, p. 902.

91   Labalme 1984: 221; Ruggiero 1985, pp. 127–9; Rocke 1996, pp. 36–7.

92   Priuli ed. Cessi 1938, IV, pp. 35–6; English version in Chambers and Pullan 1992, pp. 124–5. Cf. Martini 1986–87a: 349–50.

93   Rocke 1996, pp. 232–4.

94   Quoted in Rocke 1996, pp. 36–7.

95   See Chapter 3, notes 90–2.

96   For Bologna, see Zuccarello 2000: 47; for Florence, Rocke 1996; for Lucca, Grassi
     2007: 156–8; for Palermo, Pizzolato 2006: 450–1; for Venice, Pavan 1980: 276–7; Labalme
     1984: 232–3, 242–3; Ruggiero 1985, pp. 127–48; Martini 1986: 160–1, 169–78; Martini
     1986–87a: 351–5.
97   Lansing 1997: 38–43.
98   Rocke 1996, pp. 30–2, 122. See also Trexler 1981: 983–4; Brackett 1993: 280–7.
99   D.M.S. XI, cols. 84–5, 27 March 1511: English version in Chambers and Pullan 1992, p. 189.
100 Grassi 2007: 131–2.
101 Marcello 1992: 126–8; Rocke 1996, pp. 10–15, 87–93, 106–10, 121–2; Pizzolato
     2006: 459–64.
102 Brackett 1993: 288.
103 Mazzi 1991, pp. 222, 240–2, 359–60.
104 Rocke 1996, pp. 215–16.
105 *Leggi e memorie* 1870–72, p. 233; English version in Chambers and Pullan 1992, pp. 123–4.
106 D.M.S. III, col. 683, 28 August 1500; Canosa and Colonnello 1989, pp. 37–8; Davidson 2002,
     pp. 68–9.
107 Camerano 1998: 662; Storey 2008/2012, pp. 105–6, 112–13.
108 Davidson 2002, pp. 68–9.
109 Aretino trans. Rosenthal 1972, pp. 284–6.
110 Pallavicino ed. Marchi 1984, xlviii, pp. 118–19; Pallavicino ed. Coci 1992, pp. 56–7, 110.

3

Prostitutes, courtesans and
public morality

During the sixteenth century, many French and German cities officially closed their brothels, as though yielding to the demands of Protestant reformers that they form godly societies dominated by civic righteousness.[1] No more should public authorities connive at sexual relationships outside marriage, let alone extract revenue from them. Choice of the lesser evil should give way to a new kind of moral absolutism. Some Protestant critics called whorehouses 'schools that teach more shameful things than they prevent'.[2] Augustine's opinion, or so Luther said in his *Table Talk*, had doubtless made sense in the fourth century, but there was no reason to follow it in the sixteenth.[3] In London, after the closure of Southwark's public stews in 1546, the vice trade survived by dispersing and going underground. But it was officially banned; at intervals the authorities launched offensives against brothels if not against street-walkers, and had strumpets and harlots carted off to the new workhouse at Bridewell, there to be instructed in honest and industrious habits.[4]

Italian cities, by contrast, did not switch from regulating to banning prostitution. Their version of Christian order depended on maintaining holy and unholy quarters within the city, with an everyday sinful world, the territory of ordinary, mingled good and bad, lying between them. Female virtue at its purest, distilled into the chastity of nuns, must be defended from worldly contamination, confined within the strict cloisters required by Tridentine and post-Tridentine ecclesiastical law. The world itself must be protected against disorderly, unchristian or immoral groups of people. Magistrates should stigmatise and control these minorities, but they could also make use of them and should not regard them as beyond redemption. Jews, prostitutes, beggars, should have their proper places within the city walls and sometimes within walls of their own – ghettoes, districts of ill-fame, hospitals. In these reservations they could be exposed to conversion campaigns, which would be unlikely to reach them if they were driven from the city; transition from the brothel or the vice district to the nunnery for penitents would not be unthinkable.

In Bologna, Florence and Rome, from the 1550s to the 1570s, moves to concentrate Jews in ghettoes were made within a few years of renewed attempts to define the areas in which public prostitutes would be entitled to live and work. However, prostitutes would, as in the past, prove difficult to contain, for they were inclined to put forth new colonies and became increasingly reluctant to register with magistrates and pay their special taxes. Clandestine and part-time prostitution threatened to frustrate attempts to impose order on the industry. Some prostitutes changed residence repeatedly, flitting from parish to parish and quarter to quarter to elude constables, creditors, scandalised neighbours and anyone else who knew too much about them.

Much legislation on prostitution in the sixteenth and seventeenth centuries was not new in principle: it was still preoccupied with keeping common prostitutes within set boundaries and away from decent and godly women. The more original measures were aimed at ambitious freelancers working independently from their own lodgings. Campaigns were also – especially after the Council of Trent – launched against unmarried couples living in protracted relationships. Prostitutes, who often had personal lovers and protectors as well as fee-paying clients, were among their targets. Outbreaks of the notorious 'French evil', the venereal pox, had relatively little impact on laws governing prostitution: by and large, clients were left free to risk their own health by loose behaviour and to infect their wives and children if they would.

The restraint of the courtesan

In principle, laws recognised no difference between common prostitutes and courtesans. From 1524 onwards, Venetian legislation often expressly applied to both, as if to fend off legalistic quibbles.[5] Even cultivated and stylish courtesans incurred suggestions that they be forced to wear the yellow veil and live in the mean streets of the prostitutes' quarter – as did Tullia d'Aragona in Siena and Florence in the 1540s, though she was saved by Duke Cosimo's instruction to spare her because she was a poet.[6] In Rome, Isabella de Luna overstepped the mark by insulting an officer of the governor's court and ripping up a judgement summons and making as though to wipe her elegant behind with the shredded paper, an offence which earned her a public thrashing, as described by Bandello, who had an eye for the sensational.[7] But there were also complaints that courtesans' powerful patrons enabled them to defy the law, as witness the lament written for common prostitutes in a Florentine carnival song of the mid-sixteenth century:

> How weird it is that wealthy whores
> Don't wear the signs of shame,
> For money talks and opens doors
> And plays a different game.[8]

When, in Florence in 1563, a Venetian nobleman complained to the Onestà about Giulia Napoletana, he found to his chagrin that the judge openly favoured her and tolerated the crowd that came to cheer her on in court.[9] Nostalgic for the days before Pope Paul IV (1555–9) cramped the style of the whores of Rome, Du Bellay's courtesan boasts of going about by night and day, equipped with no licence and paying no taxes, fearing neither arrest nor imprisonment, because cardinals and other grandees would protect her.[10] Denouncing Veronica Franco of Venice, published poet and entertainer of King Henry III of France, her son's tutor grumbled that she had 'too many people in this city helping her and is supported by many who ought to hate her.'[11] Reports of Naples in the late sixteenth century complained that 'the secretaries and the civil and criminal officials of the High Court of Justice protect some of the whores, who are their friends and concubines'.[12]

Many regulations were directed against the ostentation of professional ladies, lest they be confused with true-born ladies, suggest too blatantly that vice was a way to social advancement, and extract too much in gifts and fees from gullible clients. Much of their apparent wealth was perhaps an illusion, and not all of them encouraged it – Pallavicino would write that some Venetian courtesans combed the second-hand shops of the Ghetto in search of furniture and finery for hire (borrowed plumage to dazzle guests), but others concealed their possessions in order to feign poverty and spin hard-luck stories to generous visitors.[13] False poverty could perhaps raid a client's purse just as effectively as false wealth, but vanities were an easier target for the law. In 1537 the nine prelates selected by Pope Paul III to advise on the reform of the Church turned their attention to the blemishes of Rome itself, from the scruffy and ignorant clergy officiating in St Peter's to the extravagance displayed on the streets. They complained that 'in this city harlots walk about like rich matrons or ride on mules, attended in broad daylight by noble members of the cardinals' households and by clerics. In no city do we see this corruption except in this model for all cities. Indeed they even dwell in fine houses. This foul abuse must also be corrected.'[14] Similar sentiments inspired Venetian legislation of 1543, concerned with dress, furniture and interior decoration.[15] Pearls became a prominent target in Venice, carriages in Rome.[16] Here a succession of edicts, from 1558 to 1674, forbade prostitutes to ride in them, lest a client's carriage be used to convey them at improper times to and from improper places.[17] A well-dressed woman on foot in Rome and one wearing no pearls in Venice would probably prove to be a courtesan, though some in Venice evaded the law by taking the surnames of patrician lovers and posing as married women. Seventeenth-century legislation forbade courtesans to lease apartments overlooking the Grand Canal or pay annual rents of more than a hundred ducats. Perhaps they treated fines as a necessary professional expense which could be passed on to their clients. Between 1579 and 1618 nearly two hundred well-to-do prostitutes paid them to the Provveditori alle Pompe (magistrates who enforced the sumptuary laws), mostly sums of between ten and fifty ducats but occasionally as much as three hundred.[18]

A story by Fortini satirises the tension in Rome between women of rank and courtesans. At issue is the right to wear a short pleated mantle of very fine linen. The courtesan Doralice, sporting this garment in the church of the Minerva, is insulted by a gentlewoman (herself no moral exemplar) who fancies one of Doralice's clients. The courtesan answers that if you cannot tell the courtesans from the gentlewomen it is the courtesans who suffer, for they are not the mimics: they have merely helped themselves to one item of dress, 'but you gentlewomen have acquired the skills, the habits and the actions of us courtesans, and for that reason we are in a bad way'. Encouraged by Doralice's victory in this exchange, other courtesans follow her lead and the mantle catches on. The Roman authorities try to stop them, but are repulsed by pasquinades accusing the female gentry of being 'thieves and robbers of the courtesan's trade' and naming several ladies as 'worse than courtesans'.[19] Theatregoers may be reminded of

Lady Would-Be's heavy-handed attempts, in Jonson's *Volpone*, to imitate the ways of high-class Venetian whores.

It was perhaps in churches that courtesans were most likely to mingle with respectable or honourable women. They were not all impious, though many doubtless hoped to be seen by the gallants who hung about places of worship; by way of self-advertisement, courtesans made triumphal entries to, say, Sant' Agostino or Santa Maria della Pace in Rome – moves which boosted the numbers in the congregation and were perhaps not unwelcome to the clergy.[20] Towards 1540, however, Venetian magistrates tried to specify the times at which 'courtesans or prostitutes' might enter churches, and to separate them on arrival from noblewomen and citizenesses, reserving certain benches and pews, perhaps all the seating, for women of rank. Prostitutes were forbidden to visit churches offering indulgences at any time except between nones and vespers, 'so as not to contaminate persons who enter those places with good intentions'.[21] The implication seemed to be that prostitutes would not have good intentions, and would never be entirely capable of keeping business and piety apart.

High-class courtesans sometimes annoyed authority far more than did common prostitutes with no social aspirations: where ordinary prostitutes were segregated, courtesans were expelled. In 1566–7, Pius V singled out groups of prominent courtesans and ordered them to leave Rome unless they undertook either to marry or to enter penitential convents. A newsletter of August 1566 reported the departure of over three hundred courtesans. The regime added to their troubles by also oppressing the Jews of Rome, so that women on short notice to leave could not raise cash by pawning their possessions or selling them to second-hand dealers. It was said that some courtesans were murdered, either by highway robbers as they left Rome, or by their own relatives, or by persons charged with looking after their goods. Quite likely, though, the protests of Roman residents at losses caused by the expulsion of so many customers, debtors and tenants prevented these measures from being fully pursued. Similar episodes occurred under later popes; under Sixtus V, the withdrawal of deposits by courtesans in 1585 may have set in motion a fatal run on a leading Roman bank. In 1592, Clement VIII attempted a mass expulsion of Spanish prostitutes, but desisted when eighteen of the women concerned were murdered on their way to Naples.[22]

Some families of high standing feared that their more impetuous men would lose their hearts to courtesans, defy family wishes and friends' counsel, succumb to enchantment (love potions and spells were sometimes suspected), and marry one of these adventurers. A successful courtesan might bring a dowry and help to replenish an aristocratic fortune, but this was unlikely to compensate for the dishonour she inflicted by upsetting the social order. Cornelia Griffo brought a substantial sum in 1526 to her marriage with a noble widower, Andrea Michiel, a union which, said the diarist Sanudo, brought 'great shame to the Venetian nobility'.[23] The irregular marriage of the courtesan Andriana Savorgnan to the noble Marco Dandolo in 1581 caused consternation and scandal, only partly because she was thought to have trapped him by sorcery. In 1589, Zaccaria Vendramin was said to be living on his estate at Latisana in Friuli because his wife had been a courtesan and they were not accepted in Venice.[24] When, between 1612 and 1614, the pope exiled Fillide Melandroni from Rome, he was probably obliging the family of Giulio Strozzi, who were dismayed at the possibility that the man might marry her.[25]

'A detestable vice which creeps like a cancer'

Mistresses threatened marriage and clerical celibacy far more seriously than did transactions with a commercial prostitute. In the later sixteenth and seventeenth centuries, concubinage showed signs of becoming a new greater evil which called for repression and contrasted with the indispensable lesser evil of prostitution, which could only be tolerated. Studies of southern dioceses suggest that within a few years of the Council of Trent, lay and ecclesiastical authorities began systematically pursuing clerics who were keeping mistresses. A decade or two later, they began to focus on lay couples living in sin, ordering them to marry or sever relations. In one revealing case, in Teramo (Abruzzi) in 1575, a priest, Don Colantonio, was caught by constables of the bishop and the local *capitano* in bed with Agnesina, a prostitute newly arrived from Urbino. Was this just a one-night stand, or was there evidence (her clothes had been found in a cupboard) that a longer stay was in prospect? Was she, indeed, mutating from a prostitute into a more subversive concubine?[26] In the same diocese, action against the laity gathered momentum during the 1590s, when a former inquisitor, Fra Vincenzo da Montesanto, became bishop. An edict of 1598 called concubinage a 'detestable vice which creeps like a cancer and, with its deadly example, destroys good customs and despatches souls to the house of the Devil'.[27]

In the archdiocese of Naples the most determined campaigns against lay concubinage were launched by Pietro Antonio Ghiberti, who in 1613 became vicar-general to the new archbishop of Naples, Decio Carafa: in 1613–14, proceedings involved 343 couples, compared with a mere 65 in the previous forty-one years, and the assault on concubinage was sustained until the mid-eighteenth century. By that time, at least seven thousand couples had been ordered to separate; the real total may have exceeded ten thousand.[28] Action against *conviventi* or *coppie di fatto*, living together outside marriage and guilty, if not of adultery, of continuous fornication, would often intensify during Lent, with the approach of the mandatory Easter confession and communion. Some couples would part for just long enough to qualify for communion, and then reunite. If they flouted orders to separate, they were liable to excommunication and then to harsher punishments, which might include imprisonment and exile, or whippings for the women. Most resented in seventeenth-century Naples was the use of notices [*cedulones, cartelli infamanti*] announcing an excommunication, which were affixed to the offending couple's house or posted in the immediate neighbourhood. Some young women were punished for treating them with the contempt that Isabella de Luna had once shown for a Roman judgement summons.[29] Defiant couples who persisted in seeing each other were liable to night visits from the *scoppettelle*, guards of the archbishop's court, forever hopeful of catching them *in flagrante*.[30] Mistresses, discarded on court orders or for other reasons, were in danger of being forced into prostitution unless their former partners helped them to marry someone else or a benevolent bishop took an interest in their fate.

No doubt, effective action against concubinage depended on the determination of individual bishops and their deputies, as well as on the diligence of parish clergy in reporting 'scandalous' behaviour. How far were remote country dioceses touched by moral campaigns, at least in the intervals between visits from missionary priests? When Alfonso de' Liguori, founder of the Redemptorists, became bishop of Sant' Agata dei Goti in the kingdom of Naples in 1762, he found clerical and other concubinage being openly practised and soon had to discipline two powerful families, the Raineri and the Petti, both represented in the cathedral chapter. Canon Marco Petti, who had kept two mistresses, was arrested and imprisoned and eventually retired to do penance in a monastery, while one of his mistresses was reunited with her husband, and the bishop, more compassionate than many, arranged for the maintenance of the illegitimate children sired by Don Marco.[31]

In other societies the question of lay concubinage could be approached more discreetly, at least at upper social levels. In seventeenth-century Venice, women of modest status who had lived in lasting, exclusive relationships with noblemen enjoyed some respect, and their daughters, if their fathers had acknowledged them and brought them up, could be deemed worthy to marry noblemen and to produce offspring who would be officially recognised as noble.[32] By the 1680s, however, conscience-stricken Venetians were taking the decision to marry after spending some years together, sometimes responding to clerical exhortations not to risk dying in mortal sin. Sometimes they married secretly, to conceal the evidence of so many years living together outside matrimony; occasionally they made a secret marriage into an open one, to remove doubts about their status.[33]

Prostitution and the French evil

War, wandering and promiscuity contributed to the outbreak of venereal sickness, or sicknesses, generally known as the French evil [*mal francese, morbus gallicus*], which began during the military invasions of Italy in the 1490s. Much greater physical risks now attended sexual transactions and adventures, though they had never, perhaps, been entirely free from exposure to gonorrhoea and other venereal infections. But the epidemic did not inspire magistrates to shut many brothels or criminalise prostitution on charges of spreading disease. 'The French pox which puts Death himself to terrified flight' was a formidable and disgusting sickness, especially in its first half-century, before it began to flag a little and be widely regarded as curable.[34] But it was not on a par with pestilence. The new scourge was a chronic, potentially disabling affliction likely to bring life in pain and disfigurement, perhaps for one year, perhaps for ten, rather than death within five days, and there was no prospect of the French evil destroying a third of a city's population in a few months if allowed to rampage unchecked. Prostitutes were widely if unjustly blamed for the epidemic and legend sometimes traced it to a single beautiful whore – for dramatic effect, to an aristocratic courtesan and her congress with a leper. But it was not ascribed only to sexual contagion and other means of transmission were recognised.[35] Brothel closure alone would never succeed in containing the epidemic.

In 1500, a papal physician, Gaspar Torrella, urged rulers to have matrons inspect prostitutes for signs of the disease and, if need be, compel them to enter a hospital for treatment – prefiguring, it may seem, the degrading vaginal examinations and the grim *sifilicomi* which they encountered in nineteenth-century Italy.[36] Not much systematic action was taken on Torrella's proposal, though at intervals several authorities (at Palermo in 1543, at Turin in 1588) issued orders that known prostitutes should undergo medical inspections and that any diagnosed with the French evil should be expelled from the city. More methodical than many were arrangements made in 1599 at Livorno, the free port launched by the Medici grand dukes, where prostitutes were to appear for medical examination at the Hospital of the Galleys on 19 April and thereafter at intervals of fifteen days. Here, too, expulsion rather than treatment awaited the sick.[37] But in the eighteenth century, a Neapolitan priest, Gennaro Sarnelli, praised an attempt to organise in Livorno a responsible public brothel, described both as a ghetto and as a *postribolo*, where applicants would be advised to think the matter over for eight days before entering. In this establishment, the matron, a midwife and a doctor were to examine the inmates every week and send to hospital anyone found to be diseased; it was as if Torrella's proposal had not been entirely forgotten.[38]

Public measures to control the disease might not be very extensive. Individuals, though, could take their own precautions. The passion of many pleasure-seekers for young girls, the high price set upon virgins, sprang not from paedophilia alone but also from a desire for intercourse with a partner unlikely to be infected – to say nothing of the supposition that sex with a virgin could cure a man of venereal disease, no matter what harm it inflicted on the girl.[39] Certain physicians in Venice and Padua and their followers were happy to advise men on the art of avoiding infection and sometimes to supply protective devices.[40] In a play of Pietro Fortini, the Roman courtesan Doralice, having arranged to sleep with Oresto, a gentleman of Siena, suggests that they should visit the baths at Piazza Ridolfi, there to inspect each other in the nude and assure themselves that neither has the dreaded sickness.[41] Possibly the disease itself – and the treatment, most agonising when it depended on mercury and cauterisation – could seem a stronger deterrent to loose conduct than any the law could devise, though it was clear that many people were willing to take the risks involved.

Fornication administered its own penalties, but did not punish the fornicators alone. By about 1600, some authorities were being reminded that a husband who had picked up the French evil was a menace to his wife and children. Wives pleaded to the archbishop's court in Siena that they should not have to return to husbands allegedly suffering from the disease. Especially poignant was the case which Livia made in 1602 against her husband, Mario Ragnone, who had not only given her the French evil but had also forced her to submit to painful and degrading treatment – by bathing vaginal sores with spirit and compelling her to take 'a certain powder' at an advanced stage of pregnancy, thereby endangering the life of the unborn child. It seems likely that, although the court generally tried to 'reconcile' separated couples and bring them together again, they did not insist on doing so in cases complicated by this disease.[42]

In this field charity achieved more than law. There was some organised care for victims, much of it in the hospitals for 'incurables' (sufferers from chronic diseases, including the French evil but not that alone) founded from the early sixteenth century onwards.[43] A decree of the Venetian board of health in 1522 tried to insist that beggars 'sore of the French pox or other ill' should go to the hospital for incurables, not languish on the streets and infect others by the poisonous stench which they exuded.[44] In moralistic tales portraying the downfall of bumptious courtesans, the pox hospital became a symbol of disgrace and hopelessness, providing the scene for the last pathetic act in the self-inflicted tragedy. One of these hospitals, the Misericordia at Verona, was first opened on premises which had formerly housed a brothel.[45] But it did not herald a general movement to close brothels down.

Prostitution: a defence against adultery?

Some Catholic authors, however, were critical of traditional arguments on behalf of organised or tolerated prostitution. Among them was the casuist Martín de Azpilcueta, otherwise 'Dr Navarre', who spent the last years (1567–86) of a long life in Rome and served as a consultant in the Supreme Tribunal of the Penitentiary. Once called the greatest theologian among lawyers and the greatest lawyer among theologians of the sixteenth century, he compiled a hefty manual for confessors and penitents, translated into Latin in Rome in 1573, which passed through sixty editions and reprints in the second half of the century.[46] Dr Navarre concluded that public authorities were entitled to tolerate prostitutes, pimps, procuresses and their clients and allow them to function in a certain part of the city. But they could not encourage them by building and leasing them houses and sharing in their profits, without themselves committing a sin. He was sceptical of the old contention that, if prostitutes were available, greater evils would be averted. It was as though lust, in his opinion, was not some form of bodily waste of which men could be relieved by dumping it at intervals in some appropriate place. Rather, it was an appetite which grew by what it fed on and became more voracious by being indulged in a whorehouse. Philanderers would never be satisfied with the tame experience of paying for sex, but, when this began to pall, would graduate to plotting the conquest of respectable women, 'all the more for being driven by nature and vice'. Brothels encouraged 'many boys' to commit sexual sins at an early stage in life; he wrote from personal experience of university students from quiet places who had, by consorting with prostitutes, wrecked their studies, lost their souls to sin, and ruined their health. Another hazard was that retired prostitutes became 'the means to a thousand evils' – presumably by becoming procuresses or go-betweens and entrapping innocents, possibly also by practising superstitious love magic. And why should a double standard be allowed, and men alone be provided with brothels, when as the stronger sex they ought to be more capable of self-control? In short, he concluded, the only proper cure for lust was 'the burning love of chastity', together with 'abstinence, sobriety, hard work, and above all the grace of God', all of which things were the enemies of brothels.[47] Some years later, in 1609, the Toledo Jesuit Juan de Mariana (better known for his views on regicide) took up several of Navarre's arguments and added the opinion that public brothels were no defence against unnatural vice – 'we know that in the provinces or cities in which that evil most prevails there is also the largest number of female prostitutes, and that the hunger for depravity passes from one thing to the other, burgeoning as it goes, without ever restraining or correcting itself'.[48]

Evidence from court proceedings may lend weight to the argument that prostitution was no antidote to adultery. There were plenty of courtesans in Rome in 1559. But Camillo Mantoano still found it exciting to seduce Giulia, the wife of his neighbour Gieronimo Piccardi, a notary of the Rota – an adventure which needed the collusion of Giulia's servant and confidante, Camilla of Parma, and involved making a hole through the party wall between their houses into Gieronimo's attic. Devious Camilla, who thought Gieronimo jealous, tight-fisted ('a man who would divide a louse in half') and a delight to deceive, implied that Camillo was not Giulia's only suitor.[49] Some libertines were inclined both to frequent prostitutes and to attack other women. At Montefollonico near Montepulciano in the seventeenth century, the sexual predator most dangerous to females was Lorenzo Barbieri, unmarried until he was almost forty, who regularly visited village prostitutes, was accused of rape on two occasions, and was once put on trial for attacking a married woman.[50] Coryat, the English traveller, wondered why, if the strategy of tolerating prostitutes achieved its aims, it was also necessary for Venetians to keep honourable women in near-oriental seclusion.[51] Very likely it was true that the honour of middle- and upper-class women owed much to inhabiting well-locked houses, to being veiled and chaperoned in public places, to being kept away from windows so that even amorous looks could not be exchanged with men outside, and to their instinctive rejection of flirtatious advances. But working-class women, bound to live much more in public, were probably glad of the formal division between the honourable and the dishonourable and of the diversions created by public prostitutes.[52]

Conservative opinion, though, was not generally shaken and the old arguments endured. In 1566, when Pius V was attacking the prostitutes of Rome, representatives of the citizenry again asserted that prostitutes protected wives and virgins from 'men's incontinence'. Withdraw toleration and prostitution would merely take cover behind legitimate female occupations. Arguably, too, human beings ought not to be so regimented that they forfeited any choice between good and evil; the law should not refuse women the chance to sin habitually and later repent, since prostitutes offered splendid opportunities for soul-saving. 'If the wicked women, like the Jews and all the other people ... were to leave the city, your holiness would have no-one to convert to goodness and no-one to punish.'[53] The sacrament of penance might accomplish what the law could not. A few years later, Gregory Martin, the English eulogist of Gregory XIII's Rome, acknowledged the views of 'Dr Navarre', but in the end sided with St Augustine or one of his disciples: 'Loe here is another doctor's opinion, that harlots do serve the order of the whole, whiles some certain being by themselves placed in that vile service, in the meane time honest wemen live the more void of temptations, and mayntayne not under the pretence of matrones, the filthy life of queanes.'[54] No doubt he took comfort from the belief that harlots had chosen their occupation freely and had not been cajoled or tricked into taking it up.

'An occupation which has always had to be tolerated'

Between the mid-sixteenth and the eighteenth centuries, city governors, magistrates and councils seemed less inclined to run official brothels or lease them to managers. Direct public involvement in the vice trade was harder to justify in a stricter moral climate. No doubt, too, official brothels were foundering because they could not maintain their monopoly of prostitution and were ceasing to be profitable. Toleration combined with segregation was more acceptable and more feasible, though still difficult to achieve. Some authorities designated run-down areas and back streets, preferably far from the town's show places, convents and churches, in which landlords would be permitted (indeed expected) to let premises to common prostitutes. The term *postribolo* or *luogo di postribolo* could come to mean a vice district rather than a brothel.[55] At intervals, citizens would complain that whores and their clients had yet again broken bounds and magistrates would attempt to drive them into vice quarters which were already overcrowded. At Milan in 1572 and 1640, prostitutes were instructed to approach the Capitano di Giustizia and he to find them accommodation 'with the smallest scandal possible', 'so that none of the prostitutes may complain of having no place to live'.[56] Occasionally, an old vice district had to be demolished and a new one to be found – because, at Cremona in 1550, the area had become attractive to prosperous merchants, or because, at Ferrara in 1498 or Genoa in 1551, a new street was to be driven through the fifteenth-century brothel quarter.[57] Very likely, the measure which scattered the prostitutes of a hardy public brothel in Milan, grudgingly tolerated even by Archbishop Carlo Borromeo, was the construction of the New Prisons from 1578 onwards.[58] A memorandum of about 1616 would state that 'there is no brothel [*lupanars ... sive postribulum*] in Milan today'.[59]

Some city governments did not succeed in confining prostitution within designated areas. Sometimes they stopped trying; at intervals, reformers urged them to resume this labour of Sisyphus. Unintended consequences flowed from some measures. From the early sixteenth century at least, a levy on prostitutes in Naples was entrusted to a tax-farmer on the understanding that he would only exact it from women working in public brothels and would therefore have every reason to ensure that they operated from the proper places. But, according to Galanti, the eighteenth-century economist, 'the effect was quite the opposite, because the city was filled with prostitutes in order to increase the yield of the tax, and many extortions were unjustly practised by the owners' until a fiscal reform of 1635 put an end to the arrangement.[60]

In Venice, prostitutes were spreading through the city from the mid-fifteenth century onwards. San Marco, the seat of government, could not keep them away, the brothel at Rialto could not maintain its monopoly of the trade, and a proclamation of 1502 listed another thirty-one places where prostitutes could be found. They favoured taverns, and their presence boosted the wine trade, an incidental benefit not unwelcome to the State. The Malipiero family, owners of the official brothel, pleaded for tax reductions, around 1496 and 1537, on the grounds that the property was not paying. In about 1600, censuses provided more evidence that prostitutes had been settling in parishes far from the original base; thirteen were living together in one of these neighbourhoods.[61] During the eighteenth century, the trade was dispersed through many miniature enterprises known as *scolette, casini* or *ridotti*, some owned or rented by prostitutes, dancers, singers or actors, others by artisans. Between 1750 and 1800, there were more than 130 in the city; lists of bawdy houses drawn up in 1798 suggested that one of Venice's six principal districts, Castello, then contained 44 such establishments, and that they harboured 80 women.[62] Moreover, a woman told magistrates in 1766, there were innumerable low-grade prostitutes in the city who had no incentive to reduce their takings by joining a brothel, from the whores at their doors in the via del Carbone to the 'barefoot, ragged beggar girls' looking to do business in wineshops and taverns 'with artisans' apprentices and the lowest of the low'.[63]

Both in Florence and in Bologna, the practice of registering women as prostitutes, and with it the magistrates' capacity to tax and control the more visible side of the industry, appeared to be declining in the seventeenth century. Between 1606 and 1650, 767 prostitutes registered in Florence, but at very uneven rates, in that 571 were entered on the books between 1606 and 1626, and only 196 between 1627 and 1650.[64] In Bologna, the Ufficio delle Bollette grew less vigorous in pursuing women reported to them, the women more determined to defend themselves. Of 27 women who, between 1688 and 1696, admitted to the archbishop's court that they were full or part-time prostitutes, only 8 were officially registered.[65]

Proclamations issued in Bologna in 1567 and 1568 identified seven zones to which prostitutes should be confined, together with a church for their use and edification, 'that they may no more be scattered throughout the city, where by their bad example and treacherous inducements they can all too easily persuade poor neighbours to take up the trade of a whore'.[66] The Senate had recently begun to enforce the policies of Pope Paul IV by imposing a ghetto on the city's Jews; the authorities, charging Jewish bankers and others with gross misconduct, progressed from segregation to expulsion in 1569.[67] Segregation of prostitutes within the city continued. The registered prostitutes of Bologna in 1583 were concentrated in an area between the via San Felice and the via Saragozza. But their successors gradually dispersed to other districts, to judge by the comments of a reformer, Carlo Grassi, in 1750. He urged a return to the practice of compelling public prostitutes to live in certain streets 'as is laid down by our statutes and confirmed by many proclamations of our former legates', the papal governors of the city. Renewed strictness would relieve parish priests and show disapproval of 'an occupation which is undoubtedly disreputable but has always had to be tolerated'.[68] In Florence, by the mid-sixteenth century, the Onestà were naming a number of streets in which prostitutes could lawfully reside. There may have been eighteen of these in 1547, eleven streets and three bath-houses in 1560.[69] In 1570, a government decree converted one of the districts open to prostitutes into a place of compulsory residence for Jews who wished to remain within the Florentine State, effectively moving another body of marginalised people into an already disreputable area.[70]

Pope Paul IV's creation in 1555 of a ghetto for Roman Jews was followed in 1566 by Pius V's attempt to impose a new order on the city's prostitutes. His assault was both on prominent courtesans (see above), whom he proposed to banish, and on common prostitutes, whom he wished to see herded across the river and resettled in the

Trastevere, much to the alarm of their future neighbours. The pope's deepest concern was that prostitutes were desecrating

> the finest streets of Rome, where the blood of so many martyrs has been shed, where there are so many relics and acts of devotion, where the Apostolic See and such intense religious fervour are to be found – a city which, as an example to the world, ought to be entirely free of vice and sin, to the confusion of infidels and heretics [and, presumably, to the edification of pilgrims].

At first the pope was deaf to objections, but banishment to back alleys eventually proved more practicable than deportation across the Tiber. Plans began to focus on the Ortaccio, the 'nasty garden', an unsavoury quarter close to the Mausoleum of Augustus and also to Rome's river port, the Ripa. As though establishing a second ghetto, builders put up makeshift walls to enclose this area in 1569, with the object of keeping the women in and the clients out at appropriate times. Prostitutes could now be forbidden to transact business during Lent, although the pope had to have food sent in at his own expense to keep them alive.[71] Describing the place a few years later, Gregory Martin applauded the strategy of harassing and ridiculing not only prostitutes but their clients as well, and making the trade appear as sordid as possible without actually forbidding it.

> See how they are plagued by lawes and Ordinances, and how small comforts they have toward their beastly living. Their dwellings are together as it were pent up into one place of the citie in corners and bylanes and small outhouses, for this very purpose, that the place should be notoriously infamous, thereby to restrayne men that esteme of their honour and honesty, to abstayne from such hauntes, where no man is seen (as in other streetes) but he is pointed at as a Rascal and Ribbauld, reproched, and stayned, and very infamous.[72]

To cram all the prostitutes of Rome into the squalid Ortaccio proved to be an impossible task. Under Clement VIII (1592–1603) they were given 'the run of most of a broad area in a newly built section of the city' around the Campo Marzio and the three parishes of San Lorenzo in Lucina, Sant' Andrea delle Fratte, and Santa Maria del Popolo, the Ortaccio lying to the west of this zone. Known as the *luoghi*, the whole district included streets such as the Schiavonia, which was within the Ortaccio and densely settled by common prostitutes, and, by contrast, the more elegant via Lata and the streets near Piazza della Trinità del Monte, which were favoured by the more prosperous courtesans.[73] Inhabitants of Rome had their own views on who should live in the designated areas; enmities and friendships influenced the fate of some women. In the 1590s, members of Caravaggio's fast set subjected a tailor's wife to an inverted serenade sung to lutes and guitars, urging her to move to the Ortaccio. But on another occasion, they chose to defend their own sweethearts against 'respectable' neighbours who wanted them removed to a suitably sordid place.[74]

Prostitutes' quarters were seldom true ghettoes in the same sense as those assigned to Jews, for only professing Jews could live within ghetto walls, and Christians, though often visiting to transact business with pawnbrokers and second-hand dealers, were forbidden to spend nights in the ghetto. Prostitutes were seldom so isolated: they often lived among 'respectable' people who paid similar rents, and were sometimes on good

and sometimes on bad terms with their neighbours. Rarely did governments evict other
inhabitants, although Sixtus V (1585–90) did order Spaniards living in the Ortaccio to
depart and make room for immoral women.[75] Moralists did not object if neighbours
put in hostile petitions or otherwise harassed women whose bad habits and disreputable histories they knew or suspected. Problems arose if they got on too well with each
other. In the 1730s, Gennaro Sarnelli, a forceful Redemptorist priest in Naples whose
mission, as he saw it, lay in the city rather than in remote rural areas, argued that one
reason for the current increase in prostitution was the failure to isolate or ostracise such
women. Where respectable women were already living in quarters of ill-fame, not only
did they suffer from prowling men who mistook or pretended to take them for whores,
but they could easily become 'public prostitutes' without changing their dwellings or
their dresses if their husbands died or disappeared.[76]

Dues and taxes

Since public prostitution was a legal if despised activity, public authorities could feel
themselves entitled to draw revenue from it. Sometimes, in the late middle ages, this
took the form of payments from the successful applicant for the privilege of running an
official brothel; sometimes, then and later, it took the form of taxes paid by registered
prostitutes themselves. These could be defended as legitimate charges for disciplining
and protecting them. Receipts from the vice trade, however, exposed the commune
to accusations of raking in immoral earnings, of itself turning pimp. But perhaps it
could launder its takings by earmarking them for public-spirited uses. In Genoa, Doge
Gabriele Adorno's ordinances of 1363 prescribed that income from communal brothels should go towards the construction and upkeep of the harbour and breakwater, in
accordance with the parable of the crafty steward: 'use money, tainted as it is, to win
you friends, and thus make sure that when it fails you, they will welcome you into the
tents of eternity'.[77] In Venice in 1514, the doge and Collegio listened attentively to the
suggestion that building works or excavations in the government shipyard be subsidised by taxing 'all the whores in the city', a proposal which the diarist Sanudo thought
promising. What became of it is not known.[78] In Rome, where surprisingly large sums
seem to have flowed in from tolerated prostitution, at least from the time of Sixtus IV,
courtesans were also taxed at intervals to pay for improving streets and bridges, such
as the street of the Madonna del Popolo in Ripetta (1519) or the Ponte Santa Maria
(1548).[79] Florence and Bologna exacted modest contributions from registered prostitutes, though they were seldom capable of paying a great deal.[80]

  Bemused by myths of Venetian vice and the city's reputation for soft, effeminate luxury and Spartan political shrewdness, English travellers around 1600 fell for the story
that the Venetian government derived vast sums annually from prostitution – enough
to maintain a dozen galleys, said Coryat; 'the tribute to the State from Cortizans was
thought to exceede three hundreth thousand Crownes yearely', said Moryson.[81] But
there is no trace of any such taxes in the State's accounts of income and expenditure
at the time.[82] Tall tales apart, though, it seems likely that, if they and their admirers
really were big spenders, high-class prostitutes in any city could swell State revenues by

boosting the consumption of taxable goods such as food and wine and by stimulating luxury imports. When Pius V attempted to expel hundreds of courtesans from Rome, customs officers asked for a reduction of 20,000 ducats in the revenues they were supposed to collect, especially from imports.[83] The Venetian government undoubtedly derived a few hundred ducats annually from fines levied on prostitutes who had broken the sumptuary laws.[84] In Rome in 1582, forty-two courtesans were fined for riding in coaches.[85]

From the sixteenth century onwards, however, some exactions from prostitutes or former prostitutes, especially from their possessions at the time of their deaths, were destined for the support of penitential nunneries for repentant sexual sinners. The public would not profit directly from an immoral woman's accumulated wealth, such as it was, but the money would help to atone for the sins which the public authorities chose to tolerate. These arrangements will be discussed in a later chapter.

Conclusion

In the early modern centuries there were always critics who argued that the disorder surrounding prostitution outweighed any benefits it might bestow on society. In Milan in 1593, a rescue charity declared that from prostitutes 'spring enmities and murders, thefts and drunkenness, blasphemies, slanders, incurable diseases, and numberless other evils. Well says the Wise Man, stay away from the disreputable woman, and do not approach her door'.[86] In 1624, inhabitants of a Roman street complained to the governor that prostitutes scandalised matrons and maidens, and spoke of 'the great noise and disturbance which breaks out when they start quarrels and throw stones, at the risk of killing bystanders who stop to watch and those who pass through the street on business of their own'.[87] In eighteenth-century Naples, prostitutes would never stay in their proper places and wait for custom. They were notorious for forcing themselves on the troops, 'even in their billets and at the sentry posts', and, according to Sarnelli, they had transmitted venereal disease to three hundred soldiers. The argument that prostitutes infected and partially disabled the armed forces in garrison towns and naval bases would become familiar in the nineteenth and twentieth centuries and would be used to support the case for medical inspections and compulsory treatment.[88]

In the eighteenth century, some moral theologians, following much the same paths as Navarre and Mariana, and some writers on good government and political economy, abandoned any simple pretence that heterosexual prostitution either protected marriage or discouraged unnatural vice. But they still warned against naive attempts to prohibit it, continued to hint at greater evils which would break loose if repressive laws, failing to take human nature as they found it, were put into operation. Regulation, for the time being, was the only realistic choice, and 'public incontinence' would be eliminated only in the wake of profound social changes that could hardly be made in the immediate future.

Muratori, the duke of Modena's archivist, writing of public happiness in about 1748, argued that there were 'Sound reasons why human laws should tolerate simple fornication, leaving the supreme tribunal of God to punish it' as a moral transgression which did not in itself disturb the public peace. 'Good and evil have to be perpetual dwellers in the world and to be distributed' according to the will and permission of the almighty. The prince's direct role should be confined to the suppression of homosexual practices; to the punishment of scandalous conduct and procuring; to occasionally making examples of mothers who sold their own daughters; and to the removal of prostitutes from inns and taverns where they put temptation in the way of customers seeking a drink and perhaps a night's lodging – perhaps with tragic consequences for their health and the wellbeing of their wives and families. 'Let these wretched people sell their rotten goods in their own hovels.' Muratori recommended no departures from traditional policies, save perhaps for the appointment of lay censors in the Greek and Roman tradition, who would single out and remonstrate with evil livers, including brothel-haunters and gamblers. It was true that preachers were already acting as 'zealous censors', but they spoke in general terms only, pierced nobody's armour, and could too easily be ignored.[89]

Other writers, including Genovesi, the professor of political economy at the university of Naples, and Filangieri, the philosopher of legislation, attacked prostitution as a force for depopulation and hence an enemy of public welfare (a charge once brought, for different reasons, against sodomy). For Genovesi at least, the largest possible population, containing the smallest possible proportion of idle and impoverished people, was an unquestionable good: acting upon, and stimulated by, a developing economy, it was the mainspring of the prince's power and the public wealth. Prostitution stunted demographic growth in that it reduced the birth rate by discouraging marriage and allowing free rein to 'unbridled lust [*la venere vaga e ferina*]', which knew nothing of bringing up children. It also raised the death rate by spreading a debilitating hereditary sickness, blighting the health of the people. For Genovesi, the most fearful killers at large were the smallpox, which bore off 'the twelfth and thirteenth part of those who are born', and the venereal pox, which was scarcely less lethal.[90] Prostitution was a concomitant of a general decline in the marriage rate which had set in throughout Europe. Whether it was a cause or a consequence of this, or both, was open to debate. In some societies, living on inherited wealth and devoted to ostentatious consumption, marriage was discouraged among the younger sons of aristocratic families in order to spare estates from division among heirs.[91] Here prostitution was not a prime mover. Arguably, though, prostitution exerted an especially pernicious influence by enabling men of all social classes to enjoy sexual pleasures without the responsibilities of marriage: who would favour marriage and children when they could hire and discard partners at will? As Filangieri put the matter about 1780,

> the rich man shuns marriage wilfully, the poor man out of wretchedness. The artificer prefers to divide his earnings with a prostitute whom he can abandon, whom he can change whenever he wants, rather than with a wife, who becomes tiresome as soon as the taste for innocent pleasures has been lost. In the end all social classes come to think of marriage as the tomb of freedom and happiness.[92]

For these reformers, however, no remedy could be found in simple repression, in imitating the emperor Theodosius, who had ordered the brothels of Rome to be closed.

'To do this', wrote Filangieri, adhering to traditional arguments, 'is to turn a whole country into a brothel; it is to imperil the honour of married folk; it is to cure a disorder with one that is even greater.' If a cure lay anywhere, it was in a profound social change through a drastic reduction of the bachelors in the population and the encouragement of marriage – whether by what Genovesi vaguely described as 'rewards, concessions [*franchigie*], honours' or, in Filangieri's view, by a more equal distribution of wealth and property, which would enable the people in general to contract stable and happy marriages. Prostitution, he argued, had never taken root in the Anglo-American colonies, where men married early and were not debilitated physically and mentally by long spells of licentious bachelordom.[93] Perhaps, in the absence of far-reaching changes raising the status and feasibility of marriage, which would presumably take many years to introduce, there was still a temptation to fall back on quasi-Augustinian arguments. Measures in eighteenth-century cities consisted, as before, mostly of attempting to confine prostitutes to suitable places – in Livorno (1719) to the district of the Three Kings, in Naples (1738) to the *borghi* of Loreto and Sant'Antonio, where they were not to dwell on 'the broad and dignified street' and had to stay away from inns and taverns.[94]

Criticisms of the evils attending prostitution were never persuasive enough to inspire attacks on deep-seated social problems, though they did inspire voluntary organisations to try to rescue individuals and protect children. The ancient, hardy assumption that prostitution was indispensable, and that some women of low character must always be available to serve the physical needs of 'normal' young men (and perhaps to make sure that they remained 'normal'), survived into the reports and debates of the Italian parliament and the pronouncements of sociologists until well into the late nineteenth century. It would leave a mark even on the debate in 1958 on the Merlin law which abolished regulation in Italy. The old principle was stated, for example, by Giovanni Catella, who belonged to a commission co-ordinated in 1876 by the then Minister of the Interior: 'Prostitution, a real social cautery, must be tolerated in order to avoid greater evils; prostitution is protean in its manifestations, very mobile, hard to discipline, and infests the human race with a terrible virus, of which it is the most active propagator'. And, in the words of Guglielmo Ferrero, collaborator of the criminologist Cesare Lombroso, 'given the present difficulty of contracting marriage at an early age, without prostitution, in which all the energy of the male genetic instinct finds an outlet, an enormous number of young men would be thrown into desperation from the inability to satisfy such a keen need'.[95]

Notes

1 Roper 1985; Otis 1985, pp. 40–5; V. and B. Bullough 1987, pp. 142–3, 152–3; Rossiaud 1988, pp. 49–51.
2 Ozment 1983, pp. 55–6.
3 V. and B. Bullough 1987, pp. 140–2.
4 Griffiths 1993: 39–63.
5 Pavan 1980: 263.
6 Masson 1975, pp. 108–9, 119–21.

7   Bandello ed. Flora 1934, IV.xvii, vol. II, pp. 743–5.
8   Adapted from the verses quoted in Brackett 1993: 292: 'Perche ci pare strano,/che molte nos-
     tre pari/Per aver più danari/Non vestan come vuol vostra Fiorenza.' See also Terpstra 2010,
     pp. 12–13.
9   Ruggiero 1993, pp. 40–1.
10   Du Bellay ed. Saulnier 1947, lines 256–68, p. 158.
11   Rosenthal 1992, pp. 153–7, 198.
12   Calabria 1991, p. 29.
13   Pallavicino ed. Marchi 1984, Letter xxv, p. 62; cf. also Allerston 1998 and Storey 2008/2012,
     pp. 192–3.
14   *Consilium de emendanda ecclesia*, as translated in Olin 1969, p. 196.
15   Chambers and Pullan 1992, p. 127.
16   E.S. and T.V. Cohen 1993, pp. 89–90, testimony of 1 May 1560; Bassani and Bellini 1994, p. 16;
     E.S. Cohen 1998: 399.
17   Storey 2008/2012, pp. 97, 109–13.
18   Lawner 1987, p. 17; Scarabello 2004: 70–2, 79, 84–5.
19   Fortini ed. Mauriello 1995, Second Day, Novella xix, vol. II, pp. 1128–33. The courtesan is iden-
     tified as Doralice in the Commedia of the Seventh Night, scene vi, vol. II, pp. 1163–4, where the
     story of the *batticulo* is repeated.
20   Cf. Aretino ed. Rosenthal 1972, pp. 212, 312–17, 338–41; Masson 1975, pp. 28–30.
21   *Leggi e memorie* 1870–72, doc. 99, pp. 101–2.
22   Pastor XIV, pp. 90–1, 397, 398; Larivaille 1975, pp. 177–80, 183–4, 186.
23   D.M.S. XLI, col. 166, 11 April 1526; Brown 2004, pp. 166–7; Scarabello 2004, p. 66.
24   Ruggiero 1993, pp. 26–9, 42–3, 55–6, 135.
25   Bassani and Bellini 1994, pp. 243–4.
26   Basilico 2008: 121.
27   *Ibid.*, 127–32. See also Pizzolato 2007: 231–59, on events in the diocese of Monreale in Sicily.
28   Romeo 2008, pp. 124–5, 129, 165–6.
29   *Ibid.*, pp. 114, 131–3, 173–6, 243–6.
30   Pizzolato 2007: 254–6; Romeo 2008, pp. 3–6, 28–30, 166, 223–4.
31   Jones 1992, pp. 372–5.
32   Cowan 2007, pp. 14, 29–30, 71, 117–31.
33   Martini 1986–87: 313–14, 320–9.
34   See the opening lines of the 'Lamento d'una cortigiana ferrarese' of the mid-1520s, ed.
     Aquilecchia 1974, p. 21: 'O Dio, ah Dio, ah cielo, o sorte, ah sorte/o furia infernale, morbo
     franzese/che'mpaurita fai fugir la morte!'
35   Foa 1984: 32–3, n. 38; Schleiner 1995, pp. 184–5; McGough 2011, pp. 45–53, 65–9. For a gen-
     eral historical account of syphilis, see Quétel trans. Braddock and Pike 1990.
36   Arrizabalaga *et al.* 1997, pp. 34–6, 129–30; cf. Gibson 1986, pp. 34, 58–61, 191–9.
37   Canosa and Colonnello 1989, pp. 125–6, 194; see also p. 144, for Naples in 1781.
38   De Spirito 1978: 61.
39   See, for example, McGough 2011, p. 43.
40   Schleiner 1994: 398–404.
41   Fortini ed. Mauriello 1995, Seventh Night, Commedia, Scene viii, vol. II, p. 1170; Scene xi, *ibid.*,
     pp. 1179–80.
42   Nardi 1989: 103–5, 140–2.
43   For accounts of these hospitals, see Malamani 1978: 193–216; Arrizabalaga *et al.* 1997,
     pp. 145–233.
44   Translated in Chambers and Pullan 1992, pp. 308–9.

45 Cantù 1996, p. 81; Palmer 1999, pp. 93, 94.
46 For his career and writings, see, for example, Muñoz de Juana 1998 (especially pp. 92–108) and Lavenia 2003 (136–48 for his Roman period).
47 Navarro 1584, XVII.195, pp. 424–6.
48 De Mariana ed. Pí y Margall 1854, XVII, pp. 444–6. For a discussion of Mariana's treatise on public shows and public brothels, see Soons 1982, pp. 86–91.
49 For the tale of 'Camilla the go-between', see E.S. and T.V. Cohen 1993, pp. 159–87.
50 Hanlon 2009: 29.
51 Coryat 1905 edn., I, pp. 402–3.
52 See, for example, Martines 1998: 257–8, 262, 268–72.
53 Storey 2008/2012, pp. 81–2, 84–5.
54 G. Martin ed. Parks 1969, pp. 148–50.
55 Canosa and Colonnello 1989, pp. 236–7.
56 *Ibid.*, pp. 132–6.
57 *Ibid.*, pp. 131–2, 167; Ghirardo 2001: 415–16.
58 D'Amico 1989: 396–8; D'Amico 1994, p. 142.
59 Canosa and Colonnello 1989, p. 135, n. 8.
60 Galanti 1786–90, II, pp. 29–30; cf. De Spirito 1978: 40–1.
61 Pavan 1980: 250–5; Ruggiero 1993, pp. 48–9; Chojnacka 2001, pp. 23–4, 54; Scarabello 2004: 30–2.
62 Scarabello 2004: 91–2, 100.
63 Canosa 1993, pp. 227–9; also Gozzi ed. Zardi 1915, p. 414 and Tassini ed. Moretti 1964, pp. 136–8.
64 Brackett 1993: 299–300.
65 Ferrante in Ciammitti *et al.* 1980, pp. 455–8; Ferrante 1985, pp. 7, 12, 16; Canosa and Colonnello 1989, pp. 79–87, 90.
66 Canosa and Colonnello 1989, pp. 78–9.
67 Dall'Olio 1999: 153–204.
68 Ferrante in Ciammitti *et al.* 1980, pp. 455–8; Giacomelli 1986, pp. 248–9.
69 Brackett 1993: 291; cf. Terpstra 2010, p. 20.
70 Siegmund 2006, pp. 201–9.
71 Pastor XIV, pp. 92, 396–8, 407–8 (giving the texts of newsletters of 27 July, 3 and 17 August 1566, 5 and 17 October 1569); Larivaille 1975, pp. 177–81; E.S. Cohen 1992: 611; E.S. Cohen 1998: 401–3; the ample account in Storey 2008/2012, pp. 68–80.
72 G. Martin ed. Parks 1969, pp. 145–8.
73 E.S. Cohen 1998: 403–6; Storey 2008/2012, pp. 89–90, 167–8, 171–2.
74 Bassani and Bellini 1994, pp. 7–8, 14–16.
75 Larivaille 1975, p. 183; E.S. Cohen 1991: 204–5; E.S. Cohen 1998: 406–7.
76 De Spirito 1978: 39–40, 56–7, 61; Valenzi 1995, pp. 112–16; for Sarnelli see also Jones 1992, pp. 128–30, 154, 159–63, 189, 212.
77 Polonio 2004, 330–1; the biblical reference is to Luke 16:9.
78 D.M.S. XIX, coll. 165–6, 25 October 1514; Rosenthal 1992, p. 268, n. 44.
79 Aquilecchia 1974, pp. 13–14, 15–16, 24; Masson 1975, pp. 79, 133–6; Storey 2008/2012, pp. 63–4.
80 Ferrante 1985, p. 2; Brackett 1993: 291–2.
81 Coryat 1905 edn., I, p. 403; Moryson ed. Hughes 1903, pp. 130, 411–12.
82 Chambers and Pullan 1992, pp. 148–56 (translated and annotated version of documents in Besta 1912, covering the years 1587, 1594 and 1602). The largest single source of revenue was the wine duty, which in each of these years fell a little short of 300,000 ducats.

83   Pastor XIV, p. 90; above, n. 22.

84   See above, n. 18.

85   Storey 2008/2012, pp. 63–4.

86   From the regulations of the Deposito di Santa Maria Maddalena, quoted in D'Amico 1989: 395. Cf. Ecclesiasticus 9:3 – 'Do not keep company with a harlot, lest you get entangled in her snares.'

87   Complaint by residents in the Campana in the district of Monte Giordano, quoted in Paglia 1980, pp. 68–9, and in Storey 2008/2012, pp. 91–2.

88   De Spirito 1978: 48; Valenzi 1995, p. 113. For Napoleon's measures, see Gibson 1986, p. 24.

89   Muratori ed. Mozzarelli 1996, pp. 12, 193–202. On the general theme see Sampaoli 1950; De Spirito 1978: 38–40; Canosa and Colonnello 1989, pp. 180–6, 199–213.

90   Genovesi ed. Perna 1984, I, pp. 126–32, 348, 352, 364.

91   *Ibid.*, I, p. 514.

92   Filangieri 1819, II.8, vol. I, p. 305; compare the similar remarks in Fabbroni ed. Venturi 1958, pp. 1127–8.

93   Filangieri 1819, II.8, vol. I, pp. 306–9; Genovesi ed. Perna 1984, I, p. 129.

94   De Spirito 1978: 66–8; Canosa and Colonnello 1989, pp. 195–8.

95   Gibson 1986, pp. 55–6, 140, 223–5.

4

Extenuation and rescue

Gregory Martin, in about 1580, had written of certain women 'being by themselves placed' in the 'vile service' of public prostitution, as if they had volunteered for an unpleasant task but deserved no thanks for doing so.[1] How far did observers and commentators in the early modern centuries believe that prostitutes and other dishonoured women were entirely responsible for their own predicament, ascribing this solely to their weakness and depravity rather than to the pressure of their circumstances? Or could a woman be, if not absolved, at least understood? Might she be seen as a victim, perhaps of traitors in her own family circle, perhaps of predators, traffickers or false lovers, and possibly even of an economic system which underpaid women for 'respectable' work? Could she be rescued, not just by the ancient method of exhorting her to join a religious community and do penance, as if the fault had been entirely hers, but by taking action against some of her oppressors?

In the late sixteenth century, Sperone Speroni (1500–88), a literary gentleman of Padua, acknowledged three standard excuses for becoming a prostitute, only to brush them aside. Some women, he said, would plead their fear of starvation – 'if, on account of her hunger, a young woman may steal from another person, how can she be forbidden to sell herself to escape her own penury?' But the function of poverty, said Speroni, was to spur people to industry, not excuse their vicious behaviour: all arts and crafts were 'the children of poverty' and the distaff, the needle and the loom were women's proper defences against it. Poor girls who guarded their honour would, he predicted complacently, be assisted by charities, presumably by the many confraternities which contributed to dowries for virtuous maidens, and get to make good marriages or find safe havens in convents. Girls tarnished by 'infamy' could look forward to no such happy destiny. Being no economist but a moralist, Speroni did not mention the uncertainty of employment in the textile and garment trades, the poor wages they paid, or the frequency with which they were combined with occasional prostitution.

Another girl would invoke her widowed mother, who had pressed her to become a prostitute to keep her in old age: 'we must honour the mother who bore us; to honour her is to obey her'. 'Reason would have it', said Speroni, 'that if in her commands a mother is no longer a mother but has turned into a fiend, the daughter who disobeys her shall be reckoned, not a guilty child, but an angel in the flesh'.

Then, forming a third category for him, there were women who claimed to have been betrayed by seducers, so that, having lost their honour and marital prospects, they could only survive through immoral earnings. These Speroni depicted as man-haters and deceivers rather than innocent victims:

> if the lover to whom I gave everything he desired proved to be ungrateful and unfaithful to me, what can I expect from the others whom I spurned for the love of him? It is better then, so long as I can find buyers, to sell to all comers the remnants of my honour, which I wanted to give to one man alone, and revenge myself on that villain through every one of his fellows, and love none of them out of the goodness of my heart. Rather, while pretending to love all of them, I too will sneer, steal and betray, no matter who is before me.[2]

Other commentators proved, in time, more willing to listen to explanations and to analyse the underlying causes of prostitution. Sarnelli, who campaigned against prostitution in Naples in the 1730s, called for a register of prostitutes and for inquiries into their motives and situations.[3] During the nineteenth century, the official Neapolitan registers would divide prostitutes into three classes not unlike those unsympathetically identified by Speroni: women whom unscrupulous lovers had seduced and then abandoned; destitute women, to whom the trade was a means of survival; women introduced to prostitution or sold to its organisers by feckless husbands or heartless parents bent on their exploitation.[4] An enlightened Italian committee in 1903, campaigning against what was then called the white slave trade, thought similarly, but put more blame on the clients than on the women who obliged them: traffickers flourished, surely, only because men could not or would not discipline their sexual desires or desist from their unending quest for 'depraved enjoyments'.[5]

Children in danger

Central to the literature of prostitution was the scheming mother who corrupted her own daughter. At least as numerous in real life were less calculating parents who could not or would not protect their children against precocious sexual experiences, some of them incestuous. Overcrowding, lack of privacy and shared beds in rented rooms had much to answer for, as had the kind of casual work which poor girls were called upon to do; seldom could they stay at home all day under a parent's eye. Girls were expected to reach puberty at twelve, but believed to be already at high risk several years earlier. In 1614, the administrators of a leading Roman charity tried to discriminate between respectable girls who would qualify for the dowries which the charity dispensed and others who, having been unsupervised and exposed to sexual molestation, had no reputation to lose. They were particularly interested in a girl's experiences from the age of ten upwards and looked askance at those who had gone to wash clothes in public places, to harvest grapes in other people's vineyards, to hoe, to cut wood, to gather chicory, or to spend time for any reason in remote vineyards and orchards. Equally suspect were girls who, after completing their tenth year, lived in taverns or inns or in rooming-houses, even if these belonged to their own parents (the lecherous lodger being a known hazard). So were girls of the same age who ventured out alone to make purchases in taverns or marketplaces; and likewise any girl of ten or more who lived or consorted with 'any person of ill-fame, even if he or she is a relative'.[6] By a kind of self-fulfilling prophecy, these girls would probably be written off and denied the help towards making a 'good' marriage that Speroni had envisaged. It was also notorious that a spell of domestic service would expose girls, some as young as nine, to sexual interference by employers, sons of the house, or fellow servants. Employers often undertook to provide dowries for girls who had served them for several years, but such contracts were not always honoured, either by the master or mistress or by the servant.[7]

Between 1590 and 1680, the Council of Ten in Venice tried a number of culprits for sexually assaulting girls aged between three and sixteen. The average age of their victims, so far as it can be known, was ten-and-a-half. Among them was Virginia, aged eight, held captive and assaulted by the owner of a shop to which she had been sent on an errand.[8] In some eighteenth-century cases before Venice's court of morals, the Esecutori contro la Bestemmia, witnesses suggested that girls had been *mal custodite*, 'poorly watched', by their families. One or two of the accused pleaded in their defence that the parents were so negligent that the girls were fair prey. But it was hard for poor families to protect or control children or adolescent daughters. Anzola Zelante's father was a porter, her mother a water-carrier, and they had no time to stop her promenading with sweethearts and acquiring a dubious reputation. Domenica Florissa, on becoming a live-in nurse to a noble household, had to entrust her six-year-old daughter Lucia to an aunt living in lodgings shared by two families, in which a man interfered with the child and infected her with the French evil.[9] Sarnelli lamented the fate of children aged eight to ten in the vice districts of Naples; holding that prostitution, like begging, quickly became addictive, he declared that 'having tasted the pleasure, no longer restrained by shame, the wretched creatures live as whores'.[10] In Venice in 1730, the governors of a rescue institution for reformed prostitutes set the minimum age of entry at twelve, but had to admit that girls could well be 'deflowered and ruined' long before they reached it.[11]

The unfit mother

A godsend to satirists was the mature, cynical, worldly-wise woman who expounds to a promising pupil the dodges of the courtesan's trade and incidentally warns male readers to beware of them. She was an almost timeless figure whose advice did not vary greatly; the second-century Greek dialogues of Lucian left their mark on the worlds of Aretino and Pallavicino in the sixteenth and seventeenth centuries, especially, perhaps, through Lucian's Lyra, the courtesan who 'wouldn't do anything wanton or unseemly' at bed-time. Sometimes the tutor is the girl's mother, a widow in dire financial straits, enlisting a pretty daughter in a joint moneymaking enterprise and instilling business sense – by urging the importance of taking on a range of clients, including repulsive ones who will pay handsomely for gratification, and not confining herself to pretty boys, idlers and dandies who expect to pay 'just by being good-looking'.[12] Sometimes the mother has herself been a resourceful whore, as has Aretino's Nanna, who gives her daughter Pippa the benefit of her vast experience. 'I who know it all too well am in no great haste to have you reamed. Yes indeed, a girl must know something more than just lifting her skirt and crying "Stick it in, I'm ready" …'[13]

The tutor may be no blood relation to the student, as witness Pallavicino's old beggar woman, who comes upon a frustrated, dowerless, hungry noble girl, skulking at home without prospects, and persuades her to chance her arm as a prostitute.[14] But the crafty mother recurs more often in the literature. The courtesan mother of Francesco Pona's heroine brings her daughter to Venice from Padua after the girl has lost her virginity at the age of eleven to a fickle lover from Pisa. Undaunted, she sells the child's maidenhead another six times, preferring merchants and artisans to gentry; eventually both move in with an elderly, besotted spice merchant, who takes on the daughter as a mistress and the mother as a servant.[15] Venice's most memorable courtesan-author, Veronica Franco, offers a variation on the theme (as though standing Aretino on his head) by lecturing a misguided mother who plans to launch her talentless daughter as a courtesan, warning her of the trials of a deceptively glamorous life, and pleading with the woman 'not to destroy your own soul and honour at a single blow together with your daughter's'.[16] English travellers were happy to repeat the story that the freelance prostitute's trade was commonly passed from mother to daughter – they 'doe matrizare', wrote Coryat, and his contemporary Moryson reported a Venetian prayer, 'from a Cortesan that hath a mother to teach her to spoile [i.e. fleece] her lovers, God deliver us'.[17]

The notion of the corrupting, managing mother was no mere literary conceit. In the twelfth and thirteenth centuries, the legal codes of Roger II of Sicily and the Emperor Frederick II had threatened her with savage penalties, though they distinguished between women who actively prostituted their daughters and those who merely consented to the girls selling themselves, perhaps to survive in the face of poverty.[18] In thirteenth- and fourteenth-century Bologna, prostitutes were found to be living with their mothers, who were often accused of supporting their old age by living off their daughters' earnings.[19] Trial records from the following centuries preserved traces, for example in Florence and Pistoia, of mothers and daughters acting in concert, mothers finding daughters clients or lending their premises for their immoral activities.[20] There were instances, too, of mothers influencing married daughters, to leave a spouse in Cuneo and take to the 'evil life' in Turin (1430), or, as in Florence (1565–6), to engage in prostitution for a few months in a husband's absence.[21] Perhaps in these cases the husband was abusive or a bad provider, the mother's advice born of desperation rather than depravity. At a higher level of the profession, some mothers formed lasting partnerships with their daughters which rested on a combination of affection and business interests, as did Giulia Ferrarese, the courtesan mother of Tullia d'Aragona; Tullia's daughter, Penelope, was probably destined for the same career, though any hopes pinned on her were dashed when the child died in Rome in 1549.[22]

In Rome in the early seventeenth century, about one-tenth of known prostitutes appeared to be living with their mothers, a significant proportion given the low expectation of life and the likelihood that many parents would not see their daughters grow up. Most of these mothers were aged between forty and sixty, and many were widows, apparently turning to their daughters for support.[23] In Venice, Veneranda, of the parish of the Santi Apostoli, headed a household which consisted of herself, her mother and her niece, and all three were listed as *meretrici* in a local census.[24]

It did not always follow, though, that a prostitute living with her mother had learned her trade at her hands or been pushed into it by her, or that her mother was always implicated in her activities. Young Camilla, in Bologna in 1601, met men in some-body else's house, as if to protect her widowed mother from charges of procuring.[25] Possibly significant, too, is a hint dropped by Aretino's Nanna to the effect that many of the 'daughters' groomed by the more resourceful prostitutes were not their birth chil-dren but girls selected from foundling hospitals or orphanages, and chosen for their good looks, which would begin to bloom when those of their 'mother' began to fade.[26] 'Prostituting' a daughter did not necessarily mean either training her as a courtesan to cater for a clientele or placing her in a brothel. Another method was to make her the mistress of some social superior who would 'buy' her, perhaps clothe her and help her to acquire useful accomplishments (thereby sparing the parents the trouble and expense of training her). In real life, a prostitute's mother, even if she shared the girl's earnings, was not always her tutor in the vice trade.

Severe punishment could fall on mothers convicted of corrupting their daughters; the girls themselves were not exonerated unless they were very young. In the late 1580s, according to a newsletter received in Venice, Sixtus V shocked the curia by passing an exemplary sentence on a mother who had sold her daughter's virginity to a Frenchman. This gentleman had 'enjoyed her for some time, bestowing dresses and jewellery'. The pope sent the mother to the gallows and had the daughter subjected to a terrible ordeal: resplendent in her finery, the girl must be forced to witness the execution and then stand by the gibbet for an hour, exposed to public obloquy, as though providing live evidence of the enormity of the mother's crime and sharing in some of her guilt.[27] This grim spectacle did not put a stop to the sale of daughters; in 1607, for example, the governors of the Roman rescue charity of Santa Caterina della Rosa heard tell of 'a woman who has put a price of a hundred *scudi* upon her daughter to anyone who wants to take her maidenhead'.[28] At Milan in 1671, Angela Visconti, who had abetted if not instigated her eleven-year-old daughter's career first as a concubine and then as a prostitute, was paraded round the city bearing a placard announcing her crime, and afterwards banished, while the girl, Margherita, and her aunt, Anna Castelli, were fined and then released from prison.[29]

Impoverished parents were still selling attractive children when Jean-Jacques Rousseau was secretary to the French embassy in Venice in 1743–4. His friend Carrio, secretary at the Spanish embassy, wearied of 'always going to women who belonged to others' and suggested 'an arrangement which is not rare in Venice, that we should keep one between us'. Since Rousseau feared the French evil and recoiled from ordi-nary prostitutes, he agreed to the plan to reserve for their enjoyment a fresh, unsullied child. Carrio discovered 'a little girl of eleven or twelve, whom her wretched mother wanted to sell'. They paid the price, arranged for the girl's keep, bought her a spinet, and employed a singing master to develop her talent. Rousseau's story was that they waited for her to mature, and in the interval grew very fond of young Anzoletta, accepting her as a child, so that any thought of using her sexually began to disgust them both, and their relations with the girl became gentle and paternal.[30]

Perhaps few of the children treated as saleable goods fared as well as Anzoletta, though one wonders what happened to her when the kind diplomats left Venice. Some mothers, though cast as villains, may have believed that such arrangements would not only benefit themselves but also improve their daughters' prospects. For centuries poor people had handed over girls to employers to be trained as domestic servants and work for dowries, and many had lost their virginity and fallen pregnant before their indentures expired. Less conventional contracts could have seemed more attractive. In Venice in 1785, Maria Lazara knew little about Gaetano Franceschini, to whom she entrusted her daughter, some said as a *figlia d'anima*, a cross between an adopted daughter and a servant. He paid her one ducat a month and fed and clothed the child. Other rumours had it that 'he had been advised to have sleeping by him a girl of tender years, that her heat might revive his', and the mother at last took fright on hearing that 'he was a man of pleasure with rough inclinations towards women'.[31]

Fathers and husbands

Bad mothers, immediately responsible for a daughter's upbringing, attracted more censure than did bad fathers. In practice, both parents, or a mother and stepfather, or a mother's lover, could be involved in schemes to exploit a daughter, which were not the monopoly of struggling widows or deserted wives. Conscientious parents were duty bound to provide a daughter with a marriage portion as an advance on her inheritance, although in practice the child of an impoverished family would earn much of her dowry herself. Unscrupulous couples were capable of overturning the proprieties by selling or hiring out a daughter's sexual services, thus transforming her from a financial burden into an asset, or securing favours for themselves by making her available to some influential patron. One of Bandello's realistic stories, true to life if not factually true in all respects, concerns a couple who migrate to Venice in the 1520s or 1530s and improve their fortunes by handing their dowerless daughter Cassandra over to powerful lovers – first the Dominican tutor to the nephews of Doge Andrea Gritti, and then a young nobleman who, it is hoped, will install the girl's father in a minor office of profit.[32] Giuseppe, a Roman cobbler, colluded in 1602 with his wife in a plan to make their daughter available to Captain Valerio, head constable to the governor of Rome. The captain presented Giuseppe with a gambling game (a roulette wheel or something similar?), which enabled him to make money and also to be conveniently out of the house when his daughter's lover called.[33] A girl might have reason to fear, not her undutiful father, but her mother's abusive lover: in 1596, Gregorio Arrogato, in the Sicilian archdiocese of Monreale, earned his foul local reputation not only by beating the married woman he lived with but also by selling her daughter's virginity to a gentleman from Palermo.[34]

Some daughters, no doubt, were in some degree rogues rather than victims: not all of them were pawns in some parental game, as if they had no will of their own, no initiative, and no appetite for the luxuries which misbehaviour could buy. Some were capable of behaving in ways which appalled and dishonoured their fathers, provoking them, perhaps belatedly, into imposing discipline. About 1600, Domenico

Piemontese, a carter in Rome, was so incensed by his daughters' fast-and-loose conduct in a hayloft with some of his colleagues that he pursued the female miscreants,
knife in hand, and locked them up in his house for three months. Caterina, aged
twenty-three, had earned enough to buy herself a black shawl; was this article worth
the loss of her liberty?[35]

Marriage was ideally a safe haven, to be sought by almost every virtuous young
woman. But certain husbands effectively became pimps who had entered into formal
marriage contracts, as though these agreements enabled them to exert tighter control
over their women, and as if they did not value either the sexual fidelity of their wives
or their own reputations as good providers. Court testimony depicted them as spend-
thrifts without steady employment, hoping for an income, or an extra income, from a
wife's immoral earnings; no doubt there could have been more complicated psycho-
logical reasons for their behaviour.[36] Conceivably, some chose to marry women who
were already prostitutes, though with no intention of reforming them as the Church
desired. In Ferrara in 1482, Margherita, alias The Portress [La Fachina], attracted the
term 'prostitute housewife [*meretrice casalenga*]'.[37] Shortly after his wedding in Florence
in 1417, Bartolomeo was trying to agree a price for his bride Stella with a fellow citizen
who ran a brothel in Lucca. They discussed her as a commodity, but concluded no deal,
since the husband wanted thirty florins and the prospective buyer would only offer
twelve, on the grounds that the woman was poorly dressed and would require a new
wardrobe. Bartolomeo then did what he could to hire out his wife on his own account.[38]
In sixteenth-century Verona, there were several husbands who failed to support their
wives, squandered their dowries, and sooner or later manoeuvred them into immoral
relationships with other men.[39] In Venice, about 1592, Camilla, then thirteen, was 'married' but in effect sold by her father to a fellow textile worker and soon found herself
expected to provide sexual services to a 'gentleman'. She left her nominal husband after
six months and eventually had her 'marriage' annulled by the patriarch's court on the
grounds that she had never consented to it. But it took almost thirty years to achieve this
end, and meanwhile, by her own account, she could only survive by continuing to lead
an immoral life.[40] Taken to court, husbands would assert that they had known nothing
of their wives' activities, much less inspired or planned them. One was brought to book
by solid evidence in Siena in 1602 and sentenced to five years in prison. It seemed clear
to the archbishop's court that Orazio of Urbino or Cagli, the work-shy, tavern-haunting
husband of Caterina from Rome, had agreed to her sleeping with upper-class lovers
('When the count's in the house, put a towel in the window as a sign and I will not come
in').[41] In Venice, about 1640, the husband of Isabella Novaglia had exhausted her dowry
in five years and then begun to exploit her person by 'giving her in hand' to 'a gentleman
from the house of Querini'. It seemed that this man 'helped' both of them even when
Isabella was no longer his lover.[42]

Shame might be the portion of a deceived husband, awarded cuckold's horns by
public opinion. But one whose wife was obeying his instructions, and getting him
favours by sleeping with a social superior, could believe that he was still in charge of the
woman and preserve his self-respect. Critics might well judge that he had lost control
'of that which is his'.[43]

'The prowling lion'

Beyond the treacherous family lay the sinister figures of pimps, procuresses and bawds – *lenoni, ruffiani* and *ruffiane*, parasites upon prostitutes and alleged seducers of innocent women. Though generally reviled, they could be tolerated within limits by magistrates if not by moralists. One of the milder diatribes against the eternal pimp denounced 'undisciplined young men who do not care to live by their own toil and labour, but prefer to pursue the said whores and make a living from their wretched and lamentable state'.[44] But magistrates in fifteenth-century Florence appeared to accept that some prostitutes, even if they took up residence in public brothels, would need personal champions to look after their interests, in return for a cut of their earnings. Half lovers and half business partners, pimps often lodged in the brothel themselves: four establishments in Florence's vice district in 1436 accommodated between them twenty-eight *lenoni* to about seventy *meretrici*.[45] At the 'instigation' of Carlo di Francesco, lately a wool-carder, 'a certain woman' 'lodged in the public brothel in a booth [*apotecha*] where she solicits and publicly offers her body for sexual intercourse at a price' 'on her and his behalf'.[46] Other pimps were partners of foreign prostitutes, came from the same region as their women, and had arrived in Florence with them. Some made enforceable contracts with their protégées, which bound the man to take no other lover while the agreement lasted. In 1439 a woman who tried to get away from a pimp was ordered by magistrates to pay him fifteen florins as compensation, even though she was en route for a penitential convent. Pimps enjoyed enough status to be able to form their own religious confraternity, dedicated to St Barbara and based at the church of San Leo in the vice district.[47] Magistrates sometimes accepted most of them as part of the lesser evil (so long as they paid certain dues and confined their activities to the proper area) and sometimes tried to reduce their numbers by expelling some of them from Florence.[48]

Not all pimps were responsible for leading their partners astray. But trial records commemorate certain devious men who induced other men's wives – possibly discontented ones, cheered by the prospect of escaping from miserable marriages – to run away with them, only to find themselves deposited in a brothel far from home to earn money for their cold-hearted lover. This fate overtook Nesca of Orvieto about 1300, Riguardata of Florence about 1379, and Giuliana of Bologna in 1427. Repelled by the brothel-keeper's advances and encouraged by the portraits of the Virgin Mary and St Catherine which happened to be hanging in the public brothel at Pisa, Giuliana managed to get herself out of the place. But – since she had slept with her lover at an inn on their journey – she was then sentenced to painful and humiliating punishment as an adulteress. After her ordeal she probably had little chance of returning to a respectable life.[49]

In 1588 the Jesuit Benedetto Palmio applauded the governors of Venice's principal rescue society for 'saving a great multitude of young virgins from being seized by the most cruel lion, "who is forever prowling around, looking for someone to eat [*qui circuit semper quaerens quem devoret*]"'.[50] One incarnation of this version of the Devil was the bawd [*rufiana*], commonly an ex-prostitute herself, often depicted pouncing on newcomers to the city – particularly on beggar girls and female servants in search of work.

Like Mrs Brown, the brothel madam who picks on Cleland's Fanny Hill at the 'intelligence office' for servants in eighteenth-century London, bawds kitted out likely girls, took them to lodge in disreputable places, and got them heavily into debt for the clothes they hired them at exorbitant rates. Venetian magistrates in the 1530s could only prescribe that female servants seeking situations should lodge with respectable women and that one such person should be available in every parish, while prostitutes should be forbidden to employ maids under the age of thirty.[51] Sarnelli, in the 1730s, pointed out that procurers and procuresses did not wait for young women to drift to the city, but ventured forth to recruit them in the towns and villages of the kingdom of Naples.[52] A Venetian case of 1775, which ended with the imprisonment of three brothel-keepers, Angiola Grisona, Anna Furlana and Giacomina Bassanese, suggested that methods of recruiting girls and appropriating most of their earnings had changed little since the late middle ages, and that job-seeking servants were at especially high risk.[53]

Bawdry, however, could, as much as prostitution itself, be a part-time occupation practised, not by ruthless professionals, but by impoverished women, brokers rather than bosses, who used it to eke out a precarious living. Such people assisted part-time prostitutes, for example by getting them better deals and taking a cut for themselves. Among them was the old woman of Bologna in 1606 who took in female lodgers and found them men, but also used her local knowledge to get the women work with silk merchants.[54] Pallavicino's ex-prostitute regards landladies as useful go-betweens, partly because they often lodge 'Polacks', probably soldiers and travellers from eastern Europe, who fall into their clutches with open eyes and spend whatever is asked of them.[55] When, in mid-eighteenth-century Venice, Maria Zavanterella was accused of 'evil-living', she appeared to be doing several things in order to survive. One was to keep in her house for immoral purposes servant girls who had just left their employers. But she was also thought to be a laundress or a spinner; she lived with an aged husband who went out begging; she made a little money by fostering a child from the local foundling hospital.[56] The economic gap between the procuress and the prostitute was not always enormous, and many bawds were ex-prostitutes who had lost their allure and were surviving by any means that came to hand.

False lovers and rapists

A villain often blamed for a woman's downfall, alongside the scheming parents, the feckless husband, the bawd and the pimp, was the faithless lover. As Aretino's procuress remarks of one such character,

> The rumour was soon out that he would not marry her unless she let him have a trial trip, as is the custom nowadays. And I could tell you of many, many girls who lost their cherries to lovers in the same fashion; and once their lovers had had their fill or more, they left them in the lurch without even giving them a crust of bread.[57]

Wishful thinking, fond hopes of marriage, seemed to beguile young women who, as Nanna complains in another passage, would have resisted the blandishments of bawds.[58] Three kinds of misadventure, rape, seduction and abandonment, sometimes aggravated by unwanted pregnancies, blighted a girl's reputation, dishonoured her family, and threatened to exclude her from marriage, thrusting her towards prostitution or concubinage. In Rome, about 1600, Olimpia told a concise story of her own ruin: two sexual assaults by unrecognisable predators within five days were followed by an approach within a month by an 'aunt' who manoeuvred her into bed with a member of the Flemish ambassador's entourage.[59]

Between 1589 and 1628, a rescue institution in Milan used the terms *deflorata*, *violata* and *stuprata* to indicate that the women and girls it was admitting had been unlawfully deprived of their virginity.[60] So-called 'simple' *stuprum* occurred where a woman appeared to be having sexual relations willingly with a man outside marriage, sometimes with her relatives' complicity, and to entertain no illusions that the relationship would lead to a wedding. In a more serious form of *stuprum*, a woman had succumbed to false promises of marriage which the man did not intend to keep and subsequently denied making. In another, she was a victim of physical force – not that force and fraud were wholly distinct from each other, for they could easily be combined.[61] A man might also make a promise of marriage which he sincerely intended at the time but subsequently withdrew, perhaps under pressure from relatives who regarded his betrothed as socially inferior – in which case an action might lie against him for breach of promise rather than for real or statutory rape.[62]

Two kinds of remedy were generally available to a wronged woman who proved her case in court – marriage to her seducer, and monetary compensation for the loss of her virginity, paid to her or her father, who would probably now have to provide a larger dowry to find her a husband. From the sixteenth century onwards, marriage and compensation were commonly treated as alternatives, though lawyers still cited Old Testament texts which suggested that a seducer should be compelled both to marry a girl and to compensate her father.[63] There was some reluctance to force a man to marry, partly because, in the Church's view, the essence of matrimony lay in the consent of the couple, and partly from the fear that noble youths would be lured into *mésalliances* with designing women of lower social standing. With time, a woman's chances of obtaining legal redress became negligible unless she could show that her lover had subjected her to force or fraud or both. In cases of 'simple' *stuprum*, casuists were inclined to argue that a lover was not obliged in law or justice to assist a woman when their relationship ended, but might well do so out of charity – as though to make amends for the damage to her marital prospects inflicted by the loss of her reputation.[64] Should he fail to provide for her, the woman's position would be unenviable indeed.

Unlawful defloration could be treated as a crime against the public peace, punishable by imprisonment, exile, or other harsh penalties. It might also be treated as a private wrong which could be remedied by compensation, or as a combination of the two. A woman determined enough to pursue a seducer in court could in effect be awarded a dowry or a supplement to her dowry. This would supposedly restore her honour by demonstrating that she had been a victim, and enable her eventually to marry somebody else. But she could expect the defendant to retaliate by attacking her character and would lose her case if parish priests and neighbours stigmatised her as a promiscuous woman.[65] Legislation in Venice in 1520 warned the courts against accepting too readily the allegations of servants against their employers and their families.[66] Neapolitan legislation of 1738 would take a similar view.[67]

If defaulting lovers were to be made to pay, they had to appear in court and had to be solvent. Between 1577 and 1700, almost one-third (147 of 466) of men charged in Venice with defloration under false promises of matrimony failed to appear before the judges, the Esecutori contro la Bestemmia, with the result that they were judged guilty and exiled from Venice and its surrounding territory. About 64 per cent of those who did present themselves were convicted and ordered either to marry their victims or pay a sum which would be used to contribute to the women's dowries, so long as they could arrange to wed or enter a convent in reasonable time. But some men could not pay: about 1640, Isabella Gorgo, after twenty-one years, renounced her claim to two hundred ducats from Girolamo Falvo, saying that she wished neither to marry nor to become a nun.[68] Did compensation really suffice to restore a young woman's reputation, to dispel the suspicion that she had colluded in her own misfortune? Bandello's heroine, Giulia of Gazuolo, believes that her honour has been irretrievably lost, ignores the rapist's offer to help her marry, and drowns herself in the river Olio.[69]

What constituted an enforceable promise of marriage? Should a betrothal followed by sexual relations lead inexorably towards a wedding, or could a man break his word without suffering unpleasant legal or social consequences? Was an engagement virtually equivalent to a marriage, or was it a potential trap for trusting young women? The decree on marriage enacted by the Council of Trent in 1563 tried to dispel uncertainty by dismissing statements allegedly made in private about future intentions and recognising only vows made publicly with immediate effect. It was directed against clandestine marriages, which could encourage adventurers, elopers, bigamists and rebels against parental authority. The new law established that a forthcoming marriage must normally be announced, three times in all, in the local parish church on three successive festival days. These formalities completed, 'if no legitimate impediment is revealed', the parish priest should proceed with the wedding 'in the presence of the people'. The proceedings could be curtailed should there be reason to anticipate 'that a marriage might be maliciously hindered'. But it was generally impossible to dispense with at least one publication and the presence of an authorised priest and two or three witnesses. The parish priest was to keep a register of marriages and betrothed couples to be discouraged from living together 'until they have received the sacerdotal blessing in the church'.[70]

At first, the decree may have inadvertently provided another seducer's charter, in that it allowed slippery characters to slide out of marriages by claiming that the procedures required by the council had not been followed and that nothing else could be binding. Secular magistrates in Venice in 1577 undertook to punish 'wicked men' who acquired 'wives' without observing the necessary formalities and 'having violated and enjoyed them for a while then leave them and seek dissolution of the "marriage" from ecclesiastical judges, from whom they can easily obtain it on the grounds that such "marriages" were made contrary to the decrees of the Council of Trent'.[71] A father invoked this law in 1588 in the subject city of Feltre. A local citizen had, it seemed, led the plaintiff's daughter to believe that she was married to him, but had cunningly avoided any ceremony which would be recognised by the post-Tridentine Church. The father obtained only an order to the seducer to support the woman's illegitimate child.[72]

Social pressure on young men to honour promises of marriage was probably strongest in country towns and villages, where it could spring not only from a girl's relatives but also from her 'contemporaries' [coetanei], friends and acquaintances who were not happy to see her bought off and who conveyed their displeasure to her lover. Young women who had left home for the big city could not rely on such champions.[73] Occasionally, in the countryside, aggrieved women stood up for themselves even when their families would not – as witness the spirited female in a village on the Piave in 1760, who burned down her young man's house three times, saying 'I will not be happy until I take his life, for I alone should bring death to the man who took my honour with the intention of taking me to wife and then abandoned me to grief and despair.'[74] Her rough tactics paid off, and the couple married.

Like much ecclesiastical legislation, the Tridentine decree on marriage took time, sometimes several decades, to alter accepted behaviour. But in at least one diocese, Bologna, the number of breach-of-promise cases entertained by the archbishop's court diminished rapidly. Of seventy-eight such cases considered between 1544 and 1595, fifty-four preceded the Tridentine decree and only twenty-four came after it.[75] Did this happen because more young women were learning to distrust promises and guarding their honour more carefully, or because more were realising that their cases were hopeless or being advised not to pursue them? In Piedmont, though perhaps not before the early eighteenth century, there was growing disapproval of premarital sexual relations; less inclination to rely on informal promises; more insistence on formal betrothals in the presence of witnesses which entailed an exchange of gifts, a toast to the couple and the consent of parents. In 1746 the courts heard for the first time a claim that a woman had told her lover that sex outside marriage was sinful. Women were now inclined to testify that they had been forced to have sex, not coaxed into it by promises of marriage.[76] Tuscan bishops conducting synods in the 1720s and 1730s warned girls against false promises, urged them to protect their reputations, threatened to excommunicate couples who had sex before marriage, and pointed out the dangers of long engagements.[77] In the late eighteenth century, another Tuscan prelate, Scipione de' Ricci, showed reluctance to enforce mere promises, especially those 'to which young people are inclined more as a result of fleeting passions than of a considered decision'. Rather than rely on church courts, some couples chose to draw up private agreements specifying fines for a party who broke a promise of marriage.[78]

Not surprisingly, there were still, in the eighteenth century, regions such as the Vesuvian countryside in which, despite ecclesiastical disapproval, engaged couples still lived together in anticipation of marriage. Could this lead to loss of the woman's honour if the man backed out and could not legally be held to his promise to wed her? It seemed that the woman's family often regarded this practice as a way of securing the marriage – a man was more likely to default if he had to defer sexual relations and was denied the 'trial run' of which Aretino had spoken.[79] No doubt neighbours would press him hard to marry his fiancée.

It was not inevitable that jilted young women who had lost their virginity would drift towards the 'evil life', become concubines or prostitutes. Some forms of redress were available to them, and if they had become pregnant they could, as the Church urged them, give up the child to a foundling hospital in the hope of making a new start. But any legal action they took exposed their own sexual conduct to unnervingly close scrutiny, and rural communities in particular, such as Montefollonico, examined reputations closely and had long memories for 'missteps'. These could, all too easily, consign women to the ranks of the less than respectable and land them with undesirable husbands, or no husbands at all.[80]

Poverty, prostitution and female employment

Charitable people would acknowledge that many women had been driven to prostitution not by depravity but by misery – that prostitution and destitution were close companions, or that prostitution could (in modern terms) form part of an 'economy of multiple expedients', enabling women to piece together the means of survival.[81] A seventeenth-century Neapolitan confraternity recognised that many widows were driven to 'lose their souls and fall prey to the Devil' to escape dying in want.[82] In the 1670s Mariano Sozzini called for an asylum in Rome for 'poor prostitutes who declare that they live as public sinners because they have no food and no dwelling place'.[83] In the 1730s Sarnelli called Neapolitan prostitutes 'driven more by hunger than by lechery' and deplored the neglect of young girls and orphan children, left to beg and sleep in the open, who could only sell their virtue and begin to work as child prostitutes.[84]

Of crucial importance was the plight of women struggling to support young children after the death or disappearance of husbands, or their own dismissal by men they had lived with as mistresses. The social consensus was that the proper function of lay women was to contribute labour, earnings, mother's milk and child care to households governed by male breadwinners. It should not be made easy for women to set up their own businesses or compete with men on equal terms for highly paid employment; but it was right that they should add to family income by working for outside employers (who ranged from textile manufacturers to foundling hospitals), that they should be anything from spinners to wet nurses, usually working at home and combining these occupations with child care and domestic duties. It was widely understood that they should be paid supplementary rather than living wages and be confined to the simpler industrial tasks. Who would have the patience to perform these if women did not? Italian silk industries in the seventeenth and eighteenth centuries depended heavily on low-waged female labour. Should the male head of household die, be disabled or fall chronically ill, go for a soldier, lose interest in his trade, be imprisoned or take to drink and gambling, the wife or widow would often be able to live only by combining several badly rewarded occupations (unless some of her children were old enough to look after her). These might or might not include such activities as occasional prostitution or assisting prostitutes.

It was true that an artisan's widow might be able to carry on his business at least for a while, or until a son or second husband took it over, subject to restrictions imposed by the corporation which governed the trade.[85] In theory, too, a large proportion of the dowry which the wife had brought to her marriage ought to be available to support her and her offspring after her husband's death, perhaps to enable her to marry again. But the chances were that in a working household very little of this capital would have survived the trials of years of married life.[86]

No doubt many women followed much the same course as Silvestra, a Florentine widow about 1400 whose son was described as *deviatus et vagabundus*, not the kind to hold down a steady job. She applied herself to 'spinning and laundering and looking after women in childbed and performing other services'.[87] She did not speak of anything less virtuous. Others, in equally difficult circumstances, were forced into a precarious existence in which there was only a short step from vagrancy to prostitution. Caterina Monari, from the duchy of Modena, told her story to magistrates in Bologna in 1604. About eleven years earlier, one of her brothers had found her a husband and she had lived with him for seven years, although he never had a trade. Then he left 'on account of the hunger' and she heard tell that he had died somewhere in the Veneto. By that time, however, she too had left home, en route for the towns, and for one winter in Ferrara she rented space with a 'good old woman' called Maria who 'struggled day and night' to earn a living by combing wool. Caterina herself survived by spinning 'with a distaff' and occasionally by going out begging. She did some agricultural work and then went into domestic service, first in Faenza and then in Pieve di Cento, sometimes for wages, sometimes for board and lodging alone. After that, she arrived in Bologna and drifted from one place to another, again, she said, seeking work as a servant; since her quest involved hanging about an inn or tavern, and she had no visible means of support, she excited suspicion of being a prostitute soliciting for custom and found herself before the Ufficio delle Bollette.[88]

Francesca Buttafuoco, a near contemporary of Caterina's, told her story in the diocese of Teramo (Abruzzo). At the age of seven she had arrived, from Sebenico on the Dalmatian coast, at Civitella, a small fortress town towards the north of the kingdom of Naples. She was by turns servant, concubine, mother, wife, widow and prostitute ('finding myself destitute I gave myself entirely to doing evil with my body'). Then she became servant and concubine to Gasparra, the Spanish governor of Civitella, who eventually threw her out and expelled her from the town, bashing her head with an arquebus when she did not leave fast enough. He had found a more glamorous mistress, Giovanna from Naples, whom he treated like a great lady who would brook no rival. Francesca departed first to Teramo and then to a nearby village, Montorio, 'to be with the Spanish soldiers, and then I went with them to Campli', as if, being now a camp-follower, she had descended to the lowest imaginable level.[89]

Over the centuries, women succeeded in doing virtually all the jobs commonly done by men (probably not that of public executioner), including working in the building industry, at least in the fourteenth century, and taking on agricultural work which called for enormous strength and endurance.[90] The skill and versatility of women were warmly praised by contemporaries.[91] But seldom did their appreciation mean entitlement to equal pay for the same work, or the chance to carry out the most advanced operations in manufacturing processes. By the fourteenth and fifteenth centuries, women were becoming underlings, at least in manufacturing trades regulated by corporations of merchants and artisans. They were less likely to serve apprenticeships, acquire formal qualifications, possess their own looms, set up their own establishments, though none of these things was unthinkable. They were more likely, at least in certain places at certain times, to be restricted to the primary, ill-paid tasks such as spinning and silk-winding rather than weaving,[92] or, in early modern Bologna and Gorizia, for example, to weaving veils rather than taffetas and brocades, and to be barred from operating machinery in silk-throwing mills.[93] At Turin in 1788, the female *doppiatrici*, who carried out by hand the delicate and wearisome task of twisting strands of silken thread together, were paid 8.5 soldi a day, slightly less than a male apprentice doing work which required little skill (9 soldi) and about one-third as much as a male machine operator, a *torcitore* (23.5 soldi).[94]

Gaps between male and female wages were not confined to this region, or to manufacturing industry, or to advanced economies. When the economic geographer Giuseppe Maria Galanti toured Calabria as an official government visitor, his copious jottings included information on agricultural wages for men and women. They suggested that in most districts in 1792, women were paid 40–50 per cent as much as ordinary male labourers [*bracciali, travagliatori*]. According to a note on southern Calabria, where he called agriculture primitive and inefficient, fit for the 'infancy of society', 'Workers in the fields in the province generally receive 20–25 *grana* a day. At Catanzaro they get 30. Reapers are paid more. Artisans get 3–4 *carlini* [10 *grana* = 1 *carlino*]. Women receive 10–12 *grana*.'[95]

Apart from agricultural labour, the textile industries and the garment trades, openings for women lay in domestic service, a stand-by for women of all ages, though notorious for exposing the younger ones, from very early years, to sexual interference. Where remuneration depended on sales and fees rather than on wages and piece-rates determined by male employers, women enjoyed more independence – doing washing; selling fruit and vegetables, as hawkers and pedlars or stall-holders; selling clothing and cosmetics and second-hand goods of all kinds, with or without repairing and improving them. They were active in catering and hospitality, as landladies (perhaps subletting rented accommodation), or as keepers of inns or eating houses, bakers or cooks. They did odd jobs and errands, such as pledging goods for clients at city pawnshops. They became wet nurses, relatively well paid if they worked in prosperous households, less so if they took suckling infants into their own homes or looked after weaned children for private clients or foundling hospitals. Women could set up small dames' schools for young children, though these would never bring in princely rewards and seldom do more than keep their owners at or close to the breadline. They could work on the edge of the medical profession, respectably as midwives, less so as healers, there being a large 'unofficial' field in which healing often became confused with magic and sorcery, since the line dividing legitimate medicine from superstitious or even heretical activities was hard to draw. To practise magic or divination, to help clients to attract and keep lovers, discomfit enemies, identify thieves, find lost objects or foretell the future, could be a useful source of fees or favours.[96]

Moralists in the 1520s and 1530s rejoiced in the decline of courtesans who, having lost their looks and their health, had again to do as other lone women did and rub along by letting rooms, washing clothes, cooking in taverns and selling candles in churches. Aretino, though, presented in his comedy *Cortigiana* (1525) a resourceful creature, a Figaro long before Figaro himself, who combines almost every shady feminine skill. This is Aloigia, go-between and druggist, an ex-courtesan who admittedly enjoys the unusual advantage of having acquired an arsenal of medicines and exotic properties from Madonna Maggiorina, who is about to be burned for witchcraft and murder.

> By God, I've got more business than a market place, more letters to carry than a postman, more missions than an embassy. Somebody always wants ointment for the French evil, powders to whiten his teeth, or some remedy for whatever affliction God sends him.[97]

Conclusion

Governments had recognised prostitution as, in Augustine's phrase, a 'legitimate form of wickedness', a lesser evil compared with adultery, sodomy or concubinage. But, in its public and more private forms, a dishonourable existence was a condition from which women and girls ought to be rescued. It was undesirable that unlimited numbers of innocent and respectable females should lapse into dishonour; the 'evil life' was as much a consequence of dishonour as a cause of it. Magistrates and the governors of charities made some attempts to discipline types of villain whom they blamed for corrupting and betraying young women. Bad parents, and especially bad mothers, who sought to advance their own interests by exploiting attractive daughters became targets from time to time and incurred exemplary punishment. As Chapter 6 will show, rescue societies founded during the sixteenth century proved especially eager to remove the children of disreputable women from their mothers and transfer them to protective surroundings. Courts, including ecclesiastical courts, sometimes took action against husbands who made their wives available to other men in exchange for money or favours, although, since the accused men were liable to counter that their wives had acted on their own initiative, it could be difficult to convict them.

Female victims of force, fraud or bad faith on the part of male suitors and seducers were entitled to some legal remedies. Equipped with contributions to dowries to improve their marriage prospects, they might possibly succeed in recovering their reputations, though women brave enough to pursue a case might encounter damaging and unchivalrous attempts to attack their characters in court. Clearer definitions of marriage and warnings not to trust in mere promises of a future wedding may in the end have made women more careful of their honour, less liable to betrayal. Magistrates occasionally made token efforts to protect a particularly vulnerable group of people, servant girls looking for employment, against bawds and procuresses lying in wait for an easy prey. Furthermore – see Chapters 7–11 – the development of foundling hospitals set out to make it easier for the mothers of illegitimate children to conceal their misfortunes, avoid scandal, and perhaps eventually recover their reputations. Betrayed females might be forced to accept some blame and punishment, but extenuating circumstances were to some extent acknowledged.

Even the most enlightened would-be reformers, however, could not confront problems deep-seated in economic and social systems, especially in their reluctance to pay women living rather than supplementary wages, and the consequent hardships for independent women, estranged wives and widows (above all, those with young children). Some forms of disciplinary action, such as attempts to compel unmarried couples to separate and demands that men should discard their mistresses, could well drive women towards prostitution as a condition regarded as less evil than concubinage.

It was also possible to excuse and explain very little, but to treat dishonoured women as habitual sinners of a far deeper dye than the men who used their services. They should not be abandoned, but exhorted to repent, perhaps to retreat into another, very different kind of place set apart. Societies which had established brothels and vice districts and had not pursued freelance prostitutes vigorously could atone for their presence by setting up convents for women who wished to change their ways and retreat from the world as penitents. The next chapter will discuss these establishments.

Notes

1   See Chapter 3, n. 54.
2   Speroni 1596, pp. 186–91.
3   De Spirito 1978: 49.
4   White Mario ed. Infusino 1978, p. 44.
5   Gibson 1986, pp. 73–8.
6   On the rules of the archconfraternity of the Santissima Annunziata alla Minerva, see Piazza 1698, I, pp. 422–5; Fiorani 1979: 112–13.
7   For examples see McGough 2011, pp. 41–2.
8   Martini 1986a: 804–5, 809.
9   Gambier 1980, pp. 535–6, 539–40, 544, 552–3.
10 De Spirito 1978: 54–5, 60–1.
11 McGough 2011, p. 131.
12 For a lively translation of part of Lucian's 'Dialogues of the courtesans', see Lucian ed. Costa 2006, pp. 234–47 – especially Crobyle and Corinna, and Musarion and her mother, at pp. 238–42. Cf. Aretino trans. Rosenthal 1972, pp. 169–71, and Pallavicino ed. Coci 1992, p. xliv; also Pallavicino ed. Marchi 1984, Letter xxx, pp. 72–5.
13 Aretino trans. Rosenthal 1972, pp. 167, 196.
14 Pallavicino ed. Coci 1992, pp. 11–17, 103–4.
15 Pona ed. Fulco 1973, pp. 98–115.
16 Franco ed. Croce 1949, Letter xxii, pp. 36–9.
17 Coryat 1905 edn., I, p. 407; Moryson ed. Hughes 1903, p. 152.
18 Liber Augustalis ed. and trans. Powell 1971, p. 148; K.L. Jansen et al. 2009, pp. 182–3, 432–3.
19 Rinaldi 1991, pp. 116–17; Lansing 2003, p. 98.
20 Canosa and Colonnello 1989, pp. 105–6; Weinstein 2000, pp. 40–1, 76–7, 113–17, 120; Terpstra 2010, p. 32.
21 Comba 1986: 563–4; Terpstra 2010, p. 3.
22 Masson 1975, pp. 32, 60, 96–8, 110, 129–30.

23 E.S. Cohen 1991: 205; E.S. and T.V. Cohen 1993, pp. 60, 75; Storey 2008/2012, pp. 141–7.
24 Chojnacka 2001, pp. 23–4.
25 Ferrante 1996, pp. 226–7.
26 Aretino ed. Rosenthal 1972, p. 136.
27 See the *Memorie pubbliche (Michiel)* in MS. Marciana Venice, Italiani Classe VII, 811 (7299), fo.451v., entry after 8 June 1586. On the severity of Sixtus V, see also Martelli 2002: 271–2 and Storey 2008/2012, p. 139.
28 Camerano 1993: 232–3.
29 D'Amico 2005: 110, 116–17.
30 Rousseau ed. Cohen 1953, pp.285, 296–8, 302.
31 Gambier 1980, p.553.
32 For the story of the Cretan father and the Greek mother, see Bandello ed. Flora 1934, II.iv, vol. I, pp. 691–4.
33 Storey 2008/2012, pp. 158–9.
34 Pizzolato 2007: 249–50.
35 E.S. Cohen 1988: 181–2.
36 For modern opinions concerning husbands who prostituted wives, see, for example, Benjamin and Masters 1964, pp. 183–8.
37 Ghirardo 2001: 407–8.
38 Mazzi 1991, pp. 318–19.
39 Eisenach 2004, pp. 17, 159–60, 188–9, 201–2, 206.
40 Ferraro 2001, pp. 33–8, 62–3.
41 Nardi 1989: 78–85.
42 McGough 2011, pp. 39–40.
43 Eisenach 2004, pp. 159–60, 206; Storey 2008/2012, pp. 160–1.
44 From the regulations for the public brothel in Venice (1460), as translated in Chambers and Pullan 1992, p.123.
45 Mazzi 1991, pp. 265–6.
46 *Ibid.*, pp. 312–13.
47 Trexler 1981: 1000–1; Mazzi 1991, pp. 400–1.
48 Mazzi 1991, pp. 175–6, 202–3.
49 For Nesca, see Lansing 1997: 47–8; for Riguardata, Brucker 1971, doc. 91, pp. 196–8; for Giuliana, Mazzi 1986a: 620–1.
50 Palmio 1701; Pullan 1971, p. 387. The biblical reference is to I Peter, 5:8.
51 Chambers and Pullan 1992, p. 126 (from legislation of the Council of Ten in Venice, 1539).
52 De Spirito 1978: 54–5.
53 Canosa 1993, pp. 229–30.
54 Ferrante 1996, pp. 226–7.
55 Pallavicino ed. Coci 1992, pp. 72–3.
56 Gambier 1980, p.556.
57 Aretino ed. Rosenthal 1972, p. 275.
58 *Ibid.*, pp. 376–7.
59 E.S. Cohen 1988: 176–7.
60 D'Amico 1989: 411.
61 As in the case of Camilla, described in E.S. Cohen 1988: 185–8.
62 For discussion of a case at Calcara, near Bologna, in 1554, see Ferrante 1994, pp. 920–1.
63 Alessi 1990: 805–10. The relevant texts were Exodus 22: 15–16; Deuteronomy 22: 28–9.
64 Alessi 1990: 813–14, 819–21, 826.

65 For some examples from the sixteenth century, see Nardi 1989: 33; Lazzaretti 1996: especially 66–8; from *c.*1700, Canosa 1993, pp. 201–4.

66 Romano 1996, pp. 52–3, 56–7, 243. For the use made of this piece of legislation in an eighteenth-century court case, see Gambier 1980, pp. 550–1.

67 Alessi 1990: 813–14.

68 Hacke 2004, pp. 52–63. For these activities of the Esecutori, see also Derosas 1980, pp. 454–6, and Gambier 1980, p. 531.

69 Bandello ed. Flora 1934, I.viii, vol. I, pp. 108–14.

70 *Canons and Decrees* ed. Schroeder 1941, Session 24 of the Council of Trent (11 November 1563), pp. 183–5, 454–6.

71 Lombardi 1994, pp. 150–2.

72 Ruggiero 1987: 756–61, 772, 773–4, n. 18, 775, n. 53; Ruggiero 1993, pp. 57–87.

73 Cerutti and Cavallo 1980: 346–8, 357, 363–4, 368–70.

74 Gozzi ed. Zardo 1915, pp. 234–6, 6 August 1760.

75 Ferrante 1994, p. 903; cf. Fubini Leuzzi 1990: 353–4.

76 Cerutti and Cavallo 1980: 371–4.

77 Fubini Leuzzi 1992: 126–7.

78 Lombardi 2003, pp. 432–5, 438–40.

79 Jones 1992, pp. 159–61, 252, 371–2.

80 Hanlon 2009: 12–13, 19–24.

81 Hufton 1997, pp. 327–8.

82 Lopez 1964, pp. 272–3.

83 Bonadonna Russo 1979: 279.

84 De Spirito 1978: 46–7, 54–5.

85 See, for example, Travaglini 1992: 435–6; Ago 1996, pp. 178–9; Groppi 1996a, pp. 156–8; Piccinini 1996, pp. 29–30.

86 Cf. Chabot 1988: 301–2.

87 Mazzi 1986: 367–8.

88 Ferrante 1996, pp. 206–7.

89 Basilico 2008: 138–40.

90 Piccinini 1996, pp. 29–30; Merzario 1996, p. 236.

91 Groppi 1996a, pp. 123, 129–30.

92 Greci 1996, pp. 74–8; Piccinini 1996, pp. 37–8.

93 Poni 1996, pp. 272–5.

94 *Ibid.*, p. 282.

95 Galanti ed. Placanica 1992, p. 161. See also pp. 101, 105, 109, 112, 126, 171, 183, 258, 263, 281. See p. 345 for his remarks on the 'deplorable state' of agriculture in southern Calabria.

96 For collections of essays on female employment, see, for example, Muzzarelli *et al.* 1991 and Groppi 1996. On domestic service, Klapisch-Zuber 1986 and Romano 1996. Accounts of women retailers include Mackenney 1987, p. 103 (mercers in Venice) and Travaglini 1992 (*rigattieri* in Rome). For women, witchcraft and healing, R. Martin 1989, pp. 139–47, 180–9; Gentilcore 1992, p. 224, and Gentilcore 1998, pp. 84–5; Scully 1994–5; McGough 2011, pp. 81–3. For dames' schools, Groppi 1996a, pp. 160–2. For wetnursing and fostering, see below, Chapter 10.

97 Aretino ed. Romano 1989, II.vi, pp. 94–7; III.xi, p. 120.

5

Penitent sinners

A prostitute might be indispensable to society, but she was still, in the eyes of the pious, a habitual, blatant sinner and an endangered soul. It was as if Catholic communities excused their tolerance for immoral women by urging them to repent and by supporting religious institutions which would enable a small proportion of them to do so. Cities contained enclaves devoted to special goodness and special badness: nunneries which eschewed sexual activity, at least in principle, vice districts intended for the evacuation of heterosexual lust. A woman of lost honour, be she prostitute or concubine, could redeem herself by a transition from promiscuity to chastity, from vanity to austerity, by entering a convent for 'whores repenting'. Such nunneries were commonly known in Italy as Convertite and usually dedicated to a saintly prostitute who had changed her ways and punished herself without mercy for her sins. For the Church, floods of tears, declarations of love for the Saviour and a simple change of heart and habit would hardly suffice to atone for years of sexual looseness.

But it was possible to choose another, perhaps less thorny, path. A sinful woman could also seek redemption by marrying a man ambitious to reform her. Sceptics might jeer at his naivety or doubt his motives, but in the opinion of less cynical commentators he stood to earn great spiritual merit by rescuing a lost soul. His affronted relatives, horrified at the insertion into their honourable family of a woman with a chequered past, might well prove less enthusiastic.

Penitent saints

Mary Magdalen, the 'sweet friend of Jesus', the supreme patron of fallen women, stood for the power of repentance and love of Christ to earn forgiveness for sexual sins. She was created by ecclesiastical tradition, born of imaginative reading of the New Testament – by forming one character out of at least three women in the gospels – and probably by association with a prostitute saint of the fifth century, Mary the Egyptian, who retreated from Alexandria to the deserts of the Holy Land.[1] Identified with, among others, Mary of Bethany, sister to Martha and Lazarus, the Magdalen became a symbol of the contemplative life. As Gregory Martin wrote of the reformed prostitutes of Rome, 'if leaving worldly matters to Marthaes, they wil doe continuall penance with Marie by entering into religion voluntarily … then are they placed in the Nunnery of S. Marie Magdalen.'[2] Legend cast Mary Magdalen both as a missionary who brought

Christianity to Provence and as a hermit who subsequently lived for many years in the wilderness some distance from Marseilles.[3] In the late thirteenth century, a Tuscan artist presented eight scenes from her life, which framed a central figure of Byzantine appearance, gaunt, barefoot, clad in a frayed and sack-like habit and exhorting: 'Sinners, despair not, but follow me and turn to God.' The Renaissance imagery which depicted her as a voluptuous woman contemplating a skull, a cross and a book, and set her corruptible beauty next to symbols of death and eternity, lay in the distant future.[4]

When the Lateran Council of 1215 reconstructed the sacrament of penance by calling for annual confession as the prelude to annual communion, and when preaching friars celebrated the Magdalen's tears of compunction, of contrition, of hope and compassion, she seemed to be atoning for the sins of all women and not just for the excesses of her own demons.[5] Sexual sinners had lost their physical virginity, their worldly honour. But perhaps, by means of heroic penances and divine forgiveness, through intimacy with Christ and sharing the agonies of the crucifixion, they could arrive at a higher condition of spiritual virginity. Was not the Magdalen in the choir of heavenly virgins, outranked only by the Virgin Mary herself and perhaps by St Catherine of Alexandria?[6] A few Italian women saw themselves, or were presented by their biographers, as latter-day Magdalens, treading the same path, sometimes as solitary contemplatives, sometimes as members of a disciplined religious community, and always living lives utterly opposed to the materialism and sensuality of their previous existence.

Margaret of Cortona was described by Friar Giunta Bevegnati, one of her Franciscan confessors, as a 'new Magdalen', who strove to join herself to Christ 'by meditating, praying, weeping and fasting'.[7] She was a village girl who had left home to live for nine years with a rich man in Montepulciano, described as the 'enemy of her salvation', whose son she bore. After his death, rejected by her parents, she pondered the future – still young and beautiful, should she go on living by pleasing lustful men, or choose another way? She went to Cortona, a small town in the diocese of Arezzo, worked as a servant and a midwife, and eventually joined the third order of St Francis.[8] She had been a concubine rather than a common prostitute or adulteress, and concubinage was not as sharply distinguished from formal marriage or as roundly condemned in the thirteenth century as it would be in the post-Tridentine Church.[9] Her penance was partly at least for her vanity and ostentation as she went about Montepulciano 'on foot or on horseback'.[10] Her conversion involved renouncing everything that had given her physical pleasure or comfort, shaving her head, mistreating and depriving her body to the point of wrecking her health, distancing herself from her old corrupt world – a process which for a while meant neglecting (some said cruelly ignoring) her son, who was perhaps the most constant reminder of her former life.[11] Becoming increasingly solitary, she did not, like the legendary Magdalen, retreat into the wilderness, but, to escape troublesome visitors, moved to a cell in the castle, the highest and least accessible place in the town, where, twenty years after taking the Franciscan habit and becoming 'a new woman', she died in 1297. It was said that once, in her frivolous days, when female acquaintances asked 'What will become of you, Margherita, vainest of women?', she had replied – was it a joke or an inspired prophecy? – 'the time will come when you call me a saint, for I shall have become one, and you will visit me with a pilgrim's staff'.[12] The Catholic hierarchy were not quick to recognise her sainthood, but she was eventually canonised in 1728.

In a sacred verse drama of the fifteenth century, which leans heavily on the *Golden Legend*, Mary Magdalen is unmoved by Martha's worthy but dismal exhortations:

> For piety I do not care;
> You waste your words on empty air.

But Marcella, a servant, persuades the flighty young woman to go and hear Jesus preach; talk of his handsome face impresses her more than the news that he has cured Martha of an unpleasant affliction. Splendidly dressed, Mary listens to a sermon, first on the parable of the talents, then on the lost sheep and the prodigal son. The preacher begins to address her directly: she has caught his attention, but not in the way she intended. Soon she is moved to tears and confusion, and her transformation into the passionate, sorrowful, repentant sinner begins. By way of light relief, Marcella sends Mary's followers packing, threatening to drench them in what is delicately called water, and clearing the way for the new life her mistress is about to lead.[13]

Other harlot saints figured in the *Golden Legend* or its supplement and enjoyed a more modest fame. Among them were Mary the Egyptian, Theodora of Alexandria, Pelagia of Antioch, Thais of Egypt, Afra of Augsburg.[14] Sperone Speroni, haranguing courtesans, listed these and a few minor characters; there was scarcely a city in Italy 'which has no convent of converted female sinners, generally named after one or the other'. As a first step towards redemption, he suggested, courtesans should set aside a special day for fasting and almsgiving, perhaps the first of April, the eve of the festival of St Mary the Egyptian; that woman had surely been the vilest sinner, and yet she was now a saint of such eminence that one of her arms was treasured as a relic at St Peter's in Rome.[15]

In the *Golden Legend*, one prostitute saint, Thais, who has reduced men to beggary and stained her house with the blood of quarrelling lovers, performs her gruelling penance in a women's convent, the usual setting for strenuous female repentance from the late middle ages onwards. Converted by the abbot Pafuntius, she is consigned to a narrow cell in a 'convent of virgins' where the door is sealed with lead, bread and water are passed through an opening in the wall, and she is forced to live with her own bodily waste, which symbolises the disgusting nature of her past life. Thais is instructed not to name God or the Trinity or raise her hands to heaven, but to turn eastwards and say, 'You who made me, have pity upon me.' After three years, her spiritual directors at last break down the door in response to a vision of a richly adorned bed guarded by three virgins, who represent 'the fear of future punishment, which has withdrawn her from evil; shame for the crime committed, which has earned her pardon; the love of justice, which has borne her to the heavenly heights'. Solitary penitents living on the edge of the community, enduring the harshest privations and mortifications, sometimes for far longer than Thais, occasionally figured in the annals of the Convertite.

A prostitute saint in the making for the sixteenth century was Caterina Vannini of Siena (1562–1606), who had about her something of the Magdalen, something of Thais, and something of her own name saint, Caterina Benincasa of Siena. She atoned for two or three years of sexual sinning by more than thirty years of self-punishment, twenty-two of them spent in the Sienese Convertite. Her biographer and correspondent was the cardinal archbishop of Milan, Federico Borromeo, who visited or came near to her in the course of his official journeys to Rome in the last years of her life.[16] First published in 1617 and 1618, his account probably drew on testimony from Caterina herself, her fellow nuns, and other acquaintances. Far from being a sudden change of heart like the transformations experienced by the model prostitute saints, her conversion (as he presented it) was a more gradual process: it began with secret surges of guilt and self-doubt while she worked as a courtesan in Rome and became devoted to the Magdalen, and culminated in a very public act of contrition in Siena. Despair drove her almost to suicide and Pope Gregory XIII and his agents almost forced conversion upon her. But, protesting that 'if she were to be converted, she would like that to happen in her native city', she practised for a while in Siena as a high-class prostitute. Her decisive conversion faintly echoed – had she seen the play, or did her biographer know it? – the transformation of Mary Magdalen in the medieval drama just described. Arrayed in her professional glory, she attended a Magdalen sermon, where she heard 'the Lord' addressing her: 'Do you think to bring light to this church with your worldly finery? Do you not see that you have plunged it into darkness?' But then the voice promised to pardon her, whereupon, weeping and sighing, she left the church and hastened to begin her penance by discarding her jewels and shearing her tresses. Kneeling before a crucifix at home, she flogged herself with the heavy gold chains she had thrown on the floor. She sold her possessions and gave the money to 'various poor persons, according to need', herself embracing absolute poverty.[17]

Caterina's penance was marked by pain and decrepitude, both self-inflicted and earnestly prayed for, and also by constant fasting and deprivation of sleep. Acute pains in her side served as 'a penalty for and a painful reminder of her lost virginity'. Simultaneously, though, she experienced an 'almost continuous' vision of Paradise, suffering in her own body – as Caterina Benincasa had once done – the agonies of the crucifixion and the torture of the crown of thorns.[18] To her biographer her life was a perfect demonstration of the power of penitence:

> that a poor and simple little woman, a sinner, a prostitute [*donna di mondo*], who had offended God by destroying her virginity, should be uplifted by means of this penitence to such a high degree that she deserved to hear herself called his bride by the king of kings, in whose eyes the heavens themselves are not pure, nor are the stars beautiful.[19]

After several years at home, Caterina, like her name saint, obtained from her confessor the habit of a Dominican tertiary. It took her longer to gain entry to the Convertite, which she deemed the only possible refuge for a penitent sinner with a history like hers. The nuns, or their lay governors, at first demurred, perhaps because she could no longer walk, possibly because they shrank from the trials of coping with a living saint who would hardly be an average member of their community. She was at last received into the convent in 1584 and lived there like an anchoress, in a narrow cell from which a window opened into the church to enable her to hear services and take communion.[20] Long spells of silence and utter isolation followed until the archbishop himself ordered

Caterina to have some speech with others and talk through the aperture to those who needed her counsel.[21] Her celestial wedding to Christ occurred, it seemed, 'in a little room in the new buildings of the convent, on the left hand side, when others had ascended the steps of the main staircase', on a Monday in August 1587, close to the festival of the Madonna. The ceremony lasted, the bride believed, for about half an hour.[22]

The figure of the redeemed prostitute or other sexual sinner was to some extent a work of art, even where it did not wholly depend on legend and tradition. There were conventions to be followed, rituals to be carried out; one saint could inspire or imitate another; biographers could be expected to dwell on certain familiar themes. The image of the penitent *peccatrice* appealed to the aggressive, redemptive, soul-saving charity of the sixteenth century whose targets were ignorance and sin, to a Church resolved to defend the sacrament of penance and the cloistered life against the attacks of Protestant reformers. New exemplars could be found, new stories told. Few former prostitutes can have tormented themselves so mercilessly or enjoyed such visionary consolations as Caterina Vannini. But acute pangs of guilt and the pains of withdrawal and self-denial doubtless afflicted many of them as they submitted to the discipline imposed by religious institutions and recommended in harangues not unlike the Magdalen sermon which Caterina Vannini attended on her last public appearance as a courtesan.

Redemptive marriages

Pope Gregory XIII offered his prisoner Caterina Vannini the choice of getting married, entering an institution for fallen women, languishing in gaol, or being deported – options already forced on many of the more prosperous Roman whores by his harsher predecessor, Pius V. Even zealous reformers conceded that not all remorseful prostitutes would be suited to the cloister. Nevertheless, they might be reclaimed by joining them in holy matrimony to some worthy husband. A chaste marriage would not, perhaps, expunge past sins as thoroughly as years of earthly purgatory in a nunnery, but it would admit a woman to communion and save her from dying in mortal sin. An unchaste marriage would expose an ex-prostitute, persisting in her old ways, to charges of adultery. This could be interpreted, not merely as a moral transgression, but as a criminal offence for which Pius V would have liked to impose the death penalty.[23]

Preachers in Pius V's Rome proclaimed the belief that a good man could reform a sinful woman and promised dowries to all prostitutes who agreed to marry.[24] Optimistic as ever, Speroni suggested that if a prostitute used some of her savings to dower young girls, praying to God 'that he does not allow them to be like you', other benefactors might be moved to provide the prostitute herself with a good husband.[25] Ferrante Pallavicino wrote of a certain kind of sanctimonious client, known in the trade as a 'Theatine' (after one of the strictest religious orders), who 'wanted to acquire merit even while committing a sin': this 'wryneck' would hardly marry a courtesan himself, but he was good for a generous tip if he thought the woman entertaining him had plans to marry and was assembling her own dowry with a view to giving up the 'evil life'. By this means, the prostitute's fee would become a species of almsgiving, while the client performed the remarkable feat of becoming a pious fornicator.[26]

At least since the twelfth century, students of canon law had been reminded that, although a prostitute held out 'no hope of loyalty, no certainty of chastity', even the prophet Hosea had married a promiscuous woman, and it must be presumed that his goodness had been imparted to her, not her wickedness to him.[27] Towards 1200, perhaps following earlier precedents, Pope Innocent III had recognised the special merit of those who (with honourable intentions) 'take public women out of the brothel and make them their wives'.[28] On the other hand, 'You know one doesn't believe a prostitute when she promises to be chaste', wrote the Florentine notary Lapo Mazzei, as though repeating an indisputable truth and echoing the doubts expressed in canon law.[29]

Inevitably, the unsuccessful or impious marriages were most likely to leave traces in judicial records or provide copy for litterateurs, and may give an exaggerated impression of the pitfalls involved. In Florence in 1485, Bartolomeo da Piacenza was so infuriated by the infidelities of his wife Margherita, 'the Ragusan woman', that he retaliated by poisoning her.[30] The Seigneur de Brantôme, soldier, author and courtier, mentioned a sincere belief, more prevalent in Italy and Spain than in his native France, that marriage to a harlot might indeed 'deliver a Christian soul from hell'; he had seen some women 'which did sin no more after being married, but others that could never reform, and went back to trip and stumble in the old ditch'. Revisiting Faustina, a Roman courtesan too expensive for him in his youth, he found her now married to a lawyer, but ready to oblige him, Brantôme, for 'an handful of good French crowns'. She had 'agreed with her husband for her entire liberty ... to the end the pair of them might live in affluence', on the sole condition that she should charge handsomely, and not go to bed with 'petty customers'. Such open marriages did not smack of Christian piety; 'here was a husband cuckolded out and out, in bud and blossom too', and with his full knowledge.[31] Other prostitutes' husbands were soft targets for satire, as is the obtuse Brescian in two of Bandello's short stories who plucks a girl from a Venetian brothel. She proves to be a cheerful, bibulous nymphomaniac and quite unrepentant. But perhaps her contributions to the household budget are not unwelcome and few questions are asked about them ('Had I not contrived to earn a little by helping the needy, we'd be in a bad way').[32]

Certain men proved willing to marry women of damaged reputation who were not common prostitutes or courtesans but the discarded mistresses of well-to-do and powerful men in the community. Considerate former lovers would provide such women with dowries and promise favours to the men of lower status who took them on. Agostino di Giacomo, at Giulianova in the diocese of Teramo about 1600, professed to have 'made a vow to redeem a woman from evil ways and take her for my wife'. This he tried to fulfil by marrying Diana, a former servant from a mountain village who had borne a child to her married employer, Giovan Filippo di Domenico. A problem in this case, and in at least one other in Verona, was that the woman's former consort, having abandoned her reluctantly, was suspected of continuing to see her and cuckolding her new husband. If her marriage was doomed, the fault was not entirely hers.[33]

Black comedy was not unknown. In Naples in 1589, a young Greek prostitute, Lucza, lay apparently dying and unable to speak; a man went through the motions of marrying her so that, in view of her supposed intention to reform, she could be given communion on her deathbed. When Lucza woke up unexpectedly and found a ring on her finger, both bride and groom were appalled – he at finding himself saddled with a prostitute who had failed to die as predicted, she at being married to anyone when she was unconscious. Fortunately, the ceremony had been so questionably conducted that the 'marriage' was easily annulled by the archbishop's court.[34] But there were some cases in which former prostitutes claimed to have broken successfully with the *mala vita* and to have been loyal to the marriage bed, as did Caterina Franzaroli in Bologna about 1689.[35] Marriages, though, must often have been handicapped by the suspicion that a wife would find it hard to renounce her old ways, and possibly by the notion that her husband was her moral superior, bound to watch her closely. It was not the best recipe for harmony.

Magdalen convents

By the thirteenth century it had long been possible for ecclesiastical and secular authorities to send some criminals for correction in monasteries, whose regime might be expected to reform them as exile and other forms of punishment would not. Deviant women could be confined in convents, but in the 1290s, nuns in Bologna were objecting to receiving them, seemingly with the result that 'bad women and whores do not fear to commit evil deeds'. Room would be made for female criminals in new secular prisons. By this time, though, a different kind of convent was developing, or being reborn. It was not a traditional community of virtuous women which occasionally received some delinquents. Rather, at least in principle, it was an assembly of penitent women who had asked to become part of it; who had in common, not crimes, but a particular kind of immoral behaviour or sin, a 'bad life' which they wished to renounce; and who were not virgins. It was not in any formal sense a prison, though it could begin to resemble one to some unhappy residents, and in a later century, at least one Benedictine nun guilty of fornication and complicity in murder could be sent to a convent of Convertite (Santa Valeria in Milan) for punishment. Rather, it was a penitential nunnery and a hard road to salvation, through a transition from a loose existence to a highly disciplined one, from sensual experience to rigorous self-denial.[36]

From the twelfth and thirteenth centuries onwards, penitential nunneries began to be formed with some papal encouragement in west European cities, at least in France, Germany and Italy, and in the papal enclave of Avignon, which supported the House of the Repentant Sisters of St Mary Magdalen of the Miracles.[37] Members of these communities were known as *sorores penitentes*, *répenties*, *Ruwerin*, *convertite*, and usually submitted to well-tried rules – Benedictine, Cistercian, Augustinian, Franciscan. Few of the Italian houses belonged to religious orders equipped with any central administration of their own – their ties were with the local community and the bishop, though the same would have been true of many other nunneries.[38] Their administration was often overseen by local lay confraternities or boards of trustees, and magistrates could take some interest in their affairs.

A few Italian establishments proved to be long-lasting, others much less so. Two Magdalen houses were set up in thirteenth-century Genoa, but developed into more traditional nunneries. In the mid-fourteenth century, another community, Santa Maria delle Convertite in the Mercento district of the city, began to provide a retreat for sexual sinners.[39] A citizen of Viterbo, Fardo d'Ugolino, set up an asylum for female penitents in a brothel quarter in 1313 and linked it with a hostel for potential converts of another kind, Jews who had shown interest in receiving baptism.[40]

In the 1330s, the Augustinian preacher and spiritual writer Simone da Cascia (c.1275–1348) inspired a convent for fallen women in Florence, eventually dedicated to Mary Magdalen as well as to the charitable saint Elizabeth, queen of Hungary. A local confraternity of 'singers of praise [laudesi]', Santo Spirito, undertook the practical work of collecting alms, acquiring land and building a house for the convertite, who were said to be so poor that they had to live by 'sewing and spinning and doing proper work' (no doubt this was both an economic necessity and an antidote to their previous way of life).[41] In 1447, a silk entrepreneur, Tommaso Ridolfi, instructed and employed the nuns of the Convertite in the spinning of gold thread. By Florentine standards, it was both a large convent (twenty-five residents in 1368, when many sheltered only about eleven) and a poorly endowed one, dependent on earned income – indeed, at the tax survey of 1427, it proved to be one of the nine poorest out of forty-nine in the city which reported holdings.[42] This establishment was still in being in the sixteenth century.

A similar house, the Casa di San Simone, planned at Pavia in 1399, attracted derision from some locals who seemed to have only contempt for the notion that prostitutes could or should reform, or perhaps objected to them withdrawing their labour from the brothel. There were complaints of men throwing stones and hurling obscenities from the street at the residents.[43] In Venice, Giovanni Contarini directed in his will of 1407 that a house he owned in Santa Margarita should be open to 'any woman who is a sinner in public or in secret' and 'wishes to turn to a life of good deeds and put away her sins'.[44]

Though always dependent on gifts and legacies as well as their own earnings, these asylums could attract public subsidies and be placed under public supervision. By the mid-fifteenth century, the external affairs of the Florentine convent were subject to a board of five lay governors known as Operai, recruited from the city's professional corporations, while the women enjoyed a precarious income from judicial fines levied on sodomites.[45]

More foundations followed in the sixteenth century. Among the first was the house in the Colonna district of Rome for 'nuns of the Blessed Mary Magdalen of the Penitence', formally approved in 1520 by Pope Leo X. It would provide a refuge for 'a number of loose women, devoted to the pursuit of immoral earnings' who had undertaken to do penance in the manner of 'Mary Magdalen the sinner and Mary the Egyptian' and hoped to 'earn the reward of eternal life and be worthy to meet Christ the bridegroom with their lamps alight', transformed from sexual mercenaries into the sensible bridesmaids of the parable, properly prepared for his arrival.[46] The sisters were to observe the rule of St Augustine and submit to 'perpetual enclosure'; they would take the three solemn vows of poverty, chastity and obedience; they would wear a black habit to suggest the dark and sinister nature of their previous activities, surmounted by a white mantle representing the innocence and purity of their new way of life; they were to sing the divine offices, by day and by night. The community would be subject to an abbess or prioress, appointed for a limited period (was she to be a repentant sinner herself, or a respectable woman drawn from outside?). But, like all convents, they would be under male supervision. Their spiritual directors and confessors would be the Minims of the Santissima Trinità, while their property, income and other temporal interests would be safeguarded by a confraternity with a wide range of charitable concerns, the company of the Carità recently founded by the pope's cousin, Cardinal Giulio de' Medici. Members would control admissions to the convent and hold its keys; a representative of the company must be present whenever outsiders communicated with residents in the convent.[47] On the eve of the sack of Rome in 1527, census-takers reported fifty-eight persons living in the Convertite.[48]

Though continuing an older tradition, the nunneries of the Convertite harmonised with the aggressive, moralising tone of many new charities of the sixteenth century – of the kind of missionary enterprises, fighting for souls in Europe, which sought to redeem outcasts and infidels rather than confine themselves to supporting respectable people and endowing virtuous maidens.[49] Convertite perhaps provided an alternative to brothel closure, a form of atonement for the tolerance of prostitution in Italian cities. If whorehouses and courtesans were very much in evidence, so too was their antithesis, the place of penance and purification. Preachers, solid local citizens, matrons or widows of high social standing, and lay organisations were prominent supporters of such convents. Some people were involved in several new enterprises, as was the widow Elisabetta Prato, one of the founders of the Convertite in Brescia in the 1530s and afterwards mother-general of the Ursulines in the city.[50] In Milan, also in the 1530s, one Fra Bono gathered alms and persuaded preachers to request them for 'certain women he had brought together, who called themselves the *convertite*'; he called on good Catholics who knew of girls who had 'made a little mistake [*un poco di fallo*]' and hence were in danger of going forever to the bad.[51] At Ferrara in 1537, a parish priest persuaded several women to eschew the 'evil life', and eighteen of them, including ten from a brothel in the via dell'Inferno, processed solemnly to a former monastery on 7th April.[52]

At least three communities, in Venice, Verona and Naples, were offshoots of the new hospitals for 'incurables'. Apart from their concern with victims of the French evil and other chronic illnesses, the Incurabili became bases from which several humane activities, including the care and education of orphans, were launched by influential patricians and citizens. A pox hospital could be used to warn women of the physical consequences of sexual sinning, to suggest a way of escaping these horrors, to invite them to mortify and master themselves by attending repulsively sick and sore patients, a preliminary to the austerities of the convent. In Naples, time spent working at the hospital became a kind of pre-novitiate for the Convertite, which was established as a sister institution by the governor of the Incurabili, Maria Ajerba, duchess of Tremoli, about 1538.[53] In Venice the Convertite already formed a recognised group within the Incurabili in April 1525, but in the 1530s they began crossing the water to a more remote site on the Giudecca, where a convent was built a few years later and they adopted St Augustine's rule.[54] In Verona, Convertite came, again probably during the 1530s, to form part of the complex surrounding the Misericordia, a hospital for incurables which also ran an orphanage designed to 'save [boys] from the galleys ... and [girls] from the brothel'.[55]

By 1600, convents for Convertite were features of many Italian towns. A few large cities – Naples, Milan, Bologna, Rome – had, by 1700, established more than one. Some were more genteel than others, some stricter and more determined to observe their original rules. Some were enormous, others more selective and anxious not to live beyond their means. In 1504, the Convertite at Florence sheltered 118 residents, in 1515, 162. Their population had fallen to 135 by 1575, but rose to 204 by 1620.[56] There were 72 women in Ferrara's Convertite in 1574, 80 in 1589.[57] The Venetian convent on the Giudecca reported to the Senate in 1561 a total strength of 400, including lay sisters. It was then on the verge of a scandal which would cause many women to be released, but by 1620 there were 376 residents, in 1624, 348, and in 1721, about 300.[58] The exacting San Giacomo alla Longara in Rome had only about 50 residents at the end of the seventeenth century.[59]

Missionary methods

Missions to prostitutes depended on two well-tried methods – the practice of approaching individual women and pleading with them (perhaps on one's knees) to sin no more, and the Magdalen sermon by an eloquent preacher, sometimes delivered to a captive audience. Readers of the *Golden Legend* could find, especially in the story of Thais and Pafuntius, examples of male missionaries who used bold tactics to interview prostitutes, occasionally pretending to be clients in order to secure their undivided attention. Widows, matrons and a few men prepared to risk misunderstanding set out to redeem lost souls, acting, perhaps, from the motives which long afterwards inspired the great Mr Gladstone, 'naïve to the point of recklessness about the impression this work might have upon others', to talk by the hour at night with pretty young prostitutes in Piccadilly and Soho.[60] Among the dignified ladies who reasoned with prostitutes themselves, engaged others to do so, and found them temporary accommodation were Maria Lorenzo Longo, a noble Catalan widow and first governor of the hospital for incurables in Naples; Leonor Osorio, whose husband, Juan de Vega, became viceroy of Sicily; and a wool merchant's wife in Milan, Giovana Anguillara. In many cases, they had to content themselves with affording women short respites, chances to think things over; Maria Lorenzo Longo would beseech them 'at least to abstain from sin on Fridays and Saturdays, and she paid them for those days'.[61]

Compulsory redemptive sermons, attended in theory by all known prostitutes in a community, had been delivered in the middle ages. Legislation of Amedeo VIII of Savoy, issued in 1430, had prescribed that prostitutes must abstain 'from their filth' during Easter week and assemble two or three times 'in one place in which some eminent preacher shall warn them and exhort them to convert for the sake of their salvation'.[62] Such sermons were regularly addressed to prostitutes in some cities in the sixteenth century and later and could produce at least fleeting results; a few women, sometimes dozens, promised repentance while under the preacher's spell and lodged for a while in the houses of volunteers, though some failed to persevere for more than a few weeks.[63] The Roman courtesan, in the verses which Du Bellay composed in the 1550s, toys during one Holy Week with the notion of becoming a penitent nun, her conscience being 'affected by the holy remorse which some good spirit made me feel in the midst of a sermon – so that, without thinking, I suddenly resolved to transform myself utterly'. She gives much of her fortune to the convent, but soon finds that 'my clothes had changed, my will had not', and, repenting of her repentance, resumes operations where she left them off.[64] Pope Pius V forced conversion sermons on the whores of Rome with extraordinary intensity.[65] Once, when the captive audience emerged from Sant' Ambrogio, they encountered a crowd of about two thousand loiterers, whom constables had with difficulty prevented from storming the church to see the sights. Heckling and barracking punctuated some sermons. When Nina da Prato suggested to the preacher that his duty was to expound the gospel and not to criticise the lives of others, her remarks cost her a flogging.[66] Missionary efforts on this scale were exceptional, although Clement VIII showed signs of relaunching them in December 1592.[67]

Less formally, around 1580, Jesuits would preach open-air sermons in Rome, in squares where country labourers waited to be hired or at places of special iniquity, such as the offices of moneylenders and the dwellings of prostitutes, presumably in the Ortaccio – 'yea the infamous streate of harlottes and Ribaldes lacketh not a sharpe preacher of Gods terrible judgement agaynst that abominable life, to the daylie conversion of manie great sinners'.[68] In the next century, the Jesuit Francesco De Geronimo (1642–1716) preached every Sunday of the year in a Neapolitan piazza: acrobats drew crowds to the square, but their audiences could be persuaded to turn to a different piece of theatre and be exhorted to repent of their sins. 'Women of the profession', according to a pious account, hid in their dwellings at first, but could not resist the 'celestial charmer'; some were 'transported as if by a celestial force' and cut off their long, flowing hair in accordance with time-honoured ritual, to place it like a 'trophy of victory' over sin and vanity at the foot of a large crucifix.[69]

In early modern Florence, the Magdalen sermon, delivered during Lent, developed into an annual ritual accompanied by special inducements to convert. In 1577, magistrates required registered prostitutes to assemble for a roll-call on the day of the sermon. For a time, women who volunteered on that day to enter the Convertite qualified for a discount on their dowries: in 1628 the dowry was cut from 160 to 140 scudi for a veiled nun, from 70 to 30 for a servant in the convent.[70] It became obvious, in the late 1640s, that a number of women were registering as prostitutes just before the Magdalen sermon. Were they posing as, or even becoming, prostitutes to get places in the Convertite, rather than entering the Convertite in order to renounce prostitution? Something of the sort had happened in Paris towards 1500; why not, then, in Florence towards 1650?[71]

The regime

Some regulations for Convertite affirmed that the convent was not to be used as a retirement home and that entrants must be attractive youngish women, prepared to sacrifice what remained of their careers. The Roman Compagnia della Carità warned that

We do not allow sick or elderly women to enter the convent, because their sinful trade is forsaking them, not they it; nor will we admit repulsive women or married women, because it would be impious to separate wives from husbands, and one can only suppose that ill-favoured women wish to enter the cloister, not because their heart tells them to, but on account of their ugliness.[72]

Both in Florence and in Pistoia in the seventeenth century, the average age at entry, which can be known for a few applicants, appeared to be twenty-four, which implies that they were mature but not past their best, for a successful prostitute's career would probably extend from her early teens until some point in her thirties.[73] Between 1656 and 1675, 60 per cent of women entering the Convertite of Venice were between fifteen and twenty-four.[74]

Some convents specified that candidates for entry should have been common prostitutes, working in the public domain – regulations at Ferrara stipulated that they must have plied their trade in the city for at least ten years, followed by three months of chastity as an earnest of sincere intentions to reform.[75] In practice, though, several convents were willing to accept other women of lost honour, including discarded mistresses, who were sometimes placed there and paid for by their former lovers. If they wished to remain solvent, convents could not interpret rules too rigorously.

Constitutions of the Convertite in Naples, officially approved about 1570, dwelt less on youth and beauty, more on religious orthodoxy and freedom from superstition. A candidate for entry

must not be tainted with or suspected of heresy, nor must she practise magic; she must not be married or with child; she must not be suffering from any incurable disease, be the symptoms visible or invisible; she must not be in the service of or be bound to any other religious order; she must not be over forty, and shall be a public prostitute.

In most cities, prostitutes may not have been particularly susceptible to heresy or diabolism, but they were involved in superstitious practices and some were notorious for casting spells or misusing sacred properties to ensnare desirable clients. To reject everyone who had done such things would hardly be possible – but let no-one import them to the convent, where indulgence in these rituals would earn one month's detention in the punishment cells.[76] In Venice about 1624, however, Angela Giustinian enlivened eighteen months in the Convertite by practising love magic intended to revive her lover's interest in her; alternating between orthodoxy and superstition (both had their uses), she combined her reprehensible rites with appeals to Catholic saints.[77]

Women entering the Convertite were generally expected to take perpetual vows, but seldom to do so immediately. What kind of probation should they undergo before committing themselves irrevocably to a lifetime of penitence? They were differently placed from the sheltered girls of patrician or 'civil' condition, often brought up in convents from an early age, who entered reputable nunneries chosen for them in their teens, equipped with dowries provided by their families. Ardent soul-savers would urge *meretrici* towards the cloister, but other interested parties – mockers, sceptics, clients, pimps, procuresses – would probably attempt to dissuade them. On the other hand, ex-lovers, eager to be rid of mistresses of whom they had wearied, might try to push

them prematurely into taking solemn vows. Conspiracy was suspected when, in Milan
in 1535, many of the women assembled by Fra Bono walked out of his quasi-convent,
this being then the only remedy for women who felt unsuited to religious life. A probationary period of one year was then introduced.[78] Would this suffice, or should a
pre-novitiate in some other establishment be arranged and combined with exploratory
visits to the convent? Or might there, quite the other way, be a case for shortening the
trial period?

As the Neapolitan statutes recalled, a bull of Pope Julius III (1552) had allowed
women in the Convertite to pronounce their solemn vows before a year had passed, lest
they should waver and the prize escape the missionaries' net. This concession was withdrawn by Pius IV, but later reinstated, and the Tridentine decrees on religious houses
alluded to special arrangements for Convertite, which would be allowed to stand.[79]
Years later, the question was discussed at Santa Maria Maddalena in Pistoia, when in
1638, three former prostitutes sought permission to take their vows early. Despite the
objections of professed nuns ('We waited out the year and so should others'), the petitioners won the day.[80] In the late seventeenth century, a Roman committee repeatedly
allowed women in Convertite convents to take vows after a shortened novitiate, issu-
ing, in 1681, thirteen dispensations to that effect. Two casualties of the process, teen-
age concubines placed in the Venetian convent by their former lovers, were Maddalena
Bassi and Maddalena Farner. Both had been pressed to take vows after a mere three or
four months, but were able to pursue their cases for release only by fleeing to Mantua in
1685, since the Venetian government rarely if ever allowed appeals to the pope. Farner,
professed when six weeks short of sixteen, the minimum legal age, was eventually
restored to lay status by Rome in 1696.[81]

Sixteenth-century ordinances of Santa Valeria in Milan described the questions and
arguments to be put to postulants, aiming at a balance between admonition and encouragement. They should be prepared for hardships, for 'total renunciation of oneself
and of one's own wishes', but would be faced with nothing they could not endure.[82] As
in the Roman community of 1520, regimes for penitents called for poverty of dress,
renunciation of all personal possessions, strict enclosure, recitation of the offices in
choir and of the penitential psalms, general communion at regular intervals, use of the
scourge, and manual work organised through the mother superior. This was designed
both to augment the revenues of the convent and to keep improper thoughts at bay.
'[I]dleness is the enemy of the soul and every idle woman is absorbed in the desires of
her own mind', declared the rules of Santa Valeria in Milan. Those of the Convertite of
Naples cited St Jerome's admonition, 'Always be engaged in some activity, that the Devil
may always find you busy.'[83]

In Naples particularly, the authorities seemed conscious that they were not dealing
with innocents, and were fearful that a wicked world would invade their community
unless strenuous efforts were made to stifle nostalgia for its ways. They banned remi-
niscence – 'at no time, either in public or in private, shall they speak of things to do
with the world, or of how they have been in the world, or of what they have done; it
is enough to say, in grief and humility, that one has been a sinner, without going into
details'. Among the officers were *esploratrici*, female investigators ordered to 'seek out

any excesses which may be committed in the house and to reveal them'. One or two of the lay governors were to inquire into the affairs of the community at least once a month, to put a stop to any suspicious associations or lengthy conversations with lay persons or with priests and religious, and above all with relatives, 'because these are evil times'. The statutes prescribed a disciplinary code, throwing into the scales punishments adjusted to the gravity of each offence envisaged – two months in the cells for blaspheming, two to three for assaulting or insulting officers of the convent, one year for attempting to escape or failing to inform the mother superior of a planned break-out. Should any sister actually make her escape only to be recaptured, she could in theory be sentenced to perpetual imprisonment.[84] The nuns were not convicts, but the convent had a jailhouse air, as a place of confinement for women with a rough past who might well be subject to rebellious moods and in need of something harsher than mere rebuke. One other such convent, in Palermo, reminded a Jesuit of an enclosure for wild beasts, where the women seemed to be confined by force, rather than of their own free will.[85] Caterina Vannini, at Siena, detected and discouraged six *convertite* who were planning an escape.[86] Some rebels did more than flee: Agnesina and two other nuns set fire to a building in the Venetian Convertite, an outrage which earned her eight years in the convent prison, nine months after taking her vows.[87]

Gross misconduct was not only on one side. Gian Pietro Leon of Valcamonica, a satyr in holy orders, systematically abused inmates of the Convertite in Venice for about nineteen years. This scandal showed how the absolute authority of a hypocritical spiritual director, shielded by influential friends and admirers, could be used without mercy to exploit attractive women handicapped by their own bad reputations and unprotected by powerful families of their own. In November 1561, exposed at last, the abuser was sentenced to death, and the abbess, who had colluded with him, died in prison in 1564. The papal nuncio estimated the number of women in the convent at approximately four hundred; about a quarter of them were released on the government's authority, on the grounds that they had not yet taken solemn vows, and had been 'tricked into entering, or so it is said, by the priest and others for their own ends'.[88]

Entrants and financial problems

Certain convents of Convertite admitted women who did not fit the stereotype of the repentant prostitute. Some acted as asylums which took in, at least temporarily, a number of distressed women and girls, including victims of rape and trafficking, and several others charged with misdemeanours.[89] Arguably, they were suitable places for women who had been mistresses or had been caught up in troubled relationships. At Verona in 1568, Count Guglielmo Bevilacqua told the Brescian Bartolomeo Averoldi that the Convertite was the proper place for his ex-mistress.[90] In Siena in 1571, Girolama was willing to return to her tyrannical husband only in exchange for a solemn (and probably unenforceable) promise that he would not batter her again – 'otherwise I would wish to enter the Convertite, on account of my terror of the man'.[91] In 1681, the merchant Paolo Vedova placed his young mistress among the Venetian Convertite to protect her, or so he said, from a vengeful father; the merchant Giovanni Battista Cellini did the same for his, 'so that she would not pass under anyone else's control' during his absence as consul in Amsterdam.[92] But a mistress could make the first move herself, much to the resentment of an unchivalrous lover determined not to pay for her keep, as did Maddalena Micossi about 1771. A village girl who had borne three children to her clerical cousin, Giovanni Bearzi, she was persuaded to join the Convertite of Udine by Ambrosia, the midwife at her most recent confinement, and by a confessor whom the midwife called in.[93]

Communities of *convertite* would risk insolvency or starvation if they insisted on functioning only as shelters for impoverished ex-prostitutes, plucked off the streets or bailed out of brothels by missionaries. Very likely, more money would come in with rich men's former mistresses. Convertite were not without special sources of support, other than voluntary donations, and could expect to receive contributions from dishonoured women themselves, in death if not in life. Leo X's foundation bull for the Roman Convertite established for Rome the principle that a 'courtesan or disreputable woman' would be entitled to make a will if she was prepared to bequeath or donate 'at least one quarter or one-fifth of her goods', certainly of those acquired by immoral means [*meretricando*], either to the Convertite or to some other religious or charitable cause. Should she die in Rome intestate, or without the authority to make a will, the pope would apply her estate to the Convertite.[94] Not compelled to restore their gains in full, women of lost honour were pressed to support a good cause relevant to their own interests. Let them make wills and dispose of most of their property to heirs of their choice so long as they proved themselves to be responsible testators.

But who, for these purposes, should be deemed a 'disreputable woman'? Those with a shady past, even if it was well behind them, sometimes thought it wise to appease the Convertite with a legacy or gift to fend off possible proceedings, even while protesting that they had no actual obligation to do so.[95] There was no guarantee, though, that the Convertite would always benefit. Bent on promoting urban development in the 1560s, Pope Pius IV made concessions to courtesans who were prepared to build houses worth at least five hundred scudi in the Borgo Pio, by granting them full testators' rights to dispose of their possessions and stipulating that their property would pass to their heirs even if they died intestate.[96]

Similar rules applied in Florence, which required one-quarter of a prostitute's immoral gains from 1553 onwards. Bologna proved capable of demanding as much as a half; here the Convertite and the Ufficio delle Bollette could argue as to who should be deemed a prostitute for these purposes, and the archbishop's court was entitled to inquire into the character of a deceased woman suspected of evil-living.[97] Ferrara adopted a simpler procedure: when a *publica meretrice* died, a notary would list her belongings – Lorenzo Vacchi compiled ten such inventories in 1677 – and these items would be turned over to the Convertite.[98]

In other cities, the Convertite might depend more heavily on taxation or on a share in earmarked judicial fines. In Venice from 1564 onwards, an extra 10 per cent was added to certain fines and assigned to the Convertite, though they subsequently complained of offenders who evaded paying the supplement.[99] In 1622 the Senate decreed that immoral women [*meretrici*] be taxed directly to support the Convertite and that parish priests be called upon to identify prostitutes. Public dues, however, could still be diverted or withheld, to judge by the claim of the Convertite in 1646 that the State then owed them just over three thousand ducats, which had probably been diverted to the current war effort.[100]

Solvency would inevitably depend on the convent's ability to attract dowries, the sums, destined for their own support, which nuns contributed to the community's finances. One way to secure larger portions was to admit the daughters of shabby genteel families who could not aspire to a prestigious convent, but were capable of paying more than most ex-prostitutes for places in an obscure one. In Venice the patriarch ruled in 1593 that, in general, choir or chapter nuns should be supported by an annual pension worth sixty ducats, which would require an investment of about a thousand ducats in secure funds.[101] In the seventeenth century, lump sums of no more than one or two hundred ducats would be paid on behalf of 'fallen' women entering the Convertite, but for young women said to be virgins, 350 ducats was offered in 1602, 450 in 1657. In 1621 the prioress was denounced for admitting virgins to the convent in order to raise money and then failing to discipline them, older nuns objecting that this practice violated the rules of a nunnery founded 'to raise souls from the stench of sin'.[102] The residents who had least to atone for by penance were apparently threatening to become the most disorderly. There was some danger that the original aims of the convent might be forgotten, that it might become no more than a cheap and remote alternative to the more comfortable Benedictine houses inhabited by the unmarried daughters of the aristocracy.

Seventeenth-century Turin supported two convents for penitents, Santa Maria Maddalena (1634) and Santa Pelagia (1659). But their residents had probably never been common prostitutes, concubines or courtesans: very likely they were in need of protection only because they were widowed or separated from their husbands, and were seeking shelter on the strength of modest dowries.[103] With time, many women's institutions in Naples tended in a similar fashion to go up in the world, to be taken over by families of modest status seeking places for daughters who were, for various reasons, not candidates for marriage. Neapolitan legislation of 1737 hoped that 'it may be possible to restore to their original condition the convents and conservatories which were established to receive loose women who have repented, and to find the best way of achieving this by removing the respectable women in these places to other convents'.[104] Towards the close of the century, Galanti noted that 'In the course of time many asylums for repentant sinners have become cloisters for virgins, among them the Egiziaca and the Maddalena.' He was able, however, to describe one well-endowed asylum for penitents, San Raffaele, which had been erected as recently as 1770 and had not yet followed the primrose path towards gentility.[105]

Conclusion

Convents for 'whores repenting' represented the most traditional and also the most uncompromising attempt to address the problem of immoral women, to balance tolerance with reclamation and rescue. This rested on antithesis, on the substitution of a rigorous, austere, monotonous existence for a disorderly life which had supposedly been sweetened by luxury, vanity, deception and avarice. Convents replaced the wilderness of the meretricious hermit saints with the regime of a community focused on the recitation of offices in choir and some steady manual work. Room could be made, however, for women of exceptional holiness or expiating extraordinary wickedness to live by themselves on the edge of the community. Here was a severe kind of charity concerned with saving souls by removal from the world and its temptations, not with the transformation of social undesirables into useful and active citizens. It might have been supposed that many prostitutes would not be capable of adjusting to normal life, certainly not of becoming respectable married women, and might themselves be ashamed to mix with ordinary respectable folk – that they could only change and persevere within the confines of a disciplined, celibate community, living with other women who had committed similar transgressions. At best, the Convertite helped to atone for the city's practice of licensing or at least tolerating prostitution for fear of a worse evil. At worst, they enabled unscrupulous authorities to prey on young women with much flimsier defences than the generality of nuns. Like many foundations, some made compromises over time and did not hold firmly to their original principles.

Institutions cast in this mould were still, in the late nineteenth century, offering an inflexible procedure for dealing with young women who had drifted into prostitution. Indeed, the criminologist Lombroso would suggest that young occasional prostitutes ought to be sent to convents and, by exploiting women's 'great susceptibility to suggestion', be persuaded to substitute religious devotion for sexual promiscuity, as if one obsession were conveniently replacing another.[106] Another author, however, criticised the nuns who ran such establishments for 'fanatical bigotry', for imposing an instant transition from pleasure to austerity, and for eventually 'irritating rather than converting' through rigour and lack of imagination.[107] Even in the sixteenth century, though, the penitential nunneries had begun to be complemented by new institutions which tried to encourage a more measured transition, often to respectability rather than strenuous piety, and which attempted to protect the innocent rather than redeem the fallen.

Notes

1   Haskins 1993, especially pp. 5–26, 95–7, 111.
2   G. Martin ed. Parks 1969, pp. 144–5. See especially Luke 10: 38–42; John 11: 1–46 and 12: 1–8; cf. Mark 14: 3–9.
3   Haskins 1993, pp. 127–32.
4   *Ibid.*, pp. 226–7, 230–48.
5   K.L. Jansen 1995: 1–11, 22–5.
6   Bevegnati ed. Iozzelli 1997, pp. 97–9.
7   *Ibid.*, p. 185.
8   *Ibid.*, pp. 181–4, and the editor's discussion of her life, at pp. 51–92.
9   See, for instance, Brundage 1975: 1–17; Brundage 1976: 828–9.
10 Bevegnati ed. Iozzelli 1997, pp. 204–5, 217; introduction, pp. 111–12.
11 *Ibid.*, pp. 106–8.

12 *Ibid.*, p. 184.
13 *Conversione* ed. Banfi 1963, pp. 187–268; see p. 205 for Mary's answer to Martha, 'Le tue parole niente io no curo,/ e fa' conto di averle detto al muro.'
14 For Mary the Egyptian (Maria Egiziaca), see Jacopo da Voragine ed. Graesse 1890/1965, pp. 247–9; for Theodora, *ibid.*, pp. 397–400; for Pelagia, *ibid.*, pp. 674–6; for Thais, *ibid.*, pp. 677–9; for Afra, *ibid.*, Supplement, p. 904. See also Butler ed. Thurston and Attwater 1956, III, pp. 184–7, 267–8.
15 Speroni 1596, pp. 199–200, 204.
16 Saba 1933, p. 97.
17 Borromeo 1756, pp. 9–16.
18 *Ibid.*, pp. 40–4, 47–8, 74–83, 87–90; cf. Raymond of Capua ed. Gilby 1960, pp. 186–92.
19 Borromeo 1756, pp. 33–4.
20 *Ibid.*, pp. 32–40, 51–4.
21 *Ibid.*, pp. 86, 91–3.
22 *Ibid.*, pp. 63–73; cf. Raymond of Capua ed. Gilby 1960, pp. 99–100.
23 Pastor XVII, pp. 93–5, 406–8.
24 Larivaille 1975, pp. 163–5, 177, 179–82. See also G. Martin ed. Parks 1969, p. 144, and O'Malley 1993, pp. 180–1, for a further discussion of prostitutes who chose matrimony.
25 Speroni 1596, p. 204.
26 Pallavicino ed. Coci 1992, p. 34.
27 C.J.C. *Decretum, secunda pars, causa* xxxii, *quaestiones* xiii–xiv, col. 1119. The biblical reference is to Hosea 1–3.
28 Migne P.L. 214, coll. 102–3. See also Brundage 1976: 842–3.
29 Letter to Datini, the merchant of Prato, 2 May 1407, in Mazzei ed. Guasti 1880, II, p. 82.
30 Mazzi 1991, pp. 390–2.
31 Brantôme 1934 edn., I.12, pp. 81–2.
32 Bandello ed. Flora 1934, II.xi, vol. I, pp. 779–88; II.xvii, vol. I, pp. 825–32.
33 Basilico 2008: 141–4; cf. Eisenach 2004, pp. 80, 134–5.
34 Romeo 2008, pp. 57–8, 224–6.
35 Ferrante 1996, pp. 222–3.
36 See Geltner 2008, especially pp. 23–4, 65–6; Geltner 2008a: 89–108; Geltner 2013–14: 32–3. For the famous case of Sister Virginia Maria de Leyva, the nun of Monza sent to Santa Valeria in 1608, see Mazzucchelli trans. Gendel 1963, especially pp. 200–3.
37 For lists of medieval convents of penitents, see, for example, Pansier 1910, pp. 11–14; Martínez Cuesta 1978, coll. 802–11; Cariboni 1999: 23. On Avignon, see Pansier 1910 and Rollo-Koster 2002.
38 Cf. Zarri 1986, pp. 359–61.
39 Polonio 2004: 318, 329, 337.
40 Martínez Cuesta 1978, coll. 805–6.
41 Davidsohn 1896–1908, IV, p. 422; S. Cohen 1992, p. 37; Benvenuti Papi 1996, pp. 91, 100–1, n. 29.
42 Strocchia 2009, pp. 5–6, 75–6, 121–2, 125, 226, n. 41.
43 Canosa and Colonnello 1989, pp. 114–15.
44 Semi 1983, p. 266.
45 Mazzi 1991, pp. 393–5; Rocke 1996, pp. 53, 60–2; Strocchia 2009, pp. 172–3.
46 Matthew 25: 1–13.
47 B.R., V, pp. 742–8.
48 *Descriptio Urbis* ed. Lee 1985, p. 46.

49   Cf. Pullan 1988: 193–4.
50   Mazzonis 2007, pp. 66–7, 200–1.
51   Burigozzo 1842, p. 522; Sebastiani 1995, pp. 109–11.
52   Ghirardo 2001: 421–2.
53   Francesco Saverio 1953: 196–7; Vitale 1970: 234–5.
54   Pullan 1971, pp. 235–8, 264–7, 377–8; Aikema and Meijers 1989, pp. 191–5; Nordio
      1996: 169–75, 180–1.
55   Cantù 1996, pp. 81–2, 86. For women's asylums in Verona, see also Eisenach 2004, pp. 158,
      175–6, 187, 200–1, 217–18.
56   Trexler 1972: 1333–4; S. Cohen 1982: 48; S. Cohen 1992, p. 91, 207–8, n. 58.
57   Ghirardo 2001: 421–2.
58   Pullan 1971, p. 378; Aikema and Meijers 1989, p. 195, n. 5; Sperling 1999, p. 244; Laven 2002,
      pp. 235–6.
59   Piazza 1698, I, pp. 202–3.
60   Isba 2006, pp. 114–16.
61   Pastor XV, pp. 92, 400; Francesco Saverio 1953: 196–7; G. Martin ed. Parks 1969, pp. 143–4;
      Vitale 1970: 234–5; O'Malley 1993, pp. 180–2; Lazar 2005, pp. 51, 58.
62   Comba 1986: 572–3.
63   For references to conversion sermons see, for example, Graf 1888, pp. 281–2; Tacchi Venturi
      1950–51, II ii, p. 161; Masson 1975, p. 133; De Spirito 1978: 62; Ferrante 1986, pp. 72–3;
      D'Amico 1989: 414–15.
64   Du Bellay ed. Saulnier 1947, pp. 160–1, lines 297–314.
65   Pastor XVII, p. 92.
66   Larivaille 1975, pp. 163–5, 179–80.
67   Bassani and Bellini 1994, p. 71.
68   G. Martin ed. Parks 1969, pp. 71–3.
69   Selwyn 2003, pp. 170–3.
70   S. Cohen 1992, pp. 46, 59, 88.
71   Brackett 1993: 299–300; cf. Rossiaud 1988, p. 130.
72   Tacchi Venturi 1950–51, I i, p. 384.
73   S. Cohen 1992, p. 57.
74   McGough 2011, pp. 116–17.
75   Ghirardo 2001: 421–2.
76   Vitale 1970: 232–3, 273–4, 290–1.
77   McGough 2011, pp. 120–2. On the connections between magic, prostitution and immoral
      behaviour in Venice, see also R. Martin 1989, pp. 234–6; Ruggiero 1993, pp. 90–114; Scully
      1994–5: 859–60.
78   Burigozzo 1842, p. 524; Gamba 1956, pp. 241–2.
79   Vitale 1970: 273–4; *Canons and Decrees* ed. Schroeder 1941, pp. 228–9, 496.
80   S. Cohen 1992, pp. 88–9.
81   Schutte 2010: 400–3.
82   Gamba 1956, p. 249.
83   Gamba 1956, p. 254; Vitale 1970: 287–8.
84   Vitale 1970: 273–91.
85   Canosa and Colonnello 1989, p. 119.
86   Borromeo 1756, pp. 52–4.
87   McGough 2011, p. 117.
88   Intra 1893: 103–7; Tassini ed. Moretti 1964, p. 184; Laven 2004, pp. 161–5, 236, n. 11.

89   Mazzi 1991, p. 398; S. Cohen 1992, pp. 61–2, 64–5, 70–1.
90   Eisenach 2004, pp. 175–6; cf. McGough 2011, pp. 107, 118–19.
91   Nardi 1989: 75.
92   Schutte 2010: 430–2.
93   Ferraro 2008, pp. 166–75.
94   B.R. V, pp. 745–6, 747.
95   Camerano 1998: 638, 641–6, 658.
96   Delumeau 1957–9, I, p. 236.
97   Brackett 1993: 290–1, for Florence; for Bologna, Ferrante 1985, pp. 2–3, 5–6; Ferrante 1986, p. 75.
98   Ghirardo 2001: 424, 431, n. 143.
99   Pullan 1971, p. 417.
100 McGough 2011, pp. 123–4.
101 Sperling 1999, pp. 66–8, 188–95, 217–24, 227–8.
102 McGough 2011, pp. 118–23.
103 Cavallo 1995, pp. 156–7, 160–7.
104 Valenzi 1995, p. 117.
105 Galanti 1786–90, III, pp. 138–9.
106 Quoted in Gibson 1986, p. 141.
107 *Ibid.*, pp. 83–4, 161; cf. Buttafuoco 1985, pp. 32–3.

6

Women and girls in danger

From the mid-sixteenth century, some moral campaigners began to set up rescue institutions in the form of conservatories rather than convents. These were intended to be halfway houses and boarding schools, places of transition and safe keeping. They were not designed to be places of penance, but were aimed at reconciling rather than punishing, at preventing sins rather than atoning for them, at providing refuges where women in difficulties could consider their next moves. The goals of these institutions were socially conservative. They did not equip women for economic and personal independence but set out to restore failing marriages where possible and prepare girls to be good housewives. Only a few of their charges became choir nuns or sister servants; most (over 90 per cent at establishments in Milan and Bologna) returned to the world, though one or two of the halfway houses had small convents attached to them.[1] The Roman halfway house of the 1540s was dedicated to Martha, symbol of the active life, the woman who did the housework while her sister, Mary the contemplative, somewhat to Martha's exasperation, sat at the master's feet.[2]

The new establishments fell into two categories. The first, often called Soccorso, Deposito or Malmaritate, catered for sexually experienced women, many being of tarnished reputation. Some of them had husbands and were therefore barred from taking vows in the Convertite even if they wished to do so. Some had been concubines, some prostitutes; some were at least suspected of adultery. But others were victims of marital cruelty, inadequacy, profligacy, infidelity, desertion. The second group of charities was mainly concerned with virgins, attractive girls of a dangerous age – with protecting their innocence, educating them in devout and obedient habits and practical skills, and eventually steering some of them into suitable marriages. These foundations were widely known as conservatories for 'maidens in peril' [*zitelle periclitanti* or some such phrase], i.e. virgins whose honour was in jeopardy. At first they gave special attention to rescuing the daughters of dishonoured women; in time they began to give places to girls in less immediate danger, who came from less disreputable families but were nevertheless regarded as vulnerable.

Halfway houses

Women in failing marriages were often at high moral risk and in danger of censure. A married couple who lived apart without showing due cause and obtaining ecclesiastical approval were committing an offence which could attract intrusive attention in the post-Tridentine Church. Towards 1600, the archdiocese of Siena was as much concerned with married folk who were not cohabiting as with other people who were living in concubinage: indeed, in an inquiry of 1589–90, 244 married persons were reported for improperly living apart, 141 people for living in concubinage, 21 for committing adultery. If women were not with their husbands, had they become other men's lovers or were they surviving by prostitution? Parish priests listed estranged wives who were resorting to prostitution, alleging that they had denied them 'the most holy sacraments of penance and the eucharist'.[3] In 1598, Porzia Grifi, separated from her husband, the bookseller Giulio Susini, struggled to convince the court that she was supporting herself and a seven-year-old daughter by working honestly for a hatmaker, that she had her own premises and was not living with another man.[4] Antonina Pierini, wife to the Sienese painter Ventura Salimbeni, became (to use her word) 'unwanted' by him when, about 1604, he took a mistress. She described living at five different addresses in Rome and Siena over the next three years, receiving some help from her own sisters and two brothers-in-law. Pierini was eventually convicted of living in concubinage with the well-to-do Rinaldo Specchi (the fact that she had borne a bastard did not help her defence or support her story that the man was merely employing her and giving her charity).[5]

Episcopal courts had the power to dissolve marriages by annulments or suspend them by separations of bed and board, which authorised couples to live apart but not to remarry in each other's lifetime. Marriages could be annulled on the grounds that they had been brought about by 'fear and force' and that the consent of both parties had not been freely given, or that they had not been consummated, or that they were bigamous, or that there was some relationship between the couple which ought to have been recognised as an impediment. Separations were granted, and cases for them argued, on evidence of physical and mental cruelty, which might include denial of companionship, failure to maintain a wife, gross misuse of her property; on the grounds of adultery, of mortal hatred [*odio capitale*], and, on occasion, of infection with a contagious disease.[6] But instant verdicts were not to be expected; where was a wife to go while a dispute dragged on and she was in limbo, parted in fact but not yet in law from her husband?

An early refuge for women was the Casa di Santa Marta, established as part of the early Jesuits' campaign for making Rome set a better example to lesser Catholic cities.[7] The papal bull which approved the organisation in 1543 alluded to 'a number of women who have broken free of the sacred tie of marriage and left the matrimonial household, casting off the reins of modesty and chastity and leading a loose life'. The text assumed that the fault was theirs, but hinted at extenuating circumstances – at wives tempted by the Devil in the absence of their husbands, or for other reasons. Let there be a hostel which would accept runaway wives and attempt to mediate between them and their husbands, if need be sheltering them until the men returned to Rome. Ideally, the couple would compose their quarrel, thereby 'putting an end to the scandal', or, as a regulation of the house later expressed it, 'whenever the husband wants his wife, and guarantees to be a good friend to her [*dando securtà di farli bona compagnia*], she will be obliged to go back to live with him in peace, in love, and in good conjugal loyalty'.[8]

Here and elsewhere, the task of reconciling unhappy couples would fall, not only to charities of this type, but also to clerical and lay courts and to good neighbours alarmed at the distress and violence they could not help witnessing. Given the high value which the Tridentine and post-Tridentine Church placed on formal marriage, which could be dissolved only with great reluctance and difficulty, there was a strong possibility that Church courts would be more inclined to press husbands and wives to come together again, however unhappily, than to protect wives from abuse. Perhaps charities would not always be impartial, but would lend themselves to husbands' efforts to bring protesting wives to heel and even become places of confinement and coercion.[9]

In the course of the next thirty years, Santa Marta in Rome developed into a nunnery. But another house, the Casa Pia, opened in 1563, and, according to Camillo Fanucci's account of Roman charities (published in 1602), it was usually this establishment that received unhappily married women. It was for any woman who wished to convert from a disreputable to an honourable life and, the author added, it frequently accepted 'many women who are placed there in custody by their relatives, or by courts of law', as though it were becoming a holding prison as much as an asylum. The Casa Pia had its own community of nuns, subject to the rule of St Clare, but lay women were allowed neither to see nor to speak with them.[10]

The Casa di Santa Marta in Rome was soon followed by the Casa della Carità in Naples and by the Soccorso founded in Milan in 1555 by Isabella d'Aragona. This was for 'lost women', women being harassed by seducers, and married women in difficulties, and was prepared to admit girls no more than twelve years old.[11] In Verona in the second half of the sixteenth century, places of safety were sometimes sought for former mistresses and women in matrimonial trouble, though there was no special institution for this purpose, and arrangements were improvised as the need arose.[12] Important foundations arose in the late 1570s in Milan, Venice and Florence, and similar short-stay establishments were set up at longer intervals until well into the eighteenth century. Sometimes they concentrated on the problems of married women; sometimes they catered for any wayward female who wished to change her way of life. In principle, the Deposito di Santa Maria Maddalena at Milan was for both *peccatrici* and *malmaritate*. Between 1589 and 1626, about 30 per cent of residents of identifiable status (168 of 575) were said to be in marital difficulties, while only about 5 per cent (28 of 575) were described as 'whores [*meretrici*]'.[13] Maria Pimentel, the wife of Count Olivares, the viceroy of Sicily, established a refuge for *malmaritate* in Palermo in the late sixteenth century.[14] Widowed and left with two children at the age of twenty in 1607, a Genoese aristocrat, Virginia Centurione Bracelli, rejected her father's proposals that she should marry again and devoted herself for over forty years to prayer, mysticism and practical works of charity. These included a refuge which by the 1640s had several hundred residents and opened its doors to women of every age and rank, including former prostitutes and *malmaritate*, as well as impoverished girls in general.[15]

Veronica Franco, the Venetian courtesan and poet, took an interest in the local Soccorso and drafted a petition suggesting that some prostitutes needed an asylum to which they could take their children.[16] Such proposals to keep families together were too radical to find favour. They were considered in Florence but soon dismissed – the pure and the soiled must be kept apart, evil influences curtailed, and virgins were not to be accepted 'even when their expenses will be paid and they come with *convertite* who are their mothers'.[17] This was probably widespread practice, echoed many years later in correspondence between a Roman cleric, Giovanni Battista de Rossi, and his friend, the country priest of Rocca di Papa, Pietro Santovetti. Some of their letters concerned a woman from Santovetti's parish, who was to be placed at parochial expense in Rome's *conservatorio delle malmaritate* on the understanding that her boy and girl would be taken from her within a few days and sent to separate orphanages.[18]

Later establishments for short-stay residents included the Opera del Deposito in Turin, founded in 1684 by the lay confraternity of San Paolo, for 'fallen women, women in danger, and women who cause, or are about to cause, scandal to their neighbours'.[19] In the early eighteenth century, the patriarch of Venice, Giovanni Badoer, inspired an organisation which soon became known as the Penitenti di San Giobbe. This was designed for prostitutes under the age of thirty who had repented but were in danger of relapsing because they had no money, knew no honest trade, and enjoyed no support from responsible relatives or friends. Systematic inquiries were to be made into their circumstances by 'visitors' armed with thirteen-point questionnaires. By the end of the century, it was usual to transfer to the Penitenti women who had been treated for vene-real disease at the hospital of the Incurabili and had apparently been cured. Entrants were to serve both a probationary period outside the institution and a novitiate within it, but, once fully accepted, they must be 'placed within the shortest possible time either in marriage, or in domestic service, or in a convent ... because in this manner a greater number of persons will be assisted, at smaller expense'.[20]

Halfway houses were small compared with the largest Convertite convents. Most would probably shelter between thirty and fifty women, although by 1748 the Penitenti di San Giobbe numbered eighty-three and after that year observed no fixed limits.[21] Finance, building, maintenance, admissions and fund-raising were usually in the hands of boards of deputies, part lay and part clerical, who also supplied the collectors of information about possible entrants. Chaplains, matrons and other female staff dealt with internal organisation and discipline. Wherever practicable, most halfway houses charged for the bed and board of their residents. They normally expected them to work and contribute to their keep, but might – as did the Casa del Rifugio in Naples and the Soccorso in Bologna – exempt them from working in exchange for a higher rent. A sub-stantial bequest in 1644 enabled Bologna's Soccorso to award more free places. Some residents were supported by sponsors, including former pimps and protectors and men who had once seduced or kept them as mistresses and showed some concern for their future.[22] One or two were paid for by husbands or relatives who wanted them confined.

Documents of two institutions record the arrangements made for several hundred residents, mostly during the seventeenth century – for 713 women at the Deposito di Santa Maria Maddalena in Milan (1589–1626) and 445 at the Soccorso in Bologna (1589–1662). Both establishments handed over more than 40 per cent of their charges to husbands, relatives or other persons who seemed willing to take responsibility for them. Reconciliations between *malmaritate* and their spouses would presumably account for many of these arrangements. Otherwise, the three standard destinations were familiar ones, marriage, domestic service and the convent, which were favoured in different degrees by the two foundations. A quarter of the women at Bologna were married from the Soccorso, generally to artisans, but marriages directly from the institution accounted for little more than 10 per cent at Milan. The Deposito assigned nearly a fifth of the women to domestic service, perhaps on the understanding that their employers would eventually contribute to their dowries and see them married. But only about 7.5 per cent of the women in Bologna were sent to be servants. From each institution a few, but only a few, became nuns, usually at the Convertite or at the small convent attached to the Deposito of Milan itself – twenty-seven in all at Milan, twenty-five at Bologna. Some women at both institutions absconded, were expelled, were removed to hospitals, or were sent to unspecified destinations.[23]

The halfway houses responded more flexibly, if on a smaller scale, to the needs of individual women than did the Convertite convents, and they were capable of providing for changes of mind and breakdowns in relationships. Francesca Ferrari, a cloth-merchant's daughter, entered the Deposito at Milan in 1604; she was handed over to her brother, but they did not get on well, and she then joined the household of a Marchese; eventually, in 1622, she settled down as a nun in the Deposito itself. Between 1636 and 1655, Barbara Mazzi returned several times to the Soccorso at Bologna.[24] The institutions, though, offered only a small if still valuable response to the likely need. One wonders whether they catered mostly for women with fee-paying sponsors whom their governors happened to know and wanted to please. San Giobbe in Venice aspired to help destitute women who had no patrons or protectors. Of how many other organisations was this true?

Malmaritate

The term *malmaritate* had passed into common use by about 1560. For Gregory Martin, it referred to 'wemen so-called by occasion of misliking, displeasure or falling out betweene their husbands and them'; he conceded that faults might lie on either or both sides, and that some wives were cursed with 'churlishe, cruel, fierce and wicked husbands'.[25] To Bandello, a *malmaritata* could well be a young woman stuck with an arid, jealous, older husband who could not satisfy her in bed, and who was therefore tempted to try her luck with a potent and fecund young man.[26] But in Venice, about 1560, she might be no adulteress but a woman forced to ask magistrates to protect her dowry against a husband who was mismanaging it – as was Laura Falasco, who bore witness to 'the wretchedness of being dubbed an unhappy and ill-married woman'.[27]

Both seemingly innocent and allegedly guilty women could be found in establishments which accepted *malmaritate*. Residents of the Deposito in Milan included Laura Laoziana, whose partner was keeping another wife in Venice, and some women in mortal terror of their husbands – among them Paola Albrisio, who had flung herself from a window of her house, and Orsola Rizza, who had fled 'for fear of being killed'.[28] Around 1600, Jesuits in Venice advised Paolina Businella, said to be a 'timid' young woman who had for years been resisting her husband's efforts to consummate their marriage, to take refuge in the Soccorso.[29] In Rome, Anna Maria Castelli had married

Flaminio Lucarini in October 1648, unaware that her groom had had sexual congress with her sister Isabella; when their adventure came to light, she refused to consummate the marriage and launched a nullity suit which eventually succeeded. Meanwhile, she retired into the Casa Pia, to counter any supposition that she was living as a concubine.[30] In 1729, Lucia Uslenghi, an engraver in the via dei Coronari in Rome, asked the Vicegerente to place her daughter Teresa, who was seeking a separation from her husband, in the conservatory known as the Zitelle Viperesche. This was for 'poor maidens in danger who are well born, and who on account of their age are unable to enter the other charitable institutions of Rome'.[31] Unusually, a 'free woman', Felice of Rome, resorted to the Casa Pia in 1646 to escape harassment by an unwelcome suitor, as though hoping to prevent an unhappy marriage rather than cope with its consequences.[32]

Other residents, though, were under suspicion, effectively under arrest. Some were detained by virtue of court orders. It was usual in Naples to send to the Carità women who had been accused in court of adultery. Adulteresses could be confined at the Malmaritate in Florence.[33] Camilla Savioni, daughter of a Venetian citizen, the fading former lover of an incurably ill nobleman, Andrea Marcello, was held in the Soccorso for several months in 1624 while the Inquisition investigated reports that she had bewitched him and was plotting to hasten his death in order to get her hands on his property.[34] Margherita Pellegrini, the wife of a Florentine apothecary, ran away in 1615 with one of her husband's patients, who eventually left her at the Malmaritate, perhaps to protect her against the first onslaught of her cuckolded husband's wrath.[35] Some errant wives needed protection against affronted husbands or relatives who, rather than be so unmanly as to take legal action, would avenge themselves directly on both lover and wife.[36] At the Deposito in Milan was Margherita Preboni, whose husband had died in prison after killing the man in whose company he had found her. So was Virginia Faina, caught with a priest from Monza, who was himself sent to the archbishop's prison.[37] Authorities in Bologna in 1691 feared that Maria Gandolfi's brother intended to kill her for losing her honour and damaging her family's.[38]

Artisans, servants and elderly husbands seemed inclined to rely on the law. Let a man prove adultery, and he would be entitled to claim his wife's dowry for himself. Meanwhile, he could – so long as he could pay for her keep – restrain the woman by consigning her to an institution. Camilla Nadi, a wet nurse, had an affair with an acquaintance of her employer. Since Nadi's husband, a poor cobbler, was in no position to challenge a nobleman, he sought a separation and demanded that Camilla be interned 'in some place so that she does not do evil', which proved to be the Malmaritate of Bologna.[39] Giovanni Muti, living in Venice in 1670, was seventy-five. His much younger wife Margarita, like a Bandello *malmaritata*, was so quick to seek satisfaction elsewhere that, within a month of their wedding, he caught her in a house run by a woman who arranged illicit assignations. Having deposited his wife as an adulteress in the Soccorso, the outraged husband later demanded her ejection, lest she use the place as a sanctuary, for he now wanted her punished for lewdness and ingratitude.[40]

In the course of prolonged legal argument and negotiation, husbands might confine wives in a conservatory, hoping to force a settlement on them. In 1636, Valeria Gandini, who once ran an inn in Rome with her husband, Antonio Maccatello, found herself detained at his suit in the Casa Pia. She resolved to extract herself at all costs from this 'prison', to drop further proceedings, and to accept any deal which he offered her – 'not with any inclination to do what he will force me to do, it being my sole intention to get out of this place'.[41] In Florence, many years later, Marina Falcini, the orphaned daughter of a silversmith, began an action for separation within four months of her wedding in 1773 to Andrea Lotti, who worked as a butcher in his father's shop. In the course of the litigation, which dragged on for four years, Lotti had her confined in the Malmaritate on the authority of secular magistrates, the Officio dei Pupilli, presumably to force her to reconsider her refusal to live with him and her determination to rear her child in her own mother's house rather than under the eyes of her drunken and intrusive mother-in-law. She escaped only by petitioning the grand duke for her release after five months' detention. Lotti's actions recoiled on him, however, when a judge in the court of the papal nuncio recognised that the tactics employed by both parties had stirred up 'mutual hatred and enmity', which would justify the separation that Falcini had long been seeking. In this case, resort to the Malmaritate had served, not to reconcile, but to provoke and, in the end, to divide a very unhappy couple.[42]

The Malmaritate and other halfway houses had been designed with compassionate goals that were not altogether forgotten. They were originally intended to deal sympathetically with women who were not professional prostitutes but had committed indiscretions, to save them from ruin by salvaging their marriages and encouraging husbands to moderate their own behaviour and forgive their wives. They were also meant to provide havens for women whose reputations were endangered by their reluctance to live with violent husbands or languish in bigamous or incestuous unions. They were designed to offer some form of rehabilitation to women who lacked the will and the vocation to endure the harsh penitential regimes of the Convertite, or whose circumstances barred them from entering convents. If prostitutes were sometimes believed to protect married women, reconstructed marriages could protect against a descent into prostitution. Inevitably, though, these houses, being at the disposal of magistrates and not pure charities, had another role. They could be used to discipline wives, to force them to comply at least for a time with a husband's wishes, perhaps to compel them to persevere with unhappy marriages.

Some establishments were used to protect families of standing from embarrassment at the indiscreet behaviour of certain of their members. Perhaps the very fact that these institutions were intended to be charities rather than prisons, to be therapeutic rather than punitive, made it more possible to hold women indefinitely. They had not received finite sentences for committing specific crimes, but could be kept until they showed signs of remorse and self-correction. In 1742, the Opera del Deposito in Turin was placed under direct royal protection and confusingly renamed the Opera delle Convertite. Its concerns were then extended to include immoral women who were 'not inclined to change their way of life' and had therefore to be deprived of liberty. From 1750 onwards, they were confined in a so-called Ritiro delle Forzate, where, on the authority of the chief of police, about a dozen women, the youngest twenty-eight, the oldest sixty, languished in captivity. Sensing a threat to liberty and justice, Count Benzo called for clear proof of misconduct, 'because a husband who had grown tired of his wife, or a father- and mother-in-law of their son's wife, could easily slander her to get her out of the way'.[43] A widow, Vittoria Valori, who had spent five years in the Malmaritate of Florence for allegedly leading a 'scandalous' life 'unworthy of someone of respected old lineage', claimed to be 'in a pillory and not in a conservatory' and deplored her own indefinite detention without being tried or given any opportunity to make her defence.[44]

The rescue of innocents

Beside the halfway houses, in most cities were long-stay establishments originally designed for virgins in grave moral danger. A stock character in salacious and pica-resque literature was a pretty girl being trained by her mother in the arts of the cour-tesan. A familiar image in the minds of moral campaigners was a beautiful, unsullied child, at high risk on account of her good looks, poorly protected and perhaps about to be betrayed by her family, soon to lose her innocence, her marriage prospects and her soul. From around 1540, aristocratic women, clergy and laity, nobles and citizens, courtiers and functionaries, merchants and artisans helped to establish convent-like homes to shelter and educate 'endangered' virgins, perhaps bearing both these stereo-types in mind.

In 1560, Pope Pius IV officially recognised the company responsible for the con-servatory of Santa Caterina della Rosa, set up in Rome about twenty years earlier to protect girls whose virginity, that 'priceless asset', was being sold by callous relatives.[45] An account of the Casa dello Santo Spirito in Naples, founded in the 1550s or 1560s, described an asylum for about a hundred virgins once at risk of being sold to 'lecherous men', especially foreign merchants, by desperate and debauched kinfolk – including 'prostitutes who bring up their daughters to maintain them in old age'.[46] In time, how-ever, conservatories began to accept increasing numbers of children in less immediate danger: pretty girls from families in reduced circumstances who had lost at least one parent. Their people might be respectable and well-meaning, take some interest in the girl, contribute to her board and lodging and perhaps her dowry, promise to take her back if she fell ill or misbehaved. But their ability to protect her honour could well be questioned, since her beauty would expose her to the designs of evil people who might elude their vigilance. A closed, disciplined and ever-watchful community would be bet-ter equipped to preserve her purity.

Variations on the theme were possible, but many Italian conservatories would admit girls aged between nine and twelve, keep them under surveillance for anything between four and ten years, and then arrange for them to marry or take the veil – though other destinies could be contemplated.[47] Their goal was to produce good wives and nuns, devout, practical and obedient, and to form a sound building block for society and the State. Lucrezia di Sbruglio, matron of the house in Udine from 1702 to 1733, said that her establishment served to 'foster good conduct by instructing girls in the fear of God and the skills proper to a woman ... because the happiness of families depends on the marriages of well brought-up young women, and this contributes to the glory and splendour of the prince'.[48]

Some foundations were inspired by the eloquence of missionary preachers such as the Jesuit Benedetto Palmio, who campaigned for two years in Venice from 1558 to 1560, or initiated by prelates, including Federico Borromeo, who in 1619 set up in Milan a congregation of twelve Ursulines to protect and educate a number of 'endangered girls'.[49] But they were often sustained by lay associations of local people who subscribed to their support, provided governors and counsellors, investigated deserving cases and selected candidates for admission. The company which ran the Casa della Pietà in Florence, founded in the early 1550s, consisted of women, some of them high-born and some of them widows of prominent opponents of the Medici – 'Piagnoni' who were keeping alive the republican, moralistic, charitable tradition of Savonarola many years after his downfall. A committee of 'prioresses' made rapid decisions concerning admissions to the house, which was sheltering 160–70 girls by about 1560.[50] Reminiscing in the late 1580s, when approximately two hundred females were living in the Venetian conservatory of the Zitelle, Father Palmio recited a roll of honour of thirteen women, all bearing noble names, and thirteen men, not all of them noble, who had contributed to the institution's progress.[51] The matrons or prioresses of these homes were sometimes ladies of quality and sometimes not, sometimes brought in from outside and sometimes, after the early years, chosen from among senior residents. Conservatories opened a career to women who did not wish to be wives, nuns, tertiaries, or spinsters marking time at home, and offered an absorbing occupation to a select number of widows. The prioress-matron of the Pietà in Florence for almost thirty years was Mona Alessandra (d. 1583), the childless widow of a woodworker; her successors were women who had themselves been educated and grown to middle age within the house.[52]

In Naples, the Casa dello Spirito Santo was run by a confraternity with general interests in the poor, the sick and the needy and ruled by seven leading gentlemen and citizens.[53] Individuals were more prominent in funding and managing other conservatories. Alessandro Borla, formerly in the archbishop's household, set up the Casa del Rifugio in Naples with financial help from the princess of Sulmona.[54] At Bologna, Bonifacio dalle Balle, the youngest son of a merchant, joined forces with a group of Franciscan tertiaries to set up the hostel of Santa Croce.[55] In Udine, three widows, members of the urban and rural aristocracies, inspired a house for poor and endangered virgins and themselves served in turn as its matrons between 1596 and 1620.[56]

Alternatively, hostels could be started by ordinary people who gathered children off the streets, found them places to sleep, begged alms on their behalf, and eventually, if all went well, attracted the attention of powerful patrons. These influential figures were capable of providing the assets which released the children and their champions from a hand-to-mouth existence and of setting up conventional administrative machinery – they found a cardinal protector (in Rome), recruited a governing body of solid citizens, paid for a permanent home, perhaps obtained privileges or financial contributions from government offices. In Rome, the conservatory of the Divina Provvidenza was started in 1672 by a priest, Francesco Paparetti, and eventually acquired a protector in Cardinal Benedetto Odescalchi, who became Pope Innocent XI in 1676.[57]

One such enterprise, in Venice, ended in failure. About 1648, Cecilia Ferrazzi, the orphaned daughter of a Venetian box-maker, once a receiver of charity herself, began to practise it by gathering beggar children and prostitutes' daughters and installing them in a succession of houses in four different districts of the city. The last and grandest of these was a mansion purchased in about 1658 by two noble patrons who clearly believed in her.[58] Ferrazzi's community grew until it rivalled the Casa delle Zitelle. But its finances were unsound, for it appeared to have no endowments and no means of compelling relatives to contribute to the residents' keep. An aspiring saint and in her own eyes a 'slave of Christ's passion' rather than a hard-headed philanthropist, Ferrazzi took girls 'willingly for the love of God without any compensation'. The Council of Ten subjected her enterprise to the lay commissioners for convents, who named it the Seminary of the Immaculate Conception and provided a convent-like rule. At first, Ferrazzi stayed on as superior, but she fell from favour in 1664 when the Roman Inquisition in Venice investigated her on charges of posing as a saint. Had she usurped the powers of a priest by hearing her charges' confessions, possibly to prevent them from describing abuses to an outsider? She was eventually found 'lightly suspect' of heresy.[59] After Ferrazzi's deposition and imprisonment, one of her former patrons established in her palace a boarding school for impoverished noble girls, which he entrusted to Capuchin nuns.[60]

In their early years, rescue organisations sometimes removed children forcibly from protesting relatives, aided if necessary by constables. Like beggars' hospitals, they could acquire quasi-magisterial powers of arrest and detention, but were wise to use them sparingly. The founders of the Casa dello Spirito Santo in Naples appointed thirty responsible persons to watch over thirty divisions of the city and collect or receive information about the city's endangered girls; when the governors seized children, they were sometimes opposed by local women (as in 1575), sometimes encouraged (as in 1589, when they took three little sisters from the district of San Giuseppe).[61] In Milan the Collegio del Rosario called for help on volunteers who taught children Christian doctrine and were well placed to pick up information about the circumstances of their pupils.[62] Governors of the Zitelle in Venice were invited to collaborate with the society for Poveri Vergognosi, which addressed the needs of the house poor and had reason to know what was happening behind their doors.[63] In 1588, however, the governors were advised to think hard before taking girls by force, to anticipate furious protests from their mothers, and to reflect that special favours would have to be granted to the children to help them settle down – measures bad for discipline, likely to arouse jealousy and unrest among other pupils. Indeed, the governors should authorise such drastic action only in exceptional cases, and only when at least two-thirds of them were in favour of this move.[64]

Some prostitutes, at least in Rome, agreed to part with their daughters and asked a conservatory to accept them – arguably, once free of dependants, mothers would be better placed to improve themselves. In 1592, the governors of Santa Caterina heard that

> we have visited Gentile, daughter of Elisabetta Ronda, residing with her mother, who does not lead a respectable life; in the course of our visit various kinds of people came to the house, and the girl, aged thirteen years and six months, is clearly in a dangerous

situation. It is all too possible that she has already gone to the bad. But the mother says that if the girl is rescued she will herself get married and mother and daughter be saved at the same time.

More acrimonious were events which unfolded in 1607 after constables removed Caterina Particappa, aged thirteen, from her unmarried parents, there being reason to suspect that the girl, who could sing and play beautifully, was being schooled in a courtesan's accomplishments. She was lodged in an annexe and inspected as to her virginity, but sprung from captivity by her mother (who grabbed and pinioned the prioress), her father, and two accomplices. They took the precaution of leaving Rome after this exploit.[65] By her own account, Cecilia Ferrazzi in Venice took charge of some prostitutes' daughters and, unmoved by their mothers' pleas, bribes and promises to reform, made enemies by refusing to give the girls back.[66]

Many conservatories were prepared to rescue only virgins, a policy which could have unintended consequences. Crafty mothers in Naples frustrated would-be rescuers by selling their daughters' virginity before they could be taken into care, or by rupturing their hymens themselves. Immoral behaviour became more blatant: there was now no need to fear the officers of the Spirito Santo, and mothers 'did disgraceful things in public and urged young people to sin without restraint'. By way of remedy, Alessandro Borla founded the Casa del Rifugio for girls who met the criteria of the Spirito Santo in all respects, save that they were not virgins. Tragedies might now be averted: previously, if the Spirito Santo found that girls were not virgins and sent them home, the children could well be murdered by relatives jealous of family 'honour' who had not been party to their defloration. It now became possible to transfer them discreetly to the Rifugio for their protection.[67] Perhaps it was wrong, in any case, to abandon girls to the 'evil life' on account of a physical change imposed upon them by others – though, if they were not virgins, it could well prove more difficult to arrange marriages for them in the future.

Compromise and refinement

Citizens established some conservatories expressly geared to the needs of the very poor, as was Santa Maria e San Niccolò del Ceppo in Florence in the 1550s.[68] While it was situated in the plebeian district of the Borgo Ognissanti in Florence, from 1554 to 1568, the Casa della Pietà admitted girls in great misery and poor health; nearly 60 per cent of entrants died in the establishment (they became a good deal more robust after the subsequent move to the via del Mandorlo).[69] Concern for the poorest of the poor revived at long intervals in other cities. In 1677, authorities in Lucca set up hostels intended to take beggar children of both sexes off the streets, but after two years, they determined to provide shelter only for adolescent girls in 'extreme need and manifest danger of scandal', admitting them to a residence called the Conservatorio delle Fanciulle Vagabonde, but 'leaving all other girls and all boys to beg for their living'.[70]

Many institutions, however, began in time to cater for a more select clientele, so that the daughters of prostitutes and beggars were almost forgotten. Arguably, conservatories, like convents of Convertite, would not remain solvent if they admitted only the poorest children. About 1580, Gregory Martin held that the word *zitelle* or *cittelle* now denoted 'maydes of the citie' 'that are of better parentage, but their houses fallen to decay', who were living at Santa Caterina in Rome alongside 'such whose mothers are or have been harlots'.[71] By the mid-seventeenth century, the daughters of the respectable poor appeared to be displacing the children of outcasts. The Oratorian Mariano Sozzini wrote in 1659 that the original aim of Roman conservatories had been to rescue girls sleeping on the streets, but now 'they give places only to the daughters of servants and artisans who are most strongly commended, and there is no end to their numbers'. Of Santa Caterina he remarked that 'whereas at first they sought girls out and forcibly removed them from the houses of prostitutes, now the house is filled with 136 maidens, and it is difficult to get a place, even with favours'.[72] Conservatories must needs attract donations, and their benefactors and governors were seldom content with the prospect of heavenly rewards or with an earthly reputation for disinterested generosity – they had a natural tenderness for their own impoverished relatives, for servants or other protégées and their children, coupled with a tendency to prefer the respectable to the rough, and to show special consideration for people of their own class who had fallen on hard times. In Bologna in 1609, a fellow-worker, intriguing against Bonifacio dalle Balle, the founder of Santa Croce, recruited supporters by promising that if they offered dowries or other gifts they would be entitled to nominate girls for places in the house.[73] Governors of the Divina Provvidenza in Rome agreed in the early eighteenth century that 'because the conservatory is supported by the charity of benefactors, if some benefactor who disposes of significant alms proposes a girl who has a respected father or mother, discretion may be used in admitting her to the conservatory'.[74]

To balance their books and oblige their patrons, many conservatories, sooner or later, began to accept fee-paying boarders of 'good' family, to be educated along the same lines as their charity-girls.[75] Older paying guests, occupying separate apartments and sometimes bringing their own maids, could boost the flagging income of a conservatory.[76] The internal affairs of many houses were in the hands of religious communities of nuns or quasi-nuns who, unlike the governors, lived on the premises: they were lay spinsters and widows who served as administrators and instructors, were recruited partly from former pupils and partly from outside, and could – as at the Collegio del Rosario in Milan – be relatives or protégées of the governors.[77] There was a risk that conservatories might become top-heavy as genteel spinsters joined these communities in the hope of a comfortable berth, choosing or being assigned to institutions rather than live at home.

This problem became acute in Naples during the eighteenth and early nineteenth centuries, where places were increasingly occupied by poorly disciplined women of uncertain function known as 'oblates', who were neither religious nor seculars, and certainly not in urgent need of charity.[78] At the close of the eighteenth century, Galanti explained that conservatories for *pericolanti* and *periclitanti* had proliferated in Naples as the population grew, but now, in practice, they were more for disappointed spinsters than for virgins in genuine peril. In the city, he said, 'there are now about forty-five conservatories sheltering women of every kind of status' (including those designed for reformed prostitutes). Most of these establishments were directed by priests and their residents prepared for a religious life. They could, he suggested, become more useful to society if they devoted their time to keeping schools. Rescue work was thrust aside when chaste but devious mothers passed themselves off as prostitutes in order to get their daughters into the Conservatorio dello Spirito Santo, where the girls would be well treated and become eligible after about ten years for a dowry of a hundred ducats.[79] A royal visitor in 1769 observed that Milan's Collegio del Rosario 'no longer admits girls who are truly poor and genuinely in danger'. The deputies did respond to ministerial instructions to admit a girl without payment and without the customary trousseau, but they soon, despite their healthy finances, began to make difficulties again.[80]

In 1809 a Napoleonic commissioner complained of a situation which had long been developing in Rome – that more than half of the conservatories in the city had become places of free or subsidised education for girls who were not true orphans and whose families were by no means destitute. In 1826 conservatories were said to be cluttered with fee-paying lodgers, with girls who had passed the statutory age, with old women and widows in search of cheap accommodation. They were no longer educating young women for life outside the community but becoming their final destiny. Hence their residents were ageing – in Rome in the early nineteenth century, more than half the members of most communities were over thirty. In Venice in 1597, the Zitelle had sheltered 164 females under the age of thirty, and only 20 who had passed it.[81] But for much of the nineteenth century this establishment too was occupied by ageing patrician women who treated it as a nunnery in which they were permanent residents; only in 1880 did the Congregazione della Carità resolve to enlist it once more in the task of educating attractive young women of good character.[82]

Regime and curriculum

Conservatories directed their education towards a few clear objectives – a sound knowledge of Christian doctrine; frequent communion and confession and devotion to the Virgin Mary and the saints; deference to superiors; modesty and good manners; avoidance of idleness; ability to read and write; and the acquisition of skills which would be useful to any household or convent of which they later formed part, to say nothing of the conservatory itself. These institutions were boarding schools with no holidays, designed to preserve their pupils from temptation and corruption, and to restrict and supervise all communications with the outside world, including family visits.[83]

At Udine, the regime rested partly on the rules prescribed by a Franciscan, Antonio Pagani, for a company of Dimesse at Vicenza in the 1580s, and partly on those laid down for the Zitelle in Venice by the Jesuit Benedetto Palmio. Dimesse lived together in small communities, not pronouncing vows or committing themselves to total enclosure, not wearing distinctive habits but eschewing ornaments and jewellery and contenting themselves with plain, coarsely woven dresses. Pagani's rules could apply both to the permanent residents of the house and to its pupils. Their emphasis was on interior discipline, on the correction of faults by self-examination and mutual reproof, and on a modest bearing which reflected, or ought to reflect, an inward humility. In his words, 'the true discipline of soul and body lies in being sober, well regulated and orderly in all inward and outward acts, i.e. in dressing, eating, drinking, talking, conversing, thinking, or other physical actions'.[84] At the Collegio del Rosario in seventeenth-century Milan, the rule, aiming at an equally all-embracing regime, prescribed meditations to fill the mind when mundane tasks, such as dressing and undressing, were being performed and to leave no vacant spaces for the Devil to invade.[85]

Departures from routine were few and regarded with misgiving by the authorities. But a clause in Palmio's regulations for the Venetian Zitelle envisaged a prize-giving for the girls who proved best at repeating Christian doctrine. The rules also allowed, with caution, for a slightly more imaginative form of amusement by permitting the girls to present scenes or stories from scripture, presumably as tableaux or even plays. On festivals, especially in summer, the girls were allowed not only to recite their Christian doctrine, but also to sing and experiment with versifying the psalms, 'that they may learn to read well and pass the time profitably', and 'so that idleness, the cause of all evil, may have no place in the house'. They might even, at the matron's discretion, be allowed to stroll in the gardens.[86] Music and drama seemed to be less highly valued at the Collegio del Rosario in Milan.

Most conservatory girls devoted many hours daily to acquiring and practising manual skills, as well as to the chores of sweeping, cleaning, washing and cooking, and mending their own clothes. Work was designed partly to dispel idleness and boredom, the Devil's accomplices; partly to train good wives, who might one day become help-meets for, say, mercers, tailors or stocking-makers; partly to earn money to support the conservatory and contribute to the girls' own nest-eggs. Gifts of all kinds covered less than three-quarters of the running expenses of the Casa della Pietà in Florence in the mid-sixteenth century, and the house needed to generate income to cover the shortfall.[87] Some merchant-manufacturers were happy to put out work to conservatories, which could place at their disposal a low-paid workforce subject to a kind of factory discipline; the merchants could then use or sell whatever the girls produced. Links with the woollen and silk industries were strong at conservatories in Florence, Bologna and Rome. Girls were engaged on primary tasks such as spinning wool, or raising silkworms, unwinding cocoons and preparing usable silken threads to be sent on to dyers' workshops. They might also weave the simpler kinds of fabric, including veils and ribbons, although in time certain conservatories, being a cut above the rougher establishments for beggars and foundlings, developed a capacity for more advanced and refined work.[88] Delicate activities such as making leather gloves proved more suitable to pupils of Rome's Divina Provvidenza than did the task of supplying woollen fabrics to the crews of the papal galleys.[89] The girls of the Rosario in Milan also worked in bone, making buttons, and devoted some time to laundering *panni di chiesa*, probably vestments and fabrics used in churches, such as altar-cloths.[90]

Leaving the Conservatory

In principle, conservatories sought to move most of their pupils on to other destinations and place them with other protectors when they reached a less vulnerable age.

Some girls, perhaps too many, would enter the service of the institution itself, but the traditional choices were marriage and the cloister. Many conservatories undertook to find husbands or convent places and to provide dowries themselves, as was usual in Bologna. Others preferred, as in Florence, to hand the girls over to employers or back to their more trustworthy relatives, in the expectation that these people would eventually see them married or otherwise settled.[91] Householders who took on conservatory girls as servants sometimes promised in notarised documents that they would in due course arrange their marriages.[92] The understanding in Rome towards 1700 was that noble-women and gentlewomen who took pupils of Santa Caterina into their service would maintain them for six years and eventually contribute 150 scudi to their dowries.[93] Of girls who entered the Divina Provvidenza in Rome between 1684 and 1750, 40 per cent married from the institution, 27.9 per cent returned to their families, and 5.9 per cent entered convents. Just over one-fifth (21.6 per cent) died in the conservatory; 4.6 per cent moved to another institution.[94] Only about one-sixth of entrants to the Casa delle Zitelle in Udine clearly got married from the institution – some matrons distributed dowries more generously than others – and from the 1630s onwards, an increasing pro-portion of pupils remained in the house.[95]

Conservatories which arranged marriages entertained no great social ambitions for their pupils: upward mobility was not encouraged, apart from a rise from rough to respectable. They generally sought husbands for their girls among artisans, traders and shopkeepers, occasionally looking to clerks and sometimes to servants, now and then (but rarely) to shepherds or peasant farmers. Some governors interviewed prospective husbands; others merely scrutinised written applications. About one-fifth of husbands in eighteenth-century Rome were widowers, who often applied to the establishment which had found them their first wife.[96] Marriages were arranged, often in consulta-tion with relatives, the girls, so long secluded and handicapped by inexperience and naivety, being in no position to go out and find suitable husbands for themselves. Deep acquaintance between spouses-to-be was scarcely possible, though marriages were not quite the equivalent of blind dates. Suitors were entitled to view their prospective brides from a distance, and, at least in eighteenth-century Rome, they were allowed to visit them once or twice on the premises. Forced, as distinct from arranged, marriages would have been unlawful, liable in principle to annulment, though only a bold girl would resist the match proposed to her: when Anna Giannò presumed to do so at the Divina Provvidenza in 1748, she was struck by a relative in the presence of the prioress and threatened with losing her dowry.[97]

A few marriages, inevitably, turned out badly. Certain conservatories, still acting in place of the parents, continued to take an interest in their alumnae, sometimes in a benevolent, sometimes in a disciplinary spirit. Female governors of the Venetian Zitelle were expected to pay regular visits to married women and nuns, remember-ing 'that these daughters do not have mothers other than themselves', and in the hope that husbands, seeing them 'under the protection of many matrons', would not ill-treat them. Should an ex-pupil be widowed, male officers known as Sollicitatori would seek to recover her dowry from her late husband's estate.[98] Visitors from Santa Caterina della Rosa in Rome had the power to punish former pupils who disappointed them by behaving badly – even to imprison them on a bread-and-water diet in the so-called 'house of widows', which in effect became another hostel (or lock-up) for *malmaritate*. Such was the fate of Caterina Regina, who was removed in 1583 from her prostitute mother and, after fourteen years in the institution, disastrously married to Giorgio Sogna, an innkeeper. For several years she lived sometimes with him and sometimes in the 'house of widows'. But by 1611, after his death, she had apparently become a cheap and importunate prostitute.[99]

Conclusion

In the early modern centuries, societies still resorted to traditional methods of redeeming women of lost honour – marriage to an upright man or permanent retreat into a penitential religious community which banned all sexual activity. But from about 1540, with the beginnings of the Counter Reformation (which was, in part, a campaign for the salvation of souls through redemptive charity), active missionaries began to pay more attention to the problems of women who were already married but were at least suspected of infidelity. How could they find ways of living and recovering their honour in the ordinary world? There was more recognition that the roots of prostitution or concubinage could sometimes lie in marital breakdown, for which a brutal, neglectful or absentee husband might bear some responsibility. The Tridentine Church was determined both to formalise marriage and to extol it at the expense of other kinds of partnership. It might also be important to salvage failing marriages, by attempting to reconcile unhappy couples and by providing temporary shelters for women pondering their future.

Long before the sixteenth century, the law had condemned the practice of leading children into prostitution, as witness the ferocious penalties envisaged for mothers who tried to turn their daughters into financial assets. But, again from the 1540s, new organisations tried to do more – by systematically identifying children in danger and, in extreme cases, forcibly removing them from unfit parents. In some respects, little had changed – the initial targets were still the bad mother and her pretty daughter, and the solution was still removal to a safe place which was not a convent but observed an austere religious rule designed to repel the invasions of the Devil. Usually the aim was not to prepare a budding nun for the religious life but to train a good housewife, equipped with practical skills, who could live honourably with a sober, hard-working artisan or shopkeeper and bear and bring up children.

The character of these new homes and asylums was threatened, however, by the prison and the convent, which were still close at hand. There was a danger that refuges for married women would be used to uphold a husband's authority and preserve a marriage at all costs, even by confining a protesting wife until she yielded to his wishes. Girls' homes could with time become houses mostly occupied by ageing spinsters, who had no intention of going back to the world and instead formed undemanding and undistinguished religious communities with no clear social purpose. Girls' homes were not exempt from a general law which affected many charities. At first they were supported by enthusiastic subscribers who seemed genuinely eager to rescue friendless young people. But at a certain point they became more dependent on benefactors who regarded their charity as a species of patronage and sought places for their own pro-tégées – so that prospects would be bleak for any destitute person without influential protectors, and the shamefaced or respectable poor gained at the expense of people on the margins of society.[100]

For better or worse, the conventional rescue institution for corrupted or endangered girls still tended, in the nineteenth century, to be a home run by a group of resident female staff, ruled by Catholic doctrine, and conscious of traditional notions of sin and penance. One new departure at the start of the twentieth century was the Asilo Mariuccia, opened in a Milanese suburb, inspired by practical members of the Unione Femminile and of the Milanese Committee Against the White Slave Trade. This refuge was designed to be non-confessional, founded on 'civic morality' and humane values, more inclined than other establishments to analyse the social causes of prostitution and its roots in slum housing, incest and the relationships of the workplace or domestic service. It sought to instil discipline and a sense of order and hygiene which seemed oppressive to some of its residents. But it also strove to create a family atmosphere and aimed – as some earlier homes had done – at rehabilitation within worldly society, not at retreat from the world.[101]

Notes

1   Ferrante 1983: 511; D'Amico 1989: 417.
2   Cf. Luke 10: 38–42.
3   Nardi 1989: 13–14, 23–4, 71, 90.
4   *Ibid.*, 107–9.
5   *Ibid.*, 156–7.
6   See, for example, Ferraro 1995: 494; Ferraro 2001, pp. 28–30; Hacke 2004, pp. 35–6, 89–118, 126–30; Pagano 2001, p. 75; Feci 2005: 219–20. For statistics concerning pleas before ecclesias-tical courts for annulments and separations, see Ferrante 1994, p. 903 (Bologna); Ferraro 2001, pp. 28–30 and Hacke 2004, pp. 42–3 (Venice); Chilese 2006: 11–13, 24–5, 28–9, 35 (Verona).
7   For the Jesuits' mission to prostitutes, see O'Malley 1993, pp. 178–85; for a detailed account of Santa Marta, Lazar 2005, pp. 50–69.
8   For the text of 'Divina summaque Dei', 16 February 1543, and subsequent ordinances, see Tacchi Venturi 1950–51, I.ii, docs. 77 and 78, pp. 284–94.
9   Nardi 1989: 71–4; Hacke 2004, pp. 46, 49–51, 141, 143. For attempts at reconciliation in Florence in the late eighteenth century, see Lombardi 2000, pp. 338, 346, 349.
10 Fanucci 1602, pp. 173–5, 179–81; Piazza 1698, I, pp. 203–4; Lazar 2005, pp. 66–9.
11 Francesco Saverio 1953: doc. 6, 221–2; Bendiscioli 1957, pp. 416–17.
12 Eisenach 2004, pp. 157–9, 175–6, 187, 200–1, 217–18.
13 D'Amico 1989: 409, 411.
14 Canosa and Colonnello 1989, p. 119.
15 Polonio 2004, pp. 354–5.
16 Cicogna 1824–40, V, pp. 414–16; Pullan 1971, pp. 391–3; Rosenthal 1992, pp. 131–2; Chojnacka 2001, pp. 125–9.
17 S. Cohen 1992, p. 63.
18 Fragnelli 1988: letters 6–11, 321–3.

19 Cavallo 1980: 142–3; Cavallo 1995, pp. 114–15.
20 Marcolini and Marcon 1985: 103–9, 127; Marcolini 1989, pp. 121–7; Aikema and Meijers 1989, pp. 273–80; McGough 2011, pp. 128–32.
21 Marcolini and Marcon 1985: 110.
22 Vitale 1970: 229–32, 265–72; Ferrante 1983: 501–2, 504–5; D'Amico 1989: 416–17.
23 Ferrante 1983: 511; D'Amico 1989: 417.
24 Ferrante 1983: 512–13; D'Amico 1989: 419–20.
25 G. Martin ed. Parks 1969, pp. 131–2.
26 For 'la mal maritata Cornelia', her husband and her lover, see Bandello ed. Flora 1934, i.53, vol. I, pp. 609–19. See also Martines 1998: 259–60, 284.
27 Rigo 1992–3: 263–5; Rigo 2000, pp. 534–5. Cf. Romano 1996, pp. 151–2.
28 D'Amico 1989: 413–14.
29 Hacke 2004, p. 115.
30 Feci 2005: 213.
31 Borello 2006: 84, 86–7. For the conservatory founded in 1668 by a noble Roman spinster, Livia Vipereschi, see Piazza 1698, I, pp. 197–8.
32 Feci 2005: 212–13.
33 Francesco Saverio 1953: doc. 6, 221–2; S. Cohen 1982: 54.
34 McGough 2011, pp. 90–5.
35 S. Cohen 1992, p. 76.
36 On this subject, see Brundage 1987, p. 513; Cantarella 1991, pp. 235–41.
37 D'Amico 1989: 413–14.
38 Ferrante 1983: 507.
39 Ferrante 1986, p. 85.
40 Hacke 2004, pp. 206–7, 218–22.
41 Feci 2005: 202, 205–6.
42 S. Cohen 1992, pp. 77–8; Lombardi 2000, especially pp. 342–6, and the text of the judgment of the court of the Nunziatura, at pp. 361–7.
43 Cavallo 1980: 142–3; Cavallo 1995, pp. 114–15, 247–8.
44 S. Cohen 1992, p.78.
45 Tacchi Venturi 1950–51, I.ii, pp. 314–20.
46 From a description of the house compiled about 1567, in Francesco Saverio 1953: 219–20.
47 For general studies of conservatories, see especially Groppi 1994 (on Rome) and Terpstra 2005 (on Bologna and Florence).
48 Romanello 1995, p. 73.
49 Pullan 1971, pp. 385–7; Bellettati 1988: 107–9.
50 Terpstra 2010, pp. 37–49, 110–23.
51 Palmio 1701, pp. 3–6; on numbers in the Zitelle, see Pullan 1971, pp. 390–1; Chojnacka 1998: 82. For its art and architecture, Aikema and Meijers 1989, pp. 225–39.
52 Terpstra 2010, pp. 53–4.
53 Francesco Saverio 1953, doc. 6, pp. 218–22. According to Galanti 1786–90, III, p. 136, the house was opened in 1564 and the confraternity was or became known as the Verdi.
54 Vitale 1970: 229–32.
55 Giacomelli 1986, pp. 211–12; Terpstra 2005, pp. 40–3, 77.
56 Romanello 1995, pp. 21–32, 39–40, 45, 98, 103.
57 Groppi 1994, pp. 22–5.
58 Ferrazzi ed. Schutte 1996, pp. 9–10, 22–4, 83, 87–8.
59 Ibid., pp. 58–61; Schutte 2001, pp. 208–11.

60   Ferrazzi ed. Schutte 1996, pp. 15–17, 87–8.
61   Francesco Saverio 1953: doc. 6, 218–22; Romeo 2008, pp. 53, 81.
62   Bellettati 1988: 109.
63   *Constitutioni et regole* 1701, IV.v, p. 21.
64   *Ibid.*, IV.xxxii, p. 32.
65   Camerano 1993: 233–7, 250–2.
66   Ferrazzi ed. Schutte 1996, pp. 31–2, 47–50.
67   Vitale 1970: 229–32, 265–6.
68   Gavitt 2011/2013, pp. 171–6.
69   Terpstra 2010, pp. 48–9, 127–30, 173; Gavitt 2011/2013, p. 184.
70   Russo 1984: 73–6.
71   G. Martin ed. Parks 1969, p. 131.
72   Groppi 1994, pp. 34–5, 68.
73   Terpstra 2005, pp. 40–3, 98.
74   Groppi 1994, pp. 77–83; see p. 81 for the quotation.
75   For examples, Bellettati 1988: 109, 130, 139–40, 144–5; Groppi 1994, pp. 84–5; Romanello 1995, pp. 77, 91.
76   Bellettati 1988: 125–9.
77   *Ibid.*, 120–2, 124–5, 142.
78   White Mario ed. Infusino 1978, pp. 113–42; Valenzi 1995, pp. 24–6.
79   Galanti 1786–90, III, pp. 137–8.
80   Bellettati 1988: 141–2, 146.
81   Groppi 1994, pp. 29–31, 143–4; Chojnacka 1998: 82.
82   Aikema and Meijers 1989, p. 234.
83   For the regimes at two Florentine conservatories, see Gavitt 2011/2013, pp. 177–82, 185–8.
84   Zarri 1994, pp. 260, 264–8; Romanello 1995, pp. 52–8, 167–79. For the regimes in Roman conservatories, see Groppi 1994, pp. 111–18, 124, 135–9.
85   Bellettati 1988: 109–11.
86   *Constitutioni et regole* 1701, V.lvi, lxxii, pp. 49–50, 53–5. Cf. Romanello 1995, pp. 95–6.
87   Terpstra 2010, p. 57.
88   *Ibid.*, pp. 60–79.
89   Ciammitti *et al.* 1980, pp. 471–5, 477, 481, 485–8; Ciammitti 1986, pp. 118, 131; Groppi 1994, pp. 200–1, 205–6, 243–62.
90   Bellettati 1988: 110–11, 132–3.
91   Terpstra 2005, pp. 257–8, 263, 266–7.
92   Bellettati 1988: 111.
93   Piazza 1698, I, pp. 181–4.
94   Groppi 1994, p. 152.
95   Romanello 1995, pp. 84–8.
96   Pullan 1971, p. 390; Ciammitti *et al.* 1980, pp. 485–8; Ciammitti 1986, p. 131; Camerano 1993, p. 258, n. 60; Groppi 1994, pp. 216–20, 225–6, 227–31; Romanello 1995, p. 78; Lazar 2005, p. 94.
97   Groppi 1994, p. 224.
98   Pullan 1971, pp. 389–90; Chojnacka 1998: 86–7.
99   Camerano 1993: 248–50, 252–3.
100   On this theme, see Cavallo 1991, pp. 46–62, and her study of early modern Turin (Cavallo 1995).
101   Buttafuoco 1985, pp. 25–36; Gibson 1986, pp. 78–84.

7

Foundlings and orphans:
an introduction

In the late medieval and early modern centuries, organised charities were much concerned with protecting the honour of women and girls and, incidentally, the reputation of the parents, husbands and brothers expected to take care of their morals. Among the candidates for help were young women of respectable background, innocents who, out of ill-luck or naivety rather than depravity, had become pregnant outside marriage. Some had trusted in lovers' false promises; others were victims of rape or of casual couplings with passing strangers; some were servants ill-protected against the sexual demands of employers or fellow domestics. Few misadventures could ruin a single woman more thoroughly than an unwanted pregnancy for which a putative father denied responsibility, especially if he retaliated by attacking her good name and alleging that she had lain with other men. A child born out of wedlock could destroy a mother's marriage prospects, render her unemployable as a domestic servant, perhaps force her into some form of concubinage or prostitution. Fear of disgrace could drive an isolated young woman, concealing her condition, to desperate measures, perhaps to clumsy attempts at abortion or the murder by violence or exposure of a newly born infant. These acts not only threatened the earthly lives of children but also appeared to jeopardise their souls, since no-one could be sure that a frightened mother, exhausted by solitary and unassisted labour, would see to the baptism of the child she was trying to conceal. Perhaps the most respectable woman, clinging to her reputation and terrified of family retribution, was in danger of becoming the greatest criminal, a callous child-murderer.

In the fourteenth and fifteenth centuries, by establishing licensed brothels and official vice districts, communities acknowledged the principle that the sale of sexual services, though deplorable, could be tolerated so long as it was regulated and confined to particular places. By developing foundling wards they conceded that anonymous child abandonment, though regrettable, could be allowed in extreme circumstances so long as infants were left at city hospitals and the risk to life reduced. Both processes produced victims in need of rescue and redemption. It was important that tolerance be balanced by action to protect the weak. Abandonment separated children from their natural mothers; the task of rescuing them fell to charities, which took up, at least in a rough and ready fashion, the task of feeding and educating large numbers of foundlings.

Foundling hospitals would prove to be one of the largest and least selective charities in any city.[1] Most were designed to receive children given up by their parents, either because they were illegitimate and it would be scandalous to keep them, or because their fathers and mothers, though married, claimed to be too poor to maintain them. Should hospitals be overwhelmed by numbers, they might try to accept illegitimate children only, awarding them the highest priority and, where practical, returning legitimate children to their blood parents. Foundling hospitals generally strove to protect a single mother's honour and give her another chance in life by relieving her of an unwanted child; to give the infant a better chance of surviving, by making the process of abandonment less dangerous; to save the mother from the threat of family vengeance; to ensure that the child was baptised; to make certain that families and communities were not scandalised by the presence of women openly rearing children outside wedlock. The higher the value placed on formal marriage, the sharper the distinction between the married and the unmarried state, the more unthinkable it became that single women or unwed couples should rear base-born children themselves.

Foundling hospitals were not intended to complement city brothels to provide prostitutes with opportunities for disposing of unwanted children. Indeed, in Sicily in 1750, it was suggested that prostitutes should not be allowed to abandon children, on the grounds that foundling hospitals were designed to protect honour, and prostitutes had none.[2] No doubt hospitals were sometimes used by prostitutes, whatever the rules decreed. But in principle they were designed to save respectable girls, those who had made 'a little mistake' (as Fra Bono once put it in Milan), from sinking into the 'evil life' after being publicly disgraced for bastard-bearing, and to rescue their children from criminal attempts on their lives.[3]

Foundling hospitals as a lesser evil

Arguably, foundling hospitals, or rather the forms of child abandonment which they encouraged, stood for a lesser evil. Organised abandonment, an abdication of responsibility by natural parents, was justified by the hope of avoiding much worse disasters such as abortion, infanticide, the shaming of families who might resort to 'honour' killings, the consignment of innocent souls to Limbo. Like most flirtations with a so-called lesser evil, it produced unintended results. At worst, it may, through poor organisation and inadequate funding, have done little more than replace individual murders with institutional manslaughter, the large-scale killing of young children by neglect, disease and insanitary conditions. As the great Malthus was to write in the early nineteenth century:

> it may perhaps be truly said, that, if a person wished to check population, and were not solicitous about the means, he could not propose a more effectual measure, than the establishment of a sufficient number of foundling hospitals, unlimited as to their reception of children ... An occasional child-murder from false shame, is saved at a very high price, if it can only be done by the sacrifice of some of the best and most useful feelings of the human heart ...

... by encouraging natural mothers to part from their children. His remarks were immediately inspired by the hospitals of St Petersburg and Moscow, but were no doubt intended to apply to foundling hospitals in general.[4]

Like many of the more ambitious Catholic charities, foundling hospitals were concerned with saving souls. Their primary concern, though, was not with rescuing adults and adolescents from the eternal consequences of their sinful behaviour but with saving newborn children from the hopelessness inflicted by death without baptism. For the Church's doctrine stated that only this sacrament, properly administered, could remove the taint of sin inherited from Adam's fall and admit the recipient to the Church, outside which there was no salvation. The guidance of the gospel-writers could hardly have been firmer. '[U]nless a man is born through water and the Spirit, he cannot enter the kingdom of God.'[5] 'He who believes and is baptised will be saved; he who does not believe will be condemned.'[6] Answering doubters who saw no point in baptising children too young to believe, Pope Innocent III had pronounced: 'It is unthinkable that all the little children who die every day in such numbers should perish without God in his mercy, who desires the death of no-one, providing the means of saving them.'[7] The faith of the Church or of adult Christians could surely be imparted to babies; defiled through no fault of their own by the sin of a common ancestor, they could also be rescued by the faith of others at baptism, without having to give their personal consent or to understand the ceremony. But should they die unbaptised, they would be denied burial in church and probably be interred in cellars or under the floors of houses, or under the eaves of churches, in the desperate hope that they might profit from descending rain water blessed by heaven.[8]

It was true that from the twelfth and thirteenth centuries, eminent theologians had departed from the doctrine that the souls of unbaptised infants were destined for everlasting fire. Bonaventura and Aquinas had held that they would suffer no physical or mental pain and would find themselves, not cast down into the lower depths of hell, but rather sent to its edge or border, called by Alexander of Hales the 'lembus inferni', which was also the abode of righteous folk who had died before Christ's coming. There, perhaps, they would even enjoy 'natural happiness'. But it seemed certain that they would never be among the blessed and would never see God.[9] As Virgil, Dante's guide, explains,

> Below there in the deep, a region lies
> Made sad by darkness only, not by pain,
> And where no shrieks resound, but only sighs;
> And there dwell I, with guiltless infants, ta'en
> By nipping fangs of death, untimely soon,
> Ere they were washed from sinful human stain...[10]

Even if Limbo was not a place of torment, its sighs and gloom were still to be feared and shunned. An important function of foundling hospitals was to offer spiritual survival where worldly prospects were poor, to ensure that baptism was properly administered, if need be conditionally, to unwanted and often sickly children in imminent danger of death.

Child killing by parents had been condemned as parricide, first by Christian writers and then, in the fourth century, by Roman law, when fathers lost the power of life and death over their children.[11] Some babies in any age were suffocated or drowned at birth or otherwise violently killed to conceal their existence and escape disgrace. At least as often, perhaps, they were exposed in remote and dangerous places in the expectation that they would fall victim to animals or birds of prey or starve to death. Organised abandonment, however, would make it possible to give children up with a clear intention of preserving their lives, by handing them over in comparative safety to the servants of a hospital.

To allow a child to be born, and afterwards surrender it responsibly, could seem less evil than to attempt contraception or procure a miscarriage by using 'poisons of sterility'. It was preferable to forms of birth control which qualified as sodomy, to such excesses as anal intercourse or interrupted coitus. Eminent theologians, including Jerome and Augustine, their remarks enshrined in canon law collections, had pronounced that contraception, interference with the sacred process of generation, amounted to killing a potential human being.[12] Abortion was dangerous both morally and physically, doubly wicked if it meant expelling a foetus believed to be harbouring a rational soul, and doing so to conceal sexual misconduct or limit family size. After the Council of Trent, the Catholic hierarchy strove to impress upon the faithful the gravity of this offence. Those who confessed to trying to procure miscarriages or prevent conceptions might find themselves, at least in theory, unable to obtain absolution from their regular confessors and discover that their cases had been reserved to the bishop or even – in 1588–91 – to the pope himself. True, that law was not rigorously enforced, but the Church's disapproval was emphatic, and this was no ordinary sin.[13]

'Responsible' abandonment could well seem the least wicked way out of the misfortunes created by sinful behaviour. It was broadly defined in instructions which Pope Gregory XIII issued to parish priests in 1584. Let them warn their flocks to abandon children only in the face of 'great and pressing need [*magna urgente necessitate*]', a phrase that could well refer both to the fear of shame and to the threat of starvation. If forced to abandon, they ought, if possible, to have the children baptised and to hang round their necks tickets or certificates of baptism giving their names. They must leave children only at foundling hospitals or other suitable places and not dump them at crossroads or on public ways and in other dangerous spots. The hospital's clerks must preserve the baptismal certificate in the hope that one day, in happier circumstances, this document would help the parents to recognise and recover the child (some parents had their own ideas and left objects or tokens to help possible future identification).[14] For their part, most hospitals would provide receptacles in which children could be left safely and anonymously, and instruct workers to look out for new arrivals. Beyond that reception point, children would pass into the hands of an institution which was sometimes praised (especially by its own staff) as a marvellous example of Christian charity. It could also, though, be seen as a dark tower in which ill-favoured infants began a losing battle for survival at the hands of ill-trained nurses who could provide no substitute for proper parental care.

Perhaps, viewed dispassionately, organised child abandonment was nothing more sinister than a rational process of redistributing infants – of 'circulating children' or 'delegating motherhood' from blood parents reluctant to keep them to foster parents who, with the aid of wages paid by charities, would be better equipped to bring them up. The system might work well or badly, but was neutral in itself, and should not be regarded as intrinsically evil, even as a lesser evil compared with other choices. Some scholars have warned historians against modern Western-style projections, against yielding to assumptions derived from their own culture that children are best raised by blood parents in affectionate homes.[15] Was abandonment callous when, given the likelihood of infant deaths, parents hesitated to bond with babies? In Italian communities, even children of high status were taken from their mothers and nurtured, often outside the parental home, for periods of up to two or three years. This practice has itself been called a 'form of institutionalised abandonment' on the part of parents who could love their children but not feel for them.[16] During the middle ages, child abandonment was seldom treated as a crime, unless it was clearly life-threatening. The custom had its critics, but they did not dominate the debate.[17]

Against this, however, the abandonment of illegitimate, adulterine or incestuous children could always be seen as a sorry consequence of a mortal sin. It could be argued, too, that impoverished married couples who abandoned infants were shirking their obligation, not just to procreate children, but to rear them. Officials suspected, in any case, that some parents were abandoning, not from necessity but from greed, thinking of their own comfort or foisting on hard-pressed hospitals children they could well have supported themselves. Abandonment might not be the worst conceivable sin, so long as there was a clear intention to preserve the child's life, but it was never desirable, and could at best be excused, not approved.

The vocabulary: foundlings and orphans

Towards 1508, discussing the general hospital of Milan, the administrator Antonio Gilino broached the subject of deserted infants who 'at the beginning of their lives are exposed to death by wayward parents who have begotten bastards and are bent on concealing their misdeeds, or who on account of either poverty or greed are placed by their parents outside the embrace of parental power and love'.[18] Among the commonest names for such children were *esposti, espositi, proietti, getadi* or *gettatelli*, words of classical Latin descent which described the act of casting infants out, exposing them to the vagaries of fortune and the kindness or cruelty of strangers. Sometimes, too, the children were called *trovatelli*, a word closer to the French *enfant trouvé* or the English 'foundling', which emphasised rescue rather than rejection; in the second half of the nineteenth century, *trovatelli* would eventually become the term used in parliamentary debates and official circulars.[19] Many had indeed been found in public or private places, but, as will appear later, there were other ways of arriving at a foundling hospital.

In principle, foundlings differed from orphans, who were the children of married parents and had lost at least one. Orphans stood higher in social and moral hierarchies because they had been born in wedlock and their fathers were known. Foundlings' fathers had not acknowledged them, given them surnames or patronymics, conferred respectability; until about 1800, most male foundlings took standard surnames or nicknames from the hospital which had raised them. To describe them all as bastards would have been inaccurate, and some contemporaries shrank from doing so. The people of Bologna referred to their foundling hospital as 'the Bastardini'. But the governors of the hospital in seventeenth-century Brescia refused to have the name of their register changed from 'the Book of Exposed Children' to 'the Book of Natural Children' on the grounds that some exposed children were undoubtedly legitimate as well as natural.[20] For all this, there was often a reasonable presumption, in the absence of contrary evidence, that newborn children abandoned anonymously had been doubly conceived in sin – not only in lust, as were all human beings, but also in 'illicit sexual congress' outside marriage. Even if they were not base-born, it could be said that their married parents had betrayed their own improvidence by giving the children up, revealing their failure to discipline themselves and control the size of their families by abstinence from sex, so that poverty, or corrupt motives such as laziness or greed drove them to abandon.[21] Both foundlings and orphans, however, could be received in general or foundling hospitals, which, after hearing pleas on their behalf, would agree to accept some orphans or half-orphans and some children whose fathers had gone for soldiers or sailors or deserted their families for other reasons. In 1488, the Venetian Senate described the hospital of the Pietà, designed 150 years earlier to receive abandoned children, as 'a refuge for many, indeed innumerable orphans and other children of wretchedly poor parents who have no means of supporting them'.[22]

'Abandoned children' or 'unwanted children' are possibly the most acceptable modern terms, replacing the old-fashioned 'foundling'. But Italians could mean other things by the verb *abbandonare*. Two Florentine charities of the mid-sixteenth century, the hospices for *fanciulli abbandonati* and *fanciulle abbandonate*, were actually small and selective orphanages – only eighty-eight girls passed through the female institution during its first four years (admittedly some people deposited children anonymously at the boys' home, which was soft-hearted enough to accept them).[23] In the late eighteenth century, the royal visitor to Calabria in the far south, Giuseppe Maria Galanti, wrote of children being 'abandoned', not at the moment when parents surrendered them to the care of the community, but rather at the time when the community ceased to pay nurses and foster parents to support them. 'They are abandoned at the age of seven', he said of children at Crotone; children at Catanzaro would at the same age either be adopted or become beggars or tramps; children at Nicastro would receive no public maintenance after 'the time of suckling'.[24]

The spread of foundling homes

In early medieval Europe, ecclesiastical councils, bishops, theologians and other pundits acknowledged and to some extent condoned child abandonment. They sought to regulate it, if only by prescribing that infants found exposed should be brought to churches, that priests should try to find them nurses and perhaps adoptive parents, and that, after a certain length of time, the natural parents should not be entitled to reclaim their offspring. Children, authorities warned, should never be left in unfrequented places where no-one would pick them up. But few or no organisations undertook to bring up foundlings, provide them with milk, educate them, or arrange their adoption.

Their fate depended on the personal kindness of strangers, or on something more sinister – the readiness of less humane people to use them as slaves or prostitutes.[25]

From the mid-twelfth century, in a few important cities at least, institutions became involved in the care of foundlings. In Milan in 1158, a lay confraternity [*consorzio*] joined the new hospital of the Brolo in assisting, not only the sick poor, but also *expositi infantes*.[26] By the mid-thirteenth century, the general hospital of Siena was borrowing money and selling property to pay the women who nursed the orphans and the *prohiecti* and *expositi* in its care. By 1298, it had established a foundling home [*Domus pro gittatellis*], a division of the hospital which was really a women's and children's wing.[27] In 1305, the bishop of Perugia credited the confraternity of the Blessed Virgin Mary with establishing 'the house of the Misericordia, in which pilgrims, abandoned children, and poor and sick persons would be received' – a fair description of the threefold interests of many urban general hospitals.[28] According to a legend developed and illustrated during the fifteenth century, the papal hospital of Santo Spirito in Rome was Innocent III's response to horrifying evidence of the murder of unwanted children. The hospital was in fact dedicated to all forms of hospitality. But its rule, evolving from the thirteenth century onwards, did declare that one of its works of mercy would be the task of raising orphaned and abandoned children, who, by the 1290s, were being expressly mentioned in papal documents.[29] About 1350, the hospital of Rodolfo Tanzi at Parma was looking after a hundred patients, seventy *esposti* under the age of ten, and fourteen young children whom it had sent out to nurses.[30]

In the fourteenth and fifteenth centuries, it was usual for several charities and religious houses in the same city to care for foundlings and orphans: some took charge of sucklings, some of weaned children, and some of both. With time, however, these tasks usually fell to one local hospital, often the largest. Smaller hospices sometimes merged with a bigger organisation, as the Brolo and San Celso became part of the Ospedale Maggiore in Milan in 1458.[31] Episcopal and papal legislation granted a monopoly of local foundling care to the Scaletta hospital of Imola, in 1477 and 1486.[32]

In other cities more specialised institutions began to concentrate heavily on foundlings and orphans. At Pisa, small hospitals were absorbed around 1400 into a larger body, Santo Spirito dei Trovatelli.[33] In 1336, a merchant of Venice made a bequest 'for God and my soul' to 'the boys and girls who have been cast out [*getadi*] and are known as the Pietà'. This hospital was inspired by a Franciscan from Assisi, Friar Petruccio, who 'considered himself father, son and servant of the poor', begged and pleaded on their behalf, and began operations by renting seventeen tiny houses to shelter them. Soon the male and female companies he recruited were looking after most of the foundlings of Venice; in 1360 the governors obtained a bigger grain allowance from the State by arguing that other charities once accustomed to receive foundlings were now sending them to the Pietà. The hospital acquired a special status when, removed from parochial control and exempted from paying parish dues, it became directly subject to the chief priest of St Mark's.[34]

In contrast, the Innocenti in Florence, named after the infants of Bethlehem massacred on Herod's orders, sprang from a rich man's benefaction and was planned with greater deliberation. It developed as a children's asylum after the pioneering hospital for sick people, Santa Maria Nuova, declined a bequest from Francesco Maria Datini (d. 1410), a merchant of Prato who had long been receiving advice from Lapo Mazzei, the hospital's notary, on the application of his fortune to charitable ends. Datini's legacy would have involved the institution in caring for the 'boys and girls who are called *gittatelli*' and transformed it into a general hospital. Instead, an association of silk merchants and manufacturers, the Arte della Seta, one of the seven 'major' professional corporations of Florence, prevailed on the commune of Prato to allow them to succeed to the merchant's legacy of one thousand gold florins and supervise the work in question. The new charity opened in 1445 and eventually took over two smaller Florentine hospitals with similar interests – San Gallo a few years later, Santa Maria della Scala in 1536.[35]

An ideal, 'complete' hospital would be divided into three parts: a reception ward; an organisation for placing babies, infants and young children with wet nurses and dry nurses whom the hospital paid to look after them in the nurses' own homes; conservatories for educating and training older boys and girls and providing for them when they left. Not all hospitals, though, were 'complete' in this sense, and they developed at different speeds. The general hospital at Sulmona in the Abruzzi (established in 1320) set up its foundling nursery only in 1532 and added its conservatory for growing girls as late as 1630.[36]

Organisation and revenue

In some cities, general administrative responsibility for foundling homes and their resources passed in the late middle ages from clerics and religious to confraternities or other governing bodies composed mainly of lay persons. Priests, though, still taught older children and continued to serve as chaplains. Monks in Bologna in the mid-fifteenth century, bent on joining stricter, less worldly congregations, gave up foundling care to lay confraternities; several of these combined under the name of Santa Maria degli Angeli (a brotherhood favoured by notaries) to run the hospital of San Procolo. Similar to Florence's Innocenti and probably modelled upon it, this received at least three hundred foundlings a year in the late fifteenth century.[37] Female convents, too, gave up their foundlings, who could give rise to scandal. One Venetian house, Sant' Angelo di Contorta, suffered from rumours that the infants it was still looking after, despite the existence of the Pietà, had not been left by outsiders but born in the convent. Were they the offspring of unchaste nuns and their admirers? Some sisters were rehoused, the rest not replaced; the last member of the dwindling community died in 1518.[38]

However, the laicising trend was neither universal nor uninterrupted. In Rome, a cleric, subject immediately to the pope himself, presided over the hospital of Santo Spirito; in the early sixteenth century, under the Medici, he began to take the title of Commendatore and to rank in the clerical hierarchy below bishops but above abbots. In the late sixteenth century, responsibility for the women's conservatory fell to a new order of cloistered nuns, the sisters of Santa Tecla, who were recruited from the foundlings themselves and resided in the hospital with their charges. Their regime lasted until about 1660, when serious doubts arose about their competence and integrity, and the order, its authority greatly reduced, was allowed to die out over the next forty years.[39]

Hospitals and foundling homes in northern and central Italy depended, as did other major charities, on legacies, donations, subscriptions, and alms gathered by collectors or deposited in poor boxes. Some men and women committed themselves to the service of a hospital and made over their property to it on the understanding that it would care for them when they ceased to be helpers and themselves became dependants. Generous benefactions enabled some institutions to acquire extensive landed estates outside a city, houses and commercial properties within the walls, and holdings in public debt which paid interest, albeit rather erratically, and rose and fell in value according to the market's fluctuations. Occasionally, too, in later centuries, hospitals would gain from transfers of ecclesiastical assets, including the revenues of suppressed religious houses, as at Cosenza in northern Calabria in the 1780s.[40] Foundlings' maintenance rarely depended on direct taxation or on any equivalent of the English poor rate. But governments did subsidise foundling homes in a piecemeal fashion: in the fifteenth and sixteenth centuries, Venice's Pietà received allowances of flour, firewood and wine by virtue of Senate resolutions, shared in the proceeds of some judicial fines, and was entitled to sell or hire out the use of one boat in each of the city's ferry stations.[41]

Several hospitals, since they often had ample property but little ready cash, solved some of their problems by acting as savings banks. In principle, a hospital could help ordinary people by accepting small sums of money for safe keeping; it could then help itself by drawing on these deposits in the hope that there would be no sudden and general demand for their restitution. The Innocenti in Florence set up small savings accounts, mostly for women, many of them from the surrounding countryside, and from 1545 onwards paid depositors 5 per cent interest. Hospitals in Naples and Rome engaged in similar operations, creating with varying success financial institutions from which they could themselves borrow. Their landed property, offered as a guarantee, inspired some confidence in their banks and they sometimes succeeded in devising a much-needed paper currency and in enabling customers to make payments quickly and conveniently by transfers on their books. But rumours of mounting debts could shake that confidence and provoke runs on the banks, which further damaged the hospitals' finances and blighted their reputation for probity and sound management.[42]

Struggling to balance their books, reluctant to provide a free child-minding service for ever-growing numbers of improvident or immoral people, bursarial figures dreamed of recovering some of the costs from the parents – not perhaps from penniless maidservants or village girls, but from putative fathers, or parents who had decided to reclaim their children. Their chances of tracing parents who had abandoned anonymously and had no wish to be reunited with their children were seldom robust; to pursue them too obviously would frustrate one of the aims of the charity by discouraging 'responsible' abandonment and tempting the parents into criminal acts. And parents would be less disposed to return for their children if they were liable, when they did so, to be presented with a bill for their keep. By the late eighteenth century, the general inclination was not to hold parents strictly to account.[43] But appeals could be made to consciences. In 1752, the priors of the Misericordia in Perugia attached a box to the outside wall of the hospital church to receive 'secret reimbursements [*occulte Compensationi*]' from parents of abandoned children who did not wish to declare themselves.[44]

A few hospitals began to concentrate on child care when increasing expenditure on children threatened to swallow virtually all their revenues and leave little for other uses. Such was the complaint of Padua's Casa di Dio in 1487; during the sixteenth century both this house and San Marcello in Vicenza became specialised foundling homes.[45] By 1540 Parma, too, was maintaining an Ospizio degli Esposti for charity children alone.[46] Santa Maria del Ponte in Arezzo, founded in the thirteenth century 'to take in poor travellers and wretched persons', functioned chiefly as a foundling hospital between the sixteenth and the eighteenth centuries.[47]

Some bodies, however, went to the opposite extreme and would do little for children abandoned locally other than pay for their removal to other places. At the close of the eighteenth century, Galanti complained that many hospitals in the southern kingdom were sending almost all local foundlings to the Annunziata in Naples, condemning them to gruelling journeys which often proved fatal, and diverting income intended for them to other uses which the hospitals found more appealing.[48]

There could be advantages in not specialising narrowly but rather in combining medical care and child care. Some hospitals managed to do both, or to exploit children for the benefit of patients. Older foundling children, especially girls, were a source of cheap labour. They could be put to rough work in the wards if not to skilled nursing, and be employed in cooking, cleaning and laundering for the sick. In several hospitals, unmarried women who had given birth in the wards were conscripted as wet nurses to feed other people's children. San Giovanni, a hospital for sick people in Turin, agreed to admit foundlings in the sixteenth century on the understanding that they could eventually be employed in the hospital and enable it to economise on staff wages.[49]

Foundlings, though, generally proved to be, en masse, the most expensive dependants of general hospitals. Their wet nurses, dry nurses, foster parents, schools, conservatories and dowries often claimed the lion's share of the revenues, even though many children died before reaching adolescence and even though nurses were wretchedly paid. At Imola in the mid-sixteenth century, the chief hospital contained two sick wards, one with fourteen beds for men, the other with ten for women, and probably at least two patients to a bed. At that time, the number of foundlings and orphans on the books was usually between 150 and 200, and exceeded 200 in the early seventeenth century; many of the youngest were constantly being overtaken by death but swiftly replaced by new arrivals. Accounts for 1624–5 showed that the administrators had spent 2,562 lire within the hospital, but nearly twice as much on the *baliatico*, the operation of recruiting and paying for nurses.[50] Expenditure followed a similar pattern at Santo Spirito in Rome in 1662, when the foundling hospital absorbed at least 30,000 scudi a year (about half of this sum went to the female conservatory), the hospital for sick persons only 13,000.[51] In the 1730s and 1740s, the shaky finances of the institution came under scrutiny from a papal inquiry. It seemed that in 1724–9 expenditure on the sick had accounted for only 17 per cent of outgoings, while 26 per cent went on 'nurses and children', 20 per cent on the conservatory for 'maidens', and another 8 per cent on dowries for girls who married with the hospital's help. Subsequent financial reforms boosted income, pruned expenditure, and reduced unwise reliance on the bank of Santo Spirito. But these measures did not much alter the distribution of spending. Between 1738 and 1748, 24 per cent of expenditure was on nurses' wages and allowances and 23 per cent on maintaining adolescent girls and older women, while 20 per cent reached the hospital for the sick.[52]

At the Misericordia in Perugia between 1753 and 1756, 16.9 per cent of expenditure was on the sick and 42.6 per cent on nursing foundlings.[53] At the hospital of the Annunziata at Sulmona, foundlings accounted for 27.3 per cent of expenditure in 1728, but 52.4 per cent in 1789 and a full two-thirds in 1792 (much of the increase could be attributed to a royal decree of 1762, which obliged the hospital to accept foundlings from all three provinces of the Abruzzi).[54] Galanti's scathing description of the vast and chaotic hospital of the Annunziata in Naples, c.1789, suggested that it spent 5,000 ducats annually on its church (which had recently been lavishly restored), 9,000 on its wards for feverish and injured patients, 23,000 on infant care, 'which is the principal undertaking', and 12,000 on the female conservatory. Little or nothing was done to educate and train older foundling boys.[55]

Eighteenth-century reforms

Most of the great foundling hospitals, or foundling homes within general hospitals, were creations of the late middle ages and the Renaissance. After 1500, many new establishments for children were erected, but they were generally concerned with boys and girls in moral danger rather than with infants – with orphans, waifs and strays, beggar children, the daughters of prostitutes. Efforts were eventually made to improve the arrangements for foundlings during the eighteenth century. The distribution of foundling hospitals was haphazard, since it had hitherto depended on local initiatives rather than on central State planning and had overburdened a number of metropolitan hospitals, which attracted far more children than they could care for effectively. Within the Papal States, attempts were made to reduce the demands on Santo Spirito, to increase the endowments of other important hospitals such as the Misericordia in Perugia, and to restrict admissions by forbidding married couples to abandon children.[56] During the 1780s, hospitals in Cosenza, capital of northern Calabria in the kingdom of Naples, improved dramatically after the terrible earthquake of 1783, despite the situation of Cosenza itself – clinging to a steep slope, hemmed in by hills and mountains, inhaling a cloud of noxious vapour rising from the river Crate. Now a royal hospital, the foundling home of Santa Teresa benefited by the transfer of revenues from five suppressed religious houses, while the court paid the wages of wet nurses and foster parents throughout the province from central funds.[57]

Some regions, however, had not built foundling hospitals. In the towns of southern Calabria there were few central points where unwanted children could be deposited, though the provincial capital, Catanzaro, apparently maintained one. At Monteleone, a town of some seven thousand souls which Galanti called 'the wretched emporium of an impoverished region', it was usual to leave infants 'in a midwife's house, or that of some gentleman, or on the roads'. He believed that the region had suffered from the suppression of many monasteries to which it had been usual to bring them.[58] Official assistance seldom did more than pay for children to be nursed and fostered up to a certain age, perhaps three, perhaps seven, and, where possible, arrange for them to be adopted. The local mayor and corporation would try to raise the money if they had to, but there were other possibilities. Lay religious congregations and confraternities, notorious in the eyes of rationalising reformers for indulging in 'superstitious' activities, for their enjoyment of dressing up and processing if not of flagellating themselves, were supposed to escape dissolution only if they did something socially useful and undertook either to care for foundlings or to bury the dead. Some chose the foundlings, but received little guidance in looking after them. Their performance proved to be no better than that of the mayors, though they may have raised some false expectations that the infants would now be treated more generously and have caused abandonments to increase for no sound reason.[59]

One or two communities, including Squillace on the Ionian coast, were able to draw on Monti di Esposti, charitable funds formed from gifts and legacies intended for foundlings, and similar to other Monti designed to finance marriages or funerals.[60] Here and there, too, a cathedral chapter would take up some of the burden. Exceptionally, the Cassa Sagra, restoring some of the resources it had removed by suppressions and confiscations, would finance nursing and pay a small lump sum to adoptive parents, as it did at Catanzaro.[61] But Galanti complained that local authorities were losing their power to spend on local needs at exactly the moment when they most needed it, and that communities were forfeiting pious bequests intended to benefit local people. Nicastro, for example, had been accustomed to spend two hundred ducats a year, but was now permitted only fifty, scarcely enough to pay messengers and minor officials: hence 'foundlings are allowed to perish and the aqueducts and roads are not repaired – a thing which, more than anything else, promises to turn Calabria into a wilderness'.[62] Conservatories and seminaries designed to educate and protect older foundling children were largely unknown, though some local girls may have had access to one of the five conservatories at Reggio di Calabria – perhaps the ramshackle Verginelle, which had once been a refuge for repentant female sinners and was now open to orphans.[63] Reggio maintained one of the few hospitals in the province which concerned itself with foundlings. But its obligations were confined to supplying medicines to city foundlings or their nurses, and the task of otherwise supporting the 'little bastards', both of Reggio and of its surroundings, fell to the overburdened commune.[64]

Conclusion

Citizens might build institutions for coping with unfortunate children without achieving greater humanity or efficiency. Indeed, in the opinion of some historians, foundling hospitals interfered disastrously with more informal practices which were working perfectly well. So carelessly, it is said, did they treat their charges that they may only have substituted a lingering death for actual child murder. Allegedly, like the beggars' hospitals of seventeenth-century France, in Foucault's famous thesis, they dealt with a social problem by sweeping it out of sight and mind behind institutional walls. 'The intricate, gentle complexities of the systems of transfer developed in ancient and medieval Europe were transformed into a single technique of disposal'.[65]

Fair comparisons, however, are difficult to make: how much is really known about the practice of child abandonment in the middle ages, and how successful were medieval people in finding nurses for sucklings or adoptive parents for deserted children? Medieval Europe lies beyond the reach of statisticians attempting to establish the mortality rates of abandoned children. By the sixteenth century, foundling hospitals were indicting themselves by compiling records which revealed all too starkly the number of deaths in their care. They were not, whatever their other faults, engaged in a great internment of outcast children: reception wards for babies and conservatories for older girls were enclosed, but infants and young children spent several years in the homes of their foster mothers and older boys went out to apprenticeships in towns or to work on farms. Furthermore, as Galanti's comments showed, foundling hospitals did not dominate every region. It was possible for a less centralised system, slightly reminiscent of medieval informality, to survive in remote provinces such as southern Calabria and still be in place in the late eighteenth century. From reading Galanti's notes, however, it would be hard to be sure which was the better system, since both were flawed. His harshest comments were on arrangements pivoted round the Annunziata hospital in Naples, which was receiving hundreds of children who would have been better cared for nearer to the places from which they came. But he was impressed by the relative efficiency of one new hospital, at Cosenza, which was designed to serve the population of a whole province, and provided some evidence that foundling hospitals were not to be utterly condemned.

Notes

1   For general accounts of foundling hospitals, see the wide-ranging treatises of Hügel 1863 and Lallemand 1885. For more recent surveys, see Hunecke 1985, Pullan 1989, Kertzer 1993, Hunecke 1994. Important collections of specialised essays include E.A., and also Panter-Brick and Smith 2000. For an illuminating critical discussion, see the debate between Tilly, Fuchs, Kertzer and Hansel 1992.

2   Kertzer 1993, p. 95.

3   For Fra Bono's remark, see above, Chapter 5, n. 51.

4   Malthus 1826/1996, ii.3, vol. I, p. 313.

5   John 3:5.

6   Mark 16:16.

7   For his letter, 'Maiores Ecclesiae causas', see the decretals of Gregory IX, III, tit.42, c.3, in C.J.C., II, col. 646.

8   Colucci 2003: 429–30.

9   For a recent concise history of the doctrine of Limbo, see Carpin 2006.

10 Dante trans. Sayers and Reynolds 1949–62, II, *Purgatory*, VII: lines 28–33, p. 119.

11 Noonan 1986, pp. 85–6, 91.

12 See Noonan 1986, pp. 98–101, 136, 168–9, 172–4, 178; also Noonan 1970a, pp. 15–21. On the sin of Onan, see Noonan 1986, pp. 34–6, 101–2.

13 Noonan 1970; Riddle 1996; Terpstra 2010, pp. 84–99; Christopoulos 2012.
14 Quoted in De Rosa 1978: 11 and Pagano 1979: 355.
15 For the general argument, see Boswell 1989; Panter-Brick 2000.
16 De Mause 1976, p. 34. For a more optimistic view of the affective ties between parents and children, even very young ones, see Haas 1998.
17 See Boswell 1989, pp. 147–8, 157–62, 164, 167–70, 325, 327–8.
18 Gilinus 1508, c.xxiv, 'De Expositis Infantibus'.
19 Di Bello 1997: 331.
20 Pullan 1989, p. 18.
21 Cf. Boswell 1989, pp. 81, 159, 161–2.
22 Cecchetti 1885: 142–3; Grandi 1997, p. 98.
23 Terpstra 2005, pp. 46, 48–51, 52–4, 88.
24 Galanti ed. Placanica 1992, pp. 109, 126, 154, 252–3.
25 Boswell 1989, pp. 172–4, 217–18, 222–3, 277, 349, 360–1. For criticisms of Boswell's view of these informal arrangements, see Tilly *et al.* 1992: 12 (Fuchs), 17–18 (Kertzer), 19–20 (Ransel).
26 Albini 1993, pp. 36–9.
27 Martellucci 2001: 10–11, 14, 15, 23, 28–9, 118.
28 Calzola 2003, pp. 105–7; Tittarelli *et al.* 2003, pp. 66–8.
29 See Clause 41 of the version of the rule in Migne P.L. 217, coll. 1130–58, at col.1146; Clause 36 in the version given in De Angelis 1960–2, I, pp. 259, 269; Bolton 1994: 157–8; Presciutti 2011: 762–3, 780.
30 Albini 1993, pp. 139–40.
31 Hunecke 1989, pp. 71–3; Albini 1993, pp. 164–6.
32 Galassi 1966–70, II, p. 238; Angeli 1991, p. 123.
33 Vaglini 2001, pp. 216–19.
34 Cecchetti 1885: 142–6; Grandi 1997, pp. 82–5, 90–3.
35 Gavitt 1990, pp. 35–74; Sandri 1997, pp. 52–4, 59–61. For the text of Datini's legacy see Mazzei ed. Guasti 1880, II, pp. 275–6.
36 Tanturri 2003: 149–50; Tanturri 2006: 235–6.
37 Fanti 1986, pp. 42–3; Terpstra 1994: 103–6; Terpstra 1997, pp. 210–14. For the role of lay confraternities in the care of foundlings generally, see Black 1989, pp. 200–6.
38 Ruggiero 1985, pp. 77–84.
39 Dominici 2001: 21, 24–6, 29–35, 48–9; Dominici 2003: 193, n. 11.
40 See below, n. 57.
41 Pullan 1971, pp. 416–17.
42 For the Innocenti, see Gavitt 1997: 232–3, 264–8, 270; Sandri 2001, pp. 153–78. For Naples and Rome, see *Archivi storici* 1956, I, pp. 449–99.
43 Cf. Cerutti and Cavallo 1980: 375; Kertzer 1993, pp. 95–6, 108–9.
44 Tittarelli *et al.* 2003, p. 203.
45 Povolo 1989, pp. 93–4, n. 5, 102–3; Varanini 1997, pp. 130–5, 149.
46 Dall'Aglio Maramotti 1985, pp. 37–42.
47 Sardi 2002: 94–5.
48 Galanti 1786–90, III, pp. 159–67, and below, Chapter 9, notes 59–60.
49 Cavallo 1983: 392.
50 Galassi 1966–70, II, pp. 38, 196–7, 237–47.
51 Schiavoni 1991, p. 1044; Dominici 2001: 44.
52 Colzi 2001, pp. 292, 297.

53 Tittarelli *et al.* 2003, p. 244.
54 Tanturri 2003: 154, 158, 165.
55 Galanti 1786–90, III, pp. 152–3, 158.
56 Schiavoni 1991, p. 1017; Sonnino 1991, p. 1068; Surdacki 2000: 177–8; Dominici 2003: 204–7.
57 Galanti ed. Placanica 1992: see pp. 260, 264–5 for Galanti's own account, and pp. 548–52 for reports and documents supplied by officers of the hospital.
58 *Ibid.*, pp. 126, 154, 185, 307, 348.
59 *Ibid.*, pp. 126, 160, 170, 225–6, 235, 248.
60 *Ibid.*, p. 169; see also the note on Cerchiara in northern Calabria, at pp. 104–5.
61 *Ibid.*, notes on Rossano at pp. 112, 545; on Catanzaro, p. 154.
62 *Ibid.*, pp. 305–6.
63 *Ibid.*, pp. 216–18.
64 *Ibid.*, pp. 473–6, 511, 514.
65 Boswell 1989, p. 432.

8

Natural and spurious infants: abandonment and other choices

Why did parents abandon children to foundling hospitals, and what other choices were open to them? Not all bastards were surrendered to institutions. Some were cared for by fathers or blood relations, others palmed off on pseudo-parents, others violently killed or left to die, since hospitals, whatever their good intentions, could not wholly eliminate infanticide even from places where they were easily accessible. Of crucial importance, in many cases, were the attitudes of putative fathers: how willing were they to acknowledge and maintain the children at issue? And would town neighbours and fellow-villagers be prepared to tolerate the presence of a base-born baby in their midst? Would their priest allow them to be subjected to a bad example, to witness daily the live evidence of immoral behaviour, or would he insist on the child being sent away, as quickly as possible, to a foundling hospital?

Types of illegitimacy

Laws and lawyers distinguished between types and categories of illegitimacy, some of which were less reprehensible than others and allowed the child stronger inheritance rights. They made a broad distinction between *naturales* and *spurii*. The first were the children of unmarried parents, free of other ties, living in a stable relationship as if they were man and wife but without being legally married. *Spurii* tended to be the products of brief encounters rather than prolonged relationships, and were often the children of 'unknown parents', as baptismal registers put it. Some were 'commonly begotten [*vulgo quesitos*]', the children of women who, though not necessarily common prostitutes, might well be servants or slaves who had had a series of sexual encounters. Some mothers, no doubt, had lain, or been forced to lie, with seasonal workers, rampaging soldiers or other predatory strangers.

> Immodesty and irreligion increases in the human race, above all in wartime, such as we have now, and soldiers, especially troops of soldiers, mingle all things sacred and profane. Nor do they think of supporting the children they beget in a foreign country. Hence it is vital that exposed children be cared for in this great province.

So wrote Gilino of Milan in 1508.[1] Young women may sometimes have blamed pregnancies on fictitious soldiers in the hope of shielding their real lovers, but no doubt there were genuine cases of military betrayal.[2] Among the *spurii*, too, were the children of unlawful unions – of adulterous or bigamous liaisons and incestuous relationships. So were the children of priests or nuns, sometimes called *sacrileghi*.[3] According to Baldus, a great legal authority of the fourteenth century, foundlings in general should be regarded as *spurii* in that they had no acknowledged fathers and mothers.[4]

'Natural' children could be legitimated by the subsequent marriage of their parents as those of adultery, bigamy or incest could not. Even for them there was a way to respectability, in that counts palatine of the Holy Roman Empire might be empowered to legitimate 'bastards, *manseres, nothos, spurios'* and any others 'procreated from illicit or unapproved coitus'. *Nothi* were born of a married man and an unmarried woman; *manseres*, a term derived from the Old Testament, denoted the children, of uncertain fatherhood, born of prostitutes or other promiscuous women [Deuteronomy 23:2].[5] At least one eighteenth-century legal authority held that a prostitute's child ought to be regarded as a *naturalis*, because, in view of the Church's condemnation of concubinage, there was no good reason to deem a prostitute's child inferior to a concubine's.[6]

Very likely, a large proportion of the children surrendered to foundling homes came from the ranks of the *spurii*, the least likely to be wanted and the most likely to cause scandal. But by the seventeenth and eighteenth centuries, it was becoming more difficult for unmarried couples to bring up their own 'natural' children in the face of social disapproval, even if they intended to wed. In 1773, a couple wrote to Santo Spirito in Rome: 'Notice is given that this child has been baptised and that his name is Agostino, but because the young people are not yet married and wish to hide the matter they have sent him to this venerable hospital. They will come and recover him as soon as they are married…'.[7] Since many children were abandoned anonymously, hospitals seldom received enough information to distinguish, even if they wanted to, between different types of illegitimacy. They were generally more interested in identifying children born in wedlock and returning them, where possible, to parents judged able to maintain them.

To keep or to abandon

Abandonment was generally caused by a combination of poverty and shame; a mixture of relative wealth and social confidence would make it more practicable to keep illegitimate children, at least in the fifteenth and sixteenth centuries. In fifteenth-century Florence, a number of families, usually large and prosperous ones, chose to keep illegitimate children sired by their menfolk and to treat them with varying degrees of harshness and indulgence. They could even have them legitimated with a view to their inheriting family property and providing safeguards against the extinction of the lineage. Almost a thousand illegitimate children, 651 males and 335 females, were acknowledged by Florentine taxpayers in the fiscal surveys of 1427, 1458 and 1480.[8] Some sprang from relationships formed before marriage (upper-class men generally married in their late twenties), others from couplings between the men of the household and the domestic slaves of the fifteenth century or the servant girls of a later period; a number of Florentine men fathered children on slaves belonging to other people.[9]

In Renaissance Florence, slaves were mostly female and mostly Tartars; since male slaves were few, slaves could not come together, have children mostly among themselves, and form a distinct group of unfree people. Free men could in principle beget slaves upon slave women, since the child would normally inherit the mother's status. But owners, unwilling to see their own offspring enslaved, would often choose to emancipate both the mother and her child.[10] However, a slave baby could well be sent to a hospital if the father was intent on using the mother's breast-milk, a valuable commodity in a society where women of standing seldom suckled their own infants, for the benefit of another child. He might wish her to feed one of his own legitimate children or propose to sell or hire her 'with the milk' to another family.[11] Tarsia, the daughter of Lucia, a slave belonging to Filippo Piaceti, was sent to the hospital of San Gallo in September 1427, while Lucia, who probably had no choice in the matter, became a wet nurse in the home of Piero dal Palagio.[12]

Some 60 per cent of the identifiable parents of children arriving at the Innocenti in the mid-fifteenth century appeared to be either slaves or servants.[13] They were still prominent in records of the Innocenti for 1467–85; some entries on the books mentioned the mothers only, and domestics accounted for about 40 per cent of them.[14] Another statistic suggests that 14.5 per cent of the children received between 1394 and 1485 by the hospitals of San Gallo and the Innocenti in Florence were the offspring of slaves, as were one-third of the children (55 out of 165) brought to the foundling hospital in Lucca between 1400 and 1415.[15]

Faced with embarrassing children, the living evidence of sexual misconduct, parents and relatives sometimes tried to find them false fathers and did not resort to abandonment. Most, naturally, is known about the schemes which came undone. In 1406, Francesca, a farm girl living in the district of Florence, vainly trusting in promises of marriage from a servant of the landlord, found herself pregnant and tried to escape disgrace by marrying another man, Cecco Arrighi of Ponte Boccio in the district of Pistoia. For a while she managed to dispel suspicion of her swelling stomach by feigning illness. But when a child was born to her in secret five months after the marriage, she panicked and threw 'this son and creature of God' into the river Anigne, with disastrous consequences to herself as well as to him.[16] Drawn up in 1526, the last will and testament of a Venetian gentleman, Pietro Soranzo, revealed that, having got his servant Lucia with child, he had married her off to Baldisera, his steward, falsely asserting that she was a virgin. But when Lucia gave birth to a boy, the noble father decided to come clean and have him raised in the Soranzo family, by his own son Zuane and his daughters. Pietro begged the couple's forgiveness for the subterfuge, and urged Baldisera to treat Lucia well, for the fault was not hers.[17] Less powerful people could be equally devious. In the late eighteenth century, Catterina de Vei, wife of a raftsman on the river Piave, tried to cover up her daughter's incestuous pregnancy by marrying the girl to an old man from Belluno. Both the elderly bridegroom and the baby died, but the scandal still came to light and Catterina's husband had to stand trial for sexually abusing his daughter.[18] A child conceived in adultery could sometimes be passed off on the deceived husband – although, should he be old and impotent, or jealous and unforgiving, or inclined to long absences from home, the manoeuvre would be hard to accomplish.

Some saw no need to dissemble. No secrecy surrounded the natural son of the Cavalier Count Mercurio Bua from Epirus (c.1478–c.1541–5), a famous condottiere of the Italian Wars, then in the service of the Venetian Republic as a commander of light cavalry.[19] Sixteenth-century Venetian courtesans Elisabetta Condulmer and Veronica Franco did not hesitate to acknowledge in their wills (1538, 1564, 1570) sons and daughters fathered by men other than their legal husbands.[20] In Venice respect was due to the illegitimate sons and daughters of patricians, so long as they were *naturales*, born of discreet, long-standing liaisons, and not begotten on slaves, servants or courtesans. If the natural daughters of noblemen in the sixteenth and seventeenth centuries could prove that their mothers had lived in exclusive relationships with their fathers, and that their fathers had acknowledged them from birth, they could well be considered suitable brides for noblemen and their children enjoy full political rights.[21] Lanfredino Cellesi (1518–87), a nobleman of Pistoia, had two children, Dianora and Raffaello, by his mistress Chiara, another man's wife, whom he had taken from a remote village high in the Apennines and fed and clothed for seventeen years (1561–78). One of his legitimate sons complained that 'My father cared more for her than for us', as witness his generosity towards Chiara's children – for he placed the girl in a convent and petitioned the grand duke to 'make the said Raffaello commendatario in the Order of Santo Stefano', an honourable body of knights dedicated to fighting the infidel at sea.[22]

Before bishops began to enforce the Council of Trent's decrees, priests were capable of openly acknowledging illegitimate children and treating them well. When visiting the parish of Gorzone in the Valcamonica, the bishop of Brescia discovered that the priest was living with a woman, Marina, and was told that they loved each other as though they were indeed man and wife. The priest had arranged lavish celebrations when a daughter married the previous year; one of his flock, regarding this as entirely proper, testified that the priest 'gave no scandal.'[23] From the late sixteenth century onwards, priests would be forced to dismiss the women who had openly lived as their mistresses and some examples were made of defiant clerics who refused to do so.[24] Even in the late eighteenth century, some clergy were suspected of fathering children on village girls, but perhaps they took more pains to ensure that their mistresses went elsewhere to give birth and that the children were sent to foundling hospitals or otherwise boarded out.[25]

Patchy anecdotal evidence from the later sixteenth and part of the seventeenth centuries suggests that the base-born children of a well-to-do father had a chance of escaping the hospital so long as he lived. He would be pressed, by his peers, his priest and perhaps by the hospital itself, to maintain his child – even if he could not or would not marry the mother. At first, maintenance would usually involve finding and paying a wet nurse and visiting regularly or sending a trusted agent to ensure that the child was thriving. Should the father die, however, his heirs might well be unwilling to give themselves the same trouble and the child would be sent to the hospital. That was the fate of Ottavia, natural daughter of the physician Cesare Odoni by his 'friend' Sabadina at Bologna in 1572, and also of Anna Francesca, the illegitimate daughter of a prosperous tradesman of Milan, Pietro Antonio Legnano, pork butcher, who had kept her by him for two years. His sisters, less tenderly disposed to the girl, would not save her from the hospital in 1659.[26] When, in Siena in 1606–7, Antonina Pierini, living apart from her husband, had a child by one of the rich Specchi brothers, she and they engaged three wet nurses in succession for young Andrea and appeared to have no thoughts of hiding him in the hospital, although his existence provided the archbishop's court with firm evidence of her sexual misconduct.[27]

Accusing Antonina in the archbishop's court, the procurator-fiscal declared that 'she has led a disreputable and lecherous life in this city for several years, living in concubinage and inflicting the greatest possible damage on her own soul, scandalising the people, and defying the law, the holy canons of the Council of Trent, and the constitutions of the archbishop's court'. As her ordeal suggested, it was becoming increasingly difficult for couples in ungodly relationships, and especially for the women, to maintain bastards openly. Andrea's baptismal entry of 21 October 1606 had named two parents, Eugenio Specchi and 'Antonina his doxy [*sua donnaccia*]', there being some confusion as to which of the brothers, Eugenio or Rinaldo, was the father. In the archdiocese of Bologna, at about this time, parents were becoming more reluctant to be identified as bastard-bearers in the records, while priests, as though anxious to avoid scandal, were more inclined to enter 'parents unknown'. Here, in 1570–1, 61.5 per cent of illegitimate children were said to be of unknown parentage, but by 1650–1 the proportion had risen to 90.5 per cent.

In the course of the seventeenth century, more illegitimate children seemed to be falling into the hands of the Bastardini, which demanded a contribution from the parents where practicable; no longer did the hospital hand infants back to the mother and leave her to approach the father. In 1691, when Giovan Battista Silvagni was interrogated about his three-year relationship with Lucia Bertuzzi, who had borne a child fifteen days earlier, he admitted that 'as for whose son the boy is, I can say that she charged me with it at the Bastardini, and the hospital summoned me, and I gave the usual guarantee to the hospital to pay the amount which is due, since I judge that he may be my son.'[28] In 1696 the heavily pregnant Giovanna Lazzari, who had borne several illegitimate children, was persuaded to go to the hospital officials and denounce the Venetian Francesco Patelli, putative father of the child in her womb – whereupon they sent constables to the man's house to seize goods to the value of 25 lire, to pay for the child's support.[29]

When lovers were forced to separate, the authorities concerned seldom took much interest in the fate of any children involved. There were a few exceptions; when, in 1541, Bishop Giberti of Verona heard that Caterina, the mistress of Butterino, would be happy to leave him, he found her a place to live and had her two daughters brought to her. In Naples in 1610, Vittoria de Olanda, who had six children born 'in sin [*del peccato*]', was ordered to part from her lover and to give up her children (to whom?), except for those under three years of age.[30]

There are gaps in the story, but evidence from here and there in the eighteenth century suggests that single mothers, and hospitals acting on their behalf, were becoming less eager to identify fathers and hold them to account. Mothers relied more heavily on hospitals, and hospitals generally took illegitimate children away from them. At Milan in the second half of the seventeenth century, unmarried women giving birth in the general hospital had usually been ready to name the fathers; by the late eighteenth century, they seemed less willing or perhaps less able to do so. Out of ninety-three such women in 1775–6, 48.5 per cent either did not know who the fathers were or else gave vague information from which they could not be identified.[31] Parish priests in the Papal States in the late eighteenth century, corresponding with the governor of the papal hospital of Santo Spirito, seemed anxious, above all, that a bastard be removed from the village to the foundling hospital without delay, lest parishioners be exposed to a bad example which would contaminate the community. So long as the child was removed, the mother could probably be forgiven. The stress fell on discretion and the avoidance of scandal, not on the public shaming of bastard-bearers, recording their peccadilloes for posterity, or the pursuit of fathers. Nor, on the other hand, should they be allowed to flaunt their misdeeds, and it might well seem best to attribute the infants to 'unknown parents' even when a priest knew who they were.[32]

Occasionally, local priests gave brief descriptions of the circumstances which called for child abandonment. In 1718 a parish priest in Peschiera commended a boy to the foundling hospital of Verona. Baptised Antonio, he was the son of a local girl, Caterina Marchesa, and an unknown man. '[S]he is a poor girl, and for the sake of her kinsfolk's honour it is not fitting that she should keep and suckle the child herself.'[33] A priest wrote from Castellamonte, near Turin, in 1794: 'Here is a boy begotten by a married man upon a servant-girl, who, after giving birth, left him in the adulterer's hands and fled. The man is quite incapable of having the child nursed, and would wish to avoid scandal in the neighbourhood and quarrels with his spouse, which might endanger the child's life. These are all good reasons to receive the boy into the hospital.'[34] Here was a variation on the common theme of the deserted girl; the servant had left her employer holding the baby and exposed him to grave embarrassment.

An unhappy young woman, Maria Battistella, a boatman's daughter, pleaded her case in Venice in 1777. Her story was that Zorzi Benzon, a nobleman in disfavour with his own family and forced to seek lodgings with Maria's, had pursued his rake's progress by getting her with child. When she gave birth to twins, Benzon's family were anxious to hush the matter up; his mother treated Maria with perfunctory kindness, if scarcely with generosity, by 'sending a gold ducat and some rags to cover the infants and despatch them both to the Pietà, and she also sent me a little broth'. Maria's request was 'that he give me something to live on, for I see no chance of his marrying me, because he is a rich man of the highest standing, and a first-born'. She had tried, she said, to drown herself. Disposing of the twins, even if it salvaged her public reputation, would not appease her own father. 'He is a respectable man, although a poor one, and does not want to forgive me, and even if he does he can never forget my fault.'[35]

Child murders and secret births

In theory, foundling hospitals saved souls, bodies and honour by providing a lawful means of concealing illegitimate births. The anonymous surrender of a base-born child to a hospice was a rational alternative to murder, or to negligent exposure. It might seem that any humane woman would adopt this course of action – if, or so sceptics might add, she proved capable of acting reasonably in the pain and exhaustion of childbirth and the terror of disgrace, and if a hospital happened to be close to hand.

Other societies deemed it an offence in itself for an unmarried woman to conceal a birth or an infant death, or even (as in early modern France and Prussia) to fail to register a pregnancy.[36] If she attempted to bear a child in secret, without confiding in anyone or calling for help, there might be a legal presumption, at odds with the normal presumption of innocence, that she had planned to kill her baby. Under the harsh statute of James I, on the books in England from 1624 to 1803, enforced in the seventeenth century but circumvented by judges and juries in the eighteenth, an unmarried woman guilty of concealment would face the gallows unless she could prove that her child had been stillborn or died accidentally.[37] Puritan ministers in England and New England inveighed against the concealment of sin as an offence against divine law and proof of an unregenerate spirit.[38] At the great trial scene in Scott's *The Heart of Mid-Lothian*, set in Edinburgh in 1737, the execution of Effie Deans seems inevitable even though no body has been found: her base-born child has disappeared and her upright Calvinist sister will not falsely swear that Effie disclosed her pregnancy to her.[39]

Catholic charity, as practised in Italy, leaned towards protecting personal and family reputations and avoiding scandal. To create scandal was not so much to arouse public indignation at moral offences as to cause other people to stumble, to tempt neighbours into sinning themselves. To publish a person's misconduct, to insist on public penance rather than private confession, contrition and satisfaction, would be to set a bad example before the faithful and would probably cause social disruption, a worse evil. There was much to be said for discretion, for concealment of a sin from the public eye. The Church may have been especially concerned for the good name of unsatisfactory priests, but it was not indifferent to that of young women and married couples.[40] To shame a woman publicly would reflect on her family's honour and could endanger her life, as was suggested here and there in correspondence with the hospital of Santo Spirito in Rome in the late eighteenth century. In 1786, the priest of Cesi in the Papal States commended to the hospital a baby girl, born of his parishioner Francesca di Mattè by an unknown father, in order to save Francesca from her brother's retribution. In 1789, one of the few women who wrote personally to the hospital's governor testified that 'I have given birth to a child by illicit intercourse, for I have no husband, and, for fear of being killed by my relatives, I send her to be nurtured for the time being at Santo Spirito, with the intention of recovering her when I have settled my affairs.'[41] To avoid greater evils, births outside wedlock could be hidden and the children and their parents become strangers to each other.

Tales of infanticide were central to the foundation legend of the hospital of Santo Spirito in Rome. This story developed two centuries and more after the actual foundation of the hospital around 1200: its origins were now traced to the dredging from the Tiber of the dead bodies of unwanted babies and to the pope's dream of an angel urging him to resist this great evil by building a home for foundlings. Fifteenth-century artists told the story in different styles, one in a manuscript which belonged to the hospital of Santo Spirito in Dijon, others in a sequence of frescoes set below the roof beams of the new Sistine Ward for sick patients erected in Rome in the 1470s and much more accessible to a large and varied public.[42] Most of these paintings celebrated the good deeds of the reigning Pope Sixtus IV and his rebuilding of a decayed Rome. But, by way of prologue, seven scenes commemorated the hospital's establishment by Innocent III and were placed in the part of the ward closest to the river which had given up the dead children. In the first scene, two women, apparently a mother and a confidante, perhaps an evil counsellor, collude in the murder of a newborn baby and one of the pair is beating out the child's brains against a pillar. The caption to the picture explains 'How by various means cruel mothers kill the offspring born of forbidden congress [ex damnato coitu] when they have come to light. "Their babies are dashed to pieces before their eyes", "They have no mercy on the fruit of the womb, no pity in their eyes for children" [Isaiah 13: 16, 18].'[43] In Rome the two Tiber scenes which follow have been partially obscured. But the Dijon manuscript shows two women on a bridge tossing babies, one swaddled and weighted, into a fast-flowing river; a third 'cruel mother', more opulently dressed, approaches the bridge carrying a child and looks around furtively, on the verge of committing the same detestable crime. Some of the bodies are brought to the surface by fishermen, as though to fulfil another prophecy – 'The fishermen will groan ... those who throw nets on the waters will lament [Isaiah 19:8].' In the Roman version of the drama, a fisherman brings the dead infants to the papal palace, and hangs back while a more courtly character presents two victims to the Solomon-like figure of the enthroned pope. Innocent raises his hands, palms outwards, in a stylised gesture of shock and pity; soon afterwards he builds the hospital and entrusts it to the order of Santo Spirito.[44] The officers of other hospitals would take up a similar theme. Petitioners in Florence in the 1480s declared that, but for the Innocenti, many babies would perish both in body and soul – 'They would be found dead and unbaptised on many occasions in rivers, ditches and sewers'.[45] The new hospital at Pavia in 1479 was designed to save unbaptised children from being abandoned in the city to be devoured or mutilated by pigs and dogs, or fatally exposed to the bitter cold of winter, or secretly killed by their own mothers.[46]

Centuries later, the learned Muratori of Modena followed well-trodden paths and warned of the persistent danger of infanticide: 'Abandoned by their human parents, these children of God will die, unless the charity of the faithful become their fathers and mothers and, by giving these new-born babies a kindly welcome, urge barbarous mothers to suppress the dreadful thought of concealing their own misdeeds by committing acts of parricide.'[47] Absolute secrecy was often thought desirable; a hospital which tried to pursue and expose the parents of bastards to make them pay maintenance would risk driving them to abortion and infanticide. Parish priests in Bologna in 1714 protested against their hospital's eagerness to detect abandoning mothers, and the Board of Abandoned Children in Sicily expressed similar misgivings in the mid-eighteenth century, rebuking local committees for hounding presumed parents.[48] The view was shared by Alfonso dei Liguori in his Moral Theology – the primary purpose of foundling hospitals was to save base-born children from the threat of eternal and temporal death, and hospitals should not pursue even rich parents for maintenance, lest their identity be revealed and they lose faith in the hospital's discretion.[49]

As Muratori implied, infanticide was officially regarded as an atrocious crime – not one which could be mitigated by pleading insanity produced by the strain of pregnancy

and labour, or by representing the mother as a victim of masculine abuse. In this context, the life of a bastard was not to be valued any less than that of a legitimate child.
From the early fifteenth century at least, the killing of a newborn infant was potentially
a capital crime subject to exemplary punishment. Francesca di Cristofano, convicted of
murdering her baby in 1406, was paraded through the streets of Pistoia on a donkey,
with the corpse around her neck, on her way to judicial burning. She was found guilty
both of immoral behaviour and of premeditated murder, said to have deprived the
child's father of something which belonged to him and not to her, and condemned as
a 'most cruel woman'.[50] Lucia di Boninsegna, pregnant by one of her father's brothers,
retired when her time came to a disused pigsty and there, after several hours of labour,
bore a son. According to the court record, she laid the child on the ground, naked and
unfed, hidden from view only by a couple of stones, where a dog subsequently found
it; by taking away the umbilical cord, in the hope that this might cure a goitre, she perhaps made herself seem even more heartless. The governor [*vicario*] of San Miniato
sentenced her to be beheaded in March 1427.[51]

No woman, sixteenth-century lawyers pronounced, could plead in her defence
that she had killed to defend her honour, valued though this was. Penalties imposed
by courts, at least in Venice and its dominions, were not uniformly severe, however.
From the sixteenth to the eighteenth centuries, judges inclined towards greater leni-
ency, though they were still capable of imposing long terms of imprisonment and
stretches of banishment.[52] It was often difficult to prove child murder conclusively,
even if a body could be identified and traced to a particular mother, hard to refute the
common defence that babies had been stillborn or died accidentally during or soon
after the birth.[53] In the Veneto, villagers were arrested and prosecuted more often
than townspeople. It was possible either that access to a foundling hospital genuinely
reduced the incidence of newborn-child murder or that if such a hospital were at
hand it became less believable that parents would choose to kill children when they
could resort to a bloodless alternative.[54] Fear of the angry law, erratically enforced as
it was, might not be an effective deterrent to infanticide. The hospital, on the other
hand, could provide something more positive than the fear of detection, in the form
of an incentive to save a life and an opportunity to avoid the guilt of committing a
callous murder.

Lawyers, magistrates and moralists generally assumed that illegitimate children
were killed by mothers bent on hiding their shame. This was not always true. When, on
the Capello estate in the province of Padua in 1593, Mattia bore a child to her abusive
father, Bastian Stanghelin, farm labourer, it appeared to be Bastian who baptised the
child, killed it, and buried it in the garden.[55] But women bore the brunt of prosecutions
and men were seldom pursued with the same intensity, although they could be charged
as accessories or accused of plotting to procure an abortion. Foundling hospitals could
not prevent all infanticides: conveying a child to them unseen required planning and
depended on collaboration from lovers, midwives, friends, accomplices, sometimes
hired help, not all of it trustworthy. Was it likely that a frightened woman who had con-
fided in no-one, bearing a child in solitude, exhausted by labour and perhaps panick-
ing at the cries of the infant, would succeed in herself carrying a child to a foundling

hospital with the necessary speed and secrecy? She might well be moved to silence it at once – not by opium or laudanum, but by smothering or drowning.

Law courts were told of persons charged with taking newborn children to hospitals who, out of indifference, idleness, or dissatisfaction with a paltry fee, had caused or contributed to their deaths. In Venice in 1736, a sinister, possibly fictitious old midwife was blamed for throwing Maria Franceschini's illegitimate child down a latrine rather than take her to the foundling home as requested. Better authenticated was a peasant at Villa d'Adda in the Venetian dominions in 1773, named as Domenico Fanfer, who was engaged to carry a child to hospital in Milan or Bergamo but left him to die at a farm-house on the way.[56] But in some rural communities, better organisation, a more formal procedure for sending illegitimate babies away from the village, seems to have developed in time. Parish priests could be helpful. In the Papal States in the later eighteenth century, they were often privy to secrets picked up from local gossip and the reports of midwives. Moved by compassion, or interested in scotching scandals that would reflect badly on their own pastoral care, they would baptise a bastard at home 'to avoid the scandal of having it brought to church', conceal the identities of parents, act as intermediaries between the village and the hospital, and write letters commending a child to Santo Spirito.[57]

Maternity homes and hospitals

Some lovers and protectors would remove their mistresses from the village to the city before their pregnancies began to show, perhaps putting it about that they were leaving to work as servants. Men would pay for expectant mothers to board, if necessary for several months, at houses of confinement attended by midwives. Newly born children would then be taken on short journeys to local hospitals by the midwives or their daughters. This was the procedure favoured by a clergyman, Giovanni Bearzi, for concealing the pregnancies of his cousin Maddalena Micossi, whom he sent, c.1771, to maternity homes in Udine.[58]

Birthing establishments for the use of unmarried mothers had been suppressed in seventeenth-century England, their owners and their accomplices gaoled for 'bringing lewd women abed in suspecting places'.[59] Tolerated in Italy, where the law was less hostile to concealment, they were natural auxiliaries for the foundling hospitals. The services of private establishments were doubtless beyond the means of impoverished women whose lovers would not or could not pay for them. Perhaps, though, more lives and reputations were saved during the eighteenth century when these facilities became more generally available to poor women. True, general hospitals had long provided maternity beds for single mothers and impoverished wives, from which newborn babies could be transferred to the foundling wing. But some had tried to make mothers pay or otherwise work off their debts, and some had attempted to trace the fathers. In Arezzo, the hospital of San Cristofano began to work in tandem with the city's general hospital, admitting women, most of them unmarried, who were on the point of childbirth, and sending their newborn babies on to the foundling wing of Santa Maria del Ponte. The first mother mentioned in the surviving records was Maria Angela, who 'on the 8th September 1579 came to give birth in our hospital, and on the same day gave birth to a girl, who was sent to the hospital of the Ponte as the regulations prescribe. On the 9th the woman left of her own volition [*da per se*].' At San Cristofano expectant mothers were in a minority at first, but by 1660 they were beginning to account for more than half of the patients admitted, and for 82 of 124 in 1726–9 – after which the hospital was for fifty years given over to fever patients.[60] How far it tried to preserve the anonymity of single mothers is not known, but it did reduce their isolation, unmarried mothers were evidently willing to resort to the place, and few, it seems, died in childbirth on its premises.

In certain cities, at least after 1700, attempts were made to protect the identity of 'secretly pregnant women', described as *gravide occulte* or *incinte furtivamente*. One object of the Opera dei Partorienti, attached to the hospital of San Giovanni in Turin in 1728, was 'to give a safe refuge to those young women who incautiously lose their greatest gift'. More than 80 per cent of the women in this ward were unmarried mothers, usually admitted in the seventh month of pregnancy; a woman in labour could, if she chose, wear a mask to hide her face from the midwife attending her, lest this person prove to be a gossip or a blackmailer.[61] During the eighteenth century, the Orbatello in Florence became a home for unmarried pregnant women; it was used, in the words of a contemporary, 'for endangered girls, being destined to serve, not less their honour, than the life of the creatures with whom they were pregnant'.[62] Eight women came to Verona from surrounding districts in 1772, towards the end of their pregnancies, to give birth in a ward set aside at the Santa Casa di Pietà for 'women who wish to keep their condition secret'.[63] Near Santa Maria della Scala in Siena was the hospital of Monna Agnese, which between 1763 and 1766 oversaw about sixty births a year. Visiting in 1773, the grand duke described it as cramped but clean, equipped with a kitchen and 'five or six chambers for four or five women giving birth', with a midwife and two ward maids in attendance, and food and wine supplied by the nuns of a nearby convent.[64] In 1783 a prominent local nobleman founded the Casa del Santo Bambino at Catania in Sicily, on similar lines to the maternity hospital in Turin. Eight days after giving birth, women would be able either to return to the world or to be admitted to the local refuge for repentant sinners.[65]

During the eighteenth century, the maternity section of the general hospital in Milan attracted both married and unmarried mothers-to-be; in 1775–6 just under half the entrants were married and just over one-third single. Then, in 1780, the Empress Maria Theresa established a new hospital in Milan, the Casa degli Esposti e Partorienti. The aim was not just to provide a refuge for unmarried mothers but to set up an efficient hospital for women. Treatment would be free if they brought certificates of poverty from parish priests and were willing to enter an 'unreserved' ward and become subjects of study for trainee midwives and surgeons. A mother could enter by a secret doorway and bring a sealed envelope containing her personal details: this would be opened only if she died, to enable her death to be properly registered. According to the rules of 1784, which resembled those of Vienna, one objective was to protect the identity of unmarried mothers, and another to 'grant protection to the innocent creature' by transferring newborn children to the foundling home, unless mothers were determined to keep them.[66] By that time, too, one of the many functions of the hospital of the Incurabili in Naples was to provide facilities for women who wished to 'bear children in secret'; unless they chose to keep them, their offspring would be taken to the vast foundling hospital. On average, 155 children made the journey between the two institutions each year between 1785 and 1787 and accounted for 7–8 per cent of the total entry to the Annunziata, which then admitted about two thousand children annually.[67]

Abandonment and infanticide: two stories

Artists working for Santo Spirito had dramatised child murder by cruel mothers and extolled the remedy offered by the pope's charity. Two short stories, published in collections of the mid-sixteenth century, portray between them the virtues of child abandonment and the horrors of child murder; both concern women of standing faced with unwanted pregnancies, one a gentle but resourceful girl who seeks to preserve her child's life, the other a fiend whose only thought is to destroy it utterly.

Lippa of Cremona, Giraldi Cinzio's heroine, is the victim of a spineless lover and a wicked lady's maid, who whispers evil counsel to her like the serpent in the garden. Fatally tempted, she sleeps with a rich but common young man of whom her family disapproves, despite her own misgivings – 'What if I was with child and then he rejected me? I know that my family would be so enraged that I seem to see, even at this moment, a naked knife in the hands of my father and brothers, ready to shed my blood.' The almost inevitable happens. Lippa becomes pregnant and, for fear of her brothers, her lover stops seeing her. But she ignores her maid's incitement to abort the child, somehow conceals her condition, deceives a guileless housekeeper, and eventually gives birth in her family's country retreat (fortunately, the maid has departed). 'Fearing death, and even more than death dishonour in the eyes of the world', she decides to 'leave the boy in the power of fortune' by depositing him on the trunk of a plane tree by the river. She garnishes him with violets, a gesture unlikely to protect him from birds of prey or voracious animals, but an appeal, perhaps, to the sensibilities of anyone who finds him. Her baby is rescued, as she intends, by passing shepherds. They are headed for the foundling hospital in Mantua when one of the company, whose wife has just lost a child and has the milk to nurse a foundling, decides to adopt him. The boy, whom they name Aventuroso, knows he was adopted, but comes to love the shepherd and his wife as though they were blood parents. He becomes a soldier, and during the wars finds himself in a position of power over his birth mother, her family, and his natural father, who are all taken prisoner – an event which enables him to reconcile them all to each other (a rosy birthmark on his shoulder makes him recognisable to his mother).

Lippa appears in the story as an essentially decent young woman who has made a mistake and does what she can for the child whom her honour forbids her to keep. Saved to do good in the world, perhaps moved by the noble blood on his mother's side, Aventuroso repays Lippa by rescuing her; since she has always refused to marry anyone other than his natural father, it presumably becomes possible to make him, after all, their legitimate heir. This may be a sentimental tale, packed with unlikely coincidences, inviting the comment that Aventuroso's chances of survival are hugely improved by the fact that he never arrives at the hospital but is rescued by private compassion. However, the moral is plain: a woman deserted by her lover cannot keep a natural child, but she must banish all thoughts of abortion and murder and entrust him to fortune (if not to providence) as carefully as she can. Who knows? One day he may save her as she saved him.[68]

Pandora is the villain of a 'chronicle', seemingly factual, in which Bandello points no moral but seems merely to be reporting sensational and gruesome events; he describes in detail an atrocity even more horrific than the crimes depicted for Santo Spirito in Rome. Like several of Bandello's other wayward women, Pandora is married to a middle-aged, absentee husband and takes her pleasure freely with other men. When she becomes pregnant, fear of discovery counts for something, though this is not the passion which rules her. Above all, it is wounded vanity at her lover's desertion that spurs her on to murder. She goes to great lengths to abort the child by physical force at a late stage of her pregnancy, beyond six months, when the foetus is by any reckoning a creature infused with a soul. Pandora vents her fury on her lover Cesare by savaging his offspring, crying 'See how this little beast was beginning to resemble his treacherous father', and vowing 'He will do penance for the other's sins.' Making no move to baptise the infant, depriving him of heaven as well as earth, she kills him by beating his head on the ground and ripping the body apart, disposing of the evidence by feeding the remains to a huge mastiff.

Tell this story, three centuries later, to a Victorian psychiatrist, and he might well diagnose puerperal insanity, a homicidal mania then thought to be latent in all women and brought on by the strains of pregnancy, or labour, or breastfeeding.[69] But there is no hint in Bandello's account of anything but firmness of wicked purpose, no suggestion of any attempt to fight the demonic impulse to destroy the child. Finea, the lady's maid in this story, is no temptress like the servant of Lippa, but a subordinate who carries out the most grotesque instructions. Governed by passion, impervious to any humane sentiment, Pandora could never have ordered the woman to take the child to a hospital or otherwise save his life. It may be that Bandello, though this was not his conscious aim, provided one vivid illustration of the limitations of charity, which was powerless in the face of violent and destructive emotions or fits of madness which could lead to hatred and fear of the baby.[70]

Infant murders, or the disposal of child corpses as though they were garbage or offal, still occurred in seventeenth- and eighteenth-century Venice despite the presence of the Pietà, a large hospital which allowed open entry. Margarita Serena, a widow on Burano island, threw her newborn child unbaptised into the water in 1694 and fled the scene; Francesca Preteggiani left her dead child in a graveyard in 1751, but escaped punishment because live birth could not be proved, and there were reports that on a previous occasion she had acted properly and sent the child to the Pietà.[71] In 1760, the journalist Gaspare Gozzi reported that 'Last Tuesday morning a newborn child was found dead upon a public way. Love and Shame are two powerful deities: the world can excuse the first because at least it increases the population; but the second, when it comes to such a pass, makes a woman more savage than any beast.'[72] A few weeks later, he noted that bargemen had found the corpse of a newborn girl, weighed down by a stone, 'sodden and disfigured by crabs', at the junction of the Rio di San Trovaso with the Grand Canal.[73] The children might conceivably have been stillborn and the parents have been unable to afford a funeral. But Gozzi assumed that a woman must have killed at least one of them. It may be that the murdering mothers of Santo Spirito's foundation myth and of Bandello's gruesome story would never disappear. But, arguably, a desperate woman did have, thanks to the foundling hospitals and the maternity wards, a few more choices open to her, so long as she was not completely isolated, had some honest helpers and confidants, and could to some extent master her own emotions and fears.

Children of wedlock

The effectiveness of foundling hospitals, their capacity for saving lives, depended in part on their controlling the number of entrants, so as not to overstrain their resources. Should they concentrate on the task of caring for illegitimate children alone? Or should they also accept the children of married parents who claimed to be unable to keep them – the dependants of overlarge families threatened with starvation, the children of chronically sick or disabled parents, children whose fathers or mothers had left home but were presumed to be still alive, the sucklings of milkless mothers? To receive bastards was an act of expediency: it had to be done, to avoid scandal and possible bloodshed. To receive children born in wedlock, with living parents, was one which called for discretion; this could only be exercised if the parents appeared at the hospital and proved that they were not abandoning merely for their own convenience and comfort. But if they wished to avoid interrogation, they might well be tempted to abandon anonymously as if the children were bastards, and the number of foundlings swell to the point at which the hospital became overwhelmed. There was no sure way of telling a legitimate child from a bastard, but suspicion would be aroused if the infant was more than a few days old and came with a baptismal certificate, suggesting that the child had been abandoned at leisure and not with the utmost haste.

From the late fifteenth century, high ecclesiastical authorities tried to discourage abandonment not driven by dire need. Sixtus IV (1476) and Paul III (1548) ordered that confessors should refuse to absolve parents who abandoned frivolously, or that the offenders should be excommunicated and made to reimburse the hospital for raising their children.[74] In 1487, the bishop of Padua stipulated that legitimate children should always be given openly, never anonymously, to the local hospital. 'And if a man's fortunes improve, he must take his children back, whatever state they happen to be in, and within three years he must pay the cost of bringing them up.'[75] To enforce decrees which depended so heavily on conscience and the confessional could never be a simple undertaking. Undaunted, the hospital in Milan in 1480 appointed a couple of official sleuths to track down married parents who had abandoned children without sufficient cause.[76]

Certain hospitals, as early as the sixteenth century, tried to refuse all legitimate children, certainly where both their parents were still alive, and to affirm their parents' duty to bring them up.[77] In 1560, the governor of the Trovatelli in Pisa ruled that inquiries must be made of anyone who brought a child to the hospital and that if legitimate birth was suspected the next port of call should be the priest of the parish in which the child had probably been baptised. A child shown to be legitimate must be returned to the parents, who were liable to repay any expenses incurred by the hospital.[78] In and around Ravenna in the eighteenth century, where married parents had been forbidden to abandon children since 1614, the hospital priors would do much the same thing, often using any baptismal certificates left with the children to identify their parish of origin. If both parents were alive, the baby would be returned to them, no matter how deep their poverty, though the hospital might take the child on if the mother had died and the father could not maintain it.[79] During the eighteenth century, several other hospitals declined in principle to accept legitimate children – at Parma in 1720, at Vicenza and Padua in the 1730s, at Bologna in 1740 and 1764.[80] The Board for Abandoned Children in mid-eighteenth-century Sicily could scarcely believe that any mother would be so unnatural as to 'part from her legitimate offspring', and therefore discouraged officious inquiries into the origins of babies. But the board conceded that should there be strong reason to believe that an abandoned child had been born in wedlock, it must be restored to the parents and they be charged expenses – in which case, the child might well be exposed to risk and should be watched closely lest it die or be abandoned again in another place.[81]

Attempts to overhaul the finances of Santo Spirito in Rome in the 1730s and to limit the hospital's liabilities resulted in similar measures, which applied both to Rome itself and to other centres in the Papal States. Children from villages near Viterbo would, in theory at least, be admitted to the city's new hospital only if their parish priests certified them base-born. Caracciolo, the apostolic visitor to Perugia, declared in 1740 that 'these our hospitals … are intended solely for illegitimate children of unknown parentage'. In both areas, priests were ordered to watch the young families of married couples and raise the alarm if any children mysteriously disappeared and there was no evidence of their death.[82] Formerly, in the 1650s, Santo Spirito in Rome had prided itself on receiving all children deposited at the place of collection.[83] But from the 1730s it pursued, at least fitfully, a campaign to restore children to married parents who had abandoned them improperly. Two hundred and ten foundlings were returned to married parents in 1737–9, only 15 in 1744 and again in 1749, but 113 in 1767 and 122 in 1785. The scope of the operation, however, was restricted and usually succeeded in calling only parents in Rome itself to account. Even so, Brigida, a baby from Tivoli with only one hand, was restored to her parents in 1760 with the help of the midwife who had attended her birth.[84]

Nevertheless, some foundling hospitals proved either unable or unwilling to restrict admissions, even in theory, to base-born children. In the seventeenth century, estimates of the proportion of legitimate children to the total number accepted by hospitals had been moderate, though there was much room for confusion and inaccuracy: about one child in nine was described as legitimate at the Annunziata in Naples, while at the Trovatelli in Pisa between 1695 and 1704, about 14 per cent were identified as legitimate, 16 per cent as illegitimate, the rest as the offspring of 'unknown parents'.[85] Larger figures began to be mentioned or hinted at. In Milan in 1689–90, nearly half the children left anonymously at the hospital were more than five days old, a fact which suggested that they had been abandoned at leisure and probably born in wedlock. The proportion remained at much the same level throughout the eighteenth century. Children who had already seen their first birthday accounted for about 20 per cent of admissions in the 1770s.[86] In 1700–2, 23.5 per cent of children entering the Innocenti in Florence appeared to be legitimate, but by 1762–4 the proportion had reached 48.2 per cent and by 1792–4, 71.8 per cent. During the eighteenth century, some families in rural communities near Florence, at Fiesole and San Godenzo, appeared to be sending 'surplus' children quite systematically to the Innocenti, as though they were reluctant to support more than two dependent children at any one time. By the 1790s, stricter regulations were clearly called for. Admissions to the Innocenti, it was said, must be confined to base-born children and only a few categories of legitimate ones: those whose families were delinquent or cruel or in dire poverty, or whose mothers could not produce milk, could not pay for a wet nurse, and had 'no relatives or others with a duty to meet this expense.'[87]

Conclusion

Santo Spirito's fifteenth-century foundation legend promoted the lasting idea that the supreme duty of foundling hospitals was to prevent the murder of newborn children – including 'spurious infants', born *ex damnato coitu*, who were at especially high risk. It presented child murder as the act of a cruel mother who saw her child only as the damning evidence of her own misconduct, not as a human being or a soul. She became a criminal even more depraved than the corrupting mother who groomed her daughter as a courtesan or sold her as a mistress. But appeals could be made to her reason. Charity might save lives as repressive laws and ferocious penalties could not; accommodating a lesser evil, providing opportunities to conceal an error by responsible abandonment, might achieve more than rigour. At least in the fifteenth and sixteenth centuries, it was by no means certain that the 'natural' children of well-to-do fathers and their mistresses would be abandoned while their fathers lived. In the seventeenth and eighteenth, ecclesiastical and social condemnation of concubinage made it more difficult to keep such children, while there was less tendency to hold fathers to account, more inclination to place infants with a hospital and separate them from mothers assumed to be unfit to nurse them. There were grave practical difficulties in the process of abandonment – if a mother gave birth in secret, especially in the countryside, how was the child to be conveyed to a hospital which might be many miles away? The development of discreet maternity homes, adjacent to foundling hospitals, above all in the eighteenth century, added to the possibility of concealment, and may have saved more lives.

When children were delivered to a hospital, would their lives really be saved, or would they, as social rejects, be undervalued and neglected, the hospital becoming a check to population growth? Inefficiency might prove to be an enemy as deadly as contempt, stemming as it did from overcrowding and underfunding, due partly to the competing claims of the children of married couples, and partly to over-centralisation and the disproportionate burdens thrown on some metropolitan hospitals. Suggestions that foundling hospitals, while relieving the public conscience and salvaging the honour of young women and their families, merely killed infants in a more acceptable way, were not lacking even in the seventeenth century. In 1676, noble commissioners in the Venetian dominions called the hospital of San Marcello in Vicenza 'a place of sacrifice for innocents rather than a refuge for children', as though it had become the accomplice of some latter-day Herod rather than an asylum from his cruelty; in the last nineteen years, entry to the place had meant almost certain death.[88] Writers in nineteenth-century Milan would declare that foundling hospitals enjoyed a reputation for 'putting children to death at public expense' and perpetrating 'legal infanticide'.[89] By following children's progress through hospitals, the next chapter will examine the justice of these charges.

Notes

1   Gilinus 1508, c. xxiv.
2   Ferraro 2008, pp. 1–2.
3   Kuehn 2002, pp. 36–44, 92, 132–3, 251, 255; also Povolo 1989, pp. 110–11. For the legal obligations of fathers under civil and canon law, see Arrivo 1997: 236–8; Bianchi 1997: 265–6.
4   Kuehn 2002, p. 109.
5   *Ibid.*, p. 171, and the Latin text in the Appendix, pp. 259–64.
6   Arrivo 1997: 234–5.
7   Canepari 2006: 113; see also 115–16.
8   Herlihy and Klapisch-Zuber 1985, pp. 145–6, 245–6; Kuehn 2002, especially pp. 123–31.
9   Kuehn 2002, pp. 79, 143.
10 Epstein 2005, pp. 222–4.
11 Klapisch-Zuber 1985, pp. 140–1.
12 Sandri 1991, p. 1000.
13 Gavitt 1990, pp. 20, 75–6, 84, 207. Cf. Trexler 1973–74a: 270–5.
14 Gavitt 1994, p. 74.
15 Angiolini 1996, pp. 110–11.
16 Brucker 1971, pp. 146–7; Walter 1986: 637–40.
17 Romano 1996, p. 202.
18 Ferraro 2008, pp. 74–85.
19 DMS XXIV, coll. 178–9, 20 April 1517. On the career of Mercurio Bua, see Netto 1993.
20 Rosenthal 1992, pp. 75–81; Brown 2004, pp. 173–4.
21 Cowan 2007, pp. 29–33, 71, 117–24.
22 Weinstein 2000, pp. 83–5, 89, 159–60.
23 Montanari 1987, pp. 108–10.
24 Basilico 2008: 124–5; Romeo 2008, pp. 3–6, 28–30.
25 Ferraro 2008, pp. 162–3, 166–89.
26 Bianchi 1997: 263, 267–72; Reggiani 1997: 287. For some examples of irregular relationships in which the man appeared to take charge of the children, see Nardi 1989: 85, 130–1 (Siena); Eisenach 2004, pp. 134–5 (Verona).
27 For the text of Antonina's trials, see Nardi 1989: 152–71. See also Chapter 6, n. 5.
28 Bianchi 1997: 276–9, 282–3.
29 Canosa and Colonnello 1989, p. 88.
30 Eisenach 2004, pp. 173–4; Romeo 2008, pp. 52–3, 124, n. 31. On the same theme, see Nardi 1989: 66–7.

31   Reggiani 1997: 294–9.
32   Canepari 2006: 101–2, 114, 119–20.
33   Cappelletti 1983: 428–9.
34   Doriguzzi 1983: 464.
35   Gambier 1980, pp. 539–40.
36   Jackson 2002a, pp. 5–7; Geyer-Kordesch 2002, pp. 97–100; Ferraro 2008, pp. 118–20.
37   Hoffer and Hull 1984, pp. 20–7, 68–71, 78–89; Rabin 2002, pp. 73–92.
38   Hoffer and Hull 1984, pp. 11, 49–54.
39   Scott ed. Inglis 1994, Chapters 21–4, pp. 217–52.
40   On this theme, see Fossier 2009: 317–48 and Elliott 2012, pp. 90–105.
41   Canepari 2006: 115.
42   Howe 1978, pp. 203–5, 233, n. 40, 336–42; Guerrini 2001, pp. 143–8, 160; Howe 2005. See
      also Bolton 1994, p. 139; Bolton 1994a, pp. 160–1.
43   Howe 2005, pp. 74–5, 85–6, 101–2, 143–4; 194 (for the texts of inscriptions); figs. 17–18,
      pp. 219–20. For further analysis, see Presciutti 2011.
44   Guerrini 2001, figs. 2, 3 and 5, pp. 145–9; Howe 2005, fig. 17, p. 219.
45   Trexler 1973–4: 100; 112, n. 16 and 17.
46   Presciutti 2011: 765.
47   Muratori ed. Nonis 1961, p. 558.
48   Kertzer 1993, pp. 95–6, 108; Raffaele 1997: 320–1.
49   Quoted in Arrivo 1997: 243.
50   Walter 1986: 641–8.
51   Mazzi 1986a: 629–30.
52   Povolo 1978–9: 115–30; Povolo 1979–80: 416–28; Povolo 1989, pp. 132–46.
53   See, for example, the case involving the kitchen-maid Marieta da Trieste (Venice, 1585), dis-
      cussed in Ferraro 2008, pp. 136–43.
54   Cf. Van der Spuy 2002, p. 131.
55   Ferraro 2008, pp. 45–64; see also pp. 11, 200.
56   Ibid., pp. 129–30, 135–6, 187–99.
57   Canepari 2006.
58   Ferraro 2008, pp. 166–74.
59   Hoffer and Hull 1984, p. 156.
60   Sardi 2002: 81–90.
61   Cavallo 1991, pp. 346, 348, 354–7; Cavallo 1995, pp. 199–201.
62   Trexler 1982, pp. 142–3.
63   Cappelletti 1983: 425.
64   Vigni 1985: 200, 203–4.
65   Raffaele 1991, pp. 920–2.
66   Hunecke 1991, p. 60; Hunecke 1994, pp. 121–2, 125; Reggiani 1997: 308–9.
67   Galanti 1786–90, III, pp. 142, 155–7.
68   Giraldi Cinzio 1565, I.i, vol. I, pp. 202–17.
69   Cf. Marland 2002, pp. 172–6; Quinn 2002, pp. 195, 199, 214.
70   Bandello ed. Flora 1934, III.52: vol. II, pp. 513–17. For critical comments on this story, see
      Griffith 1955, pp. 126–7; Rodax 1968, p. 88.
71   Ferraro 2008, pp. 116–36, 143–6.
72   Gozzi ed. Zardo 1915, p. 56, 15 March 1760.
73   Ibid., p. 123, 3 May 1760.
74   Hunecke 1989, pp. 74–5; Grandi 1997, pp. 68–9.

75   Povolo 1989, pp. 102–3.
76   Hunecke 1989, pp. 75–6.
77   Galassi 1966–70, II, p. 239; Viazzo *et al.* 2000, pp. 78–9.
78   Arrivo 1997: 244–5.
79   Bolognesi and Giovannini 1982, pp. 322–3.
80   Povolo 1989, pp. 107–9; Hunecke 1991, pp. 59–60; Kertzer 1993, pp. 43, 85, 87.
81   Raffaele 1997: 321–2, 324.
82   Langellotti and Travaglini 1991, pp. 747–8; Tittarelli *et al.* 2003, pp. 202–3.
83   Pagano 1979: 376.
84   Surdacki 2000: 182–6.
85   Da Molin 1991, pp. 468–70; Arrivo 1997, 246–8.
86   Hunecke 1985: 19; Hunecke 1989, pp. 86–7; Reggiani and Paradisi 1991, pp. 962–4; Hunecke
      1994, pp. 125–8.
87   Corsini 1976; Corsini 1991, pp. 83–5; Viazzo 1994, pp. 39–40; Di Bello 1997: 333–4.
88   Povolo 1989, p. 95.
89   Quoted in Dodi Osnaghi 1982, p. 428. See also Kertzer and White 1994: 452.

9

Abandonment, reception and infant mortality

Foundling hospitals and their attempts at rescuing illegitimate children can be said to have rested on three axioms. The first was that bastards, though subject to prejudice and social disapproval, had a right to life, both temporal and eternal, and that their murder was a heinous crime. The second was that, although the honour of a single mother and her family could not justify murder or exposure, it did justify the separation of base-born children from their blood parents, even from those who had the means to keep them – since their presence would cause conflict, show open disrespect for the institution of marriage, and scandalise the community. The third was that, to avoid these greater evils, their discreet abandonment should be tolerated and regulated, and the hospital should conduct an extensive rescue operation designed to save lives and turn surviving foundlings into useful members of the community. This was bound to be a hazardous undertaking, if there was any truth in Malthus's later observation that such hospitals 'encourage a mother to desert her child, at the very time when of all others it stands most in need of her fostering care. The frail tenure by which an infant holds its life will not allow of a remitted attention, even for a few hours.'[1]

Arrival

Babies and infants entered foundling hospitals by at least half a dozen different routes. Some were left at or near the premises by figures who never identified themselves. Some arrived in the arms of bearers who knew the mother's name but did not always divulge it, and others were brought by people who claimed to know nothing: in 1457 a country couple told the hospital in San Gimignano only that 'this child had passed from hand to hand and they did not know whose son he was'. Many children were discovered somewhere in towns and brought in by their finders, or by parish clergy or lay elders, or by confraternity members who made it their business to collect foundlings.[2] Exposure on open roads or fields, through malice, negligence or panic, was more dangerous to fragile lives. Only by chance did country folk come upon Maria, a babe in the wood, on Savino, who was in a basket, on Maria Prudenziana and Eusebio Maria, 'attached to a wall [*appesi ad moro*]', and set in train their journey to the hospital in Siena.[3] Fatal accidents continued to occur. In 1792 the governor of the hospital in Sulmona reported that a child had been left outside a local friary and only the head had been found, for the rest of the body had been devoured by wolfish sheep dogs – very much the kind of gruesome tragedy that foundling hospitals were supposed to prevent.[4] Children were not always left at the hospital, but they were generally brought to the hospital by the persons who picked them up.

Some children, especially orphans and half-orphans, entered 'by the door' or 'through the office', presented by relatives or friends who argued for their admission. Certain infants arrived from another part of the hospital or a nearby maternity home: they might be the offspring of unmarried or desperately poor women who had entered the wards to give birth, or the children of sick mothers who had died in hospital or who had, on recovering, chosen to leave their sons or daughters there rather than take them home. At Perugia in the early eighteenth century, 3.5 per cent of abandoned children had been born in the hospital; at Todi (1740–59), 11.4 per cent.[5] In Milan at least, confidence in the discretion and obstetric skills of the general hospital's midwives appeared to be growing during the eighteenth century, for more Milanese women, whether married or not, were choosing to give birth in hospital – in the seventeenth century 5–6 per cent of abandoned children had been born there, but in the eighteenth, 10–18 per cent. In the mid-1770s an unmarried mother very seldom took her child away with her; about half the married mothers did so, and the rest left their babies among the *esposti*.[6] Many large city hospitals accepted infants conveyed for distances of up to fifty miles by carriers employed by outlying communities, anxious to see the back of their own foundlings, eager to keep moral standards up and expenses down.

The curfew imposed at Siena in 1309–10 allowed hospitallers to emerge from their quarters, even after the third sounding of the communal bell, to rescue children left in the neighbourhood under cover of darkness.[7] Clerks at the Misericordia in Perugia and at San Gallo in Florence in the late fourteenth and early fifteenth centuries noted the manner of infants' arrival. At Perugia they were 'placed at the window' in the morning or evening or found 'at the foot of the stairs'; after a procession in 1418 somebody came upon Menecutia in the hospital church. Many were simply 'brought in [*recati*]', but one or two were described as *expositus et recommendatus* and their parents named.[8] In Florence, bearers left children at a number of favoured sites, many close to the hospital itself, including the gateway to the nearby graveyard, the boundaries of the orchard, or Piero Baccelli's lodging-house; babies might turn up at the customs point where one entered the city, or just outside the gate, or on the banks of a river where launderers, starting work at dawn, would very likely find them. Traipsing through city streets or round the walls in charge of a wailing child could be an ordeal, especially when bearers drew close to the hospital and their intentions became obvious. Bystanders barracked a woman in 1396, crying 'Where are you taking that child and where did you get it from? Mind you don't take it to San Gallo!' Discomfited, she dropped her burden in the road and fled, leaving two local women to finish the job.[9]

Even in later centuries, when hospitals had made it easier to abandon babies discreetly, irregular arrangements persisted for getting rid of children or landing other parties with the task of approaching an institution. Perhaps this was due to an unshakeable belief that the staff would attempt to identify anyone they saw abandoning a baby, demand payment for the infant's keep, or suggest that the child had been born of married parents capable of raising it themselves. In Bologna, where the authorities were notorious for demanding fees or services from unmarried mothers or fathers, it was sensible to leave babies on the altar of Santo Stefano and run away.[10] Maria Antonia Giovanna, six days old, appeared in the carriage of the Marchese di Belmonte in Naples on 23rd May 1638.[11] An unwary citizen could be left with an embarrassing burden. In March 1760 a pair of thieves snatched a cloak from a night walker on the Riva degli Schiavoni in Venice, whereupon an accomplice of theirs offered to intervene. The man asked the victim to hold a bundle for him while he gave chase and this soon began to show signs of life, much to the victim's disquiet. 'More displeased by acquiring a family than by losing a mantle, he hastened as fast as he could to the hospital of the Pietà, and having put the baby in the proper place he went home before any other misfortune could befall him.'[12]

Sooner or later, most hospitals began to provide receptacles in which bearers could leave small children in comparative safety. Hospital staff were supposed to watch them, but infants could still be exposed overnight to wind and weather, as Sienese doctors warned in 1781.[13] Practical devices were 'a little box' [casetta], a shelf or niche [scaffetta], or a basin described as a pila. This resembled a font or a holy water stoup and could be attached to a wall or mounted on columns to which an older child might be tethered.[14] Archbishop Carlo Borromeo's report on the general hospital at Brescia referred to 'foundlings who are surreptitiously carried to the cradle prepared for the purpose by the head of the infirmary towards midday', which was not the most secret hour, but not the bleakest either.[15] Coryat, on his travels in the early seventeenth century, observed at the Pietà in Venice an 'yron grate inserted into a hollow peece of the wall, betwixt which grate and a plaine stone beneath it, there is a convenient little space to put in an infant', and leave the child there anonymously if it was small enough to fit in.[16] Abandonment of older and larger children was not encouraged in Venice at this time, though not always forbidden elsewhere. A few years earlier, the governors of the Pietà had told the Senate that 'no day passes without four or five babies being brought here and left in the niche'.[17] Furtive bearers were not the only ones to use these containers: passing through a pila became part of children's initiation into the hospital community, and at San Gimignano people would place them in the stoup while they negotiated with the rector.

More sophisticated was the ruota or torno, a wooden box mounted on a turntable which enabled a child to be passed immediately through an aperture in the wall from the world outside into the hospital. There, in theory at least, a duty nurse would at once attend to it. The baby-wheel could, but did not have to, allow the bearer to pass unobserved and avoid any encounter with the staff. Sometimes it came to symbolise the hospital's all-embracing character, its readiness to receive any child of shame or poverty and ask no awkward questions. Such wheels appeared at Imola in the middle or late sixteenth century and were used at Rome and Cagliari soon after 1600, in Ravenna from 1636, at the Innocenti in Florence from 1660.[18] Milan's general hospital installed a wheel in 1594, but the device was not regularly used there until October 1689, when the porter found a child in the wheel lying on a cushion stuffed with straw.[19] This boy proved to be the first of many children to enter by this route, although – as happened in most cities – the wheel had no monopoly of the admissions process, and infants continued to be exposed in other places or presented at the door. About 40 per cent of babies admitted to the Milanese hospital during the eighteenth century had ridden on the wheel, something between 25 and 40 per cent of those who entered the hospitals at Perugia and Imola.[20] Another statistic suggested, however, that between 1778 and 1797, 1,596 children entered the hospital at Pavia by means of the wheel and 299 passed through the office.[21]

The wheel was perhaps especially popular in seventeenth-century Rome (it accepted over a thousand children a year, according to a bland account of 1623) because the guard on duty was supposed to ask only whether the child had been baptised,[22] constables were not to interrogate anyone found at night in the neighbourhood of the hospital,[23] and the apparatus would take, not only newborn babies, but also children aged up to four to six months, and very often of eighteen months to two years, thus opening the way to legitimate children. Their chances of entry were good, said a writer in 1657, because they generally had small heads and were 'very skinny [*molto estenuati*]'; if need be, hospital staff would help the bearers to manoeuvre the infants into the wheel and through the grating.[24] In Naples, entry through the *ruota* to the Annunziata conferred on the infants certain privileges as children of the Madonna, for which reason even those sent from maternity wards or found in the streets passed through it. Occasionally, children four or five years old were smeared with oil and grease in desperate attempts to slide them through the opening, and they could be injured in the process. The word for the wheel came to denote the entire foundling wing of the Annunziata – a woman who nursed foundlings was called a *notrice in Rota*, while infants who died in the hospital were described as *Morti alla Ruota*.[25]

Wheels were most used by bearers of children coming from within the city. Very likely they would receive some dead children deposited by parents reluctant to pay for their funerals.[26] They did not always guarantee anonymity. The suspicion that guards were watching and would help to trace parents – as they did in eighteenth-century Bologna and Vicenza – made some people wary of the wheels.[27] But governments recommended their general introduction in the eighteenth and early nineteenth centuries; small towns which had no hospitals of their own were urged to set up *ruote* for the purpose of collecting foundlings.[28] In Sicily in the mid-eighteenth century, a central committee hoped to see the *ruota* employed in all communities and minded by a person who knew how to baptise. She must attend to any child placed on the wheel as soon as she heard a bell ring, but should not emerge from the building lest she caught sight of the bearer.[29] Failure to provide any kind of receptacle was now regarded as a dereliction of duty. Galanti disapproved of the hospital at Capua in Campania, which gathered foundlings from six other towns and sent most of them to Naples: 'There are no rules and no good order ... in a few years they have spent 60,000 ducats on ill-conceived buildings, while at the same time we have seen foundlings dumped in the middle of the roads because there is no niche to receive them'.[30] The government issued a general directive to the southern kingdom in 1801, calling on every town and village to provide a baby-wheel.[31] Some local inhabitants were not greatly enamoured of this machinery, either in the southern or in the northern states of Italy – between 1823 and 1831, only 16 out of 100 abandoned children were left in the *ruota* at Sulmona, while between

1832 and 1837, only about a quarter of the children picked up in Ivrea (Piedmont) by the local foundling hospice had arrived by the *ruota*.[32]

Great numbers and arduous journeys

Texts on the walls of the Sistine Ward at Santo Spirito in Rome included an exhortation of the prophet Isaiah: 'To the north I will say "Give them up", and to the south, "Do not hold them." Bring back my sons from far away, my daughters from the end of the earth [Isaiah 43:6].'[33] An urban foundling hospital was a species of entrepôt, importing children despatched by the outlying villages and towns of their birth and transferring them like merchandise to other places, within or outside the city, where they could be suckled, fostered and possibly legally adopted.[34] During their grim and bumpy journey, they entered a noisome transit camp, the hospital nursery, from which many never emerged, since it proved all too difficult to honour the undertaking, 'Leave your orphans, I will keep them alive [Jeremiah 49:11]', attached to the representation in Rome of Innocent III establishing the order of the Holy Spirit.

The volume of admissions to a hospital depended on the size of the city, the distribution of other foundling hospitals throughout the province or state, and the reluctance (usually considerable) of local communities to look after their own foundlings. Many of the bigger institutions expanded fitfully from the late fifteenth until around the mid-seventeenth century. Occasionally, overwhelmed by their responsibilities, they sank into a financial morass, as did Florence's Innocenti in 1579, and had to adjust to reality, perhaps even to expel some of their older residents or transfer them to other establishments.[35] Several hospitals shrank in the first half of the eighteenth century, if only because their governors were resisting abandonment by married couples, and at least one, in Padua, closed down its *ruota*.[36] Towards the end of the century, however, particularly by 1780, some cities were experiencing a steep rise in abandonments which reversed the trend towards caution and retrenchment. This could be attributed, in varying degrees, to at least three different causes: perhaps to a rise in bastardy rates; perhaps to the practice of surrendering young children temporarily in order to free married women to do more paid work; perhaps to the facilities which cities offered for giving birth safely and in secret, so that they attracted more country women.[37]

The size of undertakings varied hugely. Even in the 1790s, towns in southern Calabria (whose populations ranged between 4,000 and 11,500) would generally deal with no more than a dozen foundlings in an ordinary year; only Tropea encountered as many as thirty or forty.[38] Marriage rates were high among the 'lowly common folk [*gente bassa*]' and fornicators were punished 'with weapons', things which made for fewer base-born children in other parts of the remote province.[39] In the fifteenth century, the children's hospital at San Gimignano in Tuscany had received about five children a year; in 1453 there were thirteen in the house and just four out at nurse.[40] But in central and northern Italy, in the mid-eighteenth century, a foundling home in a modest provincial city such as Cesena, Imola or Ravenna in the Romagna, Todi in Umbria or Viterbo in the Lazio would normally take in between twenty-five and seventy infants a year. Exceptionally, the annual figure dropped to about eighteen in Ravenna in the second half of the eighteenth century, on account of a declining bastardy rate and their rejection of most legitimate children.[41] A central provincial city would probably accept between one and two hundred, while the capital of a large state might stretch to five hundred or more, the Neapolitan Annunziata receiving the largest recorded numbers. By the 1780s, the Innocenti in Florence was admitting just over a thousand children annually, its counterpart in Milan a little less than a thousand (40 per cent more than in the previous decade), while the Annunziata exceeded two thousand in 1785, in 1786 and in 1787.[42]

Inevitably, the movements of food prices influenced the level of abandonments, especially those driven by poverty rather than shame. In famine years, as distinct from the lean months which generally recurred in late winter and spring, abandonments rose to extraordinary heights and involved more older children. They were boosted by influxes of starving crowds into the cities and outbreaks of disease, 'putrid' fevers and other illnesses which disabled parents and carers. Towards the mid-seventeenth century, between eight hundred and a thousand children were normally surrendered to Santo Spirito in Rome every year, but in a famine year, 1649, the total reached 1,133.[43] In Siena, during the poor harvest year 1766–7, 539 children, most of them between two and five years old, entered Santa Maria della Scala, where the normal annual average was about two hundred.[44] In 1764, during the same notorious famine cycle, the Annunziata received 4,675 children; over the previous five years, annual admissions had averaged 1,622.[45]

Hospital clerks could not know, or did not record, the birthplaces of many of the babies who entered their nurseries. From the incomplete information available, it seems that in fifteenth-century Florence and San Gimignano up to two-thirds of them were coming from outside the city walls, mostly from the *contado*, the city's rural domain, but a small but significant proportion from further afield.[46] Some illicit transfers were made by communities trying to foist their foundlings on each other; in 1583, exasperated officers at Imola grumbled that subject communes had sent them twenty-eight 'little bastards' with such brash impropriety that the diocesan vicar-general decided to gaol the bearers.[47] At Verona in the eighteenth century, the Domus Pietatis suffered from communes such as Legnago, forty kilometres away, which persisted in sending their foundlings to the provincial capital, and also from an obligation of uncertain origin to receive children from the prince-bishopric of Trento.[48]

Foundling care became with time an expensive, specialised enterprise concentrated in a few major centres (not all in the largest cities), sometimes designated by government decree, and hospitals here could easily become overburdened and indebted. This was especially true of Perugia in Umbria and Sulmona in the Abruzzi, whose hospitals were required to serve whole provinces rather than just their own immediate surroundings. Some relief was forthcoming; the assets of hospitals at Assisi, Foligno and Nocera were transferred to Perugia after 1739, though this did not remove the need to transport children from thence to Perugia in all weathers, and only occasionally were they allowed to take more direct routes or to be sent directly to local nurses.[49] From 1762, the hospital at Sulmona was required by royal decree to receive infants from all three parts of the Abruzzi and could solve its problems only by sending on a proportion of them, first to Naples (which protested effectively) and then to Rome, until an able administrator, Pietro Carrera, rejected this expedient as inhuman. He may have contributed to a sounder scheme introduced by the government in 1792, whereby foundlings were to be nurtured in the areas where they had been abandoned and local communes and charities required to contribute to their support.[50]

Foundling hospitals were unevenly distributed in the Papal States. Until the early eighteenth century, nearly all were concentrated in Emilia and the Romagna, Umbria and the Marches. Until new hospitals opened at Viterbo and Narni under Pope Clement XII (1730–40), 'all the country from Todi to Spoleto' and from Spoleto to the border between the Papal States and the Kingdom of Naples was sending foundlings to Santo Spirito in Rome. In 1737 this hospital was serving a population of 550,000; the Viterbo hospital did reduce Santo Spirito's load, but only by about one-seventh.[51] Misgivings about the often fatal journeys of foundlings to Rome had long troubled the authorities; in 1661 it had seemed that only one-third of the children abandoned in the provinces were still alive when they reached Santo Spirito, and many were dying shortly after arrival.[52] Economising on transport costs, provincial towns preferred to send babies to Rome in batches of eight to ten, a practice which could mean keeping them for several days in exceptionally squalid conditions.[53] Caracciolo, the papal visitor to Santo Spirito in 1738, digested reports of the abuses practised on the road by hired baby-carriers, some of whom were also smugglers, believed to be using infants to conceal the contraband goods in their baskets. Their journeys of fifty or sixty miles could last as long as five days, during which time most babies were fed on small doses of emulsion of sweet almonds. Only a few carriers would engage wet nurses to feed them at wayside inns. Many deaths from neglect and exposure occurred on the way and some murders were probably committed in the knowledge that few inquiries would be made after unwanted children and little could be proved even if they were.[54]

These practices were peculiar neither to the Papal States nor to early modern Italy, but were liable to prevail in any place where foundling care was centralised rather than practised locally, and unwanted children were hastily removed from their places of origin. Borghini, the sixteenth-century superintendent of the Innocenti, had lamented the fate of children sent from small hospices in Tuscany: 'sometimes they go two days without milk, and reach here more dead than alive, and quite often so far gone that they cannot be revived'.[55] Carriers bringing children to Milan sometimes exposed them a second time. Reluctant to complete the task, or to give the hospital any chance to refuse the babies, they would leave them in a village outside the city, or drop them somewhere within it, or slip them into the turntable, or put them down outside the hospital's walls.[56] Similar hardships were inflicted in northern Europe, where, in the 1770s, about eight thousand children were being sent annually to Paris; in their recent past some of them had come from outside the kingdom and been transported by private arrangement from Brussels, until a decree passed in the Austrian Netherlands forbade the export of foundlings.[57]

Eighteenth-century communities could send their foundlings to distant hospitals for contrasting reasons – some because a zealous government was pursuing good order and administrative neatness, others because a feeble government and a self-serving clergy were allowing local hospitals to give very low priority to foundlings. In 1751 the Grand

Duchy of Tuscany, now ruled by the house of Habsburg-Lorraine, suppressed almost seventy small traditional hospitals in the former State of Siena, partly on the grounds that they were encouraging vagrancy by harbouring bad characters masquerading as pilgrims. The State now transferred their assets to Santa Maria della Scala in the city of Siena. Many of these small establishments had been coping with local foundlings, who were henceforth loaded on to the central hospital; regulations of 1754 stipulated that 'exposed' children should be received at the fifteen granges which administered its estates and at four other designated depots, after which they should be sent to Siena.[58]

In 1785–7 an average of 967 foundlings each year entered the Annunziata from within Naples itself, from the maternity wards of the Incurabili hospital, from the suburbs, and from the villages [*casali*] within the city's territory. Forty-four creatures of unknown provenance were 'found in the Ruota' each year. On average, 1,018 foundlings arrived annually from two dozen other places in the kingdom. No-one appeared to know how many had died on the journey.[59] Galanti reproved a number of well-endowed hospitals, especially in Campania, for failing to observe their charters. They ought in theory to have cared for their local foundlings themselves. Instead they sent most of them to Naples, a carrier's fee being less than the payments due to wet nurses and foster parents, which would drag on for months and perhaps for years. Some were splashing out on churches or other buildings and spending much on the stipends of mass-priests. Where they did give charity to the laity, they preferred to care for the sick and distribute alms and medicines to the poor in general; they also preferred orphan girls to foundlings, for whom they made little room in their conservatories. At Guardia di Cerreto, the hospital enjoyed an annual income of 2,500 ducats. 'But it keeps a hospital only in name for the women and sends the foundlings to Naples. Nevertheless it has spent nine thousand ducats on decorating the church, has increased the salaries of twenty-two chaplains, and has spent another few hundred ducats on pursuing a lawsuit to get a road for its own village, without success.'[60] The largest contingents of foundlings – an average of 194 in each of the three years – came from Salerno, of whose hospital Galanti wrote: 'it has an income of 1,800 ducats. Twelve priests absorb 1,200. They give 60 ducats a year to a woman to receive foundlings, to get them baptised, and to send them on to die at the Annunziata of Naples.' Gaeta did at least maintain a 'very clean' hospital for sick males and females and a conservatory for orphaned girls. But it spent two hundred ducats from its income of ten thousand on sending infants to Naples by sea, frequently with fatal results (fifty-four arrived in 1785, forty-four in 1786, eighty-eight in 1787).[61]

Baptisms and tokens

Galanti's funereal statistics indicated that towards the close of the eighteenth century, little more than one-third of the infants who reached the Annunziata lived to see their first birthday (736 out of 2,029 in an average year, or 36.2 per cent). This hospital's record was then neither better nor worse than that of many foundling homes. But one objective could be quickly achieved: to save souls by ensuring that all its charges had been baptised. Some held that infants not only became Christians but acquired souls through baptism – or at least souls which were capable of being saved or damned, rather than lost to Limbo; at baptism, cleansed of Adam's ancestral sin, a child became an 'innocent'.[62] It was true that in emergencies a lay person could baptise a child, and in some communities midwives were not to be licensed unless they knew how to give the water and apply it even to distressed foetuses trapped in the birth canal. But the proper administration of baptism could not be taken for granted, there was generally a risk that illegitimate children had not received it, and it was the hospital's business to ensure that no child was deprived of the sacrament. If a child had received the bare minimum in an emergency it could seem important to complete the procedure by administering the 'exorcisms and holy oil' in a baptismal church.

Conscientious persons delivering children to foundling hospitals would indicate whether or not they had been baptised, attaching a coin if they had, a small bag of salt if they had not. Salt would be used in the full ceremony, when the priest applied it to the infants' mouths and cleansed them from the corruption of original sin. 'He was not baptised, but brought the salt round his neck', ran a record at San Gimignano in 1458.[63] In later centuries, documentary evidence began to replace the language of symbols and the most reliable testimony was a certificate signed by a priest, which often pointed to legitimate birth. The hospital could always, if in doubt, arrange conditional baptism – 'If you have not been baptised, I baptise you.'[64] The staff would probably have more than half of the children they admitted baptised, enlisting supervisors or nurses as godparents. About a third of children entering the Misericordia at Perugia in 1584–95 and 1640–51 had already received baptism, in 1680–9 and 1700–19, approximately a half. At the Innocenti in Florence the proportion was lower, seldom more than a fifth during the seventeenth century, but it rose to about a third in the last thirty years of the eighteenth. At Todi in the eighteenth century the proportion of previously baptised children was, likewise, about one-third.[65] There came a time, however, when baptismal certificates were used to trace married parents with a view to returning their children to them. At the start of the nineteenth century, more and more parents were sending their children unbaptised to the Innocenti in Florence, for fear of leaving tell-tale traces of their origins.[66]

Many parents left items other than salt or documents with their children. They made symbolic attempts to equip them for their new life, to place with them objects or scraps of cloth or items of clothing which would protect the child – things which glittered would repel the evil eye, sacred properties frustrate the demon – and could be used as tokens of identity. Often, from the late middle ages to the eighteenth century, messages left with the children named them, entrusted them to the hospital's care, expressed an intention to reclaim them if and when times improved. A note left at Siena towards 1500 declared that the baby's name was Archagniola Antonia and that she belonged to 'a worthy person who within a short time will make good whatever you spend on her. And so she is commended to your mercy.'[67] A few regretted their decisions and asked for the child back almost immediately; one of the earliest known documents recorded that, in 1274, Becha recovered her daughter Venturella from Santa Maria della Scala after describing the tokens [intersigna] she had left with the girl and naming the time and place at which she had exposed her.[68] Objects used through the centuries to connect children with their parents included half a rosary, half a playing card, half a coin: produce the other half, and the hospital, if it had kept proper records, might be able to reunite you with your child.[69] If a child had no distinctive birthmark a mark could be created. In a sixteenth-century story by Giraldi Cinzio, a young mother in Salerno pricks each of her baby's ears four times, so that the scars will form the points of a cross; when she and her lover are able to marry after her father's death, they succeed, not without difficulty, in recovering the boy with the help of the hospital's register.[70]

At least in the late eighteenth century, and probably in earlier times, parents could express tender feelings for the children they were giving up, as though they were not just encumbrances or embarrassments and there was some hope of seeing them again. 'He has been baptised, his name is Luca Francesco, and he is legitimate; do not mark him, for within a few months he will be reclaimed', pleaded a message addressed to Santa Maria della Scala in 1765.[71] In the 1780s, adults delivering children to the hospital of San Giovanni in Turin seemed to be equipping them for an adventure or a new life, supplying swaddling clothes, a piece of cloth (perhaps for napkins) and a bonnet, usually trimmed with lace. There might be rosaries, or medals, or cheap crucifixes with them, as though to protect the children on their journeys by invoking the powers of the cross and the saints, and there could be medicinal herbs, or packets of sugar or butter – a last contribution by blood relatives to the welfare of a child whom it was impossible to keep, an effort to present the child to the hospitallers as a fellow creature deserving of tender care.[72]

Some children came with names, recorded on certificates, mentioned or requested in accompanying notes ('call him Girolamo Crescenzio', at Siena in 1495). In the absence of instructions, hospitals bestowed their own, often using the names of popular saints: an obvious choice was the saint on whose feast-day the child had arrived at the hospital. Fina, the name of an ascetic local virgin, was usually reserved for girls from San Gimignano. Other festivals left their mark – Palm Sunday on children baptised Ulivo or Ulivetta, Easter on those named Pasqua, Pasquino or Pasquale. So, now and then, did a Saturday or Sunday, on a Sabbatino or a Domenica. Occasionally a hospital resorted to something more eloquent, a name of good omen such as Speranza or Bonaventura, or one which, like Tradita, seemed to reflect the process of handing a girl over, if not of betraying her. Alberghino suggested a child who had found some room at the inn. Classical Latin texts were used by the more advanced pupils in the school at Santa Maria della Scala and perhaps the schoolmaster was responsible for a few unchristian names adopted in that hospital – Achille, Ercole, Giulio Cesare, Annibale. Inevitably, many children bore the same name and, as they grew up, were distinguished from each other by epithets or nicknames, not always good-natured – 'the stout', 'the lame', 'the dumb', 'the crazy', and so forth. The imaginative task of inventing surnames for fatherless children was seldom undertaken before about 1800. For most of them the general designation was 'child of the house' or 'brought up in the hospital', at least until they married and sometimes even afterwards.[73]

The ordeal of the nursery

It would be unjust to suspect hospitals of concentrating on saving babies' souls from Limbo and feeling free to neglect their most urgent physical needs. But reception nurseries often became places of horror which assailed all the senses with filth, foul smells and the wailing of hungry and fretful babies. Seldom did these wards earn good reports from visitors. At least three intractable problems contributed to high mortality here: the difficulty of recruiting wet nurses of good health and character, willing to work in sordid conditions for paltry wages; the impossibility of finding adequate substitutes for human breast-milk; the high risk of cross infection, especially with skin complaints and venereal disease, which made the task of nursing sickly children especially daunting for anyone not conscripted to perform it.

Internal nurses at Santo Spirito in Rome enjoyed little liberty while serving in the hospital and were allowed out of their quarters only to go to mass or attend baptisms. Standards of hygiene were low; it was necessary in 1587 to ban doves and poultry from the premises. In the seventeenth century there were numerous reports of rickety furniture, of excessively narrow beds for the nurses, of bug infestation, of outbreaks of scabies.[74] In the 1760s, the nurses' ward of Siena consisted of a single dormitory containing nine large beds, each for two nurses and four children (more in emergencies). In the absence of cribs, babies were in danger of suffocation by overlaying.[75] Galanti took a low view of the hospital at Aquila in the Abruzzi, which distributed space incompetently – much to the rector, little to the nursery, where nurses and their charges were crammed into a small room with a tiny window:

> I found thirteen babies with three nurses and two goats. The children were all like corpses, swaddled in coarse and filthy cloths; they showed that they could scarcely stay alive. The three nurses were unfortunate women, unhealthy and misshapen, belonging to the prostitute class. To be at Santo Spirito in Aquila is a badge of shame, and given this sentiment it is hard to find nurses.[76]

Todi in Umbria did little better, according to the papal visitor who saw it in 1787 and complained of darkness, dampness and disgusting smells in the nursing rooms, and of beds, sheets and other items impregnated with scabies.[77]

There were occasional glimmers of light. Attempts to improve conditions initiated in Siena in about 1775 suggested that something better could be imagined and also, as is the way of reform schemes, reflected sadly on what had recently been tolerated. The ward was henceforth to be supervised by a head nurse, and her subordinates should now concentrate on cleaning the dormitory and the warming-room, on keeping their infants clean, and on opening the windows for a certain length of time twice a day. They should not be distracted by other tasks, for example by doing laundry, washing napkins or toting firewood, were never to enter the kitchen, and should not be compelled to spin (perhaps girls from the conservatory would now undertake these chores). A spacious loggia was to be added to the nurses' premises, so that they could walk with babies in the open air and napkins be stretched out to dry after washing.[78] Galanti bestowed rare praise on the nursery at the royal hospital of Santa Teresa in Cosenza, which had plenty of well-dressed and seemingly healthy nurses, none of whom had to suckle more than two infants.[79]

Hospitals struggled to find lactating women who had recently lost or weaned their own children. Maternity beds in general hospitals could provide cheap labour, in that women could be made to pay for the care they had received by giving up their own babies and suckling other people's children either in the maternity wards or in the nursery. The fact that internal nurses were often unmarried mothers contributed to their unsavoury reputation and aggravated the stigma attached to working in the hospital itself.[80] Borghini strove to keep the nurses, 'people of all sorts, no matter who, so long as they have milk', potentially bad influences, away from the conservatory girls of the Innocenti.[81] In its early days some wet nurses had legally been slaves, paid wages but enjoying no legal right to quit the hospital's service. In later centuries, some nurses, especially in Bologna, were almost slave labourers, *balie forzate*, for different reasons – single women who, having failed to pay in full the twenty-five lire fee demanded of one who gave up her child to the hospital, were compelled to work off their debts by serving time on the premises.[82]

In theory, nurseries ought to feed babies only for a few days or at most weeks until the hospitallers succeeded in placing them with external nurses. Smaller hospitals employed from one to six nurses on the premises, the larger ones more than ten. Santo Spirito generally kept between fifteen and seventeen nurses 'in the house' between the mid-sixteenth and the mid-seventeenth century; at times of high demand thereafter they needed anything from sixty to eighty.[83] Ideally, each nurse should give her undivided attention to just one child, but seldom was this possible; Brescia in 1580 and Florence in 1641 did well to provide two nurses for every three foundlings in the reception rooms.[84] At Santo Spirito in 1626–34 each nurse had three on her hands, and in 1635 one woman was in charge of five. Galanti estimated that about a hundred children were being nursed in the Annunziata at any time in the mid-1780s, and that each nurse had to feed four or five.[85] In Siena in the 1760s, the incessant demands made on wet nurses by three or four infants at the breast kept the milk of one or two women flowing for as much as two years.[86] At Perugia in the first decade of the eighteenth century, the average term of service for a wet nurse in the hospital was about eight months, in the course of which she would probably look after anything between eleven and twenty babies.[87] During the eighteenth century, the hospital at Ravenna employed only one nurse at a time (admittedly numbers were exceptionally small) and she had sometimes been lactating for between two and four years. Physicians occasionally complained that such 'old' milk was bound to be of poor quality, especially if the woman secreting it ate coarse food and took little exercise.[88]

Keeping frail infants alive depended on an uncertain supply of human milk, though hospitals could resort with dubious results to goats and asses. In 1302, Francesco and Vina, the sharecropping tenants of a farm belonging to Santa Maria della Scala at Siena, were instructed to raise a flock of ten goats to feed the *gittatelli*; Udine's secret council called for three nanny goats in 1558; Brescia actually kept a dozen at the Ospedale Maggiore in 1580; in 1791 the Finance Council of the Kingdom considered the use of goat's milk at the hospital in Sulmona and were prepared to approve it as an experiment.[89] Institutions were relatively slow to appreciate cow's milk, but it was used at the Innocenti in Florence towards the end of the sixteenth century.[90] However, the vitamin or protein deficiencies in much animal milk were fatal to many babies; artificial feeding of the very young was not practicable. As Galanti reflected in his commentary on the Annunziata:

They have tried to substitute animals' milk for the milk of a woman, but I think that cannot be done without deterioration of the human race. Nature has endowed the milk of each beast with a life-giving spirit related to the species. We should rather ensure that nature's most important function is not debased by our own ideas, and that mothers are rewarded for bringing up their own children.[91]

It had long been taken for granted that single mothers must be separated from their offspring; if Galanti was attacking this assumption, his ideas were too radical for his own time, although there was a slight relaxation of the rules in Florence from 1791, permitting unmarried mothers to suckle their own and other children in the hospital nursery until the babies were sent off to foster homes.[92] But many years later, after the First World War and in the wake of an acute shortage of paid wet nurses, unmarried mothers at foundling hospitals in Milan, Rome and Florence would be first urged and then compelled to suckle their own children – a procedure which would, during the 1920s, reduce infant mortality among foundlings as no measure had ever done before.[93]

Infant mortality

The high incidence of deaths on the premises was not entirely due to the hospital's inefficiency, sordid conditions and scanty resources. All children in the population were at high risk during the first few days of life, the point at which hospitals encountered large numbers of illegitimate babies. Many new arrivals were already exhausted by long journeys and blighted by exposure to the weather. Many children of temporary immigrants driven to cities by famines had almost starved before they were deposited at the hospital or on the streets. In all probability, too, married couples would abandon the least robust children, infants who were physically or mentally impaired, unlikely in future to be capable of earning their keep. Illegitimate children born in secret might have been injured by attempts to conceal pregnancies by binding the mother's abdomen, or be suffering the consequences of unattended births.[94] A few had probably experienced botched attempts at abortion. Bandello's wicked Pandora begins by 'drinking distilled waters and eating things which would have turned the stomach of a pig', and graduates to applying direct physical force by getting her maid to climb on a piece of furniture and jump off it seven times on to her back.[95] Children assaulted in the womb might well be handicapped at birth.

Promiscuous feeding in the nursery favoured the transmission of the French evil. This could be a hereditary or a congenital illness, and be transmitted to and subsequently by a wet nurse: she could pick it up from the mouth of a suckling, who was possibly the child of a promiscuous woman or of one infected by a loose-living partner. She might then convey the disease to several of the other infants she tended over a long tour of duty, if sores formed around her nipples and they had cuts or sores in their mouths. Connections between breastfeeding and 'venereal poison' were traced from the early sixteenth century onwards.[96] Should signs of the illness appear in infants, one measure, attempted in Udine, was to wean them prematurely by switching them at three or four months from breast-milk to pap (bread cooked in water and sugar) – a change of diet unlikely to do them good.[97] In Ivrea in the 1830s the hospital's organiser of wet nurses, the *levatrice*, did not send them suspect babies, but kept the sickly infants in her house and fed them there artificially until, within six days at most, they died.[98] Another method, which was proposed at Bologna in 1867 and may have been contemplated in earlier times, was to employ a syphilitic nurse to suckle syphilitic children.[99] It would be recognised in the late nineteenth century that the fear of syphilis could damage foundling children almost as much as syphilis itself, if children wrongly suspected of carrying the disease were put on to artificial, unsuitable food by nervous medical staff.[100]

Squalid, airless reception rooms and overworked, unwilling and unhealthy nurses contributed to high infant mortality but did not explain it all. Statistics supplied at the time or compiled later by painstaking scholars suggest that, in several hospitals, between 30 and 50 per cent of all children admitted died as babies on the premises. This happened partly because they were too ill or frail to be sent out to nurse; partly because external nurses could not be found promptly; partly, too, because those nurses were quick to return gravely ill babies to the hospital and it was there that they died.[101] At Florence during the 1650s, a total of 5,710 children entered the Innocenti and 2,833, just under half, died in the hospital.[102] Between the beginning of 1700 and the end of 1709, the Misericordia in Perugia admitted 1,308 children; 603 of these (46.1 per cent) died in the hospital after surviving for an average of forty-seven days. Another 438, who lived on average for about six months and represented one-third of those admitted, died when out at nurse before their first birthday.[103] Galanti's figures for the Annunziata in Naples showed that 584 of 2,029 children received during an average year from 1785 to 1787 (28.8 per cent) died in the hospital, and 709 (again about one-third of the whole) died *alle case*, in the homes of wet nurses, before their first birthday.[104]

Fair comparisons with the overall infant mortality rates for people of all social classes living in urban and rural parishes are difficult to make. It seems likely, though, that in average years, 'normal' infant mortality (deaths within the first twelve months of life) could be in the region of 30–40 per cent and hence considerably less than the 50–70 per cent often recorded for foundlings after entering hospital (to say nothing of those who had died on the way to it). In a sample of Venetian parishes, the rates were generally between 20 and 30 per cent in the seventeenth century, rising to higher levels after 1720 and just passing 40 per cent in 1770 and 1797. Around Ravenna in the eighteenth century, infant mortality among children born in wedlock varied between 25 and 45 cent; in parishes to the north-west of Milan between 1750 and 1800, overall rates ranged between 29 per cent at Nerviano and 40 per cent at Cantalupo and Vanzago.[105]

Administrators occasionally gathered evidence which suggested that external nursing was far healthier than internal; in 1660, officials at Santo Spirito, as though swayed by this testimony, tried to ensure that there were never more than twenty to thirty children in the nursery.[106] Some scholars have attributed the decline of infant mortality in certain nineteenth-century cities to greater efficiency in moving children out to nurse as quickly as possible.[107] It fell to the Annunziata of Naples to prove how deadly the opposite procedure could be. When, in 1819, the hospital broke with its usual custom and allowed 1,835 infants to be nursed on the premises, only 76 (4.1 per cent) were still alive at the age of twelve months.[108]

Conclusion

Early modern societies may perhaps be suspected of hypocrisy – of professing to value the lives of base-born children, but in practice treating them very cavalierly: not, perhaps, as Malthus half-seriously hinted, of deliberately employing foundling hospitals to dispose of surplus population, but of giving low priority to foundling children and exposing them, out of a mixture of callousness and inefficiency, to deadly ordeals. The alarming infant mortality sprang partly from parental selection, exposure of the most unfit, and partly from the dangers attending secret pregnancies and births and the consequences of attempted abortions. But there was a grim and potentially fatal logic in the process of removing newborn babies from unmarried nursing mothers and distancing them from their places of birth. It may have owed something to a desire to give children a fresh start, but more to a wish to preserve the reputation of the mother and her kin and defend moral decency. It was often inspired by a wish to use local resources for other purposes and consign foundlings, who had few champions, to some far-off authority, with little regard for their fate. Concentration of the care of foundlings, often regarded as a highly specialised enterprise, exerted intolerable strains on some overloaded institutions. They struggled to recruit nurses, both to tide infants over the first few perilous days and to remove them from the hospital into other, more salubrious, surroundings. A child in the nursery would probably become one of three or four sucklings at the breast of the same nurse, a child on its travels might lie at the mercy of ill-paid, crooked carriers with no interest in its survival and usually no nurse at all.

As Galanti implied, part of the problem lay in society's failure to reward mothers for keeping their own children; instead, hospitals paid them for looking after other people's and tempted them to give up their own. A single mother was generally condemned as an unfit mother who deserved to have her own child removed; a combination of social disapproval and poverty would make it impossible for her to keep it. In 1796 the archbishop of Florence, who had married couples in mind, instructed parish priests to point out to their flocks the inhumanity of separating children 'from the natural support of their own mothers purely for the sake of escaping the obligation to feed and maintain the babies concerned ... and to condemn them to live on milk which is not suited to their weak and delicate constitution'. It was, he said, impossible for the beleaguered Innocenti to recruit enough nurses to preserve the life and health of the exposed infants, and priests should try to revive in the hearts of parents feelings of 'natural affection, justice, and love of the public good'.[109] These sentiments, admirable though they might be, were unlikely to save illegitimate children from abandonment. One of several difficulties was that hospitals could not devise a satisfactory principle of selection. Exclude the children of all married couples, and they turned away many deserving cases. Open their doors to everyone, allow anonymous abandonment and the use of the baby-wheel, and they were overwhelmed by numbers far too great for their limited resources, merely substituting misery within an institution for misery in the world outside. Tolerance for the regulated abandonment of illegitimate children, as a lesser evil preferable to murder, called for ambitious rescue operations, designed for the benefit of the infants and their mothers. Inevitably, there was some danger that, far from allowing a defensible lesser evil, they would merely substitute one evil for another, averting the actual murders of a relatively small number of children, but replacing them with a much larger number of deaths as a result of misconceived philanthropy and inadequate funding.

Notes

1 Malthus 1826/1996, I, p. 311.
2 Trexler 1973–74a, 260–5; Sandri 1982, pp. 75–6; Black 1989, p. 200; Bussini 1991, pp. 308–9; Reggiani and Paradisi 1991, p. 940.
3 Vigni 1985: 202–3.
4 Tanturri 2003: 169.
5 Bussini 1991, pp. 308–9; Tittarelli *et al.* 2003, p. 182.
6 Reggiani 1997: 292–4, 303–6.
7 Martellucci 2001, 54–6.
8 Tittarelli *et al.* 2003, pp. 40, 44–5, 50–1, 53.
9 Sandri 1991, pp. 995–8.
10 Kertzer 1993, pp. 40 and 198–9, notes 6 and 7.
11 Da Molin 1991, pp. 462–4.
12 Gozzi ed. Zardo 1915, pp. 52–3, 12 March 1760.
13 Vigni 1985: 203–4.
14 Sandri 1982, pp. 103–6; Vaglini 2001, pp. 219, 221.
15 Montanari 1987, p. 281.
16 Coryat 1905 edn., I, p. 407.
17 Chambers and Pullan 1992, p. 313.
18 Fanucci 1602, p. 22; Galassi 1966–70, II, pp. 239, 243; Bolognesi and Giovannini 1982, pp. 320–2; Angeli 1991, p. 125; Kertzer 1993, p. 100; Viazzo *et al.* 2000, p. 70.
19 Hunecke 1989, pp. 78, 84–6.
20 Angeli 1991, pp. 125–6; Reggiani and Paradisi 1991, pp. 955–7, 963; Tittarelli *et al.* 2003, p. 182.
21 Lallemand 1885, p. 414.
22 From the account by Domenico Borgarucci in Grégoire 1979: 249–50.
23 Schiavoni 1991, pp. 1028–9.
24 Pagano 1979: 375–6.
25 Galanti 1786–90, III, pp. 155–7; Da Molin 1991, pp. 459–61, 486–7.
26 Da Molin 1983: 116–18.
27 Povolo 1989, pp. 105–6; Kertzer 1993, p. 108.
28 Kertzer 1993, pp. 95–6.
29 Raffaele 1997: 319–20, 322.
30 Galanti 1786–90, III, pp. 162–6.
31 De Rosa 1978: 26.
32 Tanturri 2003: 169; Berruti 2007: 564–5.
33 Howe 1978, pp. 338–42; Howe 2005, p. 194; Chapter 8, notes 42–44.
34 For the hospital as entrepôt – the notion comes from a Chambéry physician, *c.*1780 – see Pullan 1989, p. 9.
35 Gavitt 1997: 232–3; Sandri 2001, pp. 171, 176–7.
36 Povolo 1989, pp. 105–6.
37 Cf. Da Molin 1983: 106–7.

38   See Galanti ed. Placanica 1992: for Crotone, pp. 120, 125–6, 347; for Monteleone, pp. 185, 348; for Fiumara di Muro, pp. 198–9; for Nicastro, pp. 252–3, 305–6, 348; for Tropea, pp. 225, 348.
39   *Ibid.*, pp. 117, 169.
40   Sandri 1982, pp. 22–5, 128.
41   Bolognesi and Giovannini 1982, pp. 311–12, 321–3.
42   For Florence, Corsini 1976: 1039; for Milan, Hunecke 1994, p. 118; for Naples, Galanti 1786–90, III, pp. 155–7. See also Viazzo *et al.* 1994: Table I, 247.
43   Schiavoni 1991, pp. 1019–20.
44   Vigni 1979: 123–5; Vigni 1985: 198–9.
45   Da Molin 1983: 117–18.
46   Sandri 1982, pp. 77–9; Gavitt 1990, pp. 206–7; Sandri 1991, pp. 994–6, 1003.
47   Galassi 1966–70, pp. 240, 245, 248.
48   Cappelletti 1983:429–31; Garbellotti 1996, p. 71.
49   Da Molin 1983: 107; Tittarelli *et al.* 2003, pp. 168–9, 212–16.
50   Tanturri 2003: 154–6, 159, 165–7.
51   Schiavoni 1991, pp. 1017, 1023–4; Sonnino 1991, p. 1068.
52   Surdacki 2001: 97.
53   Pagano 1979: 357–8.
54   Langellotti and Travaglini 1991, p. 745. For evidence of similar practices in the nineteenth century, on the part of the carriers then known as 'angel-makers', see Kertzer and White 1994: 458.
55   Gavitt 1997: 242–3.
56   Reggiani and Paradisi 1991, p. 940.
57   Delasselle 1978, pp. 54–5; Winter 2010.
58   Vigni 1979: 107–9, 112.
59   Galanti 1786–90, III, pp. 155–7.
60   *Ibid.*, III, p. 165.
61   *Ibid.*, III, pp. 161–3.
62   Haas 1998, pp. 64–5; cf. Trexler 1980, pp. 368–9.
63   Trexler 1973–74a: 269–70; Sandri 1982, pp. 121–5; Sandri 1991, p. 1008; Haas 1998, p. 81; Martellucci 2001: 65. Cf. Boswell 1989, pp. 324–5.
64   Codarin Miani 1991, pp. 386–7.
65   For Perugia, Calzola 2003, pp. 134–41 and Tittarelli *et al.* 2003, pp. 196–7; for Florence, Corsini 1976: 1039; for Todi, Bussini 1991, pp. 311–12.
66   Bolognesi and Giovannini 1982, pp. 322–3; Corsini 1983: 96–7.
67   Sandri 1982, pp. 110–22; Martellucci 2001: 62–5.
68   Zdekauer 1898: 469.
69   Da Molin 1991, pp. 465–8; Sandri 1991, p. 1008.
70   Giraldi Cinzio 1565, IV.7, vol. I, pp. 701–7.
71   Vigni 1985: 234.
72   Doriguzzi 1991, pp. 516–17, 524; cf. Cappelletto 1983: 433–4.
73   Sandri 1982, pp. 100, 126–7; Martellucci 2001, pp. 64–5, 69–74, 161.
74   Surdacki 2000: 193–5.
75   Vigni 1985: 209–12.
76   De Rosa 1978: 13.
77   Bussini 1991, p. 303.
78   Corsini 1991, doc. 2, p. 94.
79   Galanti ed. Placanica 1992, pp. 264–5.

80 Hunecke 1989, pp. 93–4; Gavitt 1990, pp. 164, 167–8; Corsini 1991, pp. 93–6; Bussini 1991, p. 303; Reggiani 1997: 299–303. For individual cases see Nardi 1989: 122–4; Ferrante 1996, p. 220.

81 Fubini Leuzzi 1994, pp. 874–5.

82 Kertzer 1993, pp. 61, 124–9, 142–3.

83 Grégoire 1979: 250; Schiavoni 1991, pp. 1031–3; Surdacki 2000: 190–2.

84 In Brescia there were twelve nurses to nineteen babies in 1580 (Montanari 1987, p. 281); in Florence, eighteen ordinary nurses and two superiors to twenty-seven babies (Passerini 1853, p. 949).

85 Galanti 1786–90, III, pp. 153–4.

86 Vigni 1985: 212–13.

87 Tittarelli 1991, pp. 1140–3.

88 Bolognesi and Giovannini 1982, pp. 320, 324.

89 Montanari 1987, p. 281; Codarin Miani 1991, pp. 388–9; Martellucci 2001: 93–6; Tanturri 2003: 161.

90 Sandri 1991: 97.

91 Galanti 1786–90, III, pp. 153–4.

92 Di Bello 1997: 345–8.

93 Viazzo et al. 1994: 259–64.

94 Vigni 1985: 203–4.

95 Bandello ed. Flora 1934, III.52, vol. II, pp. 513–17. For abortifacients in sixteenth-century Florence, see Terpstra 2010, pp. 84–99; for the Venetian dominions in the eighteenth century, see Ferraro 2008, pp. 161–2, 184–5, 189–93.

96 Fildes 1988, pp. 71–2; Quétel 1990, pp. 20, 21; Kertzer 1998–9: 591.

97 Codarin Miani 1991, pp. 388–9.

98 Berruti 2007: 545–6.

99 Kertzer 1998–9: 595.

100 Viazzo et al. 1994, 258–9.

101 Cf. Kertzer and White 1994: 460, on the strength of nineteenth-century evidence.

102 Passerini 1853, p. 950.

103 Tittarelli 1991, pp. 1147–51.

104 Galanti 1786–90, III, pp. 155–7.

105 Beltrami 1954, pp. 161–71; Bolognesi and Giovannini 1982: 317–18; De Marchi 2009: 146–7. For more on the subject of general infant mortality rates, see Kertzer and White 1994: 457. See also the figures for Piacenza, 1750–1850, cited in Dodi Osnaghi 1982, p. 429: here the foundling mortality rate was 400–700 per thousand, the ordinary infant mortality rate 200–300.

106 Schiavoni 1991, pp. 1031–3.

107 Kertzer and White 1994: 467; Viazzo et al. 2000, pp. 80–6.

108 Da Molin 1991, pp. 492–3; Kertzer 1993, p. 142.

109 Corsini 1991, pp. 85–7.

10

Fostering and adoption

Foundling hospitals tried to come to terms with an ambivalent action, the abandonment of blood children in the face of necessity. From one angle, this seemed to be a reprehensible deed, a renunciation of parental responsibility; from another, it showed a proper sense of shame, a recognition that one must not try to keep a base-born child and should, in obedience to social convention and Christian morality, agree to relinquish the baby. By abandoning a child according to the rules, one avoided murder and scandal, reduced guilt, sought to preserve life, perhaps even salvaged honour. Abandonment was never commendable, but it was a lesser evil. By undertaking to rescue abandoned children, hospitals assumed the role of parents, attempting to do on a large scale what respectable fathers and mothers did on a small and intimate one – to arrange a supply of milk for up to two or three years, to instil godly habits into children, and to educate them for a proper station in life. Hospitals' ability to perform this task depended heavily on their capacity for recruiting and supervising a large, reliable force of wet nurses and foster mothers who would take on children outside the hospital walls and look after them as part of their own families. There was a danger that, if they failed to carry out this rescue operation effectively, the hospitals would merely be putting a slow death by malnutrition and neglect in the place of a swift one by smothering, drowning or dangerous exposure. Would this be a genuine lesser evil or merely an alternative abuse, perpetrated by an institution in the name of decorum?

Nurses in town and country

Should babies survive the nursery, hospitals would place them with wet nurses and foster parents in the town, or its environs, or more distant villages. They provided, for people in difficulties, a version of a service which more fortunate families arranged and paid for themselves. Parents on social strata from upper to lower middle, from aristocrats to the more prosperous artisans and shopkeepers, were inclined to hire wet nurses if they could afford them. Humanists and Christian moralists and preachers might disapprove of the practice (one ancient writer, Soranus of Ephesus, was particularly influential) and extol the advantages of feeding children with their own mother's milk. But they acknowledged several reasons, and social custom added others, why a mother should not suckle her own baby. Her health might forbid it, her milk be poor or her breasts quite dry, she ought to conserve her energy for further childbearing (well-to-do families would be anxious for heirs), she would be quicker to conceive again if she did not feed her newborn child herself. A working mother could contribute more to the family economy if she were free of a suckling child. If a nurse's pay were smaller than the mother's potential earnings, it would make good sense to hire a nurse and send the child to live with her.[1]

If a mother did choose to breastfeed, a couple ought to abstain from sexual congress while she was doing so, in deference to the belief that if she became pregnant again her milk would not be nutritious enough – the child in the womb would absorb its goodness at the expense of the child at the breast. But to deny a husband his conjugal rights for over a year would strain the marriage, and in the interests of morality and domestic peace there was good reason to hire a wet nurse, at least after the baby's first few weeks.[2] Rich households often employed live-in nurses, some of whom, at least in the fourteenth and fifteenth centuries, were slaves; in other centuries, they were well-paid and privileged servants. Less grand families sent their children to youngish married women who nursed them in their own homes. Parents of any rank who valued clean country air would place infants with farming families. Certain of the poorest people obtained nurses through foundling homes, sometimes by abandoning their children anonymously and indefinitely, sometimes (if, for example, they could not produce breast-milk themselves) by openly handing them over and agreeing to retrieve them as soon as they were weaned.

Private employers and foundling homes competed for a limited supply of suitable nurses, ideally consisting of healthy and honest lactating women who had recently buried children of their own or recently weaned them. Deals could occasionally be struck, to the advantage of both a charitable institution and a well-to-do family. At Florence in the fifteenth century, at Rome in the eighteenth, foundling homes would 'lend' a few of their sucklings to wet nurses engaged by important families, to help keep the nurses' milk flowing while they awaited their mistresses' next confinements.[3] In 1730 and 1740 the small foundling home in Ravenna sent babies to Rome in the care of wet nurses heading for aristocratic Roman households, an arrangement intended to help the nurse and her employers and relieve Ravenna of expense; at least one of the foundling children was to be sent on arrival to Santo Spirito.[4] Between about 1750 and 1850, villages to the north-west of Milan, between Rho and Legnano, catered not only for children sent by the foundling home in the city but also for progeny of the gentry, and – at least after 1800 – for the children of lower-middle or working-class parents in Milan who had made their own arrangements with local families.[5]

Hospital infants were divided into milk-children [*lattati*] and bread-children [*slattati, svezzati*]. In Siena in the fourteenth and fifteenth centuries, spells of two or even three years at the breast were thought desirable, but by the end of the fifteenth century, children were supposed to be weaned at about eighteen months. Most hospital regulations from about that time onwards called for weaning at twelve to eighteen months, although the timing could vary according to medical opinion, and weaning might take place earlier if a nurse became pregnant. Should infants survive weaning, they might, but did not have to, change nurses and be transferred to older women.[6]

Opened in 1445, the Innocenti in Florence had 456 children out at nurse in 1466.[7] In 1641 it was keeping less than 30 babies on the premises, but 935 were with foster parents (347 sucklings, 566 who had been weaned, together with 22 little boys of both sorts, *a latte e a divezzare*, at the hospital's estate at San Gimignano).[8] Borromeo's visitation of Brescia in 1580 reported 19 infants in the hospital, while 450 were boarded out.[9] At one moment in Perugia in 1766 there were only 3 babies on the premises of the Misericordia, but 551 children under other roofs.[10] In 1747, at a time of retrenchment, Santo Spirito in Rome was keeping 2,080 children at nurse (1,048 males and 1,032 females).[11]

About 1623, a hospitaller, Domenico Borgarucci, praised the charity of the poor themselves. '[W]hen their own children die, kindly people are more willing to feed infants from their own scanty resources than are other more prosperous persons, and they show them such love that they treat them better than their own children and very often adopt them as such' (shades of the good shepherd and his wife in Giraldi Cinzio's tale of Aventuroso). Affection aside, the sturdier hospital children might eventually prove very useful on the farm or about the house and be valued for that reason, though many did not live long enough to show their worth. A more jaundiced opinion was that most nurses were only interested in the money, and hospitals only in parting with as little of this as possible. '[I]n order to save money', suggested Andrea Brogiotti, three years after Borgarucci, 'they take on all kinds of nurses, even if they are diseased, and, being intent on putting something by, they do not seek the wellbeing of the poor abandoned children'.[12]

Officials made some effort to select nurses wisely. Ideally, they should be poor but honest housewives, many from the countryside, under the authority of husbands referred to as *balii* (literally male nurses), who commonly made arrangements on their behalf and received their pay as a contribution to family income. Hospitals generally sought to prevent nurses from suckling more than one infant at a time, a practice tolerated in hospital reception wards but discouraged in nursing households. Under at least one hospital, however, a minority of nurses were sometimes assigned several children – in 1771, the Annunziata at Sulmona had entrusted 362 *esposti* to 266 nurses, of whom 188 had one, 60 two, and 18 three (it is possible that some of the additional children had been, or were just about to be, weaned).[13] Hospitals would sometimes demand details of family histories; at Viterbo, towards 1740, and under Milan's regulations of 1790, prospective nurses were required to present evidence of the dates of the births and deaths of their own children.[14] In Milan and elsewhere, women underwent medical examinations intended, particularly, to detect the sores and rashes which were outward signs of venereal diseases.[15]

Pay was relatively high at first, but, as was also the custom in private households, began to shrink, often by half, as soon as a child was weaned, although clothing allowances might increase as the child grew up. Nurses' wages would probably dwindle to almost nothing when, at six to eight years of age, children began to earn their keep by doing chores. Very likely, the hospital would supply equipment at the outset – linen cloths for swaddling, perhaps cribs to prevent accidental suffocation in the family bed. After one year Santo Spirito would (in the seventeenth century) provide clothes, shoes and a habit of 'blue cloth' much like the hospital's own uniform.[16] In the eighteenth century they supplied only the cloth and expected the foster mother to do the dressmaking and tailoring; woe betide parents caught selling the materials or converting them to their own children's use.[17]

Hospital administrators and private employers shared the view that country women were stronger, healthier, capable of producing richer milk and probably cheaper to hire; humanists extolled the properties of country air even while they disparaged country people.[18] Moral dangers, such as the risk of being reared by a prostitute, groomed by a courtesan to follow in her profession, or transformed into a child beggar pleading outside a church, appeared to be fewer in villages than in corrupt, seductive towns.[19] In the city a hospital might employ such women as Virginia and Francesca Segni of Bologna, aged nineteen and fifteen in 1604, the daughters of a deceased silk-worker, who had both become pregnant out of wedlock and seen their babies die. They lived with their mother and all three did some silk-weaving and were helped out by Antonia and Ottavia ('now and then they give us bread, wine and soup'), who lived on the floor below and were suspected of being prostitutes.[20] A good reason for looking to the country was that for much of the year city women had more chances of alternative employment and relied less on nursing or fostering to top up family income. In summer, however, country women, urgently needed for agricultural labour, were capable of returning to the hospital children already in their charge; at that time, too, they were seldom free to trek to the city and pick up babies, though some hospitals increased the inducements to do so. Santa Caterina della Ruota in Milan offered travel subsidies; in 1808 they paid nurses between June and September at almost twice the normal rates. In the harvest season, and at times of economic crisis or natural disaster, other institutions fell back on women from the town. Urban nurses, too, could come to the rescue in the dead of winter, when the roads to upland villages had become impassable.[21]

Seldom, though, did a foundling home recruit more than one-fifth to one-third of its external nurses from the town. The Annunziata at Sulmona was exceptional in that, in 1793, as many as 70 per cent of its infants were being nursed in that small city.[22] Some governors, as at Milan in 1684, shunned city nurses for a time, but could not do without them indefinitely.[23] During part of the eighteenth century, inhabitants of several city parishes in Verona would take in *esposti*, as certain of the poorest families on the tax roll had done in the sixteenth. But the arrangement began to collapse in the 1770s, and by 1782, the hospital was no longer recruiting nurses from the city.[24]

Several institutions formed lasting connections with favoured regions and sent them many children. To place them with country nurses meant subjecting the frail creatures to another journey. But, unlike the ruffianly carriers who had brought some of them in, nurses did have an interest in their survival and the means to feed them on the road. Milan in 1477 strove to keep within a twelve-mile radius, the better to conduct inspections, but did not always succeed in doing so; Gorgonzola, Vimercate, Desio and Corbetta were popular places for nursing, fostering and subsequent adoptions.[25] Florence turned to the Mugello and Casentino; Turin to the Canavese; Rome to the Lazio, where it sent 60–70 per cent of its youngest children, at least in the late seventeenth and early eighteenth centuries; Todi and Sulmona to the nearby districts where the hospital held landed property; Verona to the hills around the lower basin of Lake Garda and the valleys of three rivers, the Illasi, Tramigna and Alpone.[26] In its quest for crisp, healthy air, Rome chose high places, 500–600 metres above sea level, between the foothills and the lower slopes of the mountains; during the eighteenth century, Santo Spirito sent children to about a hundred different villages and small towns, not always favouring the same ones.

Sometimes members of prominent families serving as hospital governors contrived to have babies sent to parts of the country where they and their relatives wielded influence and distributed patronage. Links of this kind were developed between the hospital of San Giovanni in Turin and Castellamonte in the Canavese. Nurses' wages injected welcome cash into the local economy, and older children could prove very useful during the spell of six to eight months in every year when the men of some communities were away in search of work.[27] In general, wages helped to clear family debts and hospitals sometimes paid creditors directly. Some nurses would come to the hospital to collect their money at short intervals, as and when it was needed; at Siena the rules provided for three-monthly payments, but nurses, as though unable to hold out for so long, would come in monthly or even every fortnight.[28]

Nursing and fostering topped up family income in rural communities where properties were fragmented and agricultural wages low. They appealed to the families of sharecroppers, small-holders and day labourers, and were often practised on hill farms where there was less demand for female labour in the fields.[29] It may have been true at all times, as it evidently was in the region of Bologna in the nineteenth century, that sharecroppers made the most dependable foster families because they went in for large, complex households and it was more likely that an adult would be at home during the day to mind a child. Very likely, the same principle applied to rural societies, near Ivrea, for example, where the law prescribed that all brothers should inherit equal shares of what was usually a small landed property – so that, to keep the farm going, relatives would live together in one household.[30] Farm labourers would offer poorer conditions, but would need the money even more, and would not have to consult their landlords before taking on the work.[31] In the parish of Tregnago in the Illasi valley in the late 1760s, about one-third of the 350 resident families were involved in bringing up *esposti* from the Pietà in Verona; the occupation passed from mother to daughter and from mother-in-law to daughter-in-law, the older women and widows caring for the bread-children. Among these senior figures was Brigida Zanfretta, wife of Giovanni Battista, who took in thirteen foundlings, already weaned, between 1735 and 1749; eight died in her house, three stayed with her until their fifth birthday, and the birth parents reclaimed the other two.[32]

From about 1750 onwards, earnings from child-rearing proved a godsend to five parishes to the north-west of Milan, when a new generation of landowners, both exploitative and entrepreneurial, invaded the countryside, imposed harsh terms on their poorer tenants, and set up cotton and silk mills in the neighbourhood. Nursing was suitable for housewives, who could mind babies and infants without disrupting their usual routines and if necessary take them to the fields; the mills paid much higher rates, but the work for spinners was seasonal and the shifts lengthy, better suited to young, unmarried women. The women earned the extra money, but the male head of the household collected their wages from the factory or from the hospital, where he was held responsible for producing the necessary documents and was expected to report twice a year.[33]

But village families did not take on infants only because they brought in a little extra money. Some doubtless knew that if breastfeeding were prolonged by suckling other people's children, the likelihood of conceiving again would be reduced, though not eliminated altogether – hospitals were conscious that nurses might become pregnant while nursing hospital children and fail to report the fact. If resorted to systematically, though, nursing hospital children could be an effective method of limiting family size, which was much to be desired in communities where partible inheritance prevailed. In a nineteenth-century village, Bialfrè, near Ivrea, a few women who took in foundling children succeeded in extending the intervals between their own pregnancies, sometimes to as much as five years, and in reducing, perhaps to a mere four, the number of children they bore over a long period of being both married and fertile, say between their early twenties and early forties.[34] If such things were possible between 1830 and 1870, could they not have been done at an earlier date?

Inspection and fraud

Hospitals showed some concern for infant lives and were anxious to ensure that nurses were honouring their contracts. They tried to set up inspection systems which would foil the ruses of poor people desperate not to lose the extra income which meant so much in a hand-to-mouth economy, and would also expose acts of cruelty or neglect. One ominous possibility was that a nurse's milk might fail and, rather than return the child and forfeit her fee, she would resort to goat's milk or pap, inadequate substitutes sometimes employed in nurseries but frowned upon outside them.[35] Poor Alessio, who seemed 'not a human child but the shadow of an animal', was returned to San Gallo in Florence in 1416 by his nurse, Monna Nanna, probably too late to save his life.[36] Institutions could require nurses to show babies to their officers, especially when they came to collect their wages (though this procedure allowed them to prepare the child for the visit or borrow another one who looked healthier); hospital emissaries might pay surprise visits to foster homes, though few hospitals, perhaps, had the staff to organise these regularly; or hospitals would rely on parish priests to report on children's welfare, especially in distant villages.[37]

From the early to mid-fourteenth century, the rector of Santa Maria della Scala in Siena was authorised to choose a hospitaller 'to seek out the children who are at nurse, and to see if they are alive or dead, and if they are well placed with the people who are looking after them'. In 1499 the chapter agreed that their agents ought to visit at least twice a year.[38] During the sixteenth century, nurses were to provide the hospital at Imola every two months with a certificate from their village priest to the effect that the child in their charge was alive and well. On the feast of Corpus Christi, as if the hospital's governors, employees and dependants were affirming their identity as one body, nurses were to parade children at the hospital for an annual review (there were ninety-eight *esposti* out at nurse in 1548). After dinner, the officers would discuss the evidence and decide whether any child should be moved.[39] Santo Spirito in eighteenth-century Rome appointed deputies in twenty-one places to ensure that babies received adequate care, stipulating that wages should be paid only against the certificates which they issued. In theory, this was supposed to happen every month but, for practical reasons, the hospital tolerated intervals of up to a year, after which arrears of pay could not be claimed. Santo Spirito, too, entertained or at least assembled its nurses at Easter and Pentecost, and payments could then be collected and babies' health checked.[40] Venetian regulations of the 1790s prescribed that nurses should produce certificates and collect pay from the Pietà every three months.[41] Some priests, as the governor of Sulmona's hospital learned in 1790, were unwilling to work for nothing and charged the foster parents a fee for testifying in writing that the children were still alive and well.[42]

Administrators understandably feared that a child's death would go unreported and the foster parents continue to claim wages and allowances until they were found out. How could official visitors know that the child shown to them when they called was the one that the hospital had assigned to the foster family? The practice of tattooing children with the hospital's emblem on one or both feet, or on the calf of a leg, was designed to prevent substitutions, and had the effect of marking them for life as foundlings.[43] At one time, the 'barbarous custom' of branding babies like cattle prevailed in Sicily, but in the late eighteenth century the authorities preferred to use a silk or cord necklace, the ends joined by a leaden seal embossed with the town's emblem to prevent removal.[44] Hospitals, though, were not always consistent – sensibly, Santo Spirito's visitors did not always assume fraud when they found the tattoo missing. When inspecting foundlings at nurse outside Rome in 1705, the hospital archivist Sebastiano Pennacchioni observed that 280 of the 1,335 infants whom he succeeded in seeing did not have the hospital's mark upon them.[45]

To keep track of the hospital's scattered children was no easy task. Pennacchioni also discovered that 98 of the total of 1,589 foundlings within his remit were no longer alive, and he could not establish the date of death of 63 of these lost children. It seemed, too, that 50 were living in unauthorised places, some had fled, and one had taken to the roads. Parish priests were not above colluding with local people to mislead the hospital – perhaps out of sympathy with their flocks, perhaps because they were sharing with them the modest profits of false claims. Don Isidoro Cerracchi, priest at Cori in the Lazio, was convicted of helping foster parents to claim for looking after deceased infants.[46]

At intervals between the fifteenth and the eighteenth centuries, hospital authorities made examples of dishonest foster parents. A labourer in the Mugello was arrested in 1469 and sent to the debtors' prison in Florence. In the 1740s the Pietà in Verona was still doggedly pursuing the heirs of a couple who had defrauded the institution twenty years earlier.[47] If hospitals could be easily deceived, criminals may have had less incentive to keep children alive. There is nothing to suggest, though, that many acted as the 'baby-farmers' of mid-Victorian England supposedly did – that they deliberately killed or neglected their youngest charges and pocketed the fees for looking after them.[48] They were paid in instalments for minding the youngest children, not lump sums for adopting them, and were subject to some kind of periodic oversight. Adoption fees were paid, if at all, only for older children, who were capable of being useful and likely to be valued more highly. None the less, horror stories were sometimes told, at least in the papers of Santo Spirito – of the couple who, about 1673, abandoned a child within a few hours of accepting him, stole his swaddling clothes and went on claiming the allowance; of the prostitute Maria Angela at Saracinesco in the diocese of Tivoli about 1739, who allegedly suffocated the babies entrusted to her. Were the local clergy always to be trusted? The archpriest here had vouched for Maria Angela's fitness to be a nurse.[49]

Some mothers gave up their own children and took on those of the hospital, which would reward them for looking after other people's children but not, without much palaver, subsidise them for nursing their own. Crafty women could (it was believed) get the best of both worlds by first abandoning their babies, then applying to be nurses, somehow recognising their own children, and selecting them from among those on offer at the hospital. Moses might have been nursed for pay by his own mother after Pharaoh's daughter picked him up, but this was not a popular precedent.[50] Bent on frustrating the manoeuvre, some hospitals, including Santo Spirito, gave children pseudonyms and concealed their baptismal names. Only Entry 197 on the hospital's secret book for 1673 connected the child known to his nurse as Marco with the child baptised Pasquale on 23rd March.[51] Brother Borgarucci had written of mothers

> trading in their own blood to the detriment of the hospital; in these cases the wary official asks them whether [their last] child was male or female, and if it was a boy he gives them a girl and vice versa, to ensure that a mother does not get her own child back. If they did otherwise, and mothers could be sure of recovering their own children and being paid, they would all put them into Santo Spirito and nobody would keep their own – they could be certain of making money and the hospital could not meet the expense.[52]

Arguably, these precautions lacked subtlety, and mothers could probably defeat them with help from corruptible staff, especially the supervisors of the babies' ward.

Infants would probably benefit from being nursed by their own mothers for pay, bad though it might be for the hospital's finances. Lives, however, were imperilled by other kinds of fraud invented by Roman traffickers known baldly as 'brokers [sensali]'. These female entrepreneurs, creating their own black economy, specialised in acquiring babies illicitly from the hospital and running a kind of human cattle-market for the use of women who would not normally have been entrusted with them.

Officials at Santo Spirito were supposed to hand over infants to an applicant only on seeing written evidence of the recent death of her youngest child. Brokers got wind of mothers who had recently lost babies and proceeded to wheedle or bribe death certificates out of their parish priests without the mothers' knowledge. Sometimes they enlisted an accomplice – a woman obviously capable of producing milk – and, with her in tow and the aid of the death certificate, they obtained a baby from the hospital. Or the broker might simply explain that the woman who supposedly wanted a child was still recovering from her recent confinement and could not come in person. The broker then took the baby home, where she usually kept two or three children 'on the bed or on the straw'. Somehow she then removed the tattoos from the baby's person and sent the child back to the hospital by means of the baby-wheel. This operation enabled her to draw pay for nursing a child no longer in her hands and almost impossible to trace. An alternative tactic was to sell the infants, two scudi for this child, three for that, to nurses who, no doubt for disreputable reasons, preferred the black market to the hospital. Should the brokers fail to move the children along promptly, they would get neighbours to feed them milk or else give them pap; if they died, their bodies would be dumped. About 1740, four *sensali* were identified, headed by a grim widow, the midwife Francesca Rastini. A parish priest claimed to have seen sixty-seven babies in Rastini's house. He had recognised as one of her charges the corpse of a child left outside his church, but had accepted her story that it was a cousin's child, for whom Rastini had been unable to afford a funeral.[53] Dealers in babies were well advised to change their lodgings frequently to avoid detection.

Restoration and adoption

Many parents leaving children at hospitals talked of reclaiming them in happier times: growing prosperity, the passing of a famine or a hard winter, or the death of a parent who had opposed a marriage, might make this move possible. Many, perhaps, were sincere, others observing the decencies, others still summoning up false optimism to soften a painful parting or trying to alleviate their guilt. Until the end of the eighteenth century, the prospects of reunion were seldom good, if only because children were unlikely to survive for more than a few months under the conditions awaiting them. Girls, more likely to be regarded as liabilities or more in need of institutional protection, were recovered less often than boys. In the first seven years of the Innocenti in Florence, about one child in sixteen returned to birth parents; at Udine between 1656 and 1755, 155 of 9,669 babies (1.6 per cent) were restored to birth parents; at Siena 60 children out of a total of 1,700 (3.5 per cent) who had been given up during years of exceptional hardship, 1763–8, were so restored.[54] Restoration would become much more common in the nineteenth century, however, at least in Florence and Milan, when, thanks to improved survival rates, the odds on recovering a child alive were better than even.[55]

After several years of nursing and fostering, most surviving foundlings embarked on a third age in which two prospects opened before them. They might be employed as servants or adopted, often by their foster parents but occasionally by other people, who were sometimes of higher rank. Or the hospital would bring them back to its own conservatory to give them an education, with a view to arranging for their subsequent employment or marriage, if they were physically and mentally fit for these destinations (see Chapter 11). In the fifteenth century, adoptions at an early age were common; in later periods, children were more likely to spend several years in seminaries, conservatories and apprenticeships.

Some adoptive parents formally bound themselves to provide for the child's upbringing and possibly trade training, and to put up a dowry for girls ripe for marriage. To adopt a child was a good work, promising spiritual rewards as well as practical benefits – domestic help, perhaps a companion and possibly an heir. Childless Francesco Pecori held out high hopes for Matteo Dicomano from the Innocenti and dreamed of making him a gentleman, a 'religious doctor' or a merchant.[56] In Rome in 1493, Sabba Bartolomei and his wife Lorenza adopted Santa, a *proietta*, vowing to raise her as if she were a daughter and eventually find her a husband; described as sickly, she perhaps would not live to claim the dowry of a hundred florins which they promised.[57] In a will made in 1539, Antonio Capello del Banco, of the Venetian parish of San Samuele, recorded that in 1526 he had adopted a child of the Pietà and named him Bonaventura; he had since apprenticed this *fio de anima* to a Rialto goldsmith, and now instructed his executors to provide for the boy until he was eighteen.[58] Straparola's *Piacevoli notti*, published in the 1550s, includes a tale in which Alchia explains to Fortunio, who is smarting at being called a bastard and the son of a whore, that he is not her 'true son, but brought up in the house for the love of God, and the lightening of her sins and her husband's'. Humiliated and resentful, he storms out to seek his fortune, denounced for ingratitude by his adoptive mother.[59]

From fostering to adoption by the same family could be a natural step, and legal adoption was the destiny of many of the children surrendered to the general hospital in Milan during the fifteenth century. Between 1475 and 1499, the Ospedale Maggiore placed 818 children, 489 girls and 329 boys, with families, about two-fifths of which had fostered them. The ages of most children were recorded: 322 were adopted at three, 287 at ages between four and nine.[60] At Padua in 1468–70 54 girls and 25 boys, protégés of the Casa di Dio, were adopted at ages which ranged from a few months to eight years; about two-fifths of them went to families living in the city's rural domain.[61]

In later centuries, however, decisions about a child's future were sometimes deferred and adoptions, especially at so early an age, became less common in northern and central Italy. Some institutions seemed determined to bring many of their children back to their own premises, as though they were anxious to supervise their education directly and had limited faith in the good intentions and Christian devotion of adopting families. The difference between an adopted child and an unpaid servant was not always clear, and some charities were conscious of the moral dangers of domestic service. The earliest age at which boys could be adopted by childless couples was raised from four to at least seven at Imola in 1529.[62] Between 1574 and 1652, the Innocenti in Florence recorded only fifteen formal adoptions.[63] However, especially in the late seventeenth and eighteenth centuries, practice again began to change and hospitals allowed children of both sexes to stay for longer periods with their country foster families, as though envisaging that they would eventually be absorbed into rural rather than urban society.

Habits varied, however, region by region. Adoption, rather than conservatory education and training, was still the principal hope for foundling children in most parts of Calabria in the late eighteenth century; otherwise, untrained and uneducated, they were liable to become beggars or vagrants when the local community ceased to pay for their support. At Catanzaro, the capital of southern Calabria, formal adoption procedures were introduced in 1791 and the central Cassa Sagra paid adopting parents a premium of eight ducats per child – a measly sum, in Galanti's view.[64] In northern Calabria it was usually boys who were adopted by fostering families, while girls entered the conservatory at Cosenza.[65] Galanti urged that rich Neapolitan families should continue and if possible extend their custom of bringing up foundlings, 'who become in a sense adoptive children'. This was all the more important because the Annunziata made no attempt to teach boys to do anything useful. 'After six years they are left to themselves, so that they grow up as fodder for the galleys and the gibbet. The same thing happens in the provincial hospitals. They save lives in order to create rogues and vagabonds and make trouble for society.'[66]

In the fifteenth century, hospitals in northern and central Italy had tended to summon back children aged between two and five, unless they were on the brink of adoption.[67] Time spent in the country grew longer, however, partly for the convenience of hospitals, and partly for the advantage of local communities. The governors of the Pietà in Verona increased the term temporarily from three years to six in 1458, and again from three to four and a half in 1495, with some possibility of staying longer in the countryside, partly because they could not hire enough assistants to look after young children in the hospital.[68] In the seventeenth and eighteenth centuries, it was customary to sing the praises of country air and extend the time spent breathing it, so that children now remained in farming communities, at first until they were about seven, in the eighteenth century until they were ten or even twelve.[69] A device used in the Papal States was *concessione a tempo nubile*, a cross between adoption and a service contract, whereby an employer-cum-surrogate-parent undertook to maintain a girl until she reached marriageable age. Under Santo Spirito, the employer would contribute something to her dowry and the hospital pay the rest; the new hospital at Viterbo expected to pay it all. Quite often the persons who took the girls on in this way had once been their nurses and had since been widowed.[70]

A report on the Innocenti in Florence in 1768 concluded that agriculture needed manpower more than did manufacturing. As if to meet this need, about two-thirds of surviving children who had once been placed with peasant nurses were remaining in the countryside, often with their foster families, especially boys.[71] Girls would more likely return to the hospital's care, but for them too some administrators recommended more years on the farm. Around 1642, Filippo Ricasoli, superintendent of the Innocenti, thought it best to leave girls to work for their foster parents and earn money towards their dowries: 'they would have a better constitution and be more experienced and hence would find husbands more easily'.[72] Like a feudal magnate procuring benefits for his vassals from a royal court, Canon Tommaso Carroccio persuaded the hospital at Turin to extend the fostering period at Castellamonte in the Canavese to ten years for boys in 1734 and for girls too (as a temporary measure) in 1739.[73] True, hospitals were usually protective of girls and inclined to enclose them. But their conservatories were filling up with females who could not or would not marry, and it could well prove cheaper and more practical to keep the younger ones in the country for longer periods. The hospital would then have to rely on local priests to assure them that the girls were living with godfearing families.

Conclusion

Foundling hospitals began by receiving babies in nurseries and went on to assign them to nursing households, as many blood parents would have done. The children passed into the hands of families which, in their own struggle to scrape a living, were in no position to pamper them. Supervision by the hospital could be loose and intermittent. Systematic criminal activity, the creation of a black market in unwanted children, as witness the Roman scandal of 1740, was not unknown. Fraudulent claims could be made, sleepy officials be deceived or corrupt ones suborned into delivering babies to racketeers. But some effort was made to keep track of the children and inquire, at least in a perfunctory fashion, after their welfare, if only to ensure that the hospital's money was not being blatantly misspent.

Can anyone tell how much affection arose between foster parents and their charges, or how far families viewed the children merely as economic assets? A few nurses may have been moved by Christian charity, or by the hope of spiritual as well as material rewards; in the late middle ages, popes had granted indulgences to women willing to suckle abandoned children and benefactors prepared to contribute to the expenses of supporting them.[74] When, in 1737, the papal visitor to Santo Spirito directed that in choosing nurses preference should be given to married alumnae of the hospital, he may have expected them to feel compassion for babies who shared their own experiences.[75] The ideal of the affectionate nurse or adoptive parent taking up the abandoned child as if it were her own was certainly present in the fiction of Giraldi Cinzio and in Borgarucci's pious account of Santo Spirito; how widely was it realised and how often did it embrace the youngest, most helpless and most demanding children, 'mewling and puking' in a nurse's arms? There were some obstacles in its path. Children, especially girls, could change nurses several times, in moves which both reflected the absence of emotional ties and prevented their formation.[76] Older, sturdier children were more likely to be valued. As they grew they could become increasingly useful to poor families and, even in the absence of much demonstrative love, there were good reasons to keep them alive and able to work. They made possible a kind of family planning, based on calculated expansion rather than limitation; a small family, short of hands to work a holding, risked losing its tenancy, and a growing boy from the hospital could save it from this fate.[77]

As children grew, their lives became less fragile, the mortality curve less steep, although, despite official faith in the properties of country air, there were still many casualties; most of the protégés of Brigida Zanfretta of Tregnago died before their fifth birthday. How would hospital children fare if they were competing with a nurse's own children? One case, from Vialfrè, near Ivrea (Piedmont), in 1850–70, is not reassuring: Marianna Gajs lost only one of the five children she herself bore during that period, but only one of the nine *esposti* entrusted to her survived. How many parallels were there to this case in earlier times, and how far was it explained by the foundlings' weakness and sickliness, rather than by the foster mother's neglect or favouritism?[78] The process of weaning was notoriously hazardous, involving a transition to less nourishing food at a time when the nurse's pay was shrinking.

It seems impossible to say how large a proportion of children survived the period of nursing and fostering and were either adopted or returned to the hospital. Most of the estimates available relate either to deaths in the first year, often held to have claimed 50–70 per cent of entrants to the hospitals, or else to deaths in the hospital's care, at any point up to about eighteen years of age. These often, eventually, amounted to more than 80 per cent, so that only about one in six of the original intake lived to go out into the world.

At least two hospitals drew up grim balance sheets in which they set the number of deaths in their care (in the nursery, out at nurse, and possibly in the conservatories and schools on their premises) against the total number of admissions over periods of five or six years. At Santo Spirito in Rome, between the beginning of 1580 and the end of November 1584, 2,672 of 3,503 children admitted (763 per thousand) died in the hospital's care.[79] At the recently reformed royal hospital in Cosenza, northern Calabria, between January 1786 and December 1791, 698 of 1,271 entrants died in care (549 per thousand).[80] These figures did not show at what ages the deaths occurred, though a very large proportion would have been in the first year or around the time of weaning. Clearer than either is a calculation made by a physician, Grillenzoni, in a critique of the foundling home at Ferrara in the 1850s: his statistics showed that about half the children admitted were dying within a year of entry, that another quarter died in the next two years, and that only a quarter of entrants were still alive at the beginning of their fourth year.[81] Hospitals could never be free of a suspicion that they were attempting the impossible – that, while making a well-intentioned attempt to save a few lives, they had placed a larger number at risk, and that their ambitious rescue campaign was doomed to failure, one evil replacing another. It could be said, though, that these charities brought modest benefits, if not always to the children they tried to protect, at least to the foster parents they provided with a small supplementary income and, incidentally, the opportunity to control the size of their own families.

Notes

1 De Mause 1976, p. 34; Ross 1976, pp. 185–6, 188; Haas 1998, pp. 90–2, 95–9.
2 Cf. Klapisch-Zuber 1985, pp. 132–64; Haas 1998, p. 243, n. 73. For mothers who suckled their children before sending them to wetnurses, see Ross 1976, p. 187; Haas 1998, pp. 113–14.
3 Gavitt 1990, pp. 205–6; Sandri 1991, p. 97; Surdacki 2002: 115.
4 Bolognesi and Giovannini 1982, p. 328.
5 De Marchi 2009: 121–2, 134–7.
6 Viazzo et al. 2000, pp. 84–5; Martellucci 2001: 109–17.
7 Gavitt 1990, pp. 86–7.
8 Passerini 1853, p. 949.
9 Montanari 1987, pp. 281–2.
10 Tittarelli et al. 2003, p. 174.
11 Piccialuti 1994, pp. 139–40; Surdacki 2001: 96.
12 Grégoire 1979: 231–2, 250–2.
13 Tanturri 2003: 155.
14 Langellotti and Travaglini 1991, p. 746.
15 De Marchi 2009: 127–8.
16 Grégoire 1979: 252; Vigni 1979: 113; Montanari 1987, p. 281; Kertzer 2000, p. 46.
17 For illustrations of pay and allowances, see Perni 1999: 164; Surdacki 2002: 113–15; De Marchi 2009: 138–9.
18 Cf. Fildes 1988, p. 105; Haas 1998, pp. 103, 244, n. 79.

19   Piccialuti 1994, pp. 137–8.
20   Ferrante 1996, pp. 209–10.
21   Sandri 1991, pp. 99–100; Kertzer and White 1994: 468; Surdacki 2002: 110–11; De Marchi
      2009: 126–7.
22   Tanturri 2003: 170.
23   Vigni 1985: 216–18; Bussini 1991, pp. 320–1; Reggiani and Paradisi 1991, pp. 974–6; Schiavoni
      1991, pp. 1034–8; Tittarelli *et al.* 2003, pp. 40–1, 48, 226–7.
24   Cappelletto 1991, pp. 330, 336; cf. Lanaro Sartori 1982: 68.
25   Albini 1993, pp. 166, 179–80.
26   For Florence see Gavitt 1990, pp. 226–30; Gavitt 1994, p. 70, Table 3.5, and pp. 80–2; for Rome,
      Schiavoni 1991, pp. 1034–6, Surdacki 2001: 97–9 and Surdacki 2002: 118–20; for Todi, Bussini
      1991, pp. 320–1; for Verona, Cappelletto 1991, p. 330.
27   Cavallo 1983: 395–403.
28   Martellucci 2001: 134–5.
29   Garbellotti 1996, p. 72.
30   Berruti 2008: 171–8.
31   Sigle *et al.* 2000: 329–30.
32   Cappelletto 1991, pp. 330–2.
33   De Marchi 2009: 120–1, 132, 139–41. Her researches relate to the five parishes of Cantalupo,
      Cerro, Nerviano, Pogliano and Vanzago.
34   Berruti 2008: 167–98.
35   Gavitt 1990, pp. 230–3; Gavitt 1994, pp. 82–3; Gavitt 1997: 245–6.
36   Sandri 1991, p. 1010. For other sad cases, see Sandri 1982, p. 166; Martellucci 2001: 116.
37   Surdacki 2001: 110–12.
38   Martellucci 2001: 117–18.
39   Galassi 1966–70, II, pp. 38, 514, 521–2 (Clause xix of the 1529–69 statutes of Santa Maria della
      Scaletta).
40   Surdacki 2002: 108–9, 116–18.
41   Perni 1999: 164.
42   Tanturri 2003: 155.
43   Grégoire 1979: 250; Vigni 1985: 234; Surdacki 2001: 102–4; Tittarelli *et al.* 2003, p. 204.
44   Raffaele 1991, pp. 911–12; Kertzer 1993, pp. 114–15.
45   Schiavoni 1991, pp. 1036–7; Surdacki 2001: 105–8. On Pennacchioni, see also Dominici
      2003: 196–7.
46   Surdacki 2001: 97, 117–18.
47   Cappelletto 1991, pp. 335–6; Gavitt 1994, p. 82.
48   Cf. Arnot 1994: 271–2.
49   Dominici 2001: 198, n. 32, 232.
50   Exodus 2: 1–10.
51   Fedeli Bernardini 2001, p. 303.
52   Grégoire 1979: 251–2.
53   Piccialuti 1994, pp. 131–8; Surdacki 2001: 112–15.
54   For Florence, Gavitt 1990, p. 204, Gavitt 1994, pp. 72–3; for Udine, Codarin Miani 1991,
      pp. 391–2; for Siena, Vigni 1985: 227–8.
55   Hunecke 1994, pp. 125–6; Viazzo *et al.* 2000, p. 88.
56   Gavitt 1990, p. 256.
57   Montenovesi 1939: 216.
58   Chambers and Pullan 1992, p. 310.

59   Straparola ed. Rua 1975, III.iv, vol. I, pp. 138–40.

60   Albini 1993, pp. 172–6.

61   Varanini 1997, p. 134.

62   Galassi 1966–70, II, p. 241.

63   Fubini Leuzzi 1994, pp. 882–4.

64   Galanti ed. Placanica 1992, p. 154.

65   *Ibid.*, pp. 260, 265.

66   Galanti 1786–90, III, pp. 154, 158.

67   For Florence see Gavitt 1990, pp. 188–9; for Milan, Albini 1993, pp. 164–7; for Siena, Leverotti 1984: 289.

68   Varanini 1996, pp. 30–1.

69   For Bologna, see Kertzer 1993, p. 85; for Cosenza, Galanti ed. Placanica 1992, p. 265; for Rome, Grégoire 1979: 252; for Siena, Vigni 1979: 113; for Todi, Bussini 1991, pp. 303–5; for Turin, Cavallo 1983: 392; for Venice, Pelizza 1997: 154–5; for Viterbo, Langellotti and Travaglini 1991, p. 747.

70   Dominici 2001: 201–4, 207, 218–19, 223–4.

71   Corsini 1983: 100.

72   Fubini Leuzzi 1994, pp. 893–4.

73   Cavallo 1983: 399–400.

74   Dall' Aglio Maramotti 1985, p. 38; Chambers and Pullan 1992, pp. 307–8; Albini 1993, p. 151; Grandi 1997, pp. 87, 99, 102–3.

75   Surdacki 2002: 109–10.

76   See, for example, Bolognesi and Giovannini 1982, pp. 326–7; Sandri 1982, pp. 149–52; Martellucci 2001: 114–17.

77   De Marchi 2009: 128–9.

78   Berruti 2008: 182–5.

79   Pagano 1979: 356–7, n. 9; Schiavoni 1991, p. 1031.

80   Galanti ed. Placanica 1992, pp. 548–51.

81   Quoted in Bolognesi and Giovannini 1982, pp. 318–19.

11

Foundlings and society

A small remnant of the children admitted to foundling hospitals returned, several years after entry, to their conservatories for training. Many had been removed by death, others by some form of adoption; a few had gone back to their blood parents. The last undertaking in the long process of rescuing foundling children was the attempt to equip them for a life in which they would become useful members of society, capable of rising above their obscure and shameful origins and of living honourably. At best, they would generally become artisans, farmworkers, housekeepers or dutiful wives and mothers (charity children were seldom encouraged to aim higher, though there were exceptions). At worst, they might encounter prejudice and distrust and be dismissed as the heirs of immoral or inadequate parents, creatures who seemed scarcely worth saving and could only form an underclass without prospects. A pessimistic writer, alarmed at the volume of abandonments in mid-nineteenth-century Milan, would complain of 'unjust prejudices which leave [on foundlings] what is almost a mark of inferior social rank', but add that 'alas, they do appear in disproportionate numbers among the criminal classes'.[1] Or foundlings might, as did some of the women who settled down in conservatories for endangered girls (see Chapter 6), simply become part of the institution itself, unable or reluctant to emerge from it, living in a world set apart from the mainstream of society and helping to keep it in being.

'Scholars or artificers'

Not surprisingly, more careers were open to boys returning to the hospital than to girls. Governors or officials could apprentice boys to local artisans with a view to their learning a 'mechanical trade' and becoming independent at the age of eighteen to twenty. Some would be employed by the hospital itself as clerks, administrators, dispensers of medicines or menial workers. A few talented youths were educated for professions. Idealists entertained the notion that a few foundlings and orphans would prove to be children of good blood and great ability who should not be confined to the lowest levels of society – could they not, for example, provide some of the capable clergy whom the Church so sorely needed? Without special concessions, base-born children would be barred from ordination and from obtaining benefices or entering religious orders. But papal privileges released pupils of Santa Maria della Scala in Siena, in principle if not always in practice, from the need to apply for individual dispensations – provided, as Paul II stipulated in 1464, 'that they do not imitate the loose lives of their parents and are of good behaviour and reputation'.[2]

Boys 'are here brought up til they be made scholars or artificers, according as they are apt and towardly', wrote Gregory Martin of Santo Spirito in Rome towards 1580.[3] In this and other hospitals, boys were minded by mistresses for a year or two and then handed over to masters. In 1657, Santo Spirito provided a combined schoolroom and dormitory equipped with fifteen beds for older boys, together with three or four rooms for younger ones still under female supervision. Such 'seminaries' taught reading, writing, grammar, arithmetic, Christian doctrine and good behaviour; a few children might pick up some Latin; a few masters taught music and looked out for choristers who would be an asset to the hospital church.[4]

Long spells in the classroom were not for everyone, however. At Florence in 1641, the Innocenti kept on its premises ninety-eight boys aged between seven and eighteen, eighty-six of whom went 'out to trades', while only twelve were 'in school'.[5] At Perugia, a local priest inspired a boys' school in 1589; a luxury in the eyes of eighteenth-century sceptics who did not believe in social advancement for foundlings, it became a soft target for austerity measures and suffered severe reductions in the number of places (from forty to fifteen, later to twelve) at the behest of the apostolic visitor after 1744.[6] A seminary at Siena, designed to prepare clever boys for occupations of higher status, sprang from a legacy of Federigo Soleti (d. 1645), accountant-general to the Apostolic Chamber under Pope Urban VIII and said to have been a resident of the hospital himself.[7] Francesco Pannolini, a silk merchant, established a college at the university of Bologna for youths from the foundling home and from two orphanages. Between 1617 and 1745, about a third of the entrants obtained doctorates, mostly in law, but sometimes in medicine or philosophy.[8]

Social advancement was contemplated for a few residents and sometimes achieved. In 1456, the governors of Santa Maria della Scala in Siena accepted a petition from Agustino di Vangelo, 'son of this house', who had proved to be 'good at grammar and especially good at rhetoric' and was bent on the study of canon law. Since he had neither books nor money, the administration made him a student loan, to be repaid after six years, to buy the necessary texts.[9] Costantino Antinori (1530–78), abandoned during the 1530s but known to be the illegitimate son of one Alessandro Antinori, received a special dispensation from the vicar of the archbishop of Florence in 1550, caught the eye of the governor of the Innocenti and became his assistant, then became a canon of San Lorenzo by means of the governor's influence and later a canon of the cathedral during the 1570s, and also took a doctorate of theology.[10] It was possible, too, to make good in a secular career. In Venice in the 1720s, Pasqual Bisson, said to be an alumnus of a 'pious hospital' and possibly of the Pietà itself, defied convention by rising from the rank of apprentice oarmaker to become admiral (superintendent) of the Arsenal, the vast shipyard which built the warships of the Venetian State.[11]

But most boys were destined to become tailors, shoemakers or carpenters, or to take up other useful trades, the hospital arranging their indentures, paying some attention to their welfare, and sometimes keeping them clothed and shod. Once trained, they usually received gratuities and were allowed to keep some of their earnings, to give them a start in the world outside the walls. Special arrangements could be made: in 1735, the foundling home at Verona resolved to have blind Andrea taught the violin, 'in the hope that by means of this occupation he may relieve the house of expense'.[12] At first, pupils could be apprenticed between the ages of five and nine, but, in time, hospitals, as though growing more protective, delayed sending them out to masters, and apprenticeship began to coincide with adolescence rather than childhood.[13]

An alternative strategy was to train children on the premises and set them to making clothes and shoes for residents of the hospital. Brescia in 1580 boasted an academy for sixty-two boys aged between eight and sixteen, which undertook to instruct them in tailoring, shoemaking and weaving: a master tailor would cut the clothes and teach the children how to 'stitch and make them up'. A few boys entered the hospital's service, as opportunities arose, to become porters, stable boys, scullions, guards or house-tailors.[14] At Siena, boys could apply to join the order of hospitallers and be employed in clerical or administrative posts. In 1483, the chapter concluded that 'Alessandro gittatello', then working in the dispensary, ought to be put to the test. Should the rector be satisfied with his ability and character, let him 'accept him as a brother of the hospital and clothe him in its habit'. Filippo, 'brought up in the house', was appointed schoolmaster in 1495. An inquiry into the morals of the inmates, launched in 1553, involved, among others, 'Martino, son of the hospital', who kept the books recording the arrangements made with nurses; 'Austino of the hospital, clerk to the chapter'; 'Paolo of the hospital, employed in the dispensary', and 'Crichetto, smith, son of the hospital'.[15] The institution would sometimes send boys out to its estates or prepare them to become stewards and administrators of the granges, forming part of an enclosed, self-perpetuating world in which the hospital, like a prestigious school or university, became one of the principal consumers of its own product.[16]

Systematic arrangements for training and educating foundling boys either within or from a city hospital were probably mostly confined to northern and central Italy. But they could at least be contemplated in parts of the southern kingdom. Pietro Carrera, administrator of the hospital at Sulmona from 1789 to 1799, wrote trenchantly in 1792 on the theme that mere almsgiving was not true charity and led only to mass dependence and degradation:

> There are a hundred beggars at the door, as naked as savages, men, women and people of all ages, but nowhere can you find anyone to make a pair of shoes, spin a bit of wool or provide the smallest service … True charity lies in obtaining for individuals the means of earning a living. In countries where begging is forbidden, nobody dies of hunger and nobody goes naked and barefoot. But in our country, where alms are plentiful, hunger, destitution and misfortune are everywhere present.

He had already sought permission to send six of his foundlings to the Marche to learn papermaking, with a view to reopening a papermill which the hospital owned. He planned to develop textile industries in Sulmona and dreamed of transforming it into 'a city of note and the treasure of the Abruzzi', though the small woollen factory he set up failed to thrive and no doubt suffered from Carrera's suspension from his post, which lasted from 1793 to 1797.[17]

Domestic service

Girls had fewer choices. They could become domestic servants, usually with the aim of earning a dowry from their employers and marrying after a few years, but occasionally of making careers as housekeepers. Or they might be married from the conservatory with the aid of a dowry provided by the hospital, acting in the place of their missing parents. Like boys, they could enter the service of the institution, and a few rose to become mistresses, instructors, superintendents of wards or even prioresses. At Santo Spirito in Rome between the late sixteenth century and about 1660, it was possible for some conservatory girls to join the order of nuns who lived with them, until it dawned on higher authority that elderly nuns were not the best people to prepare the inmates of a girls' home for married life or indeed for any activity in the world outside. However, since women in traditional convents were seldom well disposed to foundlings and would presumably have demanded dowries beyond the hospital's means (even for lay sisters), the order did in its time meet the needs of girls with a sense of religious vocation.[18] Other residents might become drudges in the kitchen and laundry, or carry out more skilled work at the loom or with the needle, earning a little money for the hospital and small sums for their own comfort. Some never ventured into the world outside, a large minority being too ill, or too gravely impaired physically or mentally, to be able to face marriage and childbearing or tackle the duties of a servant – in 1742, 37 per cent of the 583 maidens at Santo Spirito were described as ill or unfit.[19] Other women returned to the institution after a few years outside the walls. Agata died at eighty-one in Santa Maria della Scala in 1765, and Domenica was still alive at eighty-nine in 1768.[20]

By 1400, hospitals were sending some children into service on contracts resembling those made on behalf of girls from impoverished families who would have to earn much of their dowries for themselves. In that year, the Misericordia of Perugia handed Tomassina, a foundling, over to Donna Nicolutia, the wife of a resident of the city, who acquired all the hospital's rights over the girl and undertook to provide her, so long as she had given satisfaction, with a dowry worth fifty florins when Tomassina came of marriageable age – probably at her fourteenth birthday.[21] These arrangements promised to make private citizens responsible for girls' futures and to reduce overcrowding in conservatories. But there was room for misgiving, in that servant girls were notoriously vulnerable to sexual interference, and some institutions therefore hesitated to turn their charges into other people's maids-of-all-work. It would be all too easy to perpetuate the process which had created much of the need for foundling hospitals, by sending illegitimate girls off to follow their own mothers and, through no fault of their own, bear bastards whom they could not think of supporting.

By the mid-sixteenth century, some administrators seemed well aware of the hazards of domestic service and were capable of forbidding it altogether or refusing requests to be supplied with servants lest the girls be ill-used.[22] About 1579, Borghini, the superintendent of the Innocenti, wondered whether his protégées, whom he compared to 'headless chickens [*polli ebbri*]', would really make good servants. Girls would need to serve for up to twelve years in order to accumulate adequate dowries, and to achieve this end by the right time in life they would usually have to enter employment between the dangerous ages of ten and fifteen. To embark on domestic service at fifteen to twenty would not be absurd, but marriage prospects would be nearly non-existent for older women, and it was all too likely that they would return to the conservatory as disillusioned spinsters prone to unsettling fellow residents by telling them too much about life in the world outside. None the less, Borghini's successor sent 157 girls into service between 1581 and 1584. Lucrezia Pieri, a widow who followed her brother into the service of the Innocenti, placed 118 girls between 1628 and 1642. But she departed from tradition by treating domestic service, not as a transitory state and a prelude to marriage, but rather as a career. Pieri could afford, therefore, to send young women out when they were more mature and possibly less innocent, at the age of about twenty, and she based her arrangements on a new device – eight-year renewable contracts.[23]

Doubts about the wisdom of exposing young girls to domestic service persisted. The nuns of Santo Spirito obstructed the process, probably from self-interest, in that they wanted to keep the more capable girls to be their own personal servants and encouraged them to believe that entering service outside was 'like going to the slaughterhouse.'[24] At Viterbo, from the 1730s, girls were in principle to be employed only in 'a godfearing noble or gentlemanly household in which there are only women servants', an ambition probably difficult to achieve on a large scale.[25] When, in 1789, the governor of Sulmona's hospital was proposing to send girls out to serve families in the diocese, a parish priest warned him discreetly that they would be exposed to abuse by 'dissolute men [*scapestrati*]', because they had no relatives to take their part. The governor revised his plans.[26]

Female conservatories

Institutions for older girls, especially within the large metropolitan hospitals, tended to develop into vast, overcrowded pseudo-convents designed to prepare some for domestic life and to contain others until they died. Unlike genuine convents, they tested no religious vocations and demanded no dowries at entry, but they imposed a regime which rested on detachment from the world and from all masculine company, skilled manual work or grinding domestic chores, prayer, church attendance, regular communion and confession, occasional retreats, sacred readings at meals, and (officially at least) little recreation and no self-adornment. They dwarfed the more selective orphanages, the largest convents for repentant sinners and the biggest rescue homes for endangered girls.

State capitals maintained the largest conservatories. For much of the sixteenth and seventeenth centuries, the Innocenti sheltered about six hundred females at any one time (though numbers soared to an insupportable 968 in 1579 and stood at 756 in 1681).[27] From a hundred or less in the first half of the sixteenth century, the population of Santo Spirito rose to about three hundred in the late sixteenth century and four or five hundred between 1630 and 1660. Numbers fell back to just below three hundred in 1675, but mounted to their highest peaks, above eight hundred, in the late 1720s. They were reduced again to six hundred or less in the next two decades and fell to something between 350 and 420 in the second half of the eighteenth century.[28] Venice's Pietà was accommodating some 630 girls and older women in 1784, the Neapolitan Annunziata 461 in 1789.[29] Provincial centres such as Bologna, Perugia and Siena supported smaller numbers of residents, generally one or two hundred, numbers falling at Perugia during the eighteenth century.[30] Administrators could to some extent control numbers by postponing the return of younger girls from the countryside, by sending inmates out to be servants, and occasionally by moving mature women to other establishments (in Florence in 1579, transfers from the Innocenti to the Orbatello affected women aged thirty-six or older). But one expedient, sometimes ruthlessly and sometimes more gently employed, was to encourage marriages; unless many of their fitter residents moved on and became wives, numbers and expenses at conservatories would relentlessly increase.

In northern and central Italy, foundling conservatories were too plebeian to be taken over by genteel people looking for cheap berths for unappealing daughters. In parts of the south, however, foundlings could be elbowed aside to make way for children of higher status. In 1789, Galanti complained that, although the conservatory at Aversa in Campania had been intended for foundling girls, it actually had a mixed population of which they formed only a small part. The 421 residents included nuns, pupils [edu-cande], widows and married women as well as foundlings. Indeed, there were only 78 foundlings to 108 boarders of higher standing, who 'ought to be admitted for a fee of two ducats a month, but in fact pay nothing because they are favoured by the governors'. At Gaeta, the conservatory, in theory reserved for foundlings, actually met the needs of more estimable orphans. Only nine of fifty-one girls at Sessa were truly foundlings as the statutes required.[31]

Conservatory females were sometimes divided into 'families' or 'schools'. At first, these groups included girls and women of all ages and perhaps resembled the houses in a boarding school, since the system relied on seniors overseeing juniors, like prefects or monitors, and backing up the mistresses. In overall authority were women often described as sisters, who were sometimes hospitallers, sometimes tertiaries, sometimes lay persons, and were recruited wholly or partly from 'daughters of the house'.[32] In the early seventeenth century, the community at Perugia consisted of eight ordinary families and a ninth, sometimes the biggest, composed of females known to be of legitimate birth; each family was subject to two sisters, while a prioress and her deputy presided over the whole conservatory.[33] In 1742, the 583 residents of the conservatory of Santo Spirito were divided into seven schools, each headed by a matron, flanked by six female instructors or mistresses; the membership of each ranged from girls under ten to women in their seventies and eighties.[34] But in the mid-eighteenth century, some reformers, critical of the family system, wanted the generations separated, as if they feared the corrupting influence of older women on children, the development of a rival, informal authority capable of challenging the superiors. Some argued that the families themselves had become dangerously autonomous and should be abolished to make way for a uniform and featureless 'common life'.[35]

Conservatories tended to be overcrowded and unhygienic; tuberculosis ravaged more than one. Girls slept four to eight to a bed at Perugia in 1603, in Rome four to a bed in 1585 and six in 1627, while in Rome in 1660, though conditions had somewhat improved, only 158 beds were available for the 411 'maidens' and the 19 female religious in charge of them. About 1740, the infirmary at Rome was not big enough to accommodate all the sufferers from infectious diseases such as tuberculosis and scabies, some of whom therefore slept in the ordinary dormitories. But improvements were made at that time both by reducing the number of residents and by constructing a new wing, the Lungara, which contained several new dormitories together with a large new drying room, and opened into a spacious garden.[36]

In outline the regimes of the foundling conservatories differed little from those of the more select girls' homes, although many of the residents were employed in rough work for adjacent hospital wards. Much of their making and mending was intended to meet the everyday needs of the hospital, especially for clothing and bedding, but they could also produce goods for sale to the public, with some benefit to the hospital's finances and the possibility of keeping some of their earnings for themselves. Almost all their skilled work was in the garment, textile and needle trades. In the fifteenth century, the Innocenti had found it possible to place girls as well as boys to learn a trade outside the hospital, for example in the silk industry. But by the sixteenth, the protective governors preferred to have skills taught and practised in workrooms inside the walls. They defined the proper occupations in 1536 as sewing, cooking, threading and throwing silk, and weaving. A more ambitious activity, tapestry-making, entered the Innocenti in 1579, but lasted only a few years.[37] In Perugia in 1603, the women and girls span, wove and sewed 'that the city may know that they do not live in idleness'.[38] Looms for weaving cloth, linen and hemp were installed in Santo Spirito in 1661.[39]

The alternative to skilled work was back-breaking labour on housework and hospital chores, usually reserved for the strongest young women and those whom the sisters most disliked.[40] In some homes the practice of alternating between kitchen and laundry relieved the monotony slightly, while at Santo Spirito there was a little compensation in the more generous rations allocated to heavy workers and their exemption from some Lenten dietary restrictions. In the 1740s, too, scabies sufferers were removed from the wards of Santo Spirito to the hospital of San Gallicano, so that the conservatory girls no longer had to wash and pick up infection from their bedding.[41]

Music and austerity

Occasionally, children's charities developed into music schools, the conservatory mutating into a conservatoire. Alternatively, they created music schools for a small, select body of talented and privileged pupils, at some risk of upsetting their ordinary residents. In eighteenth-century Naples, four boys' orphanages became boarding schools for boys and youths of modest social standing, trained them as singers and players (especially violinists), and attempted to supply the needs of both churches and theatres. Some of their alumni became professional musicians or, in the early nineteenth century, bandsmen in line regiments. Soon after 1800, the three surviving conservatories were merged into a Royal College of Music.[42] In the mid-eighteenth century, Antonio Genovesi, professor of political economy at Naples, saw Italian music schools as pioneers of the kind of practical education that had the power to raise poor children up out of poverty and dependence, to correct the fatal tendency of Christian almsgiving to foster idleness and breed beggars. 'Why could we not have schools of painters, of sculptors, of engravers, of embroiderers, of weavers, of spinners, of tailors, of shoemakers, of smiths, and of all those crafts that prevail in civilised states?'[43]

Foundling hospitals could hardly transform the whole of their huge female conservatories into schools of music or send their girls out to perform in opera houses. But in Venice, a few musically gifted girls, perhaps forty of the six hundred females in the conservatory of the Pietà, had the chance to escape drab manual work and even become star performers acclaimed by audiences in the hospital church. In other countries, concerts of sacred music were demonstrating their power to attract fashionable audiences and raise money for charities, as did the first presentation of Handel's *Messiah* in Dublin in 1742; the composer would become a governor of the London Foundling Hospital in 1750, and the hospital benefit until 1777 from annual performances of the oratorio.[44] In Venice, the composers were employees, not governors of the establishment (Vivaldi was violin-master, concert master and prolific house composer to the Pietà), and the foundling girls themselves were the musicians and singers.[45] From the late seventeenth century, aesthetic, religious and practical motives inspired the four largest hospitals in the city (the Pietà and three others) to create a form of sacred music which made ample use both of a powerful orchestra, subject to institutional discipline and always available for rehearsal, and of the operatic virtuosity of female soloists.

After 1682, Giacomo Spada, a musician of St Mark's, began to develop a music school at the Pietà, and from 1701 onwards, the governors began to appoint full-time directors of music.[46] At the heart of the enterprise was the *choro*, choir and orchestra, which consisted of about thirty girls and women, half singers and half players, and known as 'active' members, together with a dozen or so novices under instruction.[47] Furthermore, in 1707 some of the Pietà's musicians obtained permission to take on as pupils 'little girls' from the nobility or citizenry (nobles only after 1723). These socially superior children lodged with them in the hospital and their fees helped to provide dresses for the girls of the choir-orchestra.[48] Members of the *choro* were themselves usually described as girls or children [*figliole, putte*], although some were in their twenties and thirties and appeared to have chosen music rather than marriage as a career.

In 1708, the governing body explained its strategy as follows:

> While the *choro* is the place designed to give due praise to the Lord God and ardently to beg for his holy grace and implore blessings from heaven, it also serves to induce a throng of music lovers to flock to this church. Many of them develop an affection for this charity and in life and in death bestow upon it alms and substantial legacies, which help to maintain the establishment and to feed the multitude of children whom it supports.[49]

Some cautious souls feared that the female musicians were becoming objects of 'idle curiosity' and would, if they could, have confined them to church services, forbidding them to put on anything so showy as an oratorio or cantata.[50] But during the eighteenth century, the girls became accustomed to providing entertainments (no fewer than twenty-seven in 1709) and, with the governors' permission, occasionally ventured outside the walls to grace special occasions. Some of their expeditions were impeccably virtuous, as in 1712, when Maria della Viola, Anna Maria and Dianora went to enliven the proceedings of a school of Christian doctrine held at San Francesco della Vigna; others proved less so, when, for example, a few girls and one of their teachers visited the household of Pomponne, the French ambassador, and were unsuitably entertained by the racy conversations they overheard.[51] Private performances were laid on for distinguished visitors, both royal and noble.

Some soloists, though visible to the public only through a gauze curtain which revealed the outlines of their figures but not their faces, built up a personal following.[52] About 1730–40, a critic commented on the body language of concert-goers, who suddenly came to life at the sound of their favourites; the antics of Maria la Bolognese, the writer grumbled, appealed to silly people whose appreciation spoiled the young lady. More impressive in his eyes were experienced musicians such as the soprano Apollonia and the versatile Anna Maria, who could play with equal accomplishment the harpsichord, violin, cello, viola d'amore, lute, theorbo and mandolin.[53] De Brosses, the avid French tourist, enjoyed himself most at the Pietà in 1739; Burney, the English musicologist, opined in 1770 that some of its glory had departed, but praised the girls who 'played a thousand tricks in singing, particularly in the duets, where there was a trial of skill and of natural powers, as who could go highest, lowest, swell a note the longest, or run divisions with the greatest rapidity'.[54] Gozzi, the Venetian journalist, credited the charities with instilling a love of song into all the Venetian people, so that nearly naked street urchins could sing in perfect harmony and in every house were girls who would not have known what a note of music was but could sing 'so as to ravish your ears'.[55] Had the hospitals educated the Venetian poor in general, or had they merely harnessed the talents of a select few?

Inevitably, the formation of such a privileged body as the *choro* threatened to make the ordinary girls jealous or tantalise them with ideas above their station. In 1784, when one wing of the Pietà's building was collapsing, when the other major hospitals were facing bankruptcy and radical reorganisation was contemplated, Venice's hospital commissioners saw their chance to separate the musicians and the older women from the younger girls. They argued that unless the choir and orchestra were set apart, the doge would never have 'in these children of the nation a body of industrious and mannerly subjects who are fit to become good fathers and mothers and to enter in an honourable and seemly fashion into the class of the people, to which the dubious circumstances of their birth confine them'.[56] Senators appointed to reform the Pietà in 1789 could scarcely abolish musical education, but they did revive the earlier distrust of drama and special performances and again asserted that the girls should not take part in oratorios or cantatas, but only in church services.[57]

Some clerics in other eighteenth-century cities, impervious to any notion that foundling homes ought to seek out hidden talents or offer alternatives to manual work, envisaged a regime of merciless monotony, supposedly good for discipline, fit for 'wretched girls who are supported by charity', and probably reminiscent of a very strict convent. The introduction of the so-called 'common life' meant abolishing the separate 'families' and rearranging the inmates into age groups, so that the younger children would not encounter the older residents. Let there be no 'vanities', no mockery of each other, but no displays of affection either, and no sneaking off for any reason into dark corners. There should be no music, much less any amateur theatricals, 'amusements which require study and reading' and were therefore unsuited to 'poor and wretched maidens, whose occupation must always be to live by the work of their hands'. These changes set out 'not only to preserve peace and harmony throughout the community by means of equal treatment, but also to save the maidens from the deadly sin of vanity'. Apostolic visitors contemplated this kind of levelling in the Papal States about 1739. At Perugia they took time to introduce it, and could only do so in the 1760s by setting up a second, much stricter conservatory and allowing the existing one to die out. The experiment failed, partly because girls fresh from the countryside became restive on hearing about the more relaxed regime in the old conservatory, and partly because the premises assigned to the new one were unsuitable and unhealthy. It began with between thirty and fifty girls and closed in 1777 when there were only six left and all of them were unwell.[58]

Marriage and spinsterhood

In general, foundling homes aimed at the traditional goal of preparing young women to become good wives and mothers, instilling a sense of devotion and duty and teaching a housewife's skills. But many residents remained within their own enclosed world and formed a tribe apart, some because they chose to, some because they were unfit to leave or were pressed to stay. As a visitor to the Innocenti commented in 1666, 'The girls stay there as long as they like ... They have a way of talking among themselves, with an accent not shared by others, which makes them instantly recognisable'.[59] Several conservatories sheltered significant numbers of women well past the normal age of marriage: in 1579 and 1641, about one-fifth of female residents at the Innocenti had passed their fortieth year, while in 1660, perhaps one-sixth of the females in Santo Spirito were between thirty and seventy.[60] In 1790, when some eighty spinsters were treating the conservatory of the Esposti in Parma as their permanent home, a critic complained that the interests of young children were being sacrificed to keep older women in idleness. Surely a spinster in her thirties was seldom in danger of seduction, and if a boy of fifteen could fend for himself so could a woman of thirty-five (it might be objected that one so long insulated from the world would never be able to adjust to it).[61] At the Pietà in Venice in 1793, older women, known as *giubilate*, i.e. pensioners, were unkindly described as 'unprofitable to the institution and to the nation', though moderately senior females could be employed as portresses or nursery attendants.[62]

Marriage had limited appeal for conservatory girls, many of whom preferred the familiar if squalid conditions of their mother house. Nor was there an unending supply of suitors hungry for their dowries. In Florence, Borghini complained to the grand duke in the 1570s that the world had grown 'poorer and worse' and that a decision in 1559 to double the standard dowry had done little to improve the prospects of marrying the girls off.[63] Brother Borgarucci, however, supplied a complacent account of matchmaking in Rome in the early seventeenth century. He described three occasions every year on which the nubile girls of the conservatory (like the seventy 'Young maydens mariable' of Gregory Martin's text) processed from Santo Spirito to St Peter's and prospective husbands lined the route to look them over. Should any girl take a young man's fancy, let him offer her a bouquet, a ring or a pair of gloves, a token of courtship which would entitle him to ask for her hand. The girl was supposed to like her suitor, the head of the hospital to be satisfied as to his clothes and possessions (a guide, if a superficial one, to his character, sobriety and prospects). Then, so long as arrangements for the dowry could be agreed, the couple could be married in church.

Even Borgarucci, though, had to admit that the marriageable girls had multiplied and the dowry funds were strained.[64] For these and other reasons, the numbers of marriages solemnised in the institutions of Florence, Rome and Perugia varied markedly from one period to another – 105 in Florence between 1574 and 1605, but only 35 between 1605 and 1652; only 20 marriages in Perugia in the 1590s, but 90 between 1750 and 1769.[65] At least in the later seventeenth and eighteenth centuries, certain foundling hospitals, unlike the smaller and more select homes for 'girls in danger', tended to steer their girls towards the countryside, towards their own estates or the villages where the girls had been fostered; they occasionally married men who had themselves been the hospital's pupils.[66]

To find husbands for pupils generally made economic sense: put down a lump sum for a dowry, which might (as in Rome) be the equivalent of little more than three years' maintenance, and the hospital escaped the obligation to keep the woman indefinitely. But towards 1660, arrangements in Rome, much criticised by the Commendatore Virgilio Spada, were working badly. It was not just that the nuns, inured to celibacy and perhaps believing devoutly in its superiority, saw marriage as a penalty to be inflicted on bad workers and rebels whom they did not wish to keep, 'the most ugly, ignorant and contrary'. It was also that conditions in the conservatory were preferable to those in the world outside (more eligible, as English poor law reformers of the 1830s might have put it). Girls who had come from impoverished foster homes needed no nuns to envisage for them the trials of married life, which they had already seen at first hand; in the conservatory food seemed ample and the work light, so why exchange the institution for something more gruelling? '[W]e have so much, such plenty, soup every day, wine, cheese, so many good things', Spada heard or imagined them gloating. The regime should become meaner and more strenuous, closer to that of a workhouse: inmates should want to leave as soon as possible, 'to live more comfortably and exert themselves less'.[67] Soon afterwards, the Commendatore Francesco Maria Febei, in charge from 1663 to 1681, increased the number of marriages, which had been about 25 a year in the 1650s, to as many as 138 in 1679. He encouraged youthful weddings, as if to move the girls on before they became set in their ways: during the later seventeenth century, most brides were between twelve and fifteen and took husbands aged between seventeen and twenty-two.[68]

Febei's tactics did not prevail indefinitely, however, and numbers in the conservatory swelled in the first quarter of the eighteenth century. There was still much to give marriage a bad name, particularly in the hospital's inclination to cut procedural corners (e.g. on the grounds that many suitors were peasants who could not hang about for long in Rome); to forego documents testifying to the good character and solvency of applicants; and to depend unduly on assurances given by parish priests and local worthies.

About 1740, in the village of Affile in the diocese of Subiaco, several fortune hunters were allowed to make false claims to be men of property. The hospital's dowry, though slender, could mean a good deal in the countryside and serve as a bait for scoundrels who wanted the money without the bride. An extreme example was Gregorio Trulli of Sant' Angelo in Regno, who married Orsola from Santo Spirito in 1701, obtained her dowry, murdered her, and then passed himself off as his own brother, Domenico, in order to marry Barbara, another *proietta*. Luckily for her, murder would out, and Trulli, executed in 1709, had no chance to repeat the performance.[69]

In the 1730s and 1740s, marriages multiplied again, numbers rising from the thirties in 1740 and 1742 to peaks of sixty-two in 1747 and eighty-six in 1750 and falling away thereafter as the conservatory's population contracted and stabilised.[70] The complaint against the mistresses was now the opposite of the charge laid against the sisters of the 1660s: they were not discouraging marriages but forcing too many girls into them. Hence a decree of 1737 to the effect that an administrator should ask all girls whether they wanted to marry and compile a list of those who were willing, that they might be married off in order of seniority.[71] The institution did something to help ex-pupils whose marriages had failed, but stopped short of readmitting them to the conservatory: there was no wing for *malmaritate*.[72]

Oppression and protest

Despite the high ideals proclaimed by the hospitals' apologists, abuses ranging from favouritism to sexual assault did occur within their walls. Children isolated from the world, undefended by relatives, were subject to the almost absolute power of the hospitallers and reliant on their willingness to police themselves or on the occasional intervention of a visitor. At intervals between the mid-fifteenth and the mid-sixteenth centuries, the governors of Santa Maria della Scala in Siena received reports of serious crimes committed by hospitallers, including both heterosexual and homosexual rape, which led them to deprive some offenders of office and expel others from the order. Among the accused, about 1451, was Brother Giovanni Mattei, alleged to have taken a girl of ten to a house belonging to the hospital, saying

> "Come with me and I'll give you what you want." And in that house he had carnal knowledge of her and did what he desired. Not content with a single crime … he snatched a cloak from one of the boys of the house, saying "I'll never give it you back unless you come to my bedroom". And he did not hesitate to perform with that boy every kind of lewd act which appealed to his depraved appetites.[73]

Inquiries were launched in 1553 as to how certain male residents of the hospital had caught the French evil. They elicited several bald accounts of homosexual intercourse in shared beds with infected fellow inmates. Some of these reports implicated members of the hospital staff, including a chaplain and an instructor.[74] In the same decade, Giulio, schoolmaster, was denounced to the deputy rector as unfit for his position, since he had knowingly sent a boy to serve mass with an abusing priest.[75] At Imola in 1585, there were reports of immoral relations between girls in the hospital, surgeons, a priest and at least one member of the lay company which administered the institution. The girls got much of the blame, since those who were with child were expelled without dowries as soon as they had given birth. Their chances of subsequently leading a respectable life must have been poor indeed.[76]

However, conservatories were not all places of unrelieved gloom, nor were all their residents passive and resigned to oppression. Attempts by the governors of conservatories to introduce unwelcome changes provoked at least three rebellions. One broke out at Santo Spirito in 1675, led by nuns, mistresses and older women who objected to the Commendatore's determination to push residents into marrying and to expel them from their institutional cocoon: more than that, they threatened 'to set fire to the conservatory and throw themselves out of the windows rather than obey'.[77] Indignant voices were raised at the Innocenti in 1687, when female workers were forbidden to accept commissions from outside the institution and could no longer earn pocket money and enjoy some slight contact with the world.[78] And in 1800, another attempt to impose the dreary 'common life' at Perugia provoked a rebellion which resulted in the temporary exile to Assisi of four 'aunts' (i.e. nuns) and two of the most recalcitrant girls.[79]

Innocents and outcasts

Foundling hospitals sought to insert a limited number of survivors – probably no more than 15–25 per cent of the children they received – into the lower levels of ordinary society. Most were intended to work as farmers, craftsmen and labourers, or to be the wives of working men; Italian states showed no great determination to draft large numbers of foundling boys into the army, navy or merchant marine (in Venice at least, that destiny was for beggar boys rather than foundlings).[80] In Italy, as in other European societies, there was some danger that foundling hospitals would succeed only in creating a substratum of outcasts, an underclass without prospects, still bearing the stigma of their base birth or the shame of renunciation by their parents, against whom 'respectable' people would be stubbornly prejudiced.

Foundling children were called 'innocents' in the name of the famous Florentine hospital, 'most innocent' in a petition of the governors of the Pietà in Venice in 1607.[81] Generous folk argued that, however grave the sins of their parents, the children, like the little boys of Bethlehem who suffered under Herod in the place of Christ, had themselves done no wrong. Male foundlings in fiction sometimes proved to be, if not another Romulus or Moses, adults of some ability, like the Aventuroso of Giraldi Cinzio's fable of abandonment and reunion. Galanti argued that 'If it be true that children born of burning passion receive from nature a more robust spirit, it is surely in society's interest to bring them up properly.'[82] There clearly were villages, for example in the Canavese, near Turin, where hospital children were welcome, not just as a source of extra income when they were nurselings, but because they could be genuinely useful to the family economy when they grew up. Here and elsewhere hospital children settled down, married and were absorbed into farming families or took over their tenancies. In 1765, the household of Filippo Viganò, in the village of Nerviano to the north-west of Milan, included his own sons and grandsons, and also Antonio Maria, aged thirty-three, 'from the hospital and brought up in the house', Antonio's wife Anna Maria, and their two children. In rural communities, nubile hospital girls were unlikely to be written off as paupers, since their dowries from the hospital were often bigger than any the local girls could hope to piece together, and they sometimes married earlier than the blood daughters of the couples who had taken them in.[83]

Some people, though, were clearly repelled by foundlings and suspicious of the bad character they had supposedly inherited. There was a long tradition of regarding bastards as untrustworthy, inclined to mischief-making and endowed with the same lustful tendencies as their parents – according to a fifteenth-century Venetian humanist, 'they often turn out to be inferior and infamous, and are much more prone to immorality'.[84] In 1582, Alessandro de' Medici, archbishop of Florence, warned of nuns who objected to employing foundlings as servants in their convents and would treat them cruelly if made to do so.[85] When 32 of 101 girls from Santo Spirito who married in Rome during the 1650s were described as 'cattive', 'bad' or 'nasty', and many of their marriages turned out badly, the superior-general blamed this outcome on the temperament the girls had supposedly inherited from irresponsible or immoral mothers.[86] Certain priests in the region of Siena in the 1760s objected to the presence of foundlings among their flocks.[87] It was believed at Udine in the late eighteenth century that should the circumstances of illegitimate children's birth become known, 'the poor innocent young people' would suffer great shame and damage.[88]

Even communities generally willing to receive foundling children were sometimes fearful of importing venereal disease, inherited from loose-living parents or caught at the breast from promiscuous feeding in the hospital nursery. Hospital staff could never be sure that a child was free of such illness until three months had passed. But it was quite impracticable, a recipe for many infant deaths, to keep babies for so long in unhealthy nurseries, and they were therefore sent out to nurse while the risk remained. From 1760 onwards, there were occasional panics which prompted some women, terrified of infecting both themselves and their families, to return babies to the hospitals, and deterred others from taking on new charges.[89]

For many years, little had been done to disguise the origins of foundlings and defend them against popular prejudice. Until the late eighteenth and early nineteenth centuries, most foundlings from the same hospital acquired the same name – though some may have taken the surnames of their adoptive parents, and married women eventually took those of their husbands. Between 1475 and 1825, foundlings in Milan were called Colombo, 'dove', after the hospital's emblem; degli Innocenti, plain Innocenti, Nocenzia or Nocentini were used in Florence, Scala or della Scala in Siena, Casasanta in Sulmona. The nickname Proietto clung to children of Santo Spirito in Rome. Esposito or degli Esposti were used in the southern provinces, as, occasionally, were del Frate or del Prete, which betrayed the offspring of errant clerics. In a Calabrian parish in the 1650s, one girl was registered as 'Giovanna, daughter of our first father Adam and of Caterina'; another, Ventura, as 'daughter of Adam and Eve'.[90]

The task of inventing names which would clearly distinguish children from each other called for ingenuity. In some hospitals, including the Annunziata at Naples, foundlings often received two baptismal names, and the second of these, though actually a saint's name, could sound like a surname. This practice was recommended at Udine in the late eighteenth century, where a girl might be called Maria Fedele, Paola Fortunata, Orsola Maria, or Lucia Apollonia.[91] Sulmona's hospital, quicker to act than those of Naples and Florence, dropped the general surname Casasanta in 1793. By 1796, the Misericordia in Perugia was conferring surnames and had begun to record them. In 1817, a decree of the Grand Duchy of Tuscany prescribed that each child receive an individual sur-name 'which will not reveal the status of foundling, which will be neither unseemly nor ridiculous, and will not, as far as possible, belong to any existing families, especially notable ones'.[92] It sounded like a tall order, but one not impossible to obey. Dickens fans will remember the efforts of Bumble the beadle in *Oliver Twist* ('Why, you're quite a literary character, sir!') to invent surnames in alphabetical order for the foundlings of his parish – Swubble, Twist, Unwin, Vilkins. 'I have got names ready made to the end of the alphabet, and all the way through it again when we come to Z.' While some of the names bestowed on luckless children at Sulmona, such as Asinini or Superflui, seemed to invite contempt and persecution and to change nothing, a more sensitive solution was to give the children revised versions of their nurses' names – a child entrusted to Potenza di Giovanni became Maria Giuseppa Potentini, a neutral name which sug-gested a legitimate child.[93] These were slight acknowledgements of the principle that former foundlings ought to be treated as ordinary members of society, and that found-ling status ought not to cling to them for life, as did the tattoos which marked many infants shortly after their birth.

Conclusion

Conservatories in foundling hospitals, particularly for women and girls, performed two roles which sometimes clashed with each other: to prepare for the world and to protect from the world. They were designed to equip their charges, both spiritually and practi-cally, for a position in life fit for charity children of dishonourable birth and no social aspirations, whose only family was the hospital itself. Unless they could instil in their pupils some ambition to move out into ordinary society, provide them with dowries to tempt suitors and set up households, impress on them the need to work, bear chil-dren and submit to masculine authority, live on rations scantier than those provided by the hospital, the institutions would slump into financial troubles, overcrowding and squalor rise to intolerable levels. But marriages and domestic service contracts, if hast-ily concluded, could have disastrous effects and perpetuate the cycles which foundling hospitals were designed to break, providing them with more dependants. A servant girl, unprotected against sexual interference, might bear a bastard she would be forced to abandon. A married woman, tied to a feckless, spendthrift husband, perhaps much older than herself and likely to leave her a widow, might be forced to abandon her chil-dren out of poverty.

It was also true that a conservatory was an end in itself, that one of its main object-ives was to keep itself going and serve the hospital of which it formed part, recruiting some its more promising pupils for the purpose. The least fit children were among those most likely to be abandoned, and a substantial minority of the residents at any time had little prospect of departing and sustaining life outside the walls. It could be that the greatest prospects of advancement, of wielding authority and power, attracting deference and even admiration, lay within the establishment itself, for capable and intelligent women who never married. No-one, perhaps, knew this better than did the nuns of Santo Spirito, the lay *proiette* who succeeded them as superintendents or instructors, or the singers and musicians of the Pietà in Venice.

Some governors sensed that a few talented youths could be found in their establishments and should be encouraged to make their way as professional men, as clerics, or at least as clerks and book-keepers – that there could be scholars as well as artificers, labourers and porters among them. But, as did most charities, foundling hospitals sought to preserve the social structure rather than to alter it, and did not generally promote mobility except by absorbing potential outcasts into the ranks of the honourable working poor. They did not make steady progress towards greater efficiency and enlightenment, and had forever to struggle against poor funding and uncontrollable demand. But, as Robert Browning's Waring puts it, 'certain first steps were achieved', plans made for more spacious quarters, more consideration shown for menial workers, more care taken with service contracts and arranged marriages, more respect for the dignity of alumni.

The education and training of foundlings formed part of a complicated rescue operation, a kind of compensation or atonement for social willingness to accommodate and regulate, almost to encourage and legitimate, child abandonment as a lesser evil, an alternative to much worse things. Foundlings' lives must be preserved, though luxury and ambition should be avoided, a sense of humility instilled, at least in a great majority of the pupils who lived to grow up. In the last resort, the status of foundlings remained ambiguous; perhaps it was never within the power of hospitals to expunge prejudice against illegitimate birth and transform all their surviving foundlings into useful citizens, their parents' failings forgotten.

Notes

1   Quoted in Dodi Osnaghi 1982, p. 431.
2   Martellucci 2001, pp. 17–18, 181; Kuehn 2002, pp. 46–7.
3   G. Martin ed. Parks 1969, p. 185. For boys' education at the Innocenti in Florence, see Gavitt 2011/2013, pp. 124–43.
4   Grégoire 1979: 252–3; Schiavoni 1991, pp. 1038–40; Surdacki 1998: 163–4; Surdacki 2001–2, pp. 263–4.
5   Passerini 1853, pp. 949–50.
6   Calzola 2003, pp. 108–9; Tittarelli *et al.* 2003, p. 239.
7   Vigni 1979: 113–14; Martellucci 2001, p. 20, n. 38.
8   Terpstra 2005, pp. 163–4.
9   Martellucci 2001, pp. 160–1.
10 Gavitt 1990, pp. 248–50; Gavitt 2005, pp. 114–15; Gavitt 2011/2013, pp. 150–4.
11 Davis 1991, pp. 69, 223, n. 78.
12 Garbellotti 1996, p. 73.

13　Pagano 1979: 379; Sandri 1991, pp. 1010, 1015; Gavitt 1997: 241.

14　Montanari 1987, pp. 281–4.

15　Martellucci 2001: 91, 179–80, 206–11.

16　Vigni 1985: 232.

17　Tanturri 2003: 157–8, 163–5.

18　Dominici 2001: 31–6, 42–50; Dominici 2003: 193–4; Surdacki 2009: 29.

19　Surdacki 2009: 25–7.

20　Vigni 1985: 230, n. 114.

21　Tittarelli *et al.* 2003, pp. 61–5.

22　Dominici 2001: 29, 39; cf. Terpstra 2010, pp. 48–9, 100–104, 107–8.

23　Fubini Leuzzi 1994, pp. 867–8, 874, 888–92; Gavitt 1997: 253–6.

24　Dominici 2001: 46.

25　Dominici 2003: 207.

26　Tanturri 2003: 158–9.

27　Passerini 1853, pp. 949–50; Fubini Leuzzi 1994, p. 870; Gavitt 1997: 241.

28　Grégoire 1979: 253–4; Schiavoni 1991, p. 1041; Piccialuti 1994, p. 140; Surdacki 1998: 110–12; Fedeli Bernardini 2001, pp. 306–8.

29　Galanti 1786–90, III, p. 158; Pelizza 1997: 151–2.

30　Vigni 1985: 229–30; Kertzer 1993, pp. 85–6; Calzola 2003, pp. 108–10; Tittarelli *et al.* 2003, pp. 343–5.

31　Galanti 1786–90, III, pp. 162–4.

32　Grégoire 1979: 253–4; Fedeli Bernardini 2001, pp. 306–8; Dominici 2001: 45.

33　Calzola 2003, pp. 108–10; Tittarelli *et al.* 2003, pp. 343–5.

34　Surdacki 2001–02, pp. 255–6.

35　Surdacki 1998: 153; Tittarelli *et al.* 2003, pp. 349–54.

36　Fedeli Bernardini 2001, pp. 306–9; Piccialuti 2001, pp. 277–8; Tittarelli *et al.* 2003, p. 345; Surdacki 2009: 26–7.

37　Gavitt 1990, pp. 249–50, 300; Gavitt 1994, p. 85; Gavitt 1997: 241, 260.

38　Tittarelli *et al.* 2003, p. 345.

39　Fedeli Bernardini 2001, pp. 306–8.

40　Schiavoni 1991, p. 1041.

41　Piccialuti 2001, pp. 277–8; Surdacki 2001–02, pp. 262–3; Surdacki 2009: 27, 38–9.

42　On the Neapolitan conservatories of the Pietà dei Turchini, Santa Maria di Loreto, Sant' Onofrio a Capuana and the Poveri di Gesù Cristo, see Del Prete 2009.

43　Genovesi ed. Perna 1984, I, pp. 468–9.

44　Young 1965, pp. 70–2, 81–7; McClure 1981, pp. 68–70.

45　For Vivaldi's connections with the Pietà, see Giazotto 1973 and Talbot 1984.

46　Arnold 1962–63: 33–5, 38–40.

47　See the governors' resolutions of 25 September and 4 December 1707 in the documentary appendix to Giazotto 1973, pp. 355–8, and the regulations for the *choro* (undated but evidently post-1744), *ibid.*, pp. 384–8; Talbot 1984, pp. 19–24, 135–6.

48　See governors' resolutions of 5 June 1707 and 30 April 1723, in Giazotto 1973, pp. 354–5, 373; Arnold 1962–63: 35–6.

49　Resolution of 4 March 1708, in Giazotto 1973, pp. 358–62.

50　From a decree of the supervising magistrates, the Provveditori sopra Ospedali, dated in 1704 in Giazotto 1973, pp. 48–9, but in 1740 at p. 383.

51　Giazotto 1973, pp. 67–8, 92, 366.

52　Sharp 1767, p. 28; Arnold 1962–63: 41–2.

53 For the text, whose author identified himself as 'a man from beyond the Mincio', see Giazotto 1973, pp. 389–96.
54 De Brosses ed. Bezard 1931, I, pp. 238–9; Burney 1773, pp. 145–6, 168–70, 178–82.
55 Gozzi ed. Zardo 1915, p. 85, 5 April 1760.
56 Pelizza 1997: 151–2.
57 Perni 1999: 164.
58 Tittarelli *et al.* 2003, pp. 349–56.
59 Count Galeazzo Gualdo-Priorato, quoted in Passerini 1853, p. 707.
60 Fubini Leuzzi 1994, p. 876; Fedeli Bernardini 2001, pp. 306–8.
61 Dall'Aglio Maramotti 1985, p. 38.
62 Perni 1999: 160, 161, 163, 165.
63 Fubini Leuzzi 1994, pp. 872–3.
64 Grégoire 1979: 253–4; G. Martin ed. Parks 1979, p. 85.
65 Fubini Leuzzi 1994, p. 885; Tittarelli *et al.* 2003, pp. 347–8.
66 Vigni 1985: 231–2; Surdacki 1999: 114–16.
67 Surdacki 1999: 106–7, 119–20; Fedeli Bernardini 2001, pp. 306–8; Dominici 2001: 46–8.
68 Schiavoni 1991, pp. 1041–6; Surdacki 1999: 110–12.
69 Dominici 2003: 201, 230–2.
70 *Ibid.*, 246–7.
71 Piccialuti 1994, pp. 147–51; Surdacki 1999: 105; Fedeli Bernardini 2001, p. 309.
72 Dominici 2001: 39, 228–37, 243.
73 Martellucci 2001: 216–21.
74 The record of the inquiry is printed in Martellucci 2001: 206–11.
75 Martellucci 2001: 213–14.
76 Galassi 1966–70, II, p. 243.
77 Schiavoni 1991, pp. 1043–4.
78 Fubini Leuzzi 1994, pp. 895–6.
79 Tittarelli *et al.* 2003, pp. 339–43, 357–9.
80 Pullan 1971, pp. 307–9; cf. Gavitt 2011/2013, pp. 131–2.
81 Chambers and Pullan 1992, pp. 313–14.
82 Galanti 1786–90, III, pp. 153–4.
83 De Marchi 2009: 129–31.
84 Kuehn 2002, pp. 79–80, 89–91, 95, 99–100.
85 Fubini Leuzzi 1994, pp. 880–2.
86 Surdacki 1999: 118–20.
87 Vigni 1985: 220.
88 Codarin Miani 1991, p. 390.
89 Kertzer 1998–9: 591–2; De Marchi 2009: 143–4.
90 De Rosa 1978: 24; Vigni 1985: 231–2; Da Molin 1991, p. 461; Kertzer 1993, pp. 120–1; Surdacki 1999: 116–17; Surdacki 2001: 101–2.
91 Codarin Miani 1991, p. 390; Da Molin 1991, pp. 481–3.
92 Corsini 1991, pp. 114–16; Tittarelli *et al.* 2003, pp. 155–6.
93 Tanturri 2003: 172–3, 174–9.

Conclusion

It is probably true that in almost any place and period the shapers of social action –
councillors, magistrates, philanthropists, preachers, pamphleteers – have tended to
divide into puritans and pragmatists, absolutists and relativists. Some have tried to insist on total abstinence from reprehensible activities, or at least not to condone them
openly, others have been inclined to think them impossible to uproot and to aim, more
realistically, at reducing the harm which flows from them. In modern parlance, some
of the measures described in this book could be described as forms of 'harm reduction', remote ancestors of movements which developed in the late twentieth century
around the time of the HIV epidemic to mitigate some of the consequences of drug,
alcohol and tobacco use, without wasting time and effort on 'the eradication of intractable human behaviors'.[1] The medieval *minus malum* could perhaps be translated as 'the
smaller harm', though the term 'the lesser evil' is more consonant with the language of
the past and with the moral judgements commonly pronounced at the time on dishonoured women and base-born children. Dishonoured women were generally perceived
as sinners, not practitioners of 'high-risk behaviour', as harm-reductionists would see
them, and seldom were they invited to shape their own therapy. By tolerating and regulating prostitution, authorities were supposedly using a relatively minor evil to limit
more serious transgressions such as adultery or sodomy; they were hoping to employ
a commercial transaction, making consensual sex available for a fee, to reduce rape,
seduction and subversive sexual adventures. By organising the 'safe' abandonment of
children by people unable or unwilling to keep them for moral or economic reasons or
both, by allowing the concealment of illegitimate births and protecting the anonymity
of the parents, they hoped to reduce one of the most horrendous crimes, infanticide
without baptism. Soul-saving apart, they hoped to serve society by salvaging both the
honour of young women whose reputations and marriage prospects would have been
ruined and the honour of the families duty bound to watch over their sexual conduct.

Arguably, in neither field did public policies actually reduce harm or evil. They
merely concentrated it on particular victims whom they made some show of protecting and helping – on the figures of professional prostitutes, or on illegitimate children
parted from their biological mothers and immediately handicapped in their struggle
for survival by deprivation of their own mother's milk. Both were ambivalent figures: a
prostitute might be perceived as one of the vilest members of the social order, but she
had been a person of special interest to the Christian saviour, and in one of her many

aspects she was a sinner who could reclaim herself by penance and renunciation of the world, so long as she sacrificed her career and did not wait for age and disease to put her out of business. In principle, foundlings could be perceived as innocents, the heirs of the infants martyred by Herod. But they were also thought to have been doubly conceived in sin, to have inherited their parents' immoral tendencies and perhaps also the diseases which tainted their blood. For all this, some hardy survivors could acquire a new identity as children of the hospital, not of a sinful woman, be adopted by decent, hard-working people, and, within limits, become useful members of society.

Both tolerated prostitution and organised abandonment appeared from time to time to have some impact on population levels. Were they liable to increase or reduce them and were they favoured for either reason? Many brothels and vice districts were first introduced into cities at times when population was flagging. Arguably, they were supposed to educate young men in heterosexual and potentially fecund habits, to keep unnatural vice at bay. To check population overall, to enhance the effects of plague, war and famine, would be to curtail State power, to reduce the prince's taxes: who would openly advocate such a thing? But at various times, upper-class families showed a clear interest in restricting or discouraging marriages, as if to protect their patrimonies from division. Prostitution was, or could be, a complement to late marriage or bachelordom. Malthus would later write of 'the discouragements to marriage, the consequent vicious habits' which helped to 'prevent population from increasing beyond the means of subsistence'.[2] During the eighteenth century, prostitution would be attacked by mercantilists as an enemy of marriage, a refuge from its responsibilities, the enemy of a robust and populous state, a disseminator of hereditary disease. The role of foundling hospitals was equally uncertain. It might seem that their primary purpose was to save young lives and provide State and society with useful citizens by discouraging infanticide, exposure, abortion and contraception. On the other hand, their actual procedures, and those surrounding them (such as the transportation of children to distant, overburdened centres), seemed calculated to raise infant mortality and not to reduce it. Were they half-consciously intended to control a sickly, undesirable segment of the population by subjecting them to severe survival trials and making only a pretence of rescuing them?

Some kind of bridge was needed between a Christian ethic and the realities of everyday government. The damned and the saved had to live with each other until the day of judgement, and a degree of perfection was only attainable in cloistered communities separated from the world. In late medieval and early modern Italy, nobles and citizens ruled, as it were, with a left and a right hand. The left hand accommodated a degree of evil on the pretext of avoiding social disruption. The right hand tried to atone for this realism by practising bodily and spiritual charity – by rescuing or protecting a number of individuals from the contamination of tolerated evil. Let the city have its brothels, but let it have its places of repentance too.

There was no moment at which the problems described in this book were dramatically resolved. Over five centuries, from about 1300 to 1800, contributions were made to an everlasting debate which is still in progress and often returns to the same issues. It is possible, though, if not to chart continuous movement towards any specific goal or finale in this period, at least to identify a few turning points. They were steps in a process of building up a more comprehensive apparatus for coping with social and moral problems, though new developments often took unexpected turns and were diverted from their original purposes.

In the late middle ages, mostly between the late thirteenth and late fifteenth centuries, cities put into effect three measures designed to control loose sexual activity and its consequences by accommodating rather than suppressing it. In theory, foundling hospitals enabled illegitimate children to be raised apart from their biological mothers, reducing the threat to infants' lives by removing the threat which they presented to their mothers' reputations, and feeding those in danger of starving. Cities were inclined not to expel prostitutes but to assign them their own quarters and place them under civic protection, on condition that they were distinguished from respectable women and used to divert sexual aggression from them. Foundling hospitals were not intended particularly to receive the offspring of prostitutes – many of the parents were servants or slaves – but to assist women close to the borderland between respectability and dishonour: those who had acted unwisely or been the victims of seduction and assault. The third measure consisted of establishing asylums for women of lost honour prepared to redeem themselves through penance, not in a desert but in an austere convent. This was a form of atonement for the toleration of prostitution, a gesture of the charitable right hand making up for the compromises of the pragmatic left, setting the place of virtue against the place of vice. Strenuous penance would be performed by the providers of sexual services, not by their users or exploiters, and the convents would eventually be financed, if only to a modest extent, out of the gains made from those services.

In the sixteenth century, and especially from the 1540s onwards, the more forceful missionary movements in the Church concentrated harder on the protection of endangered girls and women, and on trying to rescue them without removing them permanently from the world. Trafficking and pimping, especially of young people, had always been condemned in principle, but systematic attempts at prevention had seldom if ever been organised. Prominent targets were 'bad' parents, and especially 'bad' mothers, often inflated into monsters ready to groom and sell attractive daughters and treat them, not as claimants for dowries and drains on their resources, but rather as financial assets and staffs for their old age. More attention began to be paid to the role of marital breakdown in destroying a woman's reputation and making her depend on concubinage or immoral earnings. Could her predicament sometimes originate, not in her own inconstancy, but in her husband's brutality or fecklessness? From the mid-sixteenth century onwards, as formal marriage grew in importance, concubinage seemed to become a far greater threat to wedlock, a new greater evil than a series of transactions with a prostitute who boasted of many 'friends'. Successful courtesans sometimes suffered more brutal attacks from authority, for example in Counter Reformation Rome, than did ordinary prostitutes. Campaigns against concubinage, demands that mistresses be turned away, may have resulted in some women being driven into prostitution and in the abandonment of some children.

One likely consequence of a stricter morality was that foundling hospitals were more heavily pressed to take on base-born children, even where their unmarried parents had a lasting and affectionate relationship. Should the hospitals try to confine themselves to base-born children alone, or should they, at the risk of sinking into administrative and financial chaos, also confront the less finite problem of children abandoned out of hardship by married parents? In the interests of preserving anonymity, should they give up all attempts to inquire into a child's origins? Or should they, in the interests of balancing their books, try to secure contributions from parents, putative fathers included? During the seventeenth and eighteenth centuries, devices such as the baby-wheel encouraged anonymous abandonment. The development of maternity homes which respected the anonymity of expectant mothers encouraged the safer delivery of newborn children to foundling hospitals nearby. During the eighteenth century, attempts were made, especially in the Papal States, to create a more rational distribution of foundling hospitals and to confine some of them more rigorously to the task of coping with illegitimate children alone. Around 1800, there were signs of a more humane attitude to foundlings, of token attempts at least to counter prejudice against them by conferring individual surnames which did not immediately betray their origins. In the eighteenth century, there were some far from typical educational developments, especially in music and musical drama, which were just as emphatically rejected by conservatives – puritans who saw them as quite inappropriate to charity children destined for a humble station in life.

Seldom, though, did policies achieve their aims for long: the users of institutions, their relatives and their benefactors had ways of bending them to their own purposes. In practice, it was never possible to confine sexual commerce, in its numerous forms, either spatially or socially; to keep it within a kind of prototypical ghetto, or restrict it to licensed full-time professionals; to make it the business of marginal people who would always know and keep their places. Courtesans, though vulnerable to violence and sickness, could make at least precarious careers, dream of advancement, threaten social order by implying that vice could pay better than virtue. Prostitution could never simply be regarded as a mechanical process which disposed of animal passions in the simplest possible way, or as one which was entirely free of emotional entanglements.

Plans for the reform or protection of women depended heavily on their subjection to a husband or to a religious community, not on developing some form of 'respectable' independence which would replace the suspect independence of a 'free woman'. It was difficult to envisage such a thing in the context of an economy where female wages were low and female employment precarious. Marriage could seem profoundly unattractive, especially to girls who had been foster children in impoverished rural families; there was a danger that some pupils might resist it and cling to familiar institutional routines, helping to create an overcrowded pseudo-convent rather than a bridgehead into ordinary life. Were such establishments capable of preparing girls for the world? There was clearly a risk that marriages would be hastily arranged in order to relieve an institution of responsibility for its pupils. There was some danger that, given the sacramental nature and the near indissolubility of marriage, houses for unhappily married women would be used to maintain unhappy marriages at almost any cost.

Over time, charities tended to depart from their original purposes, if only to sustain their finances once the initial enthusiasm of their supporters had begun to subside. Some began to address the needs, not of the poorest and most endangered people, but of those protected by influential patrons; not of women of blighted reputation, but of women seeking places in an inexpensive convent. Genteel spinsters and members of the lower-middle classes began to occupy places once earmarked for courtesans' daughters and girls off the streets. In the south especially, by the eighteenth century, foundlings were being pushed aside by higher-status orphans and other boarders in local institutions and despatched on dangerous journeys to distant hospitals.

A familiar charge is that foundling hospitals, far from repelling the great evil of infanticide, merely substituted another for it and killed children by neglect. But what really brought about the high levels of infant mortality? Did the causes lie in the hospitals themselves, or in the grim experiences and poor health of the children before they reached them; in the foul conditions of the nurseries or the poverty of nursing families outside the walls; in the determination to deprive illegitimate children of the milk of their biological mothers and in the deficiencies of substitutes for human milk?

Were dishonourable female conduct and child abandonment, as described in this book, things quite alien to the twentieth and twenty-first centuries? Or were they a part of everlasting, insoluble human problems which continue to recur and to be discussed in broadly similar terms? Recent newspaper reports and personal memoirs by victims of abuse and institutional rigour, from the London Foundling Hospital to the Magdalene laundries and mother-and-baby homes of Irish convents, suggest that some of these issues are very persistent, some attitudes unchanging. Debates on prostitution and the law still tend to be conducted in terms of three possible courses of action: prohibition; regulation, combined with the imposition of stigmas and degrading treatment of the providers rather than the users of sexual services; decriminalisation, the acceptance of the sex trades as businesses like any others, satisfying human needs and appetites, providing employment much needed in hard times, calling for safeguards against exploitation but not for adverse moral judgements.

Some recent measures, though, have few clear precedents. Not many people in late medieval or early modern Italy would have believed that sexual commerce could be curbed by reducing demand rather than supply. Since 1999, several European countries, alarmed by the scale of trafficking in sexually exploited women and children and following the example of Sweden, have adopted a highly controversial strategy by making it illegal for men to pay for sexual services. Perhaps the nearest approach to this in early modern Italy (described by Gregory Martin about 1580) was the practice of jeering at the customers who hung about the Ortaccio in Rome, as well as legally harassing the prostitutes. Italians would more likely have sympathised with the arguments recently advanced – for example by sex-workers' associations – that such measures would serve only to drive the trade into dangerous shadows, to increase the vulnerability of prostitutes and blight their chances of getting help and protection, to deprive women officiously of a legitimate means of making a living.

In medieval and early modern Italy, some of the roots of prostitution, as in all times, lay in poverty and desperation, in its potential as a quick if dangerous earner, its contribution to an economy of many expedients. As presented in this book, it was, above all, a survival tactic. Associations between prostitution and drug dependence, or other addictions such as gambling, were less obvious than they have become in the twenty-first century. But links between brothel prostitution and debt servitude, tying women to the trade, were strong. Violence towards prostitutes and their premises appears to have been common. The argument that 'prostitution is, simply put, a condition that kills women' would have applied to the sixteenth century as much as to the twenty-first.[3]

Foundling hospitals in Italy contrived the separation of illegitimate children from their parents in order to avoid what seemed to be greater evils. Baby-wheels, once widely favoured in the belief that they could preserve life by assisting anonymous abandonment, began to be abolished in Italian cities from 1867 onwards (Ferrara was soon followed by Como, Milan, Turin and Ivrea).[4] But by 2012, there were reports of the return of baby boxes or hatches, similarly conceived and usually placed outside hospitals or clinics, to eleven very diverse countries of the European Union, including Germany and Czechoslovakia, and of the spread of similar 'Safe Havens' in the United States. Old discussions were reopened. Did baby hatches, as their advocates claimed, really (as in 'medieval times') save life? Did they violate the right of children to maintain personal relations with their parents? Or should it be insisted that 'the safety of children is of higher priority than their desire to know their biological parents'? Would the existence of a 'Safe Haven' have dissuaded the mother at Quakers Hill, near Sydney, who left her baby concealed at the bottom of a storm drain and was charged with attempted murder in 2014?[5] Accounts have been given of priests in Chile, mostly in the 1970s and 1980s but sometimes as recently as 2005, involved in schemes for the removal of illegitimate children from mothers reluctant to give them up – justified, not so much by solicitude for the interests of the child, as by concern for the reputation of the mother and her family. 'A young single woman who had a baby was looked at very badly', said a priest in his own defence. 'I wouldn't say it scrubbed out their life, but it was close to that. Nobody wanted to marry them.'[6] Personal memoirs and reports have brought to light stories, for example from twentieth-century Ireland, of nuns with a deeply punitive attitude to the mothers of illegitimate children and sometimes (by no means always) to the children themselves, even to the point of throwing their corpses into an unmarked mass grave.[7] Perhaps the issues described in this book will never be generally resolved, though some local successes may well be achieved.

In 1798, the great Malthus asserted the principle 'That the passion between the sexes is necessary and will remain nearly in its present state.' As Pompey, the tapster in *Measure for Measure*, more crudely puts it, 'they will to't then' unless authority intends 'to geld and spay all the youth of the city'. Sceptical of human perfectibility, Malthus wrote:

> It is the lot of man that he will frequently have to choose between two evils; and it is a sufficient reason for the adoption of any institution, that it is the best mode that suggests itself of preventing greater evils. A continual endeavour should undoubtedly prevail to make these institutions as perfect as the nature of them will admit. But nothing is so easy as to find fault with human institutions; nothing so difficult as to suggest adequate practical improvements. It is to be lamented that more men of talents employ their time in the former occupation than in the latter.[8]

Historians, whether talented or not, are seldom cut out to be social critics and must beware of patronising the past for its failure to solve intractable problems. But it can be their proper task to describe the ways in which achievements fell short of aims in an imperfect world, and to examine dispassionately some of the things that went wrong.

Notes

1   See, for example, Denning 2000; Stöver, Macdonald and Atherton 2007; Marlatt, Larimer and Witkiewicz 2012. For the quotation, see Collins *et al.* 2012, p. 19. For analogies between medieval urban policies and modern harm reduction, see Geltner 2012, pp. 29–34.
2   Malthus ed. Gilbert 2004, p. 56.
3   Tanya Gold in *The Guardian*, 17 November 2009.
4   Dodi Osnaghi 1982, p. 434; Viazzo *et al.* 1994: 247–8; Kertzer and White 1994: 453; Berruti 2007: 536.
5   *The Guardian*, 11 June 2012, 25 November 2014.
6   *Ibid.*, 16 May 2014.
7   *Ibid.*, 5 June 2014.
8   Malthus ed. Gilbert 2004, pp. 12, 106. For Pompey's exchange with Escalus, see *Measure for Measure* II.i.214–33.

Bibliography

Ago, Renata 1996: 'Oltre la dote: i beni femminili'. In Groppi 1996, pp. 164–82.

Aikema, Bernhard and Dulcia Meijers (eds.) 1989: *Nel regno dei poveri. Arte e storia dei grandi ospedali veneziani in età moderna, 1494–1797*, Venice.

Albini, Giuliana 1993: *Città e ospedali nella Lombardia medievale*, Bologna.

Alessi, Giorgia 1990: 'Il gioco degli scambi: seduzione e risarcimento nella casistica cattolica del XVI e XVII secolo', *Quaderni storici*, 25: 805–31.

Allerston, Patricia 1998: 'Wedding finery in sixteenth-century Venice'. In Dean and Lowe 1998, pp. 25–40.

Angeli, Aurora 1991: 'Caratteristiche, mortalità e destino degli esposti dell'ospedale di Imola nei secoli XVIII-XIX'. In E.A., pp. 123–49.

Angiolini, Franco 1996: 'Schiave'. In Groppi 1996, pp. 92–115.

Aquilecchia, Giovanni 1974: 'Per l'attribuzione e il testo del "Lamento d'una cortigiana ferrarese"'. In Bernardoni Trezzini *et al.* 1974, pp. 3–26.

Aquinas, Thomas ed. Thomas Gilby 1964–81: *Summa Theologiae*, 61 vols., London.

Aquinas, Thomas ed. Joseph Mathis 1971: *De regimine principum ad regem Cypri et De regimine iudaeorum ad ducissam Brabantiae*, Turin.

Archivi storici per le aziende di credito 1956: 2 vols., Rome.

Aretino, Pietro trans. Raymond Rosenthal 1972: *Dialogues*, London.

Aretino, Pietro ed. Angelo Romano 1989: *Cortigiana*, Milan.

Arnade, Peter and Michael Rocke (eds.) 2008: *Power, Gender and Ritual in Europe and the Americas. Essays in Memory of Richard C. Trexler*, Toronto.

Arnold, Denis 1962–63: 'Orphans and ladies: the Venetian conservatoires (1680-1790)', *Proceedings of the Royal Musical Association*, 89: 31–47.

Arnot, Margaret L. 1994: 'Infant death, child care and the state: the baby-farming scandal and the first infant life protection legislation of 1872', *Continuity and Change*, 9: 271–311.

Arrivo, Georgia 1997: 'Legami di sangue, legami di diritto (Pisa, secc. XVI–XVIII)', *Ricerche storiche*, 27: 231–61.

Arrizabalaga, Jon, John Henderson and Roger French 1997: *The Great Pox: The French Disease in Renaissance Europe*, New Haven and London.

Arte e pietà. I patrimoni culturali delle opere pie 1980, Bologna.

Augustine of Hippo (Aurelius Augustinus) ed. William Green 1955: *Contra academicos, De beata vita, necnon De ordine libri*, Antwerp.

Augustine of Hippo (Aurelius Augustinus) ed. and trans. Gregory J. Lombardo 1988: *St Augustine on Faith and Works*, New York and Mahwah, NJ.

Augustine of Hippo (Aurelius Augustinus) ed. and trans. P.G. Walsh 2001: *De bono coniugale. De sancta virginitate*, Oxford.

Augustine of Hippo (Aurelius Augustinus) ed. G.R. Evans, trans. Henry Bettenson 2003: *Concerning the City of God Against the Pagans*, London.

Bandello, Matteo ed. Francesco Flora 1934: *Tutte le opere*, 2 vols., Milan.

Banfi, Luigi (ed.) 1963: *Sacre rappresentazioni del Quattrocento*, Turin.

Barry, Jonathan and Colin Jones (eds.) 1991: *Medicine and Charity Before the Welfare State*, London and New York.

Basilico, Alessio 2008: ' "Li fanno pubblicamente li Signori, Dottori e Preti": concubinato e adulterio nella diocesi di Teramo (1550–1650)', *Annali dell'Istituto Italo-Germanico in Trento*, 34: 113–55.

Bassani, Riccardo and Flora Bellini 1994: *Caravaggio assassino: La carriera di un "valenthuomo" fazioso nella Roma della Controriforma*, Rome.

Bejczy, István 1997: '*Tolerantia*: a medieval concept', *Journal of the History of Ideas*, 58: 365–84.

Bellettati, Daniela 1988: 'Ragazze e donne milanesi tra XVII e XVIII secolo: il Conservatorio del Rosario', *Archivio storico lombardo*, 114: 99–150.

Beltrami, Daniele 1954: *Storia della popolazione di Venezia dalla fine del secolo XVI alla caduta della Repubblica*, Padua.

Bendiscioli, Mario 1957: 'Vita sociale e culturale'. In T.A., X, pp. 353–495.

Benjamin, Harry and R.E.L. Masters 1964: *The Prostitute in Society*, London.

Benvenuti Papi, Anna 1996: 'Mendicant friars and female *pinzochere* in Tuscany: from social marginality to models of sanctity'. In Bornstein and Rusconi 1996, pp. 84–103.

Berlinguer, Luigi and Floriana Colao (eds.) 1989: *Crimine, giustizia e società veneta in età moderna*, Milan.

Bernardino da Siena ed. Piero Bargellini 1936: *Le prediche volgari*, Milan and Rome.

Bernardoni Trezzini, Gabriella *et al.* (eds.) 1974: *Tra latino e volgare: per Carlo Dionisotti*, Padua.

Berruti, Alessia 2007: 'Un' istituzione di provincia: l'ospizio degli esposti della città di Ivrea, dal 1820 al 1870', *Bollettino storico-bibliografico subalpino*, 105: 535–82.

Berruti, Alessia 2008: 'La cura degli esposti come risorsa per una comunità contadina: il caso di Vialfrè nel Canavese dell' Ottocento', *Bollettino storico-bibliografico subalpino*, 106: 161–99.

Besta, Fabio (ed.) 1912: *Documenti finanziari della Repubblica di Venezia, serie II, I.i: Bilanci generali*, Venice.

Betteridge, Tom (ed.) 2002: *Sodomy in Early Modern Europe*, Manchester.

Bevegnati, Giunta ed. Fortunato Iozzelli 1997: *Legenda de vita et miraculis Beatae Margaritae de Cortona*, Rome.

Bianchi, Adanella 1997: 'La deresponsabilizzazione dei padri (Bologna, secc. XVI–XVII)', *Ricerche storiche*, 27: 263–86.

Bistort, G. 1912: *Il Magistrato alle Pompe nella Repubblica di Venezia: studio storico*, Venice.

Black, Christopher F. 1989: *Italian Confraternities in the Sixteenth Century*, Cambridge.

Blok, Anton 2001: *Honour and Violence*, Oxford and Cambridge.

Boccaccio, Giovanni ed. and trans. G.H. McWilliam 1995: *The Decameron*, London.

Bolognesi, Dante and Carla Giovannini 1982: 'Gli esposti a Ravenna fra '700 e '800'. In Sori 1982, pp. 307–28.

Bolton, Brenda 1994: 'Hearts not purses. Innocent III's attitude to social welfare'. In Hanawalt and Lindberg 1994, pp. 123–45. Reprinted as Item xviii in Bolton 1995.

Bolton, Brenda 1994a: ' "Received in his name": Rome's busy baby box', *Studies in Church History*, 31: 153–67. Reprinted as Item xix in Bolton 1995.

Bolton, Brenda 1995: *Innocent III: Studies in Papal Authority and Pastoral Care*, Aldershot.

Bonadonna Russo, Maria Teresa 1979: 'I problemi dell' assistenza pubblica nel Seicento e il tentativo di Mariano Sozzini', *Ricerche per la storia religiosa di Roma*, 3: 255–80.

Bongi, Salvatore (ed.) 1863: *Bandi lucchesi del secolo decimoquarto tratti dai registri del R. Archivio di Stato in Lucca*, Bologna.

Borello, Benedetta 2006: 'Lo spazio di un matrimonio: cose e contese tra marito e moglie (secc. XVII–XVIII)', *Quaderni storici*, 41: 69–99.

Bornstein, Daniel and Roberto Rusconi (eds.) trans. Margery J. Schneider 1996: *Women and Religion in Medieval and Renaissance Italy*, Chicago and London.

Borromeo, Federico 1756: *I tre libri della vita della venerabile madre Suor Caterina Vannini sanese, monaca convertita*, Padua.

Bossy, John 1985: *Christianity in the West, 1400–1700*, Oxford.

Boswell, John 1989: *The Kindness of Strangers: The Abandonment of Children in Western Europe from Late Antiquity to the Renaissance*, London.

Boulting, William 1910: *Women in Italy from the Introduction of the Chivalrous Service of Love to the Appearance of the Professional Actress*, London.

Brackett, John K. 1993: 'The Florentine Onestà and the control of prostitution, 1403–1680', *Sixteenth Century Journal*, 24: 273–300.

Brantôme (Pierre de Bourdeille, Abbé de Brantôme et d'André) English edition 1934: *Lives of Fair and Gallant Ladies*, London.

Bratchel, M.E. 1995: *Lucca 1430–1494. The Reconstruction of an Italian City-Republic*, Oxford.

Brolis, Maria Teresa 2001: 'Donne e assistenza a Bergamo nei secoli XIII e XIV: benefattrici, assistite e forme di marginalità femminile', *Nuova rivista storica*, 85: 619–50.

Brown, Patricia Fortini 2004: *Private Lives in Renaissance Venice: Art, Architecture and the Family*, New Haven and London.

Brucker, Gene (ed.) 1971: *The Society of Renaissance Florence: A Documentary Study*, New York.

Brundage, James A. 1975: 'Concubinage and marriage in medieval canon law', *Journal of Medieval History*, 1: 1–17. Reprinted as Item vii in Brundage 1993.

Brundage, James A. 1976: 'Prostitution in the medieval canon law', *Signs*, 1: 825–45. Reprinted as Item iv in Brundage 1993.

Brundage, James A. 1987: *Law, Sex and Christian Society in Medieval Europe*, London.

Brundage, James A. 1987a: 'Sumptuary laws and prostitution in late medieval Italy', *Journal of Medieval History*, 13: 341–55. Reprinted as Item xv in Brundage 1993.

Brundage, James A. 1993: *Sex, Law and Marriage in the Middle Ages*, Aldershot.

Bullough, Vern and Bonnie Bullough 1987: *Women and Prostitution: A Social History*, Buffalo.

Bullough, Vern L. and James A. Brundage 1996: *Handbook of Medieval Sexuality*, New York and London.

Burchard, Johann ed. L. Thuasne 1883–85: *Diarium sive rerum urbanarum commentarii*, 3 vols., Paris.

Burchard, Johann ed. and trans. Geoffrey Parker 1963: *At the Court of the Borgia, Being an Account of the Reign of Pope Alexander VI Written by his Master of Ceremonies, Johann Burchard*, London.

Burigozzo, Gianmarco 1842: 'Cronica milanese dal 1500 al 1544', *Archivio storico italiano*, 3: 421–552.

Burke, Peter 1987: *The Historical Anthropology of Early Modern Italy: Essays on Perception and Communication*, Cambridge.

Burney, Charles 1773: *The Present State of Music in France and Italy: or, the Journal of a Tour Through Those Countries Undertaken to Collect Materials for a General History of Music*, London.

Bussini, Odoardo 1991: 'Caratteristiche e destino degli esposti all' Ospedale della Carità di Todi nei secoli XVIII e XIX'. In E.A., pp. 301–25.

Butler, Alban ed. Herbert Thurston and Donald Attwater 1956: *Lives of the Saints*, 4 vols., London.

Buttafuoco, Annarita 1985: *Le Mariuccine: Storia di un'istituzione laica, l'Asilo Mariuccia*, Milan.

Calabria, Antonio 1991: *The Cost of Empire: The Finances of the Kingdom of Naples in the Time of Spanish Rule*, Cambridge.

Calzola, Luca 2003: 'Caratteristiche demografiche e modalità di abbandono degli esposti all'Ospedale di Santa Maria della Misericordia di Perugia nei secoli XVI e XVII'. In Tittarelli *et al.* 2003, pp. 97–150.

Camerano, Alessandra 1993: 'Assistenza richiesta e assistenza imposta: il Conservatorio di Santa Caterina della Rosa di Roma', *Quaderni storici*, 28: 227–60.

Camerano, Alessandra 1998: 'Donne oneste o meretrici? Incertezza dell'identità fra testamenti e diritto di proprietà a Roma', *Quaderni storici*, 33: 637–75.

Canepari, Eleonora 2006: 'Svelare o occultare? L'eco delle nascite illegittime (Roma, XVIII secolo)', *Quaderni storici*, 41: 101–32.

Canons and Decrees of the Council of Trent (original text with English translation) ed. H.J. Schroeder 1941: St Louis and London.

Canosa, Romano 1993: *La restaurazione sessuale: Per una storia della sessualità tra Cinquecento e Settecento*, Milan.

Canosa, Romano and Isabella Colonnello 1989: *Storia della prostituzione in Italia dal Quattrocento alla fine del Settecento*, Rome.

Cantarella, Eva 1991: 'Homicides of honor: the development of Italian adultery law over two millennia'. In Kertzer and Saller 1991, pp. 229–44.

Cantù, Bruna 1996: 'La Santa Casa di Misericordia'. In Pastore *et al.* 1996, pp. 81–7.

Cappelletti, Virginia and Franco Tagliarini (eds.) 2001–02: *L'antico Ospedale di Santo Spirito dall'istituzione papale alla sanità del terzo millennio*, 2 vols., Rome.

Cappelletto, Giovanna 1983: 'Infanzia abbandonata e ruoli di mediazione sociale nella Verona del Settecento', *Quaderni storici*, 18: 421–43.

Cappelletto, Giovanna 1991: 'Gli affidamenti di balia dei bambini abbandonati in una comunità del territorio veronese nel Settecento'. In E.A., pp. 327–40.

Cariboni, Guido 1999: 'Gregorio IX e la nascita delle "sorores penitentes" di Santa Maria Maddalena "in Alemannia"', *Annali dell' Istituto Storico Italo-Germanico in Trento*, 25: 11–44.

Carpin, Attilio 2006: *Il limbo nella teologia medievale*, Bologna.

Cavallo, Sandra 1980: 'Assistenza femminile e tutela dell' onore nella Torino del XVIII secolo', *Annali della Fondazione Luigi Einaudi*, 14: 127–55.

Cavallo, Sandra 1983: 'Strategie politiche e familiari intorno al baliatico. Il monopolio dei bambini abbandonati nel Canavese tra Sei e Settecento', *Quaderni storici*, 18: 391–420.

Cavallo, Sandra 1991: 'Bambini abbandonati e bambini "in deposito" a Torino nel Settecento'. In E.A., pp. 341–76.

Cavallo, Sandra 1991a: 'The motivations of benefactors. An overview of approaches to the study of charity'. In Barry and Jones 1991, pp. 46–62.

Cavallo, Sandra 1995: *Charity and Power in Early Modern Italy: Benefactors and Their Motives in Turin, 1541–1789*, Cambridge.

Cecchetti, Bartolomeo 1885: 'Documenti riguardanti Fra' Pietruccio di Assisi e lo Spedale della Pietà', *Archivio veneto*, 30: 141–7.

Cerutti, Simona and Sandra Cavallo 1980: 'Onore femminile e controllo sociale della riproduzione in Piemonte tra Sei e Settecento', *Quaderni storici*, 15: 346–83.

Chabot, Isabella 1988: 'Poverty and the widows in later medieval Florence', *Continuity and Change*, 3: 291–311.

Chambers, David and Brian Pullan (eds.) 1992: *Venice: A Documentary History, 1450–1630*, Oxford.

Chazelle, Celia *et al.* (eds.) 2012: *Why the Middle Ages Matter. Medieval Light on Modern Injustice*, Abingdon and New York.

Chilese, Valeria 2006: 'Le cause matrimoniali discusse presso il tribunale vescovile veronese tra XV e XVIII secolo', *Annali dell' Istituto Storico Italo-Germanico in Trento*, 32: 11–45.

Chittolini, Giorgio and Giovanni Miccoli (eds.) 1986: *Storia d'Italia. Annali 9. La Chiesa e il potere politico dal Medioevo all' età contemporanea*, Turin.

Chojnacka, Monica 1998: 'Women, charity and community in early modern Venice: the Casa delle Zitelle', *Renaissance Quarterly*, 51: 68–91.

Chojnacka, Monica 2001: *Working Women of Early Modern Venice*, Baltimore and London.

Christopoulos, John 2012: 'Abortion and the confessional in Counter Reformation Italy', *Renaissance Quarterly*, 65: 443–84.

Ciammitti, Luisa 1986: 'La dote come rendita. Note sull' assistenza a Bologna nei secoli XVI–XVIII'. In *Forme e soggetti* 1986, pp. 111–32.

Ciammitti, Luisa, Tiziana Bernardi, Fabio Giusberti and Lucia Ferrante 1980: 'Fanciulle, monache, madri. Povertà femminile e previdenza a Bologna nei secoli XV–XVIII'. In *Arte e pietà* 1980, pp. 435–520.

Cicogna, Emanuele 1824–53: *Inscrizioni veneziane*, 6 vols., Venice.

Codarin Miani, Loredana 1991: 'Santa Maria della Misericordia: un ricovero per gli esposti a Udine nel periodo 1656–1755'. In E.A., pp. 377–403.

Cohen, Elizabeth Storr 1988: 'La verginità perduta: autorappresentazione di giovani donne nella Roma barocca', *Quaderni storici*, 23: 169–91.

Cohen, Elizabeth Storr 1991: '"Courtesans" and "whores": words and behavior in Roman streets', *Women's Studies*, 19: 201–8.

Cohen, Elizabeth Storr 1992: 'Honor and gender in the streets of early modern Rome', *Journal of Interdisciplinary History*, 22: 597–626.

Cohen, Elizabeth Storr 1998: 'Seen and known: prostitutes in the cityscape of late-sixteenth century Rome', *Renaissance Studies*, 12: 392–409.

Cohen, Sherrill 1982: 'Convertite e malmaritate. Donne "irregolari" e ordini religiosi nella Firenze rinascimentale', *Memoria: rivista di storia delle donne*, 5: 46–63.

Cohen, Sherrill 1992: *The Evolution of Women's Asylums since 1500: From Refuges for Ex-Prostitutes to Shelters for Battered Women*, New York.

Cohen, Thomas V. and Elizabeth S. 1993: *Words and Deeds in Renaissance Rome: Trials Before the Papal Magistrates*, Toronto.

Collins, Susan E. *et al.* 2012: 'Current status, historical highlights, and basic principles of harm reduction'. In Marlatt *et al.* 2012, pp. 3–35.

Colucci, Silvia 2003: 'La questione della mortalità infantile e le sue testimonianze nell'arte medievale senese', *Bullettino senese di storia patria*, 110: 419–51.

Colzi, Francesco 2001: 'La gestione finanziaria dell' Ospedale di Santo Spirito nel secolo XVIII'. In Cappelletti and Tagliarini 2001–02, I, pp. 289–301.

Comba, Rinaldo 1986: '"Apetitus libidinis coherceatur." Strutture demografiche, reati sessuali, e disciplina dei comportamenti nel Piemonte tardo-medievale', *Studi storici*, 27: 529–76.

Constitutioni et regole della Casa delle Cittelle di Venetia 1701, Venice.

Conversione di Santa Maria Maddalena ed. Banfi 1963. In Banfi 1963, pp. 187–268.

Corsini, Carlo A. 1976: 'Materiali per lo studio della famiglia in Toscana nei secoli XVII-XIX: gli esposti', *Quaderni storici*, 11: 998–1052.

Corsini, Carlo A. 1983: 'L'enfant trouvé: note de démographie differentielle', *Annales de démographie historique*: 95–102.

Corsini, Carlo A. 1991: '"Era piovuto dal cielo e la terra l'aveva raccolto": il destino del trovatello'. In E.A., pp. 81–119.

Coryat, Thomas 1611/1905: *Coryat's Crudities*, reprint of 1611 edition, 2 vols., Glasgow.

Cowan, Alexander 2007: *Marriage, Manners and Mobility in Early Modern Venice*, Aldershot.

Cozzi, Gaetano (ed.) 1980–85: *Stato, società e giustizia nella Repubblica Veneta (sec.XV-XVIII)*, 2 vols., Rome.

Dall'Aglio Maramotti, Michela 1985: *L'assistenza ai poveri nella Parma del Settecento: aspetti e problemi*, Reggio Emilia.

Dall'Olio, Guido 1999: 'Ebrei, papi, vescovi e inquisitori a Bologna alla metà del Cinquecento. Le premesse dell'espulsione del 1569', *Annali dell'Istituto Storico Italo-Germanico in Trento*, 25: 153–204.

D'Amico, Stefano 1989: ' "Stà lontano della donna dishonesta." Il Deposito di San Zeno a Milano', *Nuova rivista storica*, 73: 395–424.

D'Amico, Stefano 1994: *Le contrade e la città: Sistema produttivo e spazio urbano a Milano fra Cinque e Seicento*, Milan.

D'Amico, Stefano 2005: 'Shameful mother: poverty and prostitution in seventeenth-century Milan', *Journal of Family History*, 30: 109–20.

Da Molin, Giovanna 1983: 'Les enfants abandonnés dans les villes italiennes aux XVIIIe et XIXe siècles', *Annales de démographie historique:* 103–24.

Da Molin, Giovanna 1991: 'Modalità dell' abbandono e caratteristiche degli eposti a Napoli del Seicento'. In E.A., pp. 457–502.

Dante Alighieri, *The Divine Comedy*, ed. and trans. Dorothy L. Sayers and Barbara Reynolds 1949–62, 3 vols., Harmondsworth.

Davidsohn, Robert 1896–1908: *Forschungen zur älteren Geschichte von Florenz*, 4 vols., Berlin.

Davidson, Nicholas 1994: 'Theology, nature and the law: sexual sin and sexual crime in Italy from the fourteenth to the seventeenth century'. In Dean and Lowe 1994, pp. 74–98.

Davidson, Nicholas 2002: 'Sodomy in early modern Venice'. In Betteridge 2002, pp. 65–81.

Davis, Robert C. 1991: *Shipbuilders of the Venetian Arsenal: Workers and Workplace in the Preindustrial City*, Baltimore and London.

Dean, Trevor 1998: 'Fathers and daughters: marriage laws and marriage disputes in Bologna and Italy, 1200–1500'. In Dean and Lowe 1998, pp. 85–106.

Dean, Trevor and Kate Lowe (eds.) 1994: *Crime, Society and the Law in Renaissance Italy*, Cambridge.

Dean, Trevor 1998: *Marriage in Italy, 1300–1650*, Cambridge.

De Angelis, Pietro 1960–62: *L'Ospedale di Santo Spirito in Saxia*, 2 vols., Rome.

De Azpilcueta, Martín: see Navarro, Martín.

De Brosses, Charles ed. Yvonne Bezard 1931: *Lettres familières sur l'Italie*, 2 vols., Paris.

Delasselle, Claude 1978: 'Abandoned children in eighteenth-century Paris'. In Forster and Ranum 1978, pp. 47–82.

Del Prete, Rossella 2009: 'I figlioli del Conservatorio della Pietà dei Turchini di Napoli nella seconda metà del Settecento: percorsi di studio e opportunità professionali', *Nuova rivista storica*, 93: 205–22.

Delumeau, Jean 1957–59: *Vie économique et sociale de Rome dans la seconde moitié du XVIe siècle*, 2 vols., Paris.

De Marchi, Elena 2009: 'Il mestiere di balia. Assistenza agli esposti, cura dei "figli di famiglia", ricerca di un salario nella campagna milanese in Sette e Ottocento', *Archivio storico lombardo*, 135: 119–51.

De Mariana, Juan ed. F. Pí y Margall 1854: *Obras*, 2 vols., Madrid.

De Mause, Lloyd (ed.) 1976: *The History of Childhood*, London.

De Montaigne, Michel ed. Charles Dédéyan 1946: *Journal de voyage en Italie par la Suisse et l'Allemagne en 1580 et 1581*, Paris.

De Montaigne, Michel ed. and trans. M.A. Screech 2003: *The Complete Essays*, London.

Denning, Patt 2000: *Practicing Harm Reduction Psychotherapy*, New York and London.

De Rosa, Gabriele 1978: 'L'emarginazione sociale in Calabria nel XVIII secolo: il problema degli esposti', *Ricerche di storia sociale e religiosa, nuova serie*, 13: 5–29.

Derosas, Renzo 1980: 'Moralità e giustizia a Venezia nel '500–600. Gli Esecutori contro la Bestemmia'. In Cozzi 1980–85, I, pp. 431–528.

Descriptio Urbis. The Roman Census of 1527 ed. Egmont Lee 1985, Rome.

De Spirito, Angelomichele 1978: 'La prostituzione femminile a Napoli nel XVIII secolo', *Ricerche di storia sociale e religiosa, nuova serie*, 13: 31–70.

Di Bello, Giulia 1997: 'La valorizzazione dell'amore materno. Percorsi legislativi nella Firenze dell' Ottocento', *Ricerche storiche*, 27: 331–50.

Di Blasi, Patrizia 1982: 'Onore e amore nelle novelle di Bandello'. In Rozzo 1982, pp. 145–55.

Dodi Osnaghi, Luisa 1982: 'Ruota e infanzia abbandonata a Milano nella prima metà dell' Ottocento'. In Politi *et al.* 1982, pp. 427–35.

Dominici, Silvia 2001: 'Un'istituzione assistenziale pubblica nella Roma dei papi: il conservatorio delle proiette dell'Ospedale di Santo Spirito in Saxia (secoli XVI e XVII)', *Rivista di storia della Chiesa in Italia*, 55: 19–58.

Dominici, Silvia 2003: 'Il conservatorio di Santo Spirito in Sassia di Roma: condizioni, risorsa e tutela delle donne nel Settecento', *Studi storici*, 44: 191–250.

Doriguzzi, Franca 1983: 'I messaggi dell' abbandono: bambini esposti a Torino nel '700', *Quaderni storici*, 18: 445–68.

Doriguzzi, Franca 1991: 'Vestiti e colori dei bambini: il caso degli esposti'. In E.A., pp. 513–37.

Du Bellay, Joachim ed. Verdun L. Saulnier 1947: *Divers Jeux rustiques*, Lille.

Dubuis, Pierre 1986: 'Comportamenti sessuali nelle Alpi del basso medioevo: l'esempio della castellania di Susa', *Studi storici*, 27: 577–607.

Eisenach, Emlyn 2004: *Husbands, Wives, and Concubines: Marriage, Family, and Social Order in Sixteenth-century Verona*, Kirksville, Mo.

Elliott, Dyan 2012: 'Sexual scandal and the clergy: a medieval blueprint for disaster'. In Chazelle *et al.* 2012, pp. 90–105.

Epstein, Steven A. 2005: 'Slaves in Italy, 1350–1550'. In Milner 2005, pp. 219–35.

Fabbroni, Giovanni ed. Franco Venturi 1958: 'Discorso intorno ai mezzi d'incorragimento al matrimonio'. In Venturi 1958, pp. 1099–1129.

Fanti, Mario 1986: 'Istituzioni di carità e assistenza a Bologna alla fine del Medioevo'. In *Forme e soggetti* 1986, pp. 31–64.

Fanucci, Camillo 1602: *Trattato di tutte l'opere pie dell' alma città di Roma*, Rome.

Feci, Simona 2005: 'Cause matrimoniali nella documentazione del tribunale della Sacra Romana Rota (secolo XVII)', *Annali dell' Istituto Storico Italo-Germanico in Trento*, 31: 189–224.

Fedeli Bernardini, Franca 2001–02: 'La "via lattea". I proietti forestieri e il brefotrofio tra i secoli XVIII e XIX'. In Cappelletti and Tagliarini 2001–02, I, pp. 303–30.

Ferrante, Lucia 1983: 'L'onore ritrovato: donne nella Casa del Soccorso di San Paolo a Bologna (sec. XVI-XVII)', *Quaderni storici*, 18: 499–528. Subsequently published in English translation in Muir and Ruggiero 1990, pp. 46–72.

Ferrante, Lucia 1985: 'La sessualità come ricorsa. Donne davanti al foro arcivescovile di Bologna (sec.XVII)', European University Institute Working Paper no. 85/192, Florence.

Ferrante, Lucia 1986: ' "Malmaritate" tra assistenza e punizione (Bologna secc. XVI–XVIII)'. In *Forme e soggetti* 1986, pp. 65–109.

Ferrante, Lucia 1994: 'Il matrimonio disciplinato: processi matrimoniali a Bologna del Cinquecento'. In Prodi and Peruti 1994, pp. 901–27.

Ferrante, Lucia 1996: 'Il valore del corpo, ovvero la gestione economica della sessualità femminile'. In Groppi 1996, pp. 206–28.

Ferraro, Joanne M. 1995: 'The power to decide: battered wives in early modern Venice', *Renaissance Quarterly*, 49: 492–512.

Ferraro, Joanne M. 2001: *Marriage Wars in Late Renaissance Venice*, New York.

Ferraro, Joanne M. 2008: *Nefarious Crimes, Contested Justice: Illicit Sex and Infanticide in the Republic of Venice, 1557–1789*, Baltimore and London.

Ferrazzi, Cecilia ed. Anne Jacobson Schutte 1996: *Autobiography of an Aspiring Saint*, Chicago.

Filangieri, Gaetano 1819: *La scienza della legislazione*, 5 vols., Philadelphia.

Fildes, Valerie 1988: *Wet Nursing: A History from Antiquity to the Present*, Oxford.

Findlen, Paula, Michelle M. Fontaine and Duane J. Osheim (eds.) 2003: *Beyond Florence: The Contours of Medieval and Early Modern Italy*, Stanford.

Fiorani, Luigi 1979: 'Religione e povertà. Il dibattito sul pauperismo a Roma tra Cinque e Seicento', *Ricerche per la storia religiosa di Roma*, 3: 43–131.

Florio, John 1611/1968: *Queen Anne's New World of Words*, facsimile reprint, Menston.

Foa, Anna 1984: 'Il nuovo e il vecchio: l'insorgere della sifilide (1494–1530)', *Quaderni storici*, 19: 11–34.

Forme e soggetti dell'intervento assistenziale in una città di antico regime 1986: Bologna.

Forster, Robert and Orest Ranum (eds.) 1978: *Deviants and the Abandoned in French Society*, Baltimore.

Fortini, Pietro ed. Andriana Mauriello 1995: *Le piacevoli e amorose notti dei novizi*, 2 vols., Rome.

Fossier, Arnaud 2009: '"Propter vitandum scandalum": Histoire d'une catégorie juridique (XIIe-XVe siècle)', *Mélanges de l'École Française de Rome. Moyen Âge*, 121: 317–48.

Fragnelli, Pietro 1988: '"Carità operativa" e cura d'anime nelle lettere di Giovanni Battista de Rossi, 1730–1744', *Ricerche per la storia religiosa di Roma*, 7: 289–330.

Francesco Saverio da Brusciano 1953: 'Maria Lorenzo Longo e l'Opera del Divino Amore a Napoli', *Collectanea franciscana*, 23: 166–228.

Franco, Veronica ed. Benedetto Croce 1949: *Lettere: dall'unica edizione del MDLXXX*, Naples.

Fubini Leuzzi, Maria 1990: 'Appunti per lo studio delle doti granducali in Toscana', *Ricerche storiche*, 20: 339–66.

Fubini Leuzzi, Maria 1992: 'Donne, doti e matrimonio in Toscana al tempo dei primi gran-duchi lorenesi. Studi sulla distribuzione delle elemosine dotali', *Annali dell' Istituto Storico Italo-Germanico in Trento*, 18: 121–76.

Fubini Leuzzi, Maria 1994: '"Dell' allogare le fanciulle degli Innocenti": un problema culturale ed economico, 1577–1652'. In Prodi and Penuti 1994, pp. 863–99.

Galanti, Giuseppe Maria 1786–90: *Nuova descrizione storica e geografica delle Sicilie*, 4 vols., Naples.

Galanti, Giuseppe Maria ed. Augusto Placanica 1992: *Diarii, relazioni e lettere di un visitatore generale*, Salerno.

Galassi, Nazario 1966–70: *Dieci secoli di storia ospedaliera a Imola*, 2 vols., Imola.

Gamba, Camillo Maria 1956: 'Le regole delle Pie Convertite di Santa Valeria all'epoca di Suor Virginia Maria de Leyva'. In *Archivi* 1956, I, pp. 237–61.

Gambier, Madile 1980: 'La donna e la giustizia penale veneziana nel XVIII secolo'. In Cozzi 1980–85, I, pp. 529–75.

Garbellotti, Marina 1996: 'La *Domus Pietatis*'. In Pastore *et al.* 1996, pp. 69–79.

Garzoni, Tommaso 1616: *La piazza universale di tutte le professioni del mondo*, Venice.

Gavitt, Philip 1990: *Charity and Children in Renaissance Florence: The Ospedale degli Innocenti, 1410–1536*, Ann Arbor, Mich.

Gavitt, Philip 1994: '"Perche non avea chi la ghovernasse." Cultural values, family resources and abandonment in the Florence of Lorenzo de' Medici, 1467–85'. In Henderson and Wall 1994, pp. 65–93.

Gavitt, Philip 1997: 'Charity and state building in Cinquecento Florence: Vincenzio Borghini as administrator of the Hospital of the Innocenti', *Journal of Modern History*, 69: 230–70.

Gavitt, Philip 2005: 'From *putte* to *puttane*: Female foundlings and charitable institutions in northern Italy, 1530–1630'. In Milner 2005, pp. 111–29.

Gavitt, Philip 2011: *Gender, Honor, and Charity in Late Renaissance Florence*, Cambridge. Paperback 2013.

Geltner, Guy 2008: *The Medieval Prison: A Social History*, Princeton.

Geltner, Guy 2008a: '*Detrusio*, penal cloistering in the middle ages', *Revue bénédictine*, 118: 89–108.

Geltner, Guy 2012: 'Social deviancy: a medieval approach'. In Chazelle *et al.* 2012, pp. 29–40.

Geltner, Guy 2013–14: 'A cell of their own: the incarceration of women in late medieval Italy', *Signs*, 39: 27–49.

Genovesi, Antonio ed. Maria Luisa Perna 1984: *Scritti economici*, 2 vols., Naples.

Gentilcore, David 1992: *From Bishop to Witch: The System of the Sacred in Early Modern Terra d'Otranto*, Manchester and New York.

Gentilcore, David 1998: *Healers and Healing in Early Modern Italy*, Manchester and New York.

Geyer-Kordesch, Johanna 2002: 'Infanticide and the erotic plot: a feminist reading of eighteenth-century crime'. In Jackson 2002, pp. 93–127.

Ghirardo, Dianne Yvonne 2001: 'The topography of prostitution in Renaissance Ferrara', *Journal of the Society of Architectural Historians*, 60: 402–31.

Giacomelli, Alfeo 1986: 'Conservazione e innovazione nell' assistenza bolognese del Settecento'. In *Forme e soggetti* 1986, pp. 163–265.

Giazotto, Remo, with Agostino Girard and Luigi Bellingardi 1973: *Antonio Vivaldi*, Turin.

Gibson, Mary 1986: *Prostitution and the State in Italy, 1860–1915*, New Brunswick and London.

Gilinus, Antonius 1508: *Fundationis Hospitalis Magni Mediolani ... opus*, Milan.

Giraldi Cinzio, Giovanbattista 1565: *De gli hecatommithi*, 2 vols., Mondoví.

Goldberg, P.J.P. 1999: 'Pigs and prostitutes: streetwalking in comparative perspective'. In Lewis *et al.* 1999, pp. 172–93.

Gozzi, Gasparo ed. Antonio Zardi 1915: *La 'Gazzetta Veneta'*, Florence.

Graf, Arturo 1888: 'Una cortigiana fra mille: Veronica Franco'. In his *Attraverso il Cinquecento*, Turin, pp. 217–366.

Grandi, Casimira 1997: 'L'assistenza all'infanzia abbandonata veneziana: "fantolini della pietade" '. In Grieco and Sandri 1997, pp. 67–106.

Grassi, Umberto 2007: 'L'Offitio sopra l'Honestà. La repressione della sodomia nella Lucca del Cinquecento (1551–1580)', *Studi storici*, 48: 127–59.

Greci, Roberto 1996: 'Donne e corporazioni: la fluidità di un rapporto'. In Groppi 1996, pp. 71–91.

Grégoire, Réginald 1979: ' "Servizio dell' anima quanto del corpo" nell' ospedale romano di Santo Spirito (1623)', *Ricerche per la storia religiosa di Roma*, 3, 221–54.

Grell, Ole Peter, Andrew Cunningham and Jon Arrizabalaga (eds.) 1999: *Health Care and Poor Relief in Counter-Reformation Europe*, London and New York.

Grendler, Paul F. (ed.) 1999: *Encyclopedia of the Renaissance*, 6 vols., New York.

Grieco, Allen J. and Lucia Sandri (eds.) 1997: *Ospedali e città: L'Italia del Centro-Nord, XIII-XVI secolo*, Florence.

Griffith, T. Gwynfor 1955: *Bandello's Fiction: An Examination of the Novelle*, Oxford.

Griffiths, Paul 1993: 'The structure of prostitution in Elizabethan London', *Continuity and Change*, 8: 39–63.

Groppi, Angela 1994: *I conservatori della virtù. Donne recluse nella Roma dei papi*, Bari.

Groppi, Angela (ed.) 1996: *Il lavoro delle donne*, Bari.

Groppi, Angela 1996a: 'Lavoro e proprietà delle donne in età moderna'. In Groppi 1996, pp. 119–63.

Guerrini, Paola 2001: 'La storia della fondazione dell' Ospedale di Santo Spirito in un manoscritto illustrato del secolo XV'. In Cappelletti and Tagliarini 2001–02, I, pp. 143–62.

Haas, Louis 1998: *The Renaissance Man and His Children. Childbirth and Early Childhood in Florence 1300–1600*, Basingstoke.

Hacke, Daniela 2004: *Women, Sex and Marriage in Early Modern Venice*, Aldershot.

Hanawalt, Barbara A. (ed.) 1986: *Women and Work in Preindustrial Europe*, Bloomington.

Hanawalt, Emily Albu and Carter Lindberg (eds.) 1994: *Through the Eye of a Needle: Judaeo-Christian Roots of Social Welfare*, Missouri.

Hanlon, Gregory 2009: 'The facts of life in rural Counter-Reformation Tuscany', *Journal of Interdisciplinary History*, 40: 1–31.

Haskins, Susan 1993: *Mary Magdalen: Myth and Metaphor*, London.

Henderson, John and Richard Wall (eds.) 1994: *Poor Women and Children in the European Past*, London.

Herlihy, David and Christiane Klapisch-Zuber 1985: *Tuscans and Their Families: A Study of the Florentine Catasto of 1427*, New Haven and London.

Hoffer, Peter C. and N.E.H. Hull 1984: *Murdering Mothers: Infanticide in England and New England 1558–1803*, New York.

Howe, Eunice D. 1978: *The Hospital of Santo Spirito and Pope Sixtus IV*, New York.

Howe, Eunice D. 2005: *Art and Culture at the Sistine Court: Platina's "Life of Sixtus IV" and the Frescoes of the Hospital of Santo Spirito*, Vatican City.

Hufton, Olwen 1997: *The Prospect Before Her: A History of Women in Western Europe, I: 1500–1800*, London.

Hügel, Fr.S. 1863: *Die Findelhäuser und das Findelwesen Europa's, ihre Geschichte, Gesetzgebung, Verwaltung, Statistik und Reform*, Vienna.

Hunecke, Volker 1985: 'Les enfants trouvés: contexte européen et cas milanais (XVIIIe-XIXe siècles)', *Revue d'histoire moderne et contemporaine*, 32: 3–29.

Hunecke, Volker 1989: *I trovatelli di Milano: Bambini esposti e famiglie espositrici dal XVII al XIX secolo*, Bologna.

Hunecke, Volker 1991: 'Intensità e fluttuazioni degli abbandoni dal XV al XIX secolo'. In E.A., pp. 27–72.

Hunecke, Volker 1994: 'The abandonment of legitimate children in nineteenth-century Milan and the European context'. In Henderson and Wall 1994, pp. 117–35.

Intra, G.B. 1893: 'Di Ippolito Cantilupi e del suo tempo', *Archivio storico lombardo*, 20: 76–142.

Isba, Anne 2006: *Gladstone and Women*, London.

Jackson, Mark (ed.) 2002: *Infanticide: Historical Perspectives on Child Murder and Concealment, 1550–2000*, Aldershot.

Jackson, Mark 2002a: 'The trial of Harriet Vooght: continuity and change in the history of infanticide'. In Jackson 2002, pp. 1–17.

Jacopo della Voragine ed. Th. Graesse 1890, reprinted 1965: *Legenda aurea, vulgo historia lombardica dicta*, Osnabrück.

Jansen, Katherine L. 1995: 'Mary Magdalen and the mendicants: the preaching of penance in the late middle ages', *Journal of Medieval History*, 21: 1–25.

Jansen, Katherine L., Joanna Drell and Frances Andrews (eds.) 2009: *Medieval Italy. Texts in Translation*, Philadelphia.

Jansen, Philippe 2001: *Démographie et société dans les Marches à la fin du moyen âge. Macerata aux XIVe et XVe siècles*, Paris.

Jones, Frederic M. 1992: *Alphonsus de Liguori. The Saint of Bourbon Naples 1696–1787*, Dublin.

Karras, Ruth Mazo 1996: 'Prostitution in medieval Europe'. In Bullough and Brundage 1996, pp. 243–60.

Karras, Ruth Mazo 1999: 'Prostitution and the question of sexual identity in medieval Europe', *Journal of Women's History*, 11: 159–77.

Kertzer, David I. 1993: *Sacrificed for Honor: Italian Infant Abandonment and the Politics of Reproductive Control*, Boston, Mass.

Kertzer, David I. 1998–9: 'Syphilis, foundlings and wetnurses in nineteenth-century Italy', *Journal of Social History*, 32: 589–602.

Kertzer, David I. 2000: 'The lives of foundlings in nineteenth-century Italy'. In Panter-Brick and Smith 2000, pp. 41–56.

Kertzer, David I. and Richard P. Saller (eds.) 1991: *The Family in Italy from Antiquity to the Present*, New Haven and London.

Kertzer, David I. and Michael J. White 1994: 'Cheating the angel-makers: surviving infant abandonment in nineteenth-century Italy', *Continuity and Change*, 9: 451–80.

Klapisch-Zuber, Christiane 1985: *Women, Family and Ritual in Renaissance Italy*, London.

Klapisch-Zuber, Christiane 1986: 'Women servants in Florence during the fourteenth and fifteenth centuries'. In B.A. Hanawalt 1986, pp. 56–80.

Kuehn, Thomas 2002: *Illegitimacy in Renaissance Florence*, Ann Arbor, Mich.

Labalme, Patricia H. 1984: 'Sodomy and Venetian justice in the Renaissance', *The Legal History Review*, 52: 217–54.

Lallemand, Léon 1885: *Histoire des enfants abandonnés et délaissés. Études sur la protection de l'enfance aux diverses époques de la civilisation*, Paris.

Lanaro Sartori, Paola 1982: 'Radiografia della soglia di povertà in una città della terraferma veneta: Verona alla metà del XVI secolo', *Studi veneziani, nuova serie*, 6: 45–85.

Langellotti, Alessandra and Carlo M. Travaglini 1991: 'L'infanzia abbandonata nel Viterbese (sec. XVIII–XX)'. In E.A., pp. 741–84.

Lansing, Carol 1997: 'Gender and civic authority: sexual control in a medieval Italian town', *Journal of Social History*, 31: 33–59.

Lansing, Carol 2003: 'Concubines, lovers, prostitutes: infamy and female identity in medieval Bologna'. In Findlen *et al.* 2003, pp. 86–100.

Larivaille, Paul 1975: *La Vie quotidienne des courtisanes en Italie au temps de la Renaissance (Rome et Venise, XVe et XVIe siècles)*, Paris.

Laven, Mary 2002: *Virgins of Venice: Enclosed Lives and Broken Vows in the Renaissance Convent*, London.

Lavenia, Vincenzo 2003: 'Martin de Azpilcueta (1492–1586): un profilo', *Archivio italiano per la storia della pietà*, 16: 15–148.

Lawner, Lynne 1987: *Lives of the Courtesans: Portraits of the Renaissance*, New York.

Lazar, Lance Gabriel 2005: *Working in the Vineyard of the Lord: Jesuit Confraternities in Early Modern Italy*, Toronto.

Lazzaretti, Lorella 1996: 'La donna attraverso i processi per causa matrimoniale nella diocesi di Feltre del Cinquecento', *Studi veneziani, nuova serie*, 32: 49–82.

Leggi e memorie venete sulla prostituzione fino alla caduta della Republica 1870–72: Venice, for Lord Orford.

Leverotti, Franca 1984: 'L'ospedale senese di Santa Maria della Scala in una relazione del 1456', *Bullettino senese di storia patria*, 91: 276–91.

Lewis, Katherine J., Noël James Menuge and Kim M. Phillips (eds.) 1999: *Young Medieval Women*, Stroud.

Liber Augustalis, The, or Constitutions of Melfi Promulgated by the Emperor Frederick II for the Kingdom of Sicily in 1231, ed. and trans. James M. Powell 1971, Syracuse, NY.

Lithgow, William ed. Gilbert Phelps 1974: *The Rare Adventures and Painful Peregrinations*, London.

Lombardi, Daniela 1994: 'Intervention by Church and State in marriage disputes in sixteenth- and seventeenth-century Florence'. In Dean and Lowe 1994, pp. 142–56.

Lombardi, Daniela 2000: 'L'odio capitale, ovvero l'incompatibilità di carattere. Marina Falcini e Andrea Lotti (Firenze 1773–1777)'. In Seidel Menchi and Quaglioni 2000, pp. 335–67.

Lombardi, Daniela 2003: 'Scipione de'Ricci e il matrimonio'. In Ossola *et al.* 2003, pp. 431–41.

Lopez, Pasquale 1964: *Riforma cattolica e vita religiosa e culturale a Napoli dalla fine del '500 ai primi del '700*, Naples and Rome.

Lucian [of Samosata] ed. C.D.N. Costa 2006: *Selected Dialogues*, Oxford.

McGough, Laura J. 2011: *Gender, Sexuality and Syphilis in Early Modern Venice: The Disease That Came to Stay*, Basingstoke.

Mackenney, Richard 1987: *Tradesmen and Traders: The World of the Guilds in Venice and Europe, c.1250–1650*, London.

Malamani, Anita 1978: 'Notizie sul mal francese e gli Ospedali degli Incurabili in età moderna', *Critica storica*, 15: 193–216.

Malthus, Thomas Robert 1826, reprinted 1996: *An Essay on the Principle of Population*, 6th edition, London.

Malthus, Thomas Robert ed. Geoffrey Gilbert 2004: *An Essay on the Principle of Population*, Oxford.

McClure, Ruth K. 1981: *Coram's Children: The London Foundling Hospital in the Eighteenth Century*, London.

Marcello, Luciano 1992: 'Società maschile e sodomia. Dal declino della "polis" al Principato', *Archivio storico italiano*, 150: 115–38.

Marcolini, Giuliana 1989: 'Un epilogo settecentesco. Le Penitenti di San Job'. In Aikema and Meijers 1989, pp. 121–7.

Marcolini, Giuliana and Giulio Marcon 1985: 'Prostituzione e assistenza a Venezia nel secolo XVIII: il Pio Loco delle Povere Peccatrici Penitenti di San Iob', *Studi veneziani, nuova serie*, 10: 99–136.

Marland, Hilary 2002: 'Getting away with murder? Puerperal insanity, infanticide and the defence plea'. In Jackson 2002, pp. 168–92.

Marlatt, G. Alan, Mary E. Larimer and Katie Witkiewicz (eds.) 2012: *Harm Reduction: Pragmatic Strategies for Managing High-risk Behaviors*, New York and London.

Martelli, Vladymir 2002: 'Tra tolleranza ed intransigenza. Vagabondi, zingari, prostitute e convertiti a Roma nel XVI–XVII secolo', *Studi romani*, 50: 252–78.

Martellucci, Maura 2001: 'I bambini di nessuno. L'infanzia abbandonata al Santa Maria della Scala, secoli XIII–XV', *Bullettino senese di storia patria*, 108: 9–221.

Martin, Gregory ed. G.B. Parks 1969: *Roma Sancta (1581)*, Rome.

Martin, Ruth 1989: *Witchcraft and the Inquisition in Venice, 1550–1650*, Oxford.

Martines, Lauro 1998: 'Séduction, espace familial et autorité dans la renaissance italienne', *Annales, histoire, sciences sociales*, 53: 255–90.

Martínez Cuesta, A. 1978: 'Maddalene'. In D.I.P., V, coll. 801–12.

Martini, Gabriele 1986: 'La giustizia veneziana ed il "vitio nefando" nel secolo XVII', *Studi veneziani, nuova serie*, 11: 159–204.

Martini, Gabriele 1986a: 'Rispetto dell'infanzia e violenza sui minori nella Venezia del Seicento', *Società e storia*, 9: 793–817.

Martini, Gabriele 1986–87: 'La donna veneziana del '600 tra sessualità legittima ed illegittima: alcune riflessioni sul concubinato', *Atti dell'Istituto Veneto di Scienze, Lettere ed Arti*, 145, Classe di scienze morali, lettere ed arti: 301–39.

Martini, Gabriele 1986–87a: 'Sodomia e discriminazione morale a Venezia nei secoli XV-XVII: tendenze evolutive', *Atti dell'Istituto Veneto di Scienze, Lettere ed Arti*, 145: 341–66.

Masson, Georgina 1975: *Courtesans of the Italian Renaissance*, London.

Mayhew, Henry 1861–62, reprint 1968: *London Labour and the London Poor*, 4 vols., London.

Mazzei, Lapo ed. Cesare Guasti 1880: *Ser Lapo Mazzei: Lettere di un notaro a un mercante del secolo XIV, con altre lettere e documenti*, 2 vols., Florence.

Mazzi, Maria Serena 1986: 'Ai margini del lavoro: i mestieri per "campare la vita"', *Studi storici*, 27: 359–69.

Mazzi, Maria Serena 1986a: 'Cronache di periferia dello stato fiorentino: reati contro la morale del primo Quattrocento', *Studi storici*, 27: 609–35.

Mazzi, Maria Serena 1991: *Prostitute e lenoni nella Firenze del Quattrocento*, Milan.

Mazzonis, Querciolo 2007: *Spirituality, Gender and the Self in Renaissance Italy: Angela Merici and the Company of St Ursula (1474–1540)*, Washington.

Mazzucchelli, Mario trans. Evelyn Gendel 1963: *The Nun of Monza*, London.

Merzario, Raul 1996: 'Donne sole nelle valli e nelle montagne'. In Groppi 1996, pp. 229–46.

Milner, Stephen J. (ed.) 2005: *At the Margins: Minority Groups in Premodern Italy*, Minneapolis.

Molmenti, Pompeo G. 1919: *Curiosità di storia veneziana*, Venice.

Montanari, Daniele 1987: *Disciplinamento in terra veneta: La diocesi di Brescia nella seconda metà del XVI secolo*, Bologna.

Montenovesi, Ottorino 1939: 'L'Archiospedale di S. Spirito in Roma: saggio di documentazione', *Archivio della Reale Deputazione Romana di Storia Patria*, 62: 177–229.

Mormando, Franco 1999: *The Preacher's Demons. Bernardino of Siena and the Social Underworld of Early Renaissance Italy*, Chicago and London.

Moryson, Fynes ed. Charles Hughes 1903: *Shakespeare's Europe, Being Previously Unpublished Chapters of Fynes Moryson's Itinerary*, London.

Muir, Edward and Guido Ruggiero (eds.) 1990: *Sex and Gender in Historical Perspective: Selections from Quaderni storici*, Baltimore and London.

Muñoz de Juana, Rodrigo 1998: *Moral y economía en la obra de Martín de Azpilcueta*, Pamplona.

Muratori, Ludovico Antonio ed. Piero G. Nonis 1961: *Trattato della carità cristiana ed altri scritti sulla carità*, Rome.

Muratori, Ludovico Antonio ed. Cesare Mozzarelli 1996: *Della pubblica felicità oggetto de' buoni principi*, Rome.

Muzzarelli, Maria Giuseppina 1994: 'La disciplina delle apparenze. Vesti e ornamenti nella legislazione suntuaria bolognese fra XIII e XV secolo'. In Prodi and Penuti 1994, pp. 757–84.

Muzzarelli, Maria Giuseppina, Paola Galetti and Bruno Andreolli (eds.) 1991: *Donne e lavoro nell'Italia medievale*, Turin.

Nardi, Franco Daniele 1989: 'Concubinato e adulterio nella Siena post-tridentina', *Bullettino senese di storia patria*, 96: 9–171.

Navarro, Martín (Martín de Azpilcueta) 1584: *Enchiridion sive manuale confessariorum et paenitentium*, Venice.

Netto, Giovanni 1993: 'Per una biografia di Mercurio Bua, comandante degli "stradiotti" veneti', *Archivio veneto*, 5th series, 140: 95–110.

Newett, Margaret M. 1902: 'The sumptuary laws of Venice in the fourteenth and fifteenth centuries'. In Tout and Tait 1902, pp. 245–78.

Noonan, John T., Jr. (ed.) 1970: *The Morality of Abortion: Legal and Historical Perspectives*, Cambridge, Mass.

Noonan, John T. 1970a: 'An almost absolute value in history'. In Noonan 1970, pp. 1–59.

Noonan, John T. 1986: *Contraception: A History of its Treatment by the Catholic Theologians and Canonists*, enlarged edition, Cambridge, Mass.

Nordio, Andrea 1996: 'L'Ospedale degli Incurabili nell' assistenza veneta del '500', *Studi veneziani, nuova serie*, 32: 165–84.

Olin, John C. (ed.) 1969: *The Catholic Reformation. Savonarola to Ignatius Loyola: Reform in the Church, 1495–1540*, New York and London.

O'Malley, John W. 1993: *The First Jesuits*, Cambridge, Mass. and London.

Ossola, Carlo, Marcello Verga and Maria Antonietta Visceglia (eds.) 2003: *Religione, cultura e politica nell'Europa dell'età moderna: Studi offerti a Mario Rosa dagli amici*, Florence.

Otis, Leah Lydia 1985: *Prostitution in Medieval Society: The History of an Urban Institution in Languedoc*, Chicago and London.

Ozment, Steven 1983: *When Fathers Ruled: Family Life in Reformation Europe*, Cambridge, Mass. and London.

Pagano, Emanuele 2001: 'Maltrattate, defraudate, diffamate: mogli in tribunale nella Milano di Giuseppe II', *Archivio storico lombardo*, 127: 61–105.

Pagano, Sergio 1979: 'Gli esposti dell'Ospedale di Santo Spirito nel primo Ottocento', *Ricerche per la storia religiosa di Roma*, 3: 353–92.

Paglia, Vincenzo 1980: *'La Pietà dei Carcerati'. Confraternite e società a Roma nei secoli XVI–XVIII*, Rome.

Pallavicino, Ferrante ed. Armando Marchi 1984: *Il corriero svaligiato*, Parma.

Pallavicino, Ferrante ed. Laura Coci 1992: *La retorica delle puttane*, Parma.

Palmer, Richard 1999: ' "Ad una sancta perfettione": health care and poor relief in the Republic of Venice in the era of the Counter-Reformation'. In Grell *et al.* 1999, pp. 87–101.

Palmio, Benedetto 1701: 'Alle congregationi delli magnifici signori governatori e delle magnifice signore governatrici della Casa delle Cittelle di Venetia nella Zuecca', address (1588) printed with *Constitutioni et regole* 1701.

Pannocchieschi, Francesco ed. Pompeo G. Molmenti 1919: 'Relazione'. In Molmenti 1919, pp. 310–88.

Pansier, P. 1910: *L'Oeuvre des Répenties à Avignon du XIIIe au XVIIIe siècle*, Paris.

Panter-Brick, Catherine 2000: 'Nobody's children? A reconsideration of child abandonment'. In Panter-Brick and Smith 2000, pp. 1–26.

Panter-Brick, Catherine and Malcolm T. Smith (eds.) 2000: *Abandoned Children*, Cambridge.

Parent-Duchâtelet, Alexandre ed. Alain Corbin 1981: *La Prostitution à Paris au XIXe siècle*, Paris.

Passerini, Luigi 1853: *Storia degli stabilimenti di beneficenza e d'istruzione elementare gratuita della città di Firenze*, Florence.

Pastore, Alessandro *et al.* 1996: *L'ospedale e la città: Cinquecento anni d'arte a Verona*, Verona.

Pastore, Alessandro and Maria Garbellotti (eds.) 2001: *L'uso del denaro: Patrimoni e amministrazione nei luoghi pii e negli enti ecclesiastici in Italia (secoli XV–XVIII)*, Bologna.

Pavan, Elisabeth 1980: 'Police des moeurs, société et politique à Venise à la fin du Moyen Âge', *Revue historique*, 264: 241–88.

Pelizza, Andrea 1997: 'La crisi finanziaria degli ospedali maggiori veneziani fra 1771 e 1797', *Studi veneziani, nuova serie*, 33: 123–56.

Perni, Sergio 1999: 'Una riforma dell'Istituto della Pietà di Venezia alla fine del Settecento', *Archivio Veneto*, 5th series, 152: 157–65.

Piazza, Carlo Bartolomeo 1698: *Eusevologio romano: overo, Delle opere pie di Roma*, 2 vols., Rome.

Piccialuti, Maria 1994: *La carità come metodo di governo: istituzioni caritative a Roma dal pontificato di Innocenzo XII a quello di Benedetto XIV*, Turin.

Piccialuti, Maria 2001: 'L'Ospedale di Santo Spirito nel secolo XVIII. Organizzazion e riforme'. In Cappelletti and Tagliarini 2001-2, I, pp. 269–87.

Piccinini, Gabriella 1996: 'Le donne nella vita economica, sociale e politica dell'Italia medievale'. In Groppi 1996, pp. 5–46.

Pizzolato, Nicola 2006: '"Lo diavolo mi ingannao": La sodomia nella campagna siciliana (1572–1664)', *Quaderni storici*, 41: 449–80.

Pizzolato, Nicola 2007: 'Ordinarie trasgressioni: adulterio e concubinato, dal vicinato al tribunale (diocesi di Monreale, 1590–1680)', *Quaderni storici*, 42: 231–59.

Politi, Giorgio, Mario Rosa and Franco Della Peruta (eds.) 1982: *Timore e carità. I poveri nell'Italia moderna*, Cremona.

Polonio, Valeria 2004: '"Ubi karitas, ibi pax": l'aiuto al più debole. Secoli IX-XVII'. In Puncuh 2004, pp. 311–68.

Pona, Francesco ed. Giorgio Fulco 1973: *La lanterna*, Rome.

Poni, Carlo 1996: 'Tecnologie, organizzazione produttiva e divisione sessuale del lavoro: il caso dei mulini di seta'. In Groppi 1996, pp. 269–96.

Povolo, Claudio 1978-9: 'Note per uno studio dell'infanticidio nella Repubblica di Venezia nei secoli XV–XVIII', *Atti dell'Istituto Veneto di Scienze, Lettere ed Arti*, 137, Classe di scienze morali, lettere ed arti: 115–31.

Povolo, Claudio 1979-80: 'Aspetti sociali e penali del reato d'infanticidio. Il caso di una contadina padovana nel '700', *Atti dell'Istituto Veneto di Scienze, Lettere ed Arti*, 138: 415–32.

Povolo, Claudio 1989: 'Dal versante dell'illegitimità. Per una ricerca sulla storia della famiglia: infanticidio ed esposizione d'infante nel Veneto nell'età moderna'. In Berlinguer and Colao 1989, pp. 89–163.

Presciutti, Diana Bullen 2011: 'Dead infants, cruel mothers, and heroic popes: the visual rhetoric of foundling care at the Hospital of Santo Spirito, Rome', *Renaissance Quarterly*, 64: 752–99.

Priuli, Girolamo ed. Roberto Cessi 1938: *I Diarii*, IV, Bologna.

Prodi, Paolo and Carla Penuti (eds.) 1994: *Disciplina dell'anima, disciplina del corpo e disciplina della società tra medioevo ed età moderna*, Bologna.

Pullan, Brian 1971: *Rich and Poor in Renaissance Venice: The Social Institutions of a Catholic State, to 1620*, Oxford, and Cambridge, MA.

Pullan, Brian 1988: '"Support and redeem": charity and poor relief in Italian cities from the fourteenth to the seventeenth century', *Continuity and Change*, 3: 177–208. Reprinted as Item v in Pullan 1994.

Pullan, Brian 1989: *Orphans and Foundlings in Early Modern Europe*, Reading, UK. Reprinted as Item iii in Pullan 1994.

Pullan, Brian 1994: *Poverty and Charity: Europe, Italy, Venice, 1400–1700*, Aldershot.

Pullan, Brian 2000: 'New approaches to poverty and new forms of institutional charity in late medieval and Renaissance Italy'. In Zamagni 2000, pp. 17–43.

Pullan, Brian 2005: 'Catholics, Protestants and the poor in early modern Europe', *Journal of Interdisciplinary History*, 35: 441–56.

Pullan, Brian 2008: 'Poverty, charity and social welfare'. In Witte and Alexander 2008, pp. 185–203.

Puncuh, Dino (ed.) 2004: *Storia della cultura ligure*, I (*Atti della Società Ligure di Storia Patria, nuova serie*, 44), Genoa.

Quétel, Claude trans. Judith Braddock and Brian Pike 1990: *History of Syphilis*, Cambridge.

Quinn, Cath 2002: 'Images and impulses: representations of puerperal insanity and infanticide in late Victorian England'. In Jackson 2002, pp. 193–215.

Rabin, Dana 2002: 'Bodies of evidence, states of mind: infanticide, emotion and sensibility in eighteenth-century England'. In Jackson 2002, pp. 73–92.

Raffaele, Silvana 1991: 'Il problema degli esposti in Sicilia (secc. XVIII-XIX). Normativa e risposta istituzionale: il caso di Catania'. In E.A., pp. 905–36.

Raffaele, Silvana 1997: ' "Restando proibito l'andarsi rintracciando gli occulti o incerti genitori di quei bambini che saranno portati nelle ruote": la percezione dell' abbandono nella Sicilia borbonica', *Ricerche storiche*, 27: 315–30.

Raymond of Capua ed. Thomas Gilby trans. George Lamb 1960: *The Life of St Catherine of Siena*, London.

Reggiani, Flores 1997: 'Responsabilità paterna fra povertà e beneficenza: "i figli dell' ospedale" di Milano fra Seicento e Settecento', *Ricerche storiche*, 27: 287–314.

Reggiani, Flores and Elisa Paradisi 1991: 'L'esposizione infantile a Milano fra Seicento e Settecento: il ruolo dell' istituzione'. In E.A., pp. 937–79.

Ricci, Giovanni 1983: 'Naissance du pauvre honteux entre l'histoire des idées et l'histoire sociale', *Annales: économies, sociétés, civilisations*, 38: 158–77.

Riddle, John M. 1996: 'Contraception and early abortion in the middle ages'. In Bullough and Brundage 1996, pp. 261–77.

Rigo, Angelo 1992-3: 'Giudici del Procurator e donne "malmaritate": interventi nella giustizia secolare in materia matrimoniale a Venezia in epoca tridentina', *Atti dell' Istituto Veneto di Scienze, Lettere ed Arti*, 151: Classe di scienze morali, lettere ed arti: 241–66.

Rigo, Angelo 2000: 'Interventi dello Stato veneziano nei casi di separazione: i Giudici del Procurator. Alcuni dati degli anni Cinquanta e Sessanta del XVI secolo'. In Seidel Menchi and Quaglioni 2000, pp. 519–36.

Rinaldi, Rossella 1991: ' "Mulieres publicae". Testimonianze e note sulla prostituzione tra pieno e tardo medioevo'. In Muzzarelli *et al.* 1991, pp. 105–25.

Rocke, Michael 1996: *Forbidden Friendships. Homosexuality and Male Culture in Renaissance Florence*, New York and Oxford.

Rocke, Michael 2008: ' "Whoorish boyes": male prostitution in early modern Italy and the spurious "second part" of Antonio Vignali's *La Cazzaria*'. In Arnade and Rocke 2008, pp. 113–33.

Rodax, Yvonne 1968: *The Real and the Ideal in the Novella of Italy, France and England*, Chapel Hill, NC.

Rollo-Koster, Joëlle 2002: 'From prostitutes to brides of Christ: the Avignonese *Répenties* in the late middle ages', *Journal of Medieval and Early Modern Studies*, 32: 109–44.

Romanello, Marina 1995: *Le spose del principe. Una storia di donne: la Casa Secolare delle Zitelle in Udine, 1595–1995*, Milan.

Romano, Dennis 1996: *Housecraft and Statecraft: Domestic Service in Renaissance Venice, 1400–1600*, Baltimore.

Romeo, Giovanni 2008: *Amori proibiti. I concubini tra Chiesa e Inquisizione, Napoli 1563–1656*, Bari.

Roper, Lyndal 1985: 'Discipline and respectability: prostitution and the Reformation in Augsburg', *History Workshop*, 19: 3–28.

Rosenthal, Margaret F. 1992: *The Honest Courtesan: Veronica Franco, Citizen and Writer in Sixteenth-century Venice*, Chicago and London.

Ross, James Bruce 1976: 'The middle-class child in urban Italy, fourteenth to sixteenth century'. In De Mause 1976, pp. 183–228.

Rossiaud, Jacques trans. Lydia G. Cochrane 1988: *Medieval Prostitution*, Oxford.

Rossiaud, Jacques 2010: *Amours vénales: La Prostitution en Occident, XIIe-XVIe siècles*, Paris.

Rousseau, Jean-Jacques ed. and trans. J.M. Cohen 1953: *The Confessions*, Harmondsworth.

Rozzo, Ugo (ed.) 1982: *Matteo Bandello, novelliere europeo*, Tortona.

Ruggiero, Guido 1985: *The Boundaries of Eros: Sex Crime and Sexuality in Renaissance Venice*, New York and Oxford.

Ruggiero, Guido 1987: ' "Più che la vita caro": onore, matrimonio e riputazione femminile nel tardo rinascimento', *Quaderni storici*, 22: 753–75.

Ruggiero, Guido 1993: *Binding Passions: Tales of Magic, Marriage and Power at the End of the Renaissance*, New York and Oxford.

Russo, Saverio 1984: 'Potere pubblico e carità privata. L'assistenza ai poveri a Lucca tra XVI e XVII secolo', *Società e storia*, 7: 45–80.

Saba, Agostino 1933: *Federico Borromeo e i mistici del suo tempo con la vita e la corrispondenza inedita di Caterina Vannini da Siena*, Florence.

Sampaoli, A. 1950: 'Il problema della prostituzione negli scrittori del XVIII secolo', *Nuova antologia*, 449 (May–August 1950), 170–82.

Sandri, Lucia 1982: *L'Ospedale di Santa Maria della Scala di S. Gimignano nel Quattrocento: contributo alla storia dell' infanzia abbandonata*, Società Storica della Valdelsa.

Sandri, Lucia 1991: 'Modalità dell' abbandono dei fanciulli in area urbana: gli esposti dell' Ospedale di San Gallo di Firenze nella prima metà del XV secolo'. In E.A., pp. 993–1015.

Sandri, Lucia 1997: 'La specializzazione ospedaliera fiorentina: gli Innocenti e l'assistenza all'infanzia (XV-XVI secolo)'. In Grieco and Sandri 1997, pp. 51–65.

Sandri, Lucia 2001: 'L'attività del banco di deposito dell' Ospedale degli Innocenti di Firenze. Don Vincenzo Borghini e la "bancarotta" del 1579'. In Pastore and Garbellotti 2001, pp. 153–78.

Santore, Cathy 1988: 'Julia Lombardo, "somtuosa meretrize": a portrait by property', *Renaissance Quarterly*, 41: 44–83.

Sardi, Deanna 2002: 'In nome di Maria: madri illegittime e partorienti povere nella Toscana moderna. Il caso di Arezzo fra Sei e Settecento', *Ricerche storiche*, 32: 81–99.

Scarabello, Giovanni 2004: 'Per una storia della prostituzione a Venezia tra il XIII e il XVIII secolo', *Studi veneziani, nuova serie*, 47: 15–101.

Schiavoni, Claudio 1991: 'Gli infanti "esposti" del Santo Spirito di Saxia di Roma tra '500 e '800: numero, ricevimento, allevamento e destino'. In E.A., pp. 1017–64.

Schleiner, Winfried 1994: 'Moral attitudes towards syphilis and its prevention in the Renaissance', *Bulletin of the History of Medicine*, 68: 389–410.

Schleiner, Winfried 1995: *Medical Ethics in the Renaissance*, Washington, DC.

Schroeder, H.J. (ed.) 1937: *Disciplinary Decrees of the General Councils. Text, Translation and Commentary*, St Louis.

Schuler, Carol M. 1991: 'The courtesan in modern art: historical fact or modern fantasy?', *Women's Studies*, 19: 209–22.

Schutte, Anne Jacobson 2001: *Aspiring Saints: Pretense of Holiness, Inquisition and Gender in the Republic of Venice, 1618–1750*, Baltimore and London.

Schutte, Anne Jacobson 2010: 'Between Venice and Rome: the dilemma of involuntary nuns', *Sixteenth Century Journal*, 41: 415–39.

Scott, Walter ed. Tony Inglis 1994: *The Heart of Mid-Lothian*, London.

Scully, Sally 1994–5: 'Marriage or a career? Witchcraft as an alternative in seventeenth-century Venice', *Journal of Social History*, 28: 857–76.

Sebastiani, Lucia 1995: 'Gruppi di donne tra convivenza e assistenza'. In Zardin 1995, pp. 101–15.

Seidel Menchi, Silvana and Diego Quaglioni (eds.) 2000: *Coniugi nemici. La separazione in Italia dal XII al XVIII secolo*, Bologna.

Selwyn, Jennifer D. 2003: ' "Angels of peace". The social drama of the Jesuit mission in early modern southern Italy'. In Findlen *et al.* 2003, pp. 160–75.

Semi, Franca 1983: *Gli 'ospizi' di Venezia*, Venice.

Sharp, Samuel 1767: *Letters from Italy, Describing the Customs and Manners of That Country, in the Years 1765, and 1766*, 3rd edition, London.

Siegmund, Stefanie B. 2006: *The Medici State and the Ghetto of Florence: The Construction of an Early Modern Jewish Community*, Stanford.

Sigle, Wendy, David I. Kertzer and Michael J. White 2000: 'Abandoned children and their transition to adulthood in nineteenth-century Italy', *Journal of Family History*, 25: 326–40.

Simonsohn, Shlomo 1977: *History of the Jews in the Duchy of Mantua*, Jerusalem.

Sonnino, Eugenio 1991: 'Esposizione e mortalità degli esposti nello stato pontificio agli inizi dell' Ottocento, secondo le statistiche raccolte da Leopoldo Armaroli'. In E.A., pp. 1065–96.

Soons, Alan 1982: *Juan de Mariana*, Boston.

Sori, Ercole (ed.) 1982: *Città e controllo sociale in Italia tra XVIII e XIX secolo*, Milan.

Sperling, Julia Gisela 1999: *Convents and the Body Politic in Late Renaissance Venice*, Chicago and London.

Speroni, Sperone 1596: *Orationi del Signor Speron Speroni, Dottor et Cavalier Padovano*, Venice.

Stearns, P. (ed.) 1982: *Old Age in Preindustrial Society*, New York.

Storey, Tessa 2001: 'Storie di prostituzione nella Roma della Controriforma', *Quaderni storici*, 36: 262–93.

Storey, Tessa 2008/2012: *Carnal Commerce in Counter-Reformation Rome*, Cambridge; paperback, 2012.

Stöver, Heinz, Morag Macdonald and Susie Atherton 2007: *Harm Reduction in European Prisons: A Compilation of Models of Best Practice*, Oldenburg.

Straparola, Giovan Francesco ed. Giuseppe Rua and Manlio Pastore Stocchi 1975: *Le piacevoli notti*, 2 vols., Bari.

Strocchia, Sharon T. 2009: *Nuns and Nunneries in Renaissance Florence*, Baltimore and London.

Surdacki, Marian 1998: 'La vita religiosa nel "conservatorio" dell'Ospedale di Santo Spirito in Roma, nei secoli XVII–XVIII', *Ricerche di storia sociale e religiosa, nuova serie*, 54: 149–65.

Surdacki, Marian 1999: 'Marriages of wards of Rome's Holy Spirit Hospital in the seventeenth and eighteenth centuries', *Acta Poloniae historica*, 79: 99–122.

Surdacki, Marian 2000: 'L'abbandono dei bambini a Roma e dintorni nel secolo XVIII', *Archivio della Società Romana di Storia Patria*, 123: 169–99.

Surdacki, Marian 2001: 'I trovatelli nelle famiglie affidatarie a Roma e nei dintorni nel Settecento', *Ricerche di storia sociale e religiosa, nuova serie*, 59: 91–119.

Surdacki, Marian 2001–02: 'Il "conservatorio" e la "scuola dei putti" nell' Ospedale di Santo Spirito nei secoli XVII e XVIII'. In Cappelletti and Tagliarini 2001–02, I, pp. 253–67.

Surdacki, Marian 2002: 'Le nutrici a Roma e nello stato pontificio nei secoli XVII–XVIII', *Archivio della Società Romana di Storia Patria*, 125: 105–26.

Surdacki, Marian 2009: 'Il conservatorio di Santo Spirito di Roma nei secoli XVII–XVIII', *Ricerche di storia sociale e religiosa, nuova serie*, 75: 21–42.

Tacchi Venturi, Pietro 1950–51: *Storia della Compagnia di Gesù in Italia*, 2 vols. in 4, Rome.

Talbot, Michael 1984: *Vivaldi*, London.

Tanturri, Alberto 2003: 'L'infanzia abbandonata a Sulmona nel XVIII secolo', *Ricerche di storia sociale e religiosa, nuova serie*, 64: 149–79.

Tanturri, Alberto 2006: 'Sfamare gli affamati, vestire gli ignudi: forme di assistenza a Sulmona (secoli XVI–XIX)', *Ricerche di storia sociale e religiosa, nuova serie*, 70: 235–49.

Tassini, Giuseppe ed. Lino Moretti 1964: *Curiosità veneziane, ovvero Origini delle denominazioni stradali*, Venice.

Terpstra, Nicholas 1994: 'Apprenticeship in social welfare: from confraternal charity to municipal poor relief in early modern Italy', *The Sixteenth Century Journal*, 25: 101–20.

Terpstra, Nicholas 1997: 'Ospedali e bambini abbandonati a Bologna nel Rinascimento'. In Grieco and Sandri 1997, pp. 209–32.

Terpstra, Nicholas 2005: *Abandoned Children of the Italian Renaissance: Orphan Care in Florence and Bologna*, Baltimore and London.

Terpstra, Nicholas 2010: *Lost Girls: Sex and Death in Renaissance Florence*, Baltimore and London.

Terroine, Anne 1978: 'Le roi des ribauds de l'Hôtel du Roi et les prostituées parisiennes', *Revue historique de droit français et étranger*, 4th series, 56: 253–67.

Tilly, Louise A., Rachel G. Fuchs, David I. Kertzer and David L. Ransel 1992: 'Child abandonment in European history: a symposium', *Journal of Family History*, 17: 1–23.

Tittarelli, Luigi 1991: 'Le "balie di casa" e le "balie di fuori" nell' Ospedale di Santa Maria della Misericordia di Perugia nel primo decennio del XVIII secolo'. In E.A., pp. 1139–51.

Tittarelli, Luigi, Luca Calzola and Donatella Lanari 2003: *Gli esposti all'Ospedale di Santa Maria Misericordia di Perugia dal XIV al XIX secolo*, Perugia.

Tout, Thomas F. and James Tait (eds.) 1902: *Historical Essays by Members of the Owens College*, Manchester.

Travaglini, Carlo M. 1992: 'Rigattieri e società romana nel Settecento', *Quaderni storici*, 27: 415–48.

Trexler, Richard C. 1972: 'Le célibat à la fin du Moyen Age: les religieuses de Florence', *Annales: économies, sociétés, civilisations*, 27: 1329–50.

Trexler, Richard C. 1973–74: 'Infanticide in Florence: new sources and first results', *History of Childhood Quarterly*, 1: 98–116. Reprinted in Trexler 1993, I, pp. 35–53 and Trexler 1994, pp. 203–24.

Trexler, Richard C. 1973–74a: 'The foundlings of Florence, 1395–1455', *History of Childhood Quarterly*, 1: 259–84. Reprinted in Trexler 1993, I, pp. 7–34 and Trexler 1994, pp. 225–58.

Trexler, Richard C. 1980: *Public Life in Renaissance Florence*, New York.

Trexler, Richard C. 1981: 'La prostitution florentine au XVe siècle: patronages et clientèles', *Annales: économies, sociétés, civilisations*, 36: 983–1015. In English translation in Trexler 1993, II, pp. 31–65 and Trexler 1994, pp. 373–414.

Trexler, Richard C. 1982: 'A widows' asylum of the Renaissance: the Orbatello of Florence'. In Stearns 1982, pp. 119–49. Reprinted in Trexler 1993, II, pp. 66–93 and Trexler 1994, pp. 415–48.

Trexler, Richard C. 1993: *Power and Dependence in Renaissance Florence*, 2 vols., Binghamton, NY.

Trexler, Richard C. 1994: *Dependence in Context in Renaissance Florence*, Binghamton, NY.

Vaglini, Maurizio 2001: 'L'ospedale dei trovatelli di Pisa'. In Cappelletti and Tagliarini 2001–02, I, pp. 215–24.

Valenzi, Lucia 1995: *Poveri, ospizi e potere a Napoli (XVIII-XIX sec.)*, Milan.

Van der Spuy, Patricia 2002: 'Infanticide, slavery and the politics of reproduction at Cape Colony, South Africa, in the 1820s'. In Jackson 2002, pp. 128–48.

Vanzan Marchini, Nelli Elena 1995: *I mali e i rimedi della Serenissima*, Vicenza.

Varanini, Gian Maria 1996: 'La carità del municipio. Gli ospedali veronesi del Quattrocento e nel primo Cinquecento'. In Pastore *et al.* 1996, pp. 13–41.

Varanini, Gian Maria 1997: 'Per la storia delle istituzioni ospedaliere nelle città della terraferma veneta nel Quattrocento'. In Grieco and Sandri 1997, pp. 107–55.

Venturi, Franco (ed.) 1958: *Illuministi italiani, III: Riformatori lombardi, piemontesi e toscani*, Milan and Naples.

Viazzo, Pier Paolo 1994: 'Family structure and the early phase in the individual life cycle: a southern European perspective'. In Henderson and Wall 1994, pp. 31–50.

Viazzo, Pier Paolo, Maria Bortolotto and Andrea Zanotto 1994: 'Child care, infant mortality and the impact of legislation: the case of Florence's foundling hospital, 1840–1940', *Continuity and Change*, 9: 243–69.

Viazzo, Pier Paolo, Maria Bortolotto and Andrea Zanotto 2000: 'Five centuries of foundling history in Florence: changing patterns of abandonment, care and mortality'. In Panter-Brick and Smith 2000, pp. 70–91.

Vigni, Laura 1979: 'L'ospedale senese di Santa Maria della Scala nel XVIII secolo', *Bullettino senese di storia patria*, 86: 100–43.

Vigni, Laura 1985: 'Gli esposti all' ospedale senese di S. Maria della Scala (1763–68)', *Bullettino senese di storia patria*, 92: 198–234.

Vitale, Giuliana 1970: 'Ricerche sulla vita religiosa e caritativa a Napoli tra medioevo ed età moderna', *Archivio storico per le province napoletane*, 86–87: 207–91.

Walter, Ingeborg 1986: 'Infanticidio a Ponte Bocci: 2 marzo 1406. Elementi di un processo', *Studi storici*, 27: 637–48.

Weinstein, Donald 2000: *The Captain's Concubine: Love, Honor, and Violence in Renaissance Tuscany*, Baltimore and London.

White Mario, Jessie ed. Gianni Infusino 1978: *La miseria in Napoli (1877)*, Naples.

Wiesner, Merry E. 1999: 'Prostitution'. In Grendler 1999, V, pp. 179–80.

Winter, Anne 2010: 'Abandoned in Brussels, delivered in Paris: long-distance transports of unwanted children in the eighteenth century', *Journal of Family History*, 35: 232–48.

Witte, John, Jr., and Frank S. Alexander (eds.) 2008: *Christianity and Law: An Introduction*, Cambridge.

Young, Percy M. 1965: *Handel*, London.

Zamagni, Vera (ed.) 2000: *Povertà e innovazioni istituzionali in Italia. Dal medioevo ad oggi*, Bologna.

Zardin, Danilo (ed.) 1995: *La città e i poveri. Milano e le terre lombarde dal Rinascimento all'età spagnola*, Milan.

Zarri, Gabriella 1986: 'Monasteri femminili e città (secoli XV–XVIII)'. In Chittolini and Miccoli 1986, pp. 359–429.

Zarri, Gabriella 1994: 'Disciplina regolare e pratica di coscienza: le virtù e i comportamenti sociali in comunità femminili (secoli XVI–XVIII)'. In Prodi and Penuti 1994, pp. 257–78.

Zdekauer, Ludovico 1898: 'I primordi della Casa dei Gettatelli in Siena (1238–1298), con documenti inediti', *Bullettino senese di storia patria*, 5: 452–69.

Zuccarello, Ugo 2000: 'La sodomia al tribunale bolognese del Torrone tra XVI e XVII secolo', *Società e storia*, 22: 37–51.

Index